D1566404

Literature and politics in the English Reformation

Published in our
centenary year
2004
MANCHESTER
UNIVERSITY
PRESS

Politics, culture and society in early modern Britain

General editors

PROFESSOR ANN HUGHES
DR ANTHONY MILTON
PROFESSOR PETER LAKE

This important series publishes monographs that take a fresh and challenging look at the interactions between politics, culture and society in Britain between 1500 and the mid-eighteenth century. It counteracts the fragmentation of current historiography through encouraging a variety of approaches which attempt to redefine the political, social and cultural worlds, and to explore their interconnection in a flexible and creative fashion. All the volumes in the series question and transcend traditional inter-disciplinary boundaries, such as those between political history and literary studies, social history and divinity, urban history and anthropology. They contribute to a broader understanding of crucial developments in early modern Britain.

Literature and politics in the English Reformation

TOM BETTERIDGE

Manchester
University Press

Manchester and New York

distributed exclusively in the USA by Palgrave

Published by Manchester University Press
Oxford Road, Manchester M13 9NR, UK
and Room 400, 175 Fifth Avenue, New York, NY 10010, USA
www.manchesteruniversitypress.co.uk

Distributed exclusively in the USA by
Palgrave, 175 Fifth Avenue, New York, NY 10010, USA

Distributed exclusively in Canada by
UBC Press, University of British Columbia, 2029 West Mall,
Vancouver, BC, Canada V6T 1Z2

British Library Cataloguing-in-Publication Data
A catalogue record for this book is available from the British Library

Library of Congress Cataloging-in-Publication Data applied for

ISBN 0 7190 6460 0 *hardback*
EAN 978 0 7190 6460 9

First published 2004

13 12 11 10 09 08 07 06 05 04   10 9 8 7 6 5 4 3 2 1

Typeset in Scala with Pastonchi display
by Koinonia Ltd, Manchester

Printed in Great Britain
by Biddles Ltd, King's Lynn

Contents

Preface

I have acquired many debts, personal and intellectual, in the course of completing this study. Tom Freeman has read much of this book in manuscript and his comments have always been helpful. John Ibett, Diarmaid MacCulloch, Anne McLaren, Alec Ryrie, Greg Walker and Bill Wizeman have all read large sections of this work and have made many useful suggestions that have immensely improved the final version of this study. John King's *English Reformation Literature* was the work that inspired me to write on the literature of the reign of Edward VI. John's comments on Chapter 2 of this study were invaluable, as has been his support for my work over the years. I would also like to thank Andrew Hadfield and Patrick Collinson for the support they have given me. Many people have indulged me by listening to my views on English Reformation literature during the period in which this work was being written. I would like to thank in particular Brian Cummings and David Scott Kastan. My colleague at Kingston University, Erica Longfellow, has been a constant source of support and friendship. I would like to thank Peter Lake and Anthony Milton for their support for this book, and the staff at Manchester University Press, particularly Alison Welsby and Jonathan Bevan. This book would not have been completed without the support of the AHRB who provided me with a grant to take a year's sabbatical just when I needed it. Finally I would like to thank my colleagues at Kingston University for all their help, comradeship and humour. This book is dedicated to them.

Abbreviations

EETS   *Early English Text Society* (e.s. — extra series)

EHR   *English Historical Review*

ELH   *English Literary History*

HJ   *Historical Journal*

JEH   *Journal of Ecclesiastical History*

JMEMS   *Journal of Medieval and Early Modern Studies*

LP   *Letters & Papers, Foreign and Domestic, of the Reign of Henry VIII, 1509–47*, eds J.S. Brewer, James Gairdner and R.H. Brodie (1862–1932)

MLN   *Modern Language Notes*

PP   *Past and Present*

SCJ   *Sixteenth Century Studies Journal*

SEL   *Studies in English Literature*

SP   *Studies in Philology*

Sp   *Speculum*

STC   *A Short Title Catalogue of Books Printed in England Scotland and Ireland, and of English Books Printed Abroad, 1475–1640*, eds A.W. Pollard and G.R. Redgrave, rev. W.A. Jackson, F.J. Ferguson and K. F. Pantzer, 2 vols (1986)

TRHS   *Transactions of the Royal Historical Society*

Introduction

This book is a study of the English Reformation as a poetic and political event. It examines the writing of the period 1520–80, political, religious and poetic, in relation to the effects of confessionalization on Tudor writing. The central argument of the book is that it is a mistake to understand this literature simply on the basis of the conflict between Protestantism and Catholicism. Instead one needs to see Tudor culture as fractured between emerging confessional identities, Protestant *and* Catholic, and marked by a conflict between those who embraced the process of confessionalization and those who rejected it.

Confessionalization is the process of creating and sustaining religious confessions as organized public churches. It has been developed as a concept during the last decade or so by a number of historians interested in the German Reformation. In particular, Wolfgang Reinhard and Heinz Schilling have used the idea to move beyond an understanding of the European Reformation as a conflict between Protestants and Catholics and instead to stress the continuities between the various European Reformations, German, Spanish, French and English. Schilling writes:

> I have drawn a conclusion regarding terminology from the concept of confession-alisation: instead of the Counter Reformation, Lutheran Orthodoxy, and the 'Second Reformation', we should speak of 'Catholic confessionalisation', 'Lutheran confessionalisation', and 'Reformed or Calvinist confessionalisation'. By using linguistically parallel terminology it becomes clearer that these are three processes running parallel to each other and that the concept of confessionalisation includes an over-arching political, social, and cultural change.[1]

Schilling's argument has a number of radical implications. It suggests that the European Reformation was a product of a process of confessionalization and that therefore the emergence of competing Christian confessional identities, primarily Catholic and Protestant, was an effect and not a cause of religious change during the sixteenth century. The implication of this is that aspects of early modern religion which have traditionally been seen as elements of competing denominations should instead been viewed as products of Catholicism's and Protestantism's shared confessional basis[2] This argument is particularly important as regards the English Reformation in relation to mid-Tudor politics and literature.

The politics of confessionalization at one level can be understood in terms of an increase of state power. The creation of true and false religious identities, and the process of examination and inquisition that this entailed, clearly had the potential to massively increase the power of early modern governments and ruling elites. Schilling comments: 'The framing and enforcement of innumerable laws for the protection and regulation of religious and ecclesiastical life enormously expanded the hitherto weakly developed business of the state.'[3] Reinhard and Schilling argue that confessionalization played a central role in the creation of absolutist states in early modern Europe. In England, however, the political effects of confessionalization were markedly different. The under-developed nature of the English state in comparison with those of continental Europe at this time meant that in Tudor England the process of confessionalization had rather different long-term political effects. It is, however, potentially misleading to refer to the English state in this period since such a thing can hardly be said to have existed – certainly not in a modern sense. What did exist was a series of networks of power, authority and influence that could at key times take on a consistency that gave them the appearance and indeed power of a state. John Guy has suggested that Tudor government can be understood as a series of concentric circles centered upon the monarch.[4] The trick, and it was a difficult one that became more so during the early modern period, was to get these circles moving in the same direction and at the same speed. Confessionalization created the possibility of adding a whole new force to this process. It had the ability to bind together the circles of government.[5]

At the same time confessionalization could also place new pressures on Tudor political norms. In particular it had potentially disruptive effects on the ideal, and practice, of counsel. Despite the fact that counsel was a central concept of Tudor praxis, nothing about it was coherent or fixed. Apart from a general agreement that it was desirable in itself, there was no agreement over its status, scope or boundaries.[6] This lack of definition and the endless debates that took place concerning its form, organization and potency were what made counsel such a useful concept for Tudor politicians. Counsel's usefulness within Tudor political praxis as an explanatory tool was heightened by the development of confessionalized explanations for its failure – popery / heresy. Their presence within the commonwealth could also be used to explain, and explain away, political conflict and social unrest.[7] At the same time, however, any confessionalization of counsel, and politics in general, created the possibility that voices outside the political nation could be legitimatized on the basis of their confessional purity. For example, in Mary Tudor's reign the writer Miles Hogarde used his sense of Catholicism as a confessionalized identity to valorize his artisan voice against those lukewarm members of the Marian regime who were failing to properly stamp out the dangers of heresy.[8]

It is, however, not simply in the area of politics the confessionalism had a profound impact on mid-Tudor culture. The literature of the period 1530–80 is profoundly marked by confessionalization. This is because the production of confessional purity required the control of knowledge. Gerald Strauss has suggested: 'Ideologically, the Reformation was first and foremost an exaltation of authorized texts'.[9] It would, however, be more accurate to argue that a key element of the European Reformation was a desire to authorize texts.[10] Confessionalization addressed perfectly the fears of the literati over the unregulated circulation of knowledge, particularly in the form of printed texts, by providing a perfect rationale for its regulation.[11] It legitimatized the control of all aspects of early modern culture by justifying the attempt to force language, popular culture and even selfhood into confessional moulds.[12] In particular, confessionalization embodied a specific model of selfhood based upon the struggle to achieve confessional purity and its poetics consistently valorized the plain simple truth of the Word of God against the dangers of textual play and linguistic ambiguity. In the past, studies of mid-Tudor literature tended to collapse these aspects of confessionalization into English Protestant culture. This is, however, simply a product of the eventual success of Protestantism in England during the sixteenth century.[13] In the work of Miles Hogarde one can see a Catholic sensibility being developed, which in the work of later Catholic writers, for example Robert Southwell, contains all the markers of confessional 'Protestant' writing.[14]

This study argues that confessionalization as a process pre-dated the advent of the Protestantism in England. It was evident in the early Henrician attacks on Lollardy and was part of an early Tudor clericalist reform programme that can be seen in the writings of men as diverse as Bishop John Alcock and Edmund Dudley. The Henrician Reformation created a complicated situation in which the process of confessionalization was embraced, but without any proper confessions. Injunctions, examinations and statements of doctrinal orthodoxy were established parts of Henrician government, but the confession they were designed to enforce was terrifyingly vague to all but the King himself. To be faithful to the Royal Supremacy and the Henrician Reforma-tion one had to make sure that there was no gap between one's beliefs and those of Henry, while never being quite sure what Henry would publicly claim to believe from one month to the next. It is this situation that produces the tortured poetry of writers like Sir Thomas Wyatt. With the advent of the confessionalized regimes of Edward VII and Mary one can start talking confidently about English Protestantism and Catholicism. Early Elizabethan culture reflected the trauma of the mid-Tudor period, the persecutions of Mary's reign but also magisterial Protestant horror at the breakdown of order in 1549. After 1558 reformation, the defining commitment of the government to the imposition of one particular confession upon the country, was effectively abandoned, with the result that the process of confessionalization slowed almost to a standstill – despite the best efforts of godly activists, Puritans and Jesuits, to give it a kick-start. The Elizabethan Church was unambiguously Protestant but every parish had to buy a copy of a work written by arguably the leading anti-confessional writer of the sixteenth century – Erasmus' *Paraphrase of the New Testament.*[15]

Literature and politics in the English Reformation is a study of the English Reformation as a poetic and political event: one in which hermeneutic debates could easily take a lethal turn, the boundary between heresy and orthodoxy was at once absolute and dangerously ambiguous, and the ground was mapped out for the political conflicts of the next hundred years. The texts that will be discussed in this study are an eclectic group unified by the extent to which they reflect key elements of the cultural history of the period 1510–80, political, poetic and religious. The Introduction discusses a number of texts from before the Henrician Reformation, including Edmund Dudley's *Tree of Commonwealth*, the writings of John Skelton and William Tyndale, and Sir Thomas More's *Dialogue concerning Heresies.* Chapter 1 examines Sir Thomas Elyot's seminal work of Tudor political thought, *The Governour.* It then moves on to analyse the writing of the Henrician Reformation, in particular the poetry of Sir Thomas Wyatt. The second chapter discusses the politics and literature of Edward VI's reign, concentrating on the events of 1549, Robert Crowley's poetry and William Baldwin's prose work *Beware the Cat.* Chapter 3 focuses on the literature of Mary Tudor's reign, in particular the writing of John Heywood and Miles Hogarde, while the fourth chapter discusses a number of works produced during the first decade of Elizabeth I's rule. This study concludes by briefly examining Edmund Spenser's *Shepheardes Calender.*

RELIGION, POLITICS AND PRINT

The state of religion in pre-Reformation England has been the subject of much recent historical research. In particular, studies like Eamon Duffy's magisterial *The Stripping of the Altars: Traditional Religion in England 1400–1580* have conclusively shown that the English Church entered the sixteenth century in good health, popular and dynamic.[16] There were, however, members of the early Tudor clerical and political elite who appear not to have shared Duffy's relatively sanguine view of the state of the English Church, and in particular of the role of the clergy within the commonwealth. The period 1500–10 saw the production of a number of works advocating a reforming clericalist agenda. In particular, Edmund Dudley in *The Tree of Commonwealth* argued that the clergy had a vital role to play in the control of cunning or knowledge. Dudley's work, however, also expressed a fear that the circulation of cunning within the realm had already slipped beyond the possibility of clerical control. The spectre that haunted *The Tree of Commonwealth* was print and its ability to create a world in which knowledge circulated without control or order. It is, however, precisely this printed world that was celebrated in the poetry that Robert Copland wrote during the 1520s.[17]

In 1497 one of Bishop John Alcock's sermons was published with the title *Mons Perfectionis*. The publication of this work indicates that there were members of the English Church eager to address and exploit the possibilities created by print.[18] Alcock's text is a pastoral work intended for learned lay people as well as the clergy. One of the central arguments of this work is that 'the holy scrypture is the door by which we must entre in to the knowledge of almyghty god'.[19] Alcock makes clear, however, that this door can only properly be opened by the clergy. The religious message of *Mons Perfectionis* is the need for the spirituality and laity to work together to lead Christian lives, and the extreme difficulty of doing so. During the course of his work Alcock reminds his readers, 'no man what condicion so euer he be of wylll thynke [that] he be suffycyent of hymselfe w[ith]out the grace of almyghty god whiche is the pryncipal [and] fyrst meuer to vertue in our soules without our meryte.'[20] It is this consciousness of humanity's fallen nature and complete helplessness without God's grace that leads *Mons Perfectionis* to idealize monastic life. Alcock's tract, however, is not simply an assertion of the power and authority of the spirituality over the temporality. For example Alcock quotes St Ambrose as saying, 'I prayse more a meke and an humble wyfe than a proude mayde / [and] I preferre a meke maryed man before a sturdy and a selfe wylled relygyous man.'[21] *Mons Perfectionis* celebrates monasticism as a model for Christian living open to all, laity and clergy. Alcock's sermon offers its readers the possibility of leading a godly life potentially as worthy as that led by monks or nuns. All that was required was obedience to the strictures laid down in *Mons Perfectionis*.[22] Alcock uses the possibilities created by print to imagine in this sermon the entire realm, or perhaps more accurately his entire readership, as members of a printed monastery with him as the virtual abbot.[23] *Mons Perfectionis* ends by reminding its clerical readers, regular and secular, of St Jerome's warning: 'All maysters [and] relygyous men [that] techeth one [and] done an other they ben those [that] ben cursed of Christe.'[24] Alcock's work is designed to encourage its readers, lay and clerical, to strive towards leading a Christian life in which there is no separation between belief and practice. Total and unconditional obedience to the strictures laid out in *Mons Perfectionis* is, however, essential if readers wish to achieve this result.[25]

Mons Perfectionis constructs itself as a printed sermon designed to teach the laity while emphasizing its status as a clerical text by stressing its point of origin as the spoken words of a preaching bishop. The people involved in the publication of Alcock's sermon, who were almost certainly clergymen and may well have included the bishop himself, saw the possibilities of print for enhancing their roles as teachers and preachers but also perhaps the danger that, if they did not use the new medium to disseminate their message, others might use it to less wholesome ends. The nature of these less desirable ends is suggested in the prologue to another early Tudor religious text *The Contemplacon of Synners*. This work's probably clerical author argues that 'now a dayes it lyketh best a man to here or rede compylacyons whiche ben compendious pleasau[n]te [and] prouffytable, short in sayenge [and] large in sentence ...'[26] This section of the prologue to *The Contemplacon of Synners* critiques the desire of readers, and in theory hearers, for large sentences at the expense of short sayings, to read for pleasure and not spiritual profit. The author of *The Contemplacon of Synners* goes on to claim that while he is incapable of writing the kind of work that is popular among readers he will, with the help of God's grace, produce one that is spiritually profitable to those who read it. *Mons Perfectionis* and *The Contemplacon of Synners* reflect the preparedness of members of the early Tudor Church to respond to the new situation created by print by engaging with the new technology and using it to advance a reforming clericalist agenda.

This clericalist agenda is an important part of the background to Dean Colet's famous sermon of 1511. In this sermon Colet held up an idealized image of the priesthood as the guardians of social stability and well-being. He claimed that the 'the dignity of priesthood ... is greater than either the king's or emperor's: it is equal to the dignity of angels'.[27] Christopher Harper-Bill has pointed out that the insistence on clerical reform in this sermon needs to be seen in the context of this idealization of the clergy.[28] Colet's emphasis on the need for the reform of the English Church is driven by a clericalist assumption concerning the clergy's central role in producing a reformed godly society. Colet told his listeners: 'The clergy and spiritual parts once reformed in the Church, then may we with a just order proceed to the reformation of the lay part: the which truly will be very easy to do if we first be reformed.'[29] Colet stressed the need for the clergy to reform themselves because he was committed, like the people behind the publication of *Mons Perfectionis*, to religious and social reform. Indeed in this convocation sermon Colet was probably largely preaching to the converted. The early Tudor English Church contained a number of bishops to whom the reform agenda mapped out by Colet would have been uncontroversial. Colet's clericalist arguments make complete sense in the context of an early Tudor English Church increasingly prepared to enforce religious orthodoxy as witnessed during the 1510s and 1520s by the sudden upsurge in the number of Lollards being prosecuted and condemned. It is unlikely that was a sudden increase in Lollardy during the early years of the sixteenth century.[30] What this period did witness, however, was the emergence of a clericalist agenda dedicated to religious reform, part of which included a more rigorous pursuit of orthodoxy. It was this which produced the spate of Lollard hunts in the early years of the sixteenth century as Tudor churchmen sought to fulfill their pastoral duty to instruct their flock and protect them from heresy.[31]

It is perhaps not surprising to find works like *Mons Perfectionis* or church-men like Colet expressing support for a clericalist agenda of social and religious reform. Far more surprising is the fact that Edmund Dudley's *The Tree of Commonwealth* makes similar arguments in the context of a theoretical political discussion of the English commonwealth.[32] Dudley was a clever if not over-scrupulous lawyer who rose to prominence in the period 1503–9 as a member of the Council Learned in the Law.[33] He was immediately arrested on the accession of Henry VIII, and subsequently executed, as part of a policy to make him, and his colleague Richard Empson, bear the opprobrium for policies that the new monarch wished to see firmly associated with his father's reign. It was while he languished in the Tower of London in 1510 that Dudley wrote his tract on the government of England, *The Tree of Commonwealth*.

Dudley opens his work with a discussion of the proper behaviour of a monarch.[34] He uses a number of historical examples – Harold, Henry III and Richard II – to sustain his argument that there are three main enemies to good kingship, cruelty, covetousness and lust. It is only once the text has discussed kingship within this moral framework that it moves on to deal with the status of the commonwealth as a whole through the metaphor of 'the tree of commonwealth'.[35] Dudley writes:

> The comon wealth of this realme or of the subiectes or Inhabitants therof may be resemblid to a faier and mighte tree growing in a faier feild or pasture, vnder the couerte or shade wherof all beastes, both fatt and leane, are protectyd and comfortyd from heate and cold as the tyme requireth.[36]

The tree of the commonwealth has a number of roots – justice, truth, concord and peace, as well as fruit – honourable dignity, worldly prosperity and tranquility. These fruit are associated by Dudley with specific social orders, the tree of the commonwealth's branches. For example, nobility's fruit is worldly prosperity. These fruit, however, have dangerous cores. Dudley warns the nobility not to pare the fruit of worldly prosperity too much otherwise they may reach its core, delectation. Similarly the fruit destined for the commonality is tranquillity but at its core is lewd enterprise.[37] *The Tree of Commonwealth* contains an image of a functioning polity that is carefully balanced, while at the same time dynamic. Each social order has a fixed role or fruit they must harvest in order to perform their proper function within the commonwealth, while at the same time avoiding the dangerous core at its heart. In *The Tree of Commonwealth* each social order is depicted as being in constant danger of failing, of finding the dark core at the centre of its social role. Dudley's text takes the fear of social disorder and places it at the centre of each of the orders that make up its image of the commonwealth.[38]

Two things in particular endanger *The Tree of Commonwealth*'s stable dynamism – the role of the clergy and lack of tranquillity among the commonality. *The Tree of Commonwealth* expends considerable energy discussing what happens if the commonality pare their fruit, tranquillity, too far and reach its dangerous core, lewd enterprise. Dudley claims:

> This lewd core of enterprise ... most comenly ... sendith [two] purssyfauntes or messengers before hym, chosen of the worst for our profytt. The furst of the two messengers is discontentacion or murmurr. This messenger will induce you to grudge or to make some inward displeasure in doing your Dewtie ... if ye reuerently receive this felloo then commyth the second messenger, in a gay, guilt cote, to enveigle your synne with pryde, the most perillous spectakle [that] the commynaltie may vse. Fowle is it in all men but worst in the poorest. The name of second messenger is Arrogancy, nighe cosen to pride.[39]

What is significant in this passage is the way that the commonality's fall is signified by the sudden emergence of messengers from outside the bounds of the commonwealth. The message of these agitators clearly associates them with the Peasants' Revolt in 1381. Dudley writes that Arrogance, in a clear parody of the egalitarian Christian ideology espoused by such leaders of the Peasants' Revolt as John Ball, will tell the commonality that 'ye be the children and righte inheritors to Adam aswell as thei [the gentles]'.[40]

Arrogance's behavior, in particular the 'Christian' message of his words, relates to one of the more contentious aspects of *The Tree of Commonwealth*, its attitude to the clergy. It has been argued that Dudley's work is anti-clerical.[41] This is, however, a potentially anachronistic reading of *The Tree of Commonwealth*. In this work Dudley does express a number of criticisms of the clergy. He suggests that they should be barred from holding secular positions and that there was room for greater royal power over the church. Dudley also argues that the clergy needed reform and, in *The Tree of Commonwealth*, claims the right as a layman to comment on their failings.[42] In Dudley's ideal realm the clergy should be moral Lanterns of Light teaching the gospel message by leading godly, simple lives.

The 'anti-clericalism' of *The Tree of Commonwealth* is, however, like Colet's, premised upon the centrality of the clergy to the health of the commonwealth, and in particular their role in ensuring the continual increase of knowledge or 'cunning'. This makes the clergy the one order whose role necessitates a degree of dynamism beyond the simple process of maintaining the equilibrium. Dudley writes: 'What is the paring of good example to the Clergie appointed? Encrease of vertue and conning.'[43] Behind the apparent anti-clericalism of *The Tree of Commonwealth* lies a clericalist agenda. Dudley goes on to argue that the clergy have a duty to ensure a continual increase in cunning; otherwise a decrease will inevitably follow. He writes:

I pray god hartely [that] none of you turne the paringes of the fruite from thencrease of conning to the discrease and distruction of conning ... When do ye so? When so euer you of your self that lack connyng will take no pain to haue it, nor will favour nor cherisshe other to haue it. This is one perillous stroke [that] lettyth the encrease of connyng. And other is when ye dispose your benifyces to such as ar not clerkes ...[44]

Dudley's whole approach to the question of cunning is predicated on the assumption that it is a clerical matter. His concern that the clergy are failing in their duty in this area is met with a clericalist solution. He does not consider the possibility that the failure of the clergy in the field of cunning can or indeed should be taken in hand by any other members of the commonwealth. For him the state of cunning within the commonwealth can only be addressed by the clergy. At the same time *The Tree of Commonwealth*'s representation of cunning in economic terms, constantly rising and falling, increasing and decreasing, potentially undermines Dudley's emphasis on its control by the clergy and threatens the self-sustaining stability at the heart of the tree of commonwealth. It suggests that cunning has already started to slip beyond the control of any one social group. How can cunning continuously increase without changing the balance of the tree of commonwealth? Can the clergy control something that is potentially so volatile? And if the clergy do not take cunning in hand, who will? The possibility that *The Tree of Commonwealth* implicitly raises is that it will be Arrogance and his colleagues that will take over cunning if the clergy do not; people from outside the commonwealth whose *modus operandi* is spreading rebellious rumors and corrupting texts.[45] *The Tree of Commonwealth* represents cunning as a commodity whose production and consumption is in danger of subverting the integrity of the tree of commonwealth unless controlled by the clergy. What would it mean if the circulation of cunning rested simply on the ability of printers and writers to satisfy the desires of their readers for large sentences and pleasurable texts?

It is not, however, necessary to speculate on the implications of a market in cunning since they can be discerned in a number of texts written during the 1520s. In particular, Robert Copland, a printer, translator and writer produced a number of works during this period celebrating print and the possibilities that it created. In 1521 Wynkyn de Worde published Copland's translation of St Edmund Rich's *Speculum Ecclesiae*, *The Myrrour of the Chyrche*. In his envoy to this text Copland writes:

> Almyghty lorde / o blyssed holy goost
> Whiche dide enflame / [with] vertue fro[m] on hy
> Thy chosen seruau[n]tes / [the] day of pe[n]thecost
> To preche thy worde / here vnyuersally
> This lytell boke / of maters right goostly
> Thou wylt forth se[n]de / e[n]dued with thy grace

> In vertues the reders so to occupy
> Auoydi[n]ge vyce / in heuen to haue place.[46]

In this verse Copland gives his translation an apostolic function by placing it within a Pentecostal context. In the process Copland claims for his 'lytell boke' a degree of authority that potentially puts him in competition with the clergy. If Copland's translation can partake of the universal Pentecostal mission that Christ left his followers, then what does this imply about its writer? Does he participate in the book's apostolic grace? The potentially radical nature of these questions is partly mitigated by the book's original saintly authorship. Copland is also careful in this verse to stress the extent to which it is the book that is apostolic. There is, however, a tension in this verse between the status of *The Myrrour of the Chyrche* as a material book to be sold and its godly function. The relationship of the 'lytell boke' to God's grace is further compli-cated by the possible collapse of the work's spiritual apostolic ability to cross ʰoundaries and the extent to which its literal ability to circulate relates directly to its status as a commodity. In these terms Copland's verse creates a symbolic equivalence between the market in printed books and the operation of the grace of God. This tension is reflected in another verse that Copland produced in 1521, the Invocation he printed alongside a translation of *The Passyon of Our Lord*.

> Almyghty god / that dyed vpon the rode
> Vs to redeme / by thyne extreme doloure
> And wylfully there / shedde thy precyous blode
> Of parfyte faythe: dystyll let downe thy shoure
> Vs to endewe / from all spottes of errour
> And stedy vs / in goostly medytacyon
> Of thy grete payne / of our comforte and floure
> Suche werkes to vse / that be to our saluacyon.[47]

This verse works around a number of puns. The first one is on the word 'endewe' as in moisten and endow. Copland is punning on the idea of Christ's blood washing away all spots of errour in a spiritual sense but also a physical one. The word 'werkes' is punned in a very similar way in the final verse where the two meanings are spiritual acts of remembrance of Christ's sacrifice and more specifically the book itself as a work. This punning does not in anyway undermine the orthodoxy of Copland's verse.[48] What it does illustrate, as does the envoy to *The Myrrour of the Chyrche*, is the extent to which print created new possibilities, not only in relation to the expression of Christ's teaching but also in terms of who could claim the right to put it into the public sphere.

Copland's work of the 1520s consistently shows an awareness of the implications of the emergence of print in relation to the commodification of written knowledge. In his brilliant Prologue to *The Seuen Sorowes that women*

haue when theyr husbandes be deade, Copland creates an imaginary debate
between himself and a customer which stages the effects of market forces on
the circulation of knowledge or cunning in 1520s England. The Prologue
opens with Copland questioning his role as a writer.

> Copland.
> Why should I muse suche trifles for to wryte
> Of wanton toyes, but for the appetyte
> Of wandryng braynes, that seke for thynges new
> And do not reche if they be fals or trew.[49]

These musings are, however, rudely interrupted by a barrage of questions from
exactly the kind of 'wandryng brayne' that Copland is criticizing in these lines.

> Quidam (A Buyer).
> With what newes? or here ye any tidings
> Of the pope, of the Emperour, or of kynges
> Of martyn Luther, or of the great Turke
> Of this and that, and how the world doth worke.[50]

What distinguishes the questions that make up this verse are their lack of
order or real purpose. These are the questions of someone whose desire for
news, to know, has quite outstripped their wisdom. It does not matter to
Copland's prototype Buyer what they buy as long as they do, as long as there is
some news to be had. Copland, for the moment taking part in dialogue in his
head, comments:

> Copland.
> So that the tongue must euer wagge and clatter
> And waste their wyndes, to medle of eche matter
> This ben we prynters called on so fast
> That meruayle it is, how that our wittes can last.[51]

Despite the initial representation of the Buyer as someone who seems to
desire almost any text, it becomes apparent that he actually wants to buy
something quite specific. Copland, finally breaking his silence, tells the Buyer:
'... syr I haue a very proper boke / Of morall wysdome please ye their on to loke
/ Or els a boke of comen consolation.'[52]

The Buyer is not, however, interested in moral or spiritual works.

> Quidam.
> Tusshe a straw man, what should I do therewith
> Hast thou a boke of the wydowe Edith
> That hath begyled so many with her wordes /
> Or els suche a geest that is ful of bourdes [jests]
> Let me se, I wyll yet waste a peny
> Vpon suche thynges and if thou haue eny.[53]

The upshot of the dialogue between Copland and the Buyer is that the latter promises to recount from memory the story that he wants to buy so that it can be printed and presumably sold back to him as a finished commodity. The Prologue to *The Seuen Sorowes* depicts a world in which the boundaries between spoken word and print are entirely porous. The story that the Buyer tells Copland is one that he has seen elsewhere – in other words a printed text. Copland's prologue tells the story of a text's travels from print to the Buyer's memory and then back into print. It depicts a world in which the production and consumption of knowledge is entirely market-driven and based on the arbitrary wishes of buyers. The desire of 'wandryng braynes' like the Buyer to purchase news 'of this and that, and how the worlde doth worke' is so overwhelming that printers are driven to distraction trying to satisfy it.

The Seuen Sorowes, the work that Copland goes on to produce from the Buyer's words, is replete with bawdy puns which are often based on a tension between a word's or phrase's religious and bodily meanings. For example 'The fyrst sorowe' describes a widow's grief at having her husband 'layde in the graue'. The poem, however, quickly suggests that this grief is not simply for the dead husband:

> Consyderyng her good, that is gretly spente
> And the candell well nygh wasten and brent
> She loketh on the candell wyth a dolefull gost.[54]

The burnt and wasted candle in this verse symbolizes in general the husband's death, the fact that the flame of his life has gone out, and specifically the widow's grief at the loss of his 'candell'. Copland is playing here with religious imagery in a way that provokes the reader to bawdiness. Or perhaps more accurately, in these lines, and throughout the poem, Copland consistently mixes registers so that if the reader desires they can find sexual images beneath or behind the moralizing surface of the text. The pleasure that Copland's text offers its reader is the constant possibility of reading through its banally moralizing surface to find its hidden bawdy subtext. The implication of *The Seuen Sorowes* is that print is particularly suited to the creation of this kind of text. Copland's poem plays with the relationship between reader, text and writer / printer. The Prologue raises the question of authorship and suggests that the Buyer / Reader is ultimately the author of the text. The Buyer's / Reader's authorship of *The Seuen Sorowes* is then confirmed by the way the poem consistently incites its readers to find or excavate its bawdiness from its surface moralizing. In effect Copland is suggesting in this poem that while printers may produce works of 'moral wysdome' or 'comen consolation', the desires of their readers will render even these works susceptible to being read against their efficacious grain.

The Seuen Sorowes is not, however, an attack on the world of print. The fact that knowledge has become a commodity is treated by Copland as the basis of a joke. The Buyer partakes in the commodification of his own words purely so that he can satisfy his desire to consume them in printed form. Taking cunning to the market-place is a source of humor for Copland. He does not share Dudley's fears of a world in which the circulation of knowledge and learning is out of control or even worse simply determined by the rules of the market. Copland's celebration of the possibilities created by print is shared by a number of other works produced during the 1520s. For example *A Hundred Merry Tales*, 1526, presents its readers with a collection of jests without any prefatory or editorial guidance.[55] The jests themselves depict a world of arbitrariness where meaning is left ambiguous, is reduced to a pun or is even absent entirely. In a number of jests the purpose appears to be to simply to give the reader the pleasure of reading amusing narratives replete with slap-stick humor. *A Hundred Merry Tales* presents its readers with an image of the world of the popular as comic, anarchic and driven by a materialism that makes it fundamentally unthreatening to the social order of Tudor England.[56] Many of the tales that are included in *A Hundred Merry Tales* assume a readership that shared the interests of Copland's Buyer. For example,

> There was a mayde stode by a ryuers syde in her smock washynge clothes. And as she stoupyd oft tymes her smockke devyd between her butokkes. By whome there came a fere seynge her and sayde in sport. Mayd mayde take hede for Bayard bytys on the brydyll. Nay wys mater fere quod the mayden he doth but wype hys mouth and we nyth ye wyll come and kysse hym. [57]

This tale is typical of many of those included in *A Hundred Merry Tales*. Its humour depends on a moment of reversal in which the Friar's initial witty response to the erotic image of the maid doing the washing is turned on its head and instead made a comment upon his lack of sexual potency. Bayard might be biting on his bridle but, as far as the maid is concerned, unless he is prepared actually to act he is simply talking. The moral attached to this tale, 'By thys ye may se that a womans answer is neuer toseke' does not seem to relate to the tale's content except at a relatively banal level. It is questionable if the Friar was seeking an answer to his comment but, if he was, the maid's response is pertinent and witty. The ambiguous relation between this tale and its moral is typical of the collection as a whole. *A Hundred Merry Tales* plays with the idea that reading the bawdy, witty tales it contains has a moral or educational purpose. In truth the only reason for reading its stories and jests is their humour. Adding moral tags to them, particularly ones that are often provocatively inappropriate, nonsensical or banal, reflects the work's self-conscious parodic relationship with humanism. *A Hundred Merry Tales* allows its readers to indulge the fantasy that their reading has a moral or educational motivation while at the same time mocking the idea of 'studying' the jests and stories that it contains. *The Seuen Sorowes* and *A Hundred Merry Tales* embrace a world in which the production of texts and the circulation of knowledge are determined by the desires of the reader. Indeed in both texts the idea that people might buy them for any other reason than enjoyment is ridiculed. The management and control of learning and knowledge that so concerned Dudley in *The Tree of Commonwealth*, and which he argued there should be the job of the clergy, is not relevant in terms of the way *The Seuen Sorowes* or *A Hundred Merry Tales* construct their relationship with their readers. The only thing that determines their existence, and that of the 'cunning' they contain, is their desirability as commodities to be consumed for pleasure.

HERESY AND PAPISTRY IN THE WORK OF JOHN SKELTON AND WILLIAM TYNDALE

The relationship between the clericalist agenda of men like Dudley and the world of print as represented in Robert Copland's poetry is played out in the writing of John Skelton and William Tyndale. Both men shared Dudley's concern with the regulation of cunning. In Skelton's work existing anxieties over the status of authority in early Tudor England are given an additional charge and emphasis by the poet's involvement in the campaign against heresy provoked by the condemnation of Thomas Bilney in 1527.[58] Tyndale's work, and in particular *The Obedience of a Christian Man*, adopts a radical clericalist position towards the reform of the commonwealth similar to that of Alcock or Colet. In his work, however, the nature of this reformation, although not its scope, is governed by an incipient Protestantism.

Skelton's early career was spent at court, where he was Prince Henry's tutor from 1496–1501. Between 1503 and 1512 he was rector of the parish of Diss, Norfolk, but appears to have engineered a return to court by 1515. Much of Skelton's poetry is marked by a fear of disorder: social, political and in particular linguistic. This fear is coupled with an emphasis in his work on his status as poet and the right that this gave him to speak out on matters of national importance. Andrew Hadfield comments: 'If Skelton's career does have a consistent theme ... it must surely be his insistence on his Englishness and his ability to intervene in the "public sphere" to speak for the English people.'[59] The national role that Skelton assumed as the honest voice of poetic truth was, however, potentially undermined by his apparent wariness towards print; a technology which would have ensured his work had a far greater audience.[60] It is impossible now to determine the specific reasons why, unlike for example his contemporary Stephen Hawes, Skelton appears to have been reluctant to embrace the possibilities offered by print. His poem *Speke Parott*, however, does illustrate Skelton's concern with the corruption and distortion of language. It is one of a number of satires that Skelton wrote during the

1520s in which Cardinal Thomas Wolsey is depicted as sharing the qualities of Copland's Buyer in his relentless need to consume. In *Speke Parott* Skelton argues that Wolsey's usurpation of the king's authority has created a situation in which all authorities are in danger of being undermined and even language itself is becoming unhinged.

Speke Parott opens with an announcement, in Latin, that it will enhance its author's reputation. The next section of the poem is 'spoken' by Parott who introduces himself as a 'byrde of Paradyse'.[61] As the poem progresses, however, the number of narrative voices increases. At the same time the stability of the Parott's voice becomes less certain. At one moment the Parott is quoting a popular song and the next speaking in Latin. Even at those moments when the poem's voice is relatively stable its meaning remains problematic. For example in a verse that appears to refer directly to Wolsey's diplomatic mission to France in 1521 the poem's narrator asks the Parott also to go on a mission to Calais and plead for Wolsey to come home.

> Passe forthe, Parotte, towardes some passengere;
> Require hym to convey yow ovyr the salte fome;
> Addressyng your selfe, lyke a sadde messengere,
> To owur soleyne Seigneour Sadoke, desire hym to cum home,
> Making hys pilgrimage by *Nostre Dame de Crome*:
> For Jerico and Jerssey shall mete together as sone
> As he to exployte the man owte of the mone.[62]

In this verse the poem's narrator, or more accurately one of the voices that make up the text, asks Parott to act as a messenger to Wolsey, Seigneour Sadoke. The Parott's message is that the Cardinal should come home, but via the obscure church of Nostre Dame de Crome. Things are not, however, entirely as they seem in this verse: despite its relatively straightforward meaning, one needs to question the idea of using the Parott as an ambassador. Is this a reflection on the naivety of the poem's narrator? Or is it a comment on the world created by Wolsey's corruption in which a babbling parrot can even be considered for such a role?[63] If this is the case then the implication is that even the voices that make up Skelton's text have been subverted by the 'riot' or disorder caused by Wolsey. The final two lines of this verse suggest that this is indeed the case since, while they initially seem to be making a simple satirical point, this expectation is then dashed by the final line. The reader expects that in the final line the phrase 'As he to' will be followed by a practical purpose that, owing to his incompetence, Wolsey can no more achieve then Jericho and Jersey can meet. Instead the task that Wolsey is accused of failing at is 'expelling the man out of the moon'. It is as though at this moment *Speke Parott* is acknowledging that Wolsey's failures are a result of the nonsensical world in which he is forced to work. Such a reading, however, is unduly sympathetic to the Cardinal. Instead what Skelton is suggested in these lines is that it is impossible to even imagine Wolsey being involved in any real or practical endeavour. Wolsey's world is one in which the nonsensical rubs shoulders with the fantastic and his effect on the commonwealth is to fill it with nonsense.

The all persuasive nature of Wolsey's corruption becomes apparent in the final section of the poem when the Parott describes the state of the England under the Cardinal's sway.

> So myche prevye wachyng in cold wynters nights;
> So myche serchyng of loselles, and ys hym selfe so lewde;
> So myche conjuracions for elvyshe myday sprettes;
> So many bullys of pardon publysshed and shewyd;
> So myche crossing and blyssyng and hym all be shrewde
> Suche pollaxis and pyllers, suche mulys trapte with gold –
> Sens Dewcalyons flodde, in no cronycle ys told.[64]

The accusations made against Wolsey in this verse seem specific but are potentially undermined by the way in which they are expressed. Skelton's use of such poetic devices as internal rhymes and repetition suggest that the specificity of the text's complaints against Wolsey takes second place to its status as a poem. The poem's self-reflective emphasis at this point on its poetic nature, however, is what sustains its validity and authority. The emphasis on poetic order and form in the final verses of *Speke Parott* is designed to protect this section of the poem as much as possible from the baneful linguistic effects of Wolsey's rule. This is necessary because the rest of *Speke Parott* has consistently argued that Wolsey's corrupt effect on the commonwealth is most radical and generalized in the field of language. The Cardinal's nonsense has created a nonsensical world in which meaning has become almost impossible to imagine and the truth of the situation can only be heard from a babbling parroting parrot.[65]

In *Speke Parott* Wolsey's ambition and avarice know no boundaries and in the process destroy every boundary that they meet. Skelton imagines this process of reductive levelling in terms of the creation of a world in which the structures and norms that sustain meaning have been radically simplified and reduced to the single principle of Wolsey's all-pervasive desire. Like the market in news and knowledge created by print, Wolsey in *Speke Parott* operates as a principle of arbitrariness and disorder in the linguistic realm, making the meaning of words and the status of texts dependent not on their intrinsic worth but instead entirely on their place in a process of exchange and consumption.

In his later poem *A Replycacion Agaynst Certayne Yong Scolers Adjured of Late*, Skelton takes the imagery of linguistic disorder that in *Speke Parott* he associates with Wolsey and instead applies it to heresy.[66] In the process he gives traditional understandings and representations of the heretical radical new contours. In particular, whereas it is hyperbole to blame Wolsey for an all-pervasive collapse of linguistic order, when made in relation to heresy such an accusation makes complete sense. *A Replycacion* was written to condemn Thomas Bilney and another 'yong scholar', Thomas Arthur. It was apparently commissioned by Wolsey, whom Skelton is now happy to laud as 'the most worthy cardinal'.[67] *A Replycacion* is a vicious attack on Bilney and Arthur. It spares no time in debating the status or validity of their beliefs. Instead, in a move entirely typical of almost all English Reformation polemic, it effectively denies any possibility or even grounds for engaging seriously with what Bilney or Arthur actually believed or adjured. For Skelton heretical beliefs are inherently incoherent and nonsensical. This is not to say that heresy could not be attractive or sound impressive to the unwary, uneducated or naive. But there is no point in engaging it in serious dialogue since at its most basic level heresy has no positive content; it is simply a corruption or perversion of the truth. Skelton's representation of heresy in *A Replycacion* draws on traditional tropes and motifs, in particular heresy's inherently infectious character and its origin in excessive study.[68] Skelton also, however, in this poem exploits the possibilities created by print and poetry to create a text which on the page enacts heresy's disorder and its banishment from the public sphere.

A Replycacion has a similar complex graphic form to many of Skelton's other poems, where it is used to produce a hierarchy of voices within a poem's boundaries. In *A Replycacion* Skelton creates graphically on the page a clear distinction between those sections in the poem when in a formal official voice the text recounts the events surrounding the 'Yong Scolers'' recantation, these sections are often in Latin, and those which describe their heresy. Skelton's intention here is to separate the process of inquisition from heresy's disorder and corruption. *A Replycacion*'s representation of heresy consistently constructs it as being linguistically disordered and disordering. At the opening of the poem Skelton makes his readers experience by proxy the effects of heresy on the 'Yong Scolers'' learning.

Howe yong scolers nowe a dayes enbolned with the flyblowen blast of the moche vayne glorious pipplyng wynde, whan they have delectably lycked a lytell of the lycorous electuary of lusty lernyng, in the moche studious scolehous of scrupulous philology, countyng them selfe / excellently enformed and transcendingly sped in moche high connyng, and whan they have ones superciliously caught

> A lytell ragge of rethorike
> A lesse lumpe of logyke
> A pece or a patche of philosophy
> Than Forthwith by and by
> They tumble so in theology,

> Drowned in dregges of divinite,
> That they juge them selfe able to be
> Doctors of the chayre in the Vyntre
> At the Thre Cranes.[69]

When reading this section of Skelton's poem the reader moves from prose into poetry without a pause. Skelton rushes the reader on so that they experience a fall into the linguistic nonsense of Bilney's and Arthur's heresy with its rags of rhetoric and lumps of logic.[70] *A Replycacion* integrates heresy into its formal qualities as a poem by constantly making the reader experience the tension between the work's poetic form, which is marked by order and proportion, and heresy's disorder and formlessness. For example when Skelton describes the actual events surrounding the 'Yong Scolers'' act of penance at St Paul's Cross the meaning of his poetry appears to be in danger of collapsing into heresy's nonsense. He writes:

> Ye are brought to, 'Lo, Lo, Lo!'
> Se where the heretykes go,
> Wytlesse wandering to and fro!
> With, 'Te he, ta ha, bo ho, bo ho!'
> And suche wondringes many mo.
> Helas, ye wreches, ye may be wo![71]

These lines are at one level addressed directly to Bilney and Arthur since it is they who have been 'brought' to a place of public humiliation and woe. Skelton's readers have also, however, made this journey. They too are in a sense condemned to follow in Bilney's and Arthur's footsteps and, in reading *A Replycacion*, pass through the nonsense of heresy. In the process Skelton makes his reader experience heresy's reductive effects on learning and in particular language. The reader is brought to a place where words have become just meaningless sounds; their meaning entirely located in their sound.[72] In Skelton's poem the language of heresy wanders aimlessly, without order or sense. Its lacks a firm or proper place from which to speak since it is ultimately the product of the 'Yong Scolers'' extreme solipsism. The reader's escape from this maze of meaningless words is, however, provided by the form and proportion of Skelton's poetry.

Skelton's response in *A Replycacion* to the dangers of false teaching, and in particular heresy as a form of linguistic corruption, is to advocate poetry – typically he uses his own as an example – as embodying a mystical or divine order. He writes:

> ... there is a spyrituall,
> And a mysteriall
> And a mysticall
> Effecte energiall

As Grekes do it call
Of suche an industry
And suche a pregnancy,
Of heavenly inspiration
In laureate creation,
Of poets commendation,
That of divine myseracion
God maketh his habitation
In poets whiche excelles,
And sojourns with them and dwells.[73]

In these lines Skelton claims that poetry is the natural habitation of God. This reflects a central element of Skelton's argument in *A Replycacion* which is the applicability of the grammatical metaphor to the conflict between heresy and orthodoxy. The grammatical metaphor was developed during the medieval period and was based on the idea that the rules of grammar were part of nature, discovered and not invented by man. This led to an idealization by some medieval writers of grammar as a point of eternal and divine truth within the fallen human world.[74] The grammatical metaphor also, however, had a negative side in which spiritual lack was signified by, and enacted through, linguistic failure. In particular, the grammatical metaphor effectively created a distinction between truthful language, distinguished by a fullness based upon the unity of its parts, and falsehood, which was linguistically marked by an emptiness produced by a lack of equivalence between word, meaning and intention.[75] Applying the grammatical metaphor to the distinction between heresy and orthodoxy was not a new polemical strategy. Thomas Hoccleve in his early fifteenth-century anti-Lollard poem, *Address to Sir John Oldcastle*, argued that Oldcastle's '... fals conceites renne aboute loos!'[76] For Hoccleve, however, this was a minor element of his opponent's heresy; in the case of Bilney and Arthur, Skelton makes their 'loose conceits' central. Skelton's use of the grammatical metaphor allows him to construct orthodoxy as a real language, a set of ordered interrelated natural truthful signs, while representing heresy as a jumbled mess of words which, while appearing complex, are ultimately unproductive, sterile and nonsensical.

A Replycacion represents heresy as a form of linguistic solipsism in which the meaning of works has been emptied out and rendered meaningless. This emptiness is, however, a paradox since at one level the heretical in Skelton's poem is marked by an extreme, even excessive, material productivity. Bilney's and Arthur's studies are represented by Skelton as turning learning, philosophy, rhetoric, into lumps or pieces of matter. It is heresy's material emptiness in *A Replycacion* that creates an association between it and print. Bilney and Arthur in Skelton's poem act like printers, turning words into matter and infecting the public sphere with their mass of empty meaningless words.[77] Like Wolsey's greed in *Speke Parott*, their heresy is represented by Skelton as insatiable. If not checked it would shallow up the whole world in its protean, aimless wandering. Unlike Wolsey's corruption in *Speke Parott*, however, heresy as represented in *A Replycacion* can be generalized and applied across the realm without looking like hyperbole; there could be only one Wolsey – whereas one heretic could infect the whole world.[78] The use Skelton made of the grammatical metaphor, and his equation of heresy with the effects of print on learning, set the tone for mid-Tudor attacks on heresy.[79] There is, however, no difference in symbolic terms between heresy as represented in *A Replycacion* and papistry as it appeared in the pages of its author's Protestant opponents; Tyndale's papists come from exactly the same stock as Skelton's heretics.

Papistry is the truth's constant counterpart in the work of William Tyndale. Across all fields and registers, political, ecclesiastical and hermeneutic, Tyndale's papists range. Their presence, regardless of where they appear, is marked by a linguistic excess whose result is always to reduce and stifle meaning. William Tyndale is best known as translator of the English Bible. He worked as a tutor in Gloucestershire before travelling in 1523 to London, where he asked Cuthbert Tunstall, the bishop of London, to support his plan to translate the Bible into English – in one of the great 'what if' moments of Tudor history, he was turned down. Tyndale's response was to travel to Germany and complete a translation of the New Testament which was published in 1526. From this date until his death in 1536 it is probably accurate to regard Tyndale as the leading English Protestant of his generation.[80] He went on to produce a translation of the Pentateuch as well as numerous polemical works.[81]

Tyndale's *Obedience of a Christian Man* is at one level a radical work of political theory.[82] Its solution to political and social conflict is the need for absolute obedience across all social and political registers. Tyndale tells his readers:

> I have described unto you the obedience of children, servants, wives and subjects. These four orders are of God's making, and the rules therof are God's word. He that keepeth them shall be blessed ... and he that breaketh them shall be cursed. If any person of impatiency, or a stubborn and rebellious mind, withdraw himself from any of these, and get him to any other order, let him not think thereby to avoid the vengeance of God in obeying rules and traditions of man's imagination.[83]

In this passage Tyndale reduces the complex world of early Tudor society to four orders and constructs any deviation from this structure as inherently sinful. Tyndale's argument throughout *Obedience* is based on a conflict between the coherence, singularity and absolute nature of God's truth and papistry's endless desire to subvert and deny it through linguistic anarchy.[84] Tyndale consistently represents papistry in terms of its corrupt language and its corruption of language. His papists obscure the literal truth and enact this obscurity in their words. Their language is productive but sterile, voluminous but empty, clever but meaningless.[85] Tyndale never tires of arguing that ultimately papists reduce the meaning of language to the level of the body, and in particular the belly. When commenting on how the Bible has been interpreted Tyndale writes:

> [The papists] follow the four senses of the scripture, of which three are no senses; and the fourth, that is to wit the literal sense ... hath the pope taken to himself ... We must abide his interpretation. And as his bellies think, so must we think; though it be impossible to gather any such meaning of the scripture.[86]

The papists reduce the meaning of Scripture to a single all encompassing principle – their bellies. Their reductive desires are not, however, only directed against God's word. *Obedience* argues that in both the political and social spheres the papists distort and destroy the natural God-sanctioned order by introducing linguistic complexity, sophistry and dark reasons into the public sphere. Tyndale's solution to the papist's corruption, political, social and hermeneutic, is radical and iconoclastic. It is to sweep them and their language away.

In *Obedience* Tyndale argues that 'one king, one law is God's ordinance in every realm'.[87] The implication of this is that an ideal commonwealth would be distinguished by its unity and stability. It would also, however, be strangely silent since the absolute requirement of obedience laid upon everyone from servant to monarch effectively removes the need for any kind of political sphere. This is, however, not the whole story in terms of the politics of *Obedience*, since producing a truthful ordered commonwealth demands constant vigilance. In particular, it requires the labour of those who possess the abilities needed to expound God's truth and confront the lies of the papists. *Obedience* argues for absolute obedience in the context of a rigid model of the society. At the same time the implication of this work is that the process of producing a purged godly society requires men like Tyndale, people from outside society's rigid bounds, to act as guides and protectors. Purging papistry and restoring society to a state of transparent order based upon obedience is represented in Tyndale's work as a process of violent purgation. In particular, the linguistic nature of papistry's corruption creates a need for people, like Tyndale, who can perform the linguistic iconoclasm needed to dispel papist sophistry. Despite the emphasis in *Obedience* on monarchical power implicit in this work is a clericalist agenda that in its construction of the central importance of clergy in the process of reformation would not have been out of place in the work of Colet or Alcock. The apparent tension between valorization of the role of the monarch and its clerical agenda reflects the extent to which *Obedience* is a self-consciously performative and rhetorical text – the work of a preacher not a political theorist. Richard Y. Duerden comments, with reference to *Obedience*, 'Tyndale's rendering of the monarch is not ... a description, but a ... metaphorical idealization'.[88] It is the creation of such aspirational ideals that is at the centre of Tyndale's political *and* religious agenda. He conceived of his role as a prophet in print creating aspirational images, metaphors and tropes.[89] Even the plain literal truth of Scripture is an idealization, an allegorical figure, which his work as a translator created as an object for Christians to work towards but did not, and indeed could not, make present.[90]

Papistry, with all its linguistic wiles, endangered Tyndale's work because it shared the same tools that he needed as a writer and preacher. In his prologue to Leviticus, Tyndale wrote:

> beware of allegories for there is not a more handsome or apt thing to beguile withal than an allegory, nor more subtle and pestilent thing in the world to persuade a false matter than an allegory. And contrariwise there is not a better, vehementer or mightier thing to make a man understand withal than an allegory. For allegories make a man quick witted, and print wisdom in him and maketh it to abide, where bare words go but in at one ear and out at the other.[91]

The plain truth of the Bible is a mighty allegory. Seeking to read it and understand was for Tyndale a life-time's work. He told readers of his translation of Genesis, 'As thou readest ... think that every syllable pertaineth to thine own self, and suck out the pith of scripture, and arm thyself against all assaults.'[92] The most important, indeed in some ways the only, weapon that Tyndale reader's needed in order to defend themselves was scripture – internalized and made one's own. This would leave the papists 'ever gnawing upon the bitter bark without and never attaining unto the sweet pith within'.[93]

The relative sophistication of Tyndale's papists as allegorical tropes only really becomes apparent when compared with papistry as represented in the work of writers like John Bale or in Henrician propaganda. *A litel treatise ageynste the mutterynge of some papistes in corners* was published anonymously in 1534 as part of the government's propaganda campaign in support of the Royal Supremacy.[94] It is replete with anti-papal propaganda depicting papal greed in terms of its insatiability and linguistic excess.

> What laws hath [the Pope] devised, what legations, what and how many divers courts, what dispensations, what pensions out of abbeys exempt, what Peter pens out of parishes, what reservations, what constitutions, what citations, what suspensions, what pardons, what kind of cursings and blessings and absolutions, what wyles, what gyles, what frauds, what devilish deceipts and snares are daily covertly couched to catch coin from the people.[95]

In this passage the words pile up until their meaning becomes almost redundant. It is their multiplicity that matters – adding 'what wyles' after 'what gyles' adds nothing to the meaning of this passage. The reader is not expected to think about different papist wyles and gyles. This passage performs the linguistic excess of papistry. And part of its motivation is a desire to be comic. *A litel treatise* represents papistry as a form of excessive linguistic productivity that is ultimately sterile since it fills up the political, religious, social and textual space with empty, meaningless words.

Papistry as represented by John Bale is endlessly associated with inappropriate and sterile textual production. He constantly produces lists of papist falsehood, corrupt monkish orders and false religious practices. These lists, however, are not simply important in terms of their content. Indeed at one level their content is redundant and this is the point of their appearance in Bale's text. In his play *King Johan* the character Clergy lists all the religious orders that make up the church.[96] Although in the original version of the play this list was six lines long and included twenty 'orders' Bale was apparently not satisfied with this and added another forty orders when he revised the work.[97] Clergy's list is at one level simply intended to express the diversity and inappropriate number of papist religious orders. At the same time, however, it has a function that goes beyond its actual content. It is designed to mark papistry as being inherently and deliberately wasteful of the space of religion; of filling it up with pointless and ultimately meaningless names. As in *A litel treatise*, though at far greater length and in much more detail, Bale represents papistry using tropes and figures similar to those deployed by Skelton in his depiction of heresy in *A Replycacion*. Bale's papistry, like Skelton's heresy, is ultimately nothing more then empty words and endless sentences. But at the same time it has the potential not only to undermine the social and political order but also to eat away and destroy the very fabric of language itself.

What separates Tyndale's papists from those of Bale and other later Protestant writers is his awareness of his own investment in the kind of textual strategies and tropes that in Bale's work are constructed as inherently papist. Tyndale knew that it was nonsense to argue that, for example, allegory was an unambiguous indicator of papistry. He tells readers of his Old Testament, 'the very use of allegories is to declare and open a text that it may be the better perceived and understood'.[98] Tyndale's religious agenda is driven by a desire to teach, to preach the word of God. Sometimes this meant emphasizing the plain text of the Bible while at other times it involved creating a paranoid account of papist corruption. If using allegories helped explain God's literal word then Tyndale was quite prepared to do this and to advise others to follow his lead. What is most noticeable about Tyndale's work is its sense of urgency, its insistence on the need for spiritual renewal through a return to the purity of Christ's teaching. Tyndale constructs himself in his writing as a prophet, a printed preacher, speaking from the wilderness to demand repentance and reformation. It is his assumption of this public role that links him with likes of Colet, Alcock and even Skelton.[99]

Skelton and Tyndale claimed to speak with privileged voices within the public sphere: as a writer of poetry, God's natural habitat, and as a Biblical translator, freeing God's voice from papist chains. For Skelton and Tyndale it is language, pure and divine or heretical and papist, that is the battleground of the Reformation. The poetics of confessionalization demanded two different languages – one of large empty sentences, of windy words and misty reasons and another of short sentences, order, proportion and truth. Confessional language in the hands of men less gifted then Tyndale or Skelton was coarse and reductive.[100] And it is was against the confessionalization of language that Thomas More protested in the *Dialogue concerning Heresies*.

SIR THOMAS MORE AND THE *DIALOGUE CONCERNING HERESIES*

The *Dialogue concerning Heresies* was first printed in 1529 and was almost certainly written as part of the same campaign that saw the production of Skelton's *A Replycacion*. In the canon of More's work the *Dialogue concerning Heresies* has often been seen as the moment when the learned, witty, humanist More transformed into the bigoted, boring, persecutionary More. However, the *Dialogue concerning Heresies* is not a prose version of Skelton's poem. Nor is it the first instalment of More's later polemic works against Tyndale. The *Dialogue concerning Heresies* is instead a complex work of religious polemic and literature. In it More uses his skills as a writer to teach, or perhaps more accurately remind, his readers how to read. The *Dialogue concerning Heresies* is a lesson in careful reading, but one which ultimately More thought no educated or reasonable man should need; a lesson for the doubters, for the over-clever and the easily swayed, for those already infected by the temptation to read through a simplifying confessional prism.

Sir Thomas More had a distinguished political and intellectual career before entering the King's service in 1518. He rose to prominence during the 1520s until he became Lord Chancellor in 1529. His tenure in this office was, however, uneasy as it corresponded with Henry's attack on the papacy as part of his campaign for a divorce. More resigned the office of Lord Chancellor in 1532. It appears that Henry never forgave him for his opposition to the Royal Supremacy. In 1534 More was sent to the Tower for refusing the Oath of Supremacy and a year later he was executed.[101] The *Dialogue concerning Heresies* is a massive work. It works systematically and in detail through the attitudes and beliefs that More considered were the major heresies of his time. In particular, in this work More attacks what he regarded as the heretical beliefs of Bilney and Tyndale. Despite its polemical religious agenda, the *Dialogue concerning Heresies* is a self-conscious piece of literary fiction.[102] It consistently places in the foreground its fictionality, reflects on its status as a piece of writing and embodies a complex hermeneutic model.[103]

More opens the *Dialogue concerning Heresies* with a proverb. 'It is an olde sayd saw / that one busynes begettyth and bringeth forth a nother.'[104] He then goes on to recount how the *Dialogue concerning Heresies* came to be printed. He tells how a 'secrete sure frende' sent to him a messenger to question the credence to be given to some matters which, although 'certayne and owt of doute', had recently been 'put to question'. Having answered his friend through his messenger, More then had doubts about the messenger's ability to remember the whole of their discussion: 'me thought I had not well done / without wrytynge / to truste onely his memory / namely syth some partys of the mater be such of them selfe / as rather nede to be attentely redde and aduysed / than houerly harde and passyd ouer'.[105] More's decision to commit his words to writing is also motivated by a concern over the messenger's trustworthiness. Having written an account of the dialogue between him and the messenger, More then finds that this text has been copied and circulated. Indeed his words have even been carried over the sea and have there fallen into the hands of English heretics. It is in order to forestall the production by these 'shrewde apostates' of corrupt versions of his text that More produces a printed version of the *Dialogue concerning Heresies*. However, before printing the final version of his dialogue with the messenger, More has his work checked for accuracy and orthodoxy: 'I determyned that I wolde nothynge alowe nor defende / that the iudgement of other vertuouse [and] connynge men wold in any wyse mysse lyke.'[106] Finally the finished text of the *Dialogue concerning Heresies* is put before its readers as an accurate and full account of the discussion between More and his friend's messenger.

Of course none of this is true. The 'More' of this preface is as much as textual construct as the messenger. More opens the *Dialogue concerning Heresies* quoting a proverb and the rest of the preface goes on to illustrate perfectly the truth of this saying. In particular, More's preface applies the principle of this saying to the process of producing knowledge in the world of print. There is an inexorable logic behind the preface's story of how and why the *Dialogue concerning Heresies* was printed, as if once spoken the dialogue between More and the messenger was destined to end up in print. The More of the preface adopts a weary and resigned attitude to this inevitability. He claims that it is only a series of doubts, over the messenger's ability to remember the whole dialogue and his trustworthiness, that led to the production of a written record of the dialogue. Further anxieties over the circulation of this work then made More produce a finished printed version of the *Dialogue concerning Heresies*. The effect of this story is to create a series of recessions that separate the initial dialogue between More and the messenger from the work in its final form. In particular, the preface to the *Dialogue concerning Heresies* raises doubts over More's authorship. Not in an absolute sense – of course More wrote it – but in terms of intention. The preface to the *Dialogue concerning Heresies* creates a number of surrogate authors, the secret friend whose letter provides the initial impetus for the work, the messenger whose questions provide the text's motivation, More's doubts over the messenger's trustworthiness and even the 'shrewde apostates' whose probable desire to produce a corrupt version of the *Dialogue concerning Heresies* leads to its final publication. In this preface More makes Doubt, the friend's, the messenger's, More's and the apostates', the author of his work.[107]

This authorial doubt is not, however, shared by More the actual writer of the *Dialogue concerning Heresies*, although it is at times by his fictional persona. The whole preface can be read as one long joke. In particular, the story it tells of the work's journey from speech to writing before ending in print can be compared with the Robert Copland's similarly convoluted account of the process by which *The Seuen Sorowes* came to be printed. One of the effects of the ironic and comic tone of the preface is to remind the attentive reader that they are reading a work of fiction. For example, the fictional More claims that one reason for producing a written version of his dialogue with the messenger was a concern that parts of their discussion needed to be read and considered and not simply heard. But at this point in the story no written version of the work in theory exists. More's irony here, partly directed at his own fictional self, emphasizes the necessary fictionality of his, and indeed all, printed dialogues – no dialogue between two real, as opposed to printed, people could resemble that between More and the messenger. This moment is also, however, exemplary of the serious argument of More's text. The preface to the *Dialogue concerning Heresies* opens with a piece of simple oral wisdom that it then shows to be true. But this truthfulness is one that is beyond the written printed world depicted in the preface – one suffused by doubt. It is this all-pervasive doubt that the *Dialogue concerning Heresies* is written to disperse but also to critique.

Much of the *Dialogue concerning Heresies* is taken up with a detailed exam-ination of the case of Thomas Bilney.[108] This discussion relates directly to the issues raised in the work's preface since what is exposed during its course is the messenger's radical, almost ontological, state of doubt. The messenger doubts everything and anything about Bilney's case. The only thing that he appears to believe is that Bilney was innocent but even this is a largely negative belief based upon scepticism concerning the trustworthiness and honesty of the authorities. What More argues in the *Dialogue concerning Heresies* is that the messenger's doubt is corrosive not only in terms of accepted religious beliefs or practices but ultimately of all knowledge. In particular, it creates a world which truth resides with the individual and doubt runs havoc every-where else; tearing up the social order, destroying learning and undermining belief. At the beginning of Book III of the *Dialogue concerning Heresies*, More gives the messenger an account of how Bilney fell into heresy.

> [Bilney] ... after [that] he fell from [the] study of the law (wherin he was proctour and partely well lernyd) vnto the studye of scrypture / he was as I say very ferefull and scrupulouse / [and] began at the furste to fall in to such a scrupulouse holynes / that he rekenyd hym self bounden ... to kepe ... the wordys of Cryst after the very letter / that bycause our lorde byddeth vs when we pray enter oure chamber and shyt the dore to vs / he thought it therefore synne to say his seruice abrode / and alway wold be sure to haue hys chamber dore shyt vnto hym whyle he sayd hys matins.[109]

In More's account Bilney's attempt to follow the letter of Christ's words led him to retreat into the solitary space of his chamber. It is this solitariness that ultimately leads to his downfall, since, as More argues, it created the conditions for Bilney to pass through scrupulous religiosity into heresy:

> wyth the werynesse of that superstycyous fere and seruyle drede / he fell as farre to the contrary. And vnder pretexte of loue and lyberty waxed so dronke of [that] new must of lewd lyghtnes of mynd [and] vayn gladnesse of harte / whyche he toke for spyrytuall consolacyon / [that] what so euer hym self lysted to take for good / that thought he forthwith approued by god. And so framed hym selfe a fayth / framed hym selfe a conscyence / framed hym / selfe a deuocion wheryn hym lyste / and wherin hym lyked he sette hym selfe at lybertye.[110]

In this version of Bilney's fall into heresy, the over-scrupulous private study of the Bible, which took the place of public worship, led to him creating his own personal fantasy religion. More's use of the word 'frame' to describe Bilney's construction of his new religion is designed to suggest its mechanical and artificial nature. The idea of framing a new religion also relates Bilney's methods to those of printers who used frames to produce texts.[111] What Bilney frames is, however, created entirely for his own consumption. Like Copland's Buyer he makes his own text which he can then consume in a process of continual self-intoxication and self-consumption.

Chapter Three of Book III of the *Dialogue concerning Heresies* addresses the messenger's doubts concerning Bilney's trial. During the course of this discussion More tells the story of another examination he had attended.

> I was also my selfe synce his [Bilney's] abiuracyon (as it happed) with an honorable prelate at suche tyme as one that was an auncyent heretyke had been examyned / and there had confessed [that] he had holden / taught / and in diverse countries spredde about almost all the heresyes / that any lewd heretyke holdeth.
> May ye not tell his name quod he? [the messenger]
> Which of them quod I. For he had mo names than halfe a lefe can holde.
> Where dwellyd he quod your frende?
> Euery where and no where quod I. For he walked about as an apostle of the deuyll from shyre to shyre and towne to towne thorowe the realme.[112]

This passage is accompanied by a marginal gloss, 'Heretikes most comenly haue divers names'. It is not clear who this ancient heretic is or was. Indeed the way More describes him indicates that he is less a real person then a personification of the principle of heresy. More's ancient heretic is distinguished by his lack of fixity. Diversity is his main characteristic, of beliefs, names and places. He is an image of heresy's lack of purpose – its aimless, pointless wandering.

More's ancient heretic, however, represents more then simply the protean quality of heresy. He also expands the focus of the discussion at a point when it was in danger of getting too specific. This is typical of More's polemical strategy in the *Dialogue concerning Heresies*. Sometimes it is a merry tale or a piece of proverbial wisdom that changes the focus of the text. In this case, however, More's intention is more serious. His ancient heretic can be related directly to the Old Man who plays such a significant but ultimately ambiguous role in Chaucer's *The Pardoner's Tale*. Chaucer was one of More's favourite writers. In one of the last letters More wrote from the Tower of London he quoted Chaucer's *Troilus and Criseyde*, presumably from memory.[113] *The Pardoner's Tale* is about corrupt false preaching. Chaucer's Pardoner, like More's heretics, distorts religion to make it serve his own ends. In particular, the 'moral' tale at the centre of the Pardoner's 'sermon' turns out to have no real moral or even purpose. Its complexity hides its essential spiritual sterility.[114] In this work Chaucer is criticizing readers who in their desire for complex texts lose sight of the morality of what they are reading, who put large sentences before worthy sayings. The Old Man at the centre of *The Pardoner's Tale* is a strange doomed figure condemned to wander the earth endlessly unable to die. In a recent article on this poem Lee Patterson has discussed the religious implications of the Old Man's fate, commenting:

> It is as a figure of despair driven by incestuous yearnings that the Old Man of *The Pardoner's Tale* invokes the figure of Judas. And he also invokes him, and his Old Testament prefiguration, Cain, in his condition of endless wandering.[115]

More's ancient heretic and Chaucer's Old Man share many characteristics, most notably their endless pointless wandering. What links them most directly is, however, that they both refer to those archetypal rebels against God, Cain and Judas. The ancient heretic in the *Dialogue concerning Heresies* has no name – or rather he has half a page of them – all false; he lives nowhere – or again more accurately he lives in every shire and town; like heresy he is potentially everywhere and everyone. This lack of definition and protean quality is, however, an aspect of his despair. The ancient heretic's endless wandering, like that of Chaucer's Old Man, relates to a specifically hermeneutic failure. Despite the fact that they appear to be constantly on the move, their failure properly to understand Christ's teaching means they are actually stuck in a sterile non-productive state. Like Bilney, their failure to read the spirit of the word means they are caught in a world they have made; framed in their own fantasies. The *Dialogue concerning Heresies* ends with a vision of Judgement Day:

> Cryst shall at [the] last restrayne [and] destroy his Idoll Anticryst with [the] spyryte of his holy mouth / repayryng [and] delatyng his chyrche agayne / [and] gathering therinto as well the remenaunt of the Iewes / as all other sectes abrode aboute the worlde / shall make all folke one flocke vnder hym selfe the shepeherde / and delyuer a gloryous kyngdome to his father of all the saued people from our foremare father Adam to [the] last day.[116]

This apocalyptic vision, however, seems to sit oddly alongside the prosaic nature of the final words of the *Dialogue concerning Heresies*: 'And after dyner he [the messenger] departed home towarde you / and I to the courte.'[117] The apparent disjuncture between the Apocalypse and the details of everyday human life is, however, illusionary. More knew, as a good Augustinian, that each moment of time is shot through with the truth of Christ's teaching. By the end of the *Dialogue concerning Heresies* the messenger too has learnt this lesson, as have More's readers. It is easy as one works through the complexities of the debate between the messenger and More to lose sight of the ultimate purpose of their discussions. At the end of the work, however, More reminds his readers that outside the closed logic of the dialogue exists the reality of people's daily lives and the promise of Christ's return – both of which are far more real then the doubt-filled dialogue of More and the messenger.

In the *Dialogue concerning Heresies* More is attempting to achieve two potentially contradictory results. His first aim is the explicit one of confounding heresy. His approach to this is, however, unusual in terms of English Reformation writing since throughout the *Dialogue concerning Heresies* he attempts to engage in detail with the actual beliefs and attitudes of those he regarded as heretics. It was far more common in writing of this kind to adopt the approach of Skelton or Tyndale and simply dismiss one's opponents as either papists or heretics. And the fact that this dismissal could be lengthy, humorous and detailed did not diminish the extent to which it ultimately depended on characterizing one's doctrinal enemies as speakers of the nonsensical language of papistry / heresy. More's work is not in anyway non-polemical or fair to his opponents. But it does treat their views seriously. This accounts for the important similarities, but also differences, between the representation of Bilney in *A Replycacion* and in the *Dialogue concerning Heresies*. Skelton and More agree that Bilney's fall into heresy was initially as a result of too much study. But whereas Skelton's Bilney is portrayed in mocking tones as a fool, More's is a more sophisticated, plausible and therefore dangerous figure.[118] For More, simply producing a tropological précis of one's opponents and their beliefs, allowing the label heretical to work as an over-reaching hermeneutic tool, was to encourage precisely the kind of hasty superficial reading that led people into spiritual peril.

The *Dialogue concerning Heresies* is a long and detailed work because it wants its readers to take their time and grapple with all the implications of the beliefs of a man like Bilney before rejecting them.[119] It is this learning process through reading that reflects More's other aim in this work, which was to resist the poetics of confessionalization. The *Dialogue concerning Heresies*, despite all its polemics against heretics, is an anti-confessional text. It resists the kind of simplified and effective strategies adopted in *A Replycacion* or *The Obedience of a Christian Man*. Instead in this work More argues that he can combine a multiplicity of different genres and forms, he can discuss heresy in detail, he can produce passages of allegory, visions of Judgement Day, he can refer to the works of the Fathers, and all this can come together in a coherent whole without resorting to the imposition of the radically simplified confessional hermeneutics of Skelton or Tyndale. Instead he trusts his readers, as the messenger does at the end of the *Dialogue concerning Heresies*, to go into their chambers, read his work and understand its message.[120] It is this confidence, and the demands it makes on the reader, that the events of the 1530s drained from Tudor culture.[121] In place of More's confidence, one has the anxious fraught poetry of men like Sir Thomas Wyatt and the banality of official Henrician propaganda.

More's *A Dialogue of Comfort Against Tribulation*, written in the Tower in 1534–35, takes the form of a dialogue between two Hungarians, Anthony and Vincent.[122] During the course of their discussions they deal with a whole range of possible tribulations that can befall a Christian. Their nationality makes them particularly aware of the dangers posed by war and armed invasion since their dialogue is overshadowed by the knowledge that the Great Turk will probably attack again soon. Towards the end of *A Dialogue of Comfort Against Tribulation*, More produces a terrifying image of hell to illustrate that nothing in earth, not even the sight of the Turkish army drawn up ready for battle, should be enough to make a Christian renounce their faith.

> if yon shuld sodaynly than [look] on the tother side [away from the Turkish army], the grownd quake [and] ryve atwayne, [and] the devilles rise out of hell, [and] shew themselfe in such vgly shappe as dampnid wretchis shall see them / [and] ... we shuld loke downe into that pestilent pitt [and] se the swarme of sely soules in the terrible tourmentes there: we wold wax so ferd of that sight, that as for the Turkes hoste, we shuld scantly remember we saw them.[123]

In this passage More plays a trick on his reader since one can hardly fail to forget the Turkish army when confronted with an image of hell opening at one's feet. *A Dialogue of Comfort Against Tribulation* is one of More's final expressions of his confidence in the power of writing. One can read the Turks as Protestants or heretics, and indeed many modern critics and historians have made this assumption. But More's work clearly indicates that this is a false over-reductive reading.[124] Or more accurately to read it in this way is to reduce the meaning and significance of the text, forcing it to fit into a simplified confessional mould and thereby to be far less challenging as a Christian work. More wants his work to make his readers think. In this, as in much else, he is a profoundly un-Henrician writer since for Henry what mattered was obedience, not thought.

CONCLUSION

In 1534 Germen Gardynare, probably Gardiner, was credited as the author of a work entitled, *A letter of a younge gentleman named mayster Germen Gardynare, wryten to a frend of his, wheron men may se the demeanour [and] heresy of John Fryth late burned.*[125] This is a curious text. It is a rare example of an account of an examination written from the perspective of the authorities, or at least someone in sympathy with them. It mocks John Frith as an arrogant young man incapable of understanding the most obvious points of Christian teaching.[126] Gardynare comments that 'it were not possible for all the doctors that be and haue ben to wryte so playn as to make Firth call them playne'.[127] Later Gardynare reports that Frith refused to answer a question relating to the role of the church in defining heresy, telling his inquisitors 'he wolde not answere directely, but sayde take me as you wyll'. Gardynare's response to this attempt to evade the question was to remind Frith that 'we must order our wyll iff we wold do well'.[128] *A letter of a younge gentleman* presents Frith in an unflattering light as an arrogant young man who, despite his youth and lack of learning, is prepared to argue over serious matters of religion that he does not properly understand. *A letter of a younge gentleman* is, however, also surprisingly critical of the person it was allegedly sent to, Gardynare's unnamed friend, probably Edward Fox.[129] Whomever the letter was allegedly addressed to, in it Gardynare speculates about the effect hearing Frith's heretical views on the mass will have upon them. 'Me thynke I se hereat your ioyntes tremble, your / eyes stare, your heares stert up, and all the behauour of your body alter, abhorynge these deuelyshe wordes of thys cursed wretche. But who can let the deuyll to be lyke hym selfe.'[130] Gardynare's depiction of the likely response of his friend, and by implication his readers, to Frith's heresy serves to remind one that the title of this tract includes a promise that it would display the 'demeanour [and] heresy of John Fryth'. It is how Frith behaved during his examination at least as much as his actual views that Gardynare wishes to bring to his reader's attention.[131] The sub-text of *A letter of a younge gentleman* is the comforting one that it is possible to tell if someone is a heretic by their demeanour. However the other implication of Gardynare's work is that heresy can produce a violent disordered response even in the most orthodox person.

A letter of a younge gentleman is an entirely typical piece of English Reformation writing. Its representation of the process of inquisition is a mirror image of the far more numerous Protestant accounts of examinations and trials. In the latter it is the inquisitors that are unreasonable, cannot sustain a coherent argument and whose bodies announce the truth of their violent disordered natures. In *A letter of a younge gentleman* it is Frith's inner disorder that is announced unwittingly by his body. When confronted by a passage from saint Hilary that he can not answer, he 'began as yt had ben in a tragedye, to ruffle and crye why had not the byshoppe told hym this'.[32] It is not only, however, the depiction of Frith in this text, but also the way that *A letter of a younge gentleman* asks to be read, that is typical of much of the writing produced between 1530 and 1580. Gardynare's work has a clear polemical agenda, which is to incite the reader to position themselves alongside those examining Frith. At the same time *A letter of a younge gentleman*'s slightly mocking construction of the friend to whom it is allegedly addressed suggests that they are not an appropriate model for the reader to imitate. Gardynare's work seeks to position its readers in the examination room between the heretical Frith, the easily seduced friend who appears not to be prepared to play a full part in the struggle against heresy, and those actually examining Frith.[33] It consistently incites the reader to side with the examiners against Frith and in comparison with the absent friend.

A letter of a younge gentleman equates a subjectivity based on reason, coherence and order with its own religious position while at the same time representing its opponents, like Frith, as unreasonable disordered people, who, when faced with an argument they cannot answer, behave like tragic actors, crying and ranting. It argues that those who fail to embrace its own specific religious position are themselves in danger of being seduced by heresy. Gardynare's work illustrates a tension produced by confessionalization between religious polemic and pleasure. Reading *A letter of a younge gentleman* was meant to be instructive and pleasurable. The rules of the market place were not suspended for religious writing. As a commodity, *A letter of a younge gentleman* offered its readers not only religious polemic but also the frisson of experiencing the process of examination. Those who bought it got the gothic excitement and voyeuristic thrill of owning a text that promised to display the notorious heretic Frith and the truth about his shocking heresy. These readerly pleasures, however, ultimately endanger the tract's polemical agenda since they relate to the performative world of Frith and heresy. *A letter of a younge gentleman* presents its readers with the stark choice of aligning themselves with its confessional position or remaining in a state of lukewarm orthodoxy and therefore, like the friend, holding a dangerously naïve view as regards the seductive nature of heresy – and the pleasures of the text. The confessionalized world depicted in *A letter of a younge gentleman* is one in which writing and reading have taken on dangerous, reductive, even lethal qualities; in which reading can suddenly become inquisition and to write is potentially to place oneself in the examination chamber. This is the context for the writing of the period 1530–47, a world in which one word out of place could lead to either the martyr's pyre or the traitor's block.

NOTES

1 Heinz Schilling, *Religion, Political Culture and the Emergence of Early Modern Society* (Leiden: 1992), pp. 209–210.

2 Reinhard argues that confessionalization, 'the establishment of pure doctrine and its handy formulation in a confession of faith, which could be used to measure everybody's orthodoxy', took place right across Western Europe during the period 1530–80. He goes on to suggest that, despite the different confessions being produced, Lutheran, Catholic and Calvinist, the effects of confessionalization were fundamentally the same across Europe (Wolfgang Reinhard, 'Reformation, Counter-Reformation, and the Early Modern State: A Reassessment', *The Catholic Historical Review*, 75 (1989), pp. 383–404, p. 391).

3 Heinz Schilling, 'Confessional Europe', in *Handbook of European History 1400–1600 Late Middle Ages: Renaissance and Reformation*, Vol. 2, eds Thomas A. Brady, Heiko A. Oberman and James D. Tracy (Leiden: 1995), pp. 641–681, p. 659.

4 John Guy, *Tudor England* (Oxford: 1991), pp. 166–171.

5 Michael Braddick comments: 'The state is not a purely institutional phenomenon ... The state creates and is created by a degree of normative consensus and organizational co-ordination.' Confessionalization strengthened the state not just in institutional terms but perhaps far more importantly in relation to the homogenization of political classes, often across wide social divides. See Michael Braddick, 'State Formation and Social Change in Early Modern England', *Social History*, 16 (1991), pp. 1–17, p. 2.

6 See John Guy, 'The Rhetoric of Counsel in Early Modern England', in *Tudor Political Culture*, ed. Dale Hoak (Cambridge: 1995), pp. 292–310, p. 293.

7 For the seminal discussion of popery as a concept see Peter Lake, 'Anti-Popery: The Structure of a Prejudice', in *Conflict in Early Stuart England: Studies in Religion and Politics 1603–1642*, eds Richard Cust and Ann Hughes (London: 1989), pp. 72–106. Despite the early Stuart focus of Lake's essay, its description of the essential qualities of popery can be applied across the early modern period. This is because, even though there were important changes to reflect the political situation, popery (just like its twin, heresy) in terms of its practices and effects within the polity remained constant from 1533–1688.

8 It is sometimes assumed that there was something specifically egalitarian or even democratic about Protestantism. This is not the case. Confessionalization, whether it produced Protestantism or Catholicism as the state religion, had the potential to legitimize the eruption of non-elite voices into the political sphere. The classic example of this is the way in which resistance theory was passed back and forth by Catholics and Protestants during the French religious wars. The argument that a monarch could be resisted on confessional grounds was a potential within all confessionalized religious identities and not the property of one or the other.

9 See Gerald Strauss, *Enacting the Reformation in Germany: Essays on Institution and*

Reception (Aldershot: 1993), p. 5.

10 On the Reformation as a pan-European process leading to the creation of authorized texts see John Bossy, *Christianity in the West 1400–1700* (Oxford: 1985), p. 103.

11 Reinhard points out that the control of education was invariably a key aspect of confessionalisation. See Reinhard, 1989, p. 396.

12 Reinhard comments: 'The alliance of Church and State during the process of "Confessionalisation" reached its culmination in the field of ideas and emotions, where it secured the consent of the subjects to their own subjugation.' In the English context this subjugation did not take place at state level since the Church of England effectively defined itself as non-confessional, despite its Protestantism. Instead it took place among those who embraced a fully confessionalized Protestant religious identity – the Puritans. Ibid., p. 403. On the relation of confessionalization and popular culture see Schilling, 1995, p. 663.

13 One example of this is the idea that the emergence of Petrarchan poetry under Henry VIII was related to Protestantism. Gary Waller has done some very interesting work on the relationship between the Protestant and the Petrarchan self. He writes: 'The Protestant self, curiously analogous to the Petrarchan self, is always in flux, always changing even while it articulates an ideal of stasis. So the Protestant poet, whether he was as obsessive as Greville or as ambitious as Spenser, would inevitably find himself writing out his contradictions and anguish in his poetry, at once fascinated by words and aware of their untrustworthiness and suspicious of their promiscuous materiality.' This state of being caught between a fixed self and one in flux, and the need it produces constantly to work through the tension between these two poles is not, however, a product of Protestantism so much as it is of confessionalization. See Gary Waller, *English Poetry of the Sixteenth Century* (Harlow: 1993), p. 95.

14 The confessional aspects of Southwell's poetry are discussed by Brian Cummings in *The Literary Culture of the Reformation: Grammar and Grace* (Oxford: 2002), pp. 346–355.

15 For Erasmus' implicit but clear rejection of confessionalization see Desiderius Erasmus, 'Erasmus' Letter to Carondelet: The Preface to His Edition of St Hilary', trans. John C. Olin, in *Six Essays on Erasmus*, ed. John C. Olin (New York: 1979), pp. 93–120, pp. 104–105.

16 See Eamon Duffy, *The Stripping of the Altars: Traditional Religion in England 1400–1580* (New Haven: 1992). For an important criticism of Duffy's work see David Aers, 'Altars of Power: Reflections on Eamon Duffy's *The Stripping of the Altars: Traditional Religion in England 1400–1580*', *Literature and History*, n.s. 3:2 (1995), pp. 90–105. For a perceptive article that seeks to explain both the vitality of the pre-Reformation English Church and its eventual demise see G.W. Bernard, 'Vitality and Vulnerability in the Late Medieval Church: Pilgrimage on the Eve of the Break with Rome', in *The End of the Middle Ages? England in the Fifteenth and Sixteenth Centuries*, ed. John Watts (Stroud: 1998), pp. 199–233. For the early history of English Protestantism see A.G. Dickens, 'The Early Expansion of Protestantism in England 1520–1558', *Archiv für Reformationsgeschichte*, 78 (1987), pp. 187–222, and Peter Marshall and Alec Ryrie, eds, *The Beginnings of English Protestantism* (Cambridge: 2002).

17 On the effects and implications of printing on early modern European culture see Elizabeth L. Eisenstein's seminal study *The Printing Press as an Agent of Change: Communications and Cultural Transformations in Early-Modern Europe* (Cambridge: 1994). Although there have been a number of criticisms of Eisenstein's work, it is hard

to dispute the key argument of her study that: 'The advent of printing transformed the conditions under which texts were produced, distributed and consumed ... The most revolutionary impact of the new technology was initially exerted simply by increasing the output of extant texts – whatever their original provenance' (p. 168).

18 On the use of print by the early Tudor Church see Julia A. Smith, 'An Image of a Preaching Bishop in Late Medieval England: The 1498 Woodcut Portrait of Bishop John Alcock', *Viator*, 21 (1990), pp. 301–322, p. 322.

19 John Alcock, *Mons Perfectionis: otherwyse in englysshe the hyl of perfeccon* (1497), STC 279, A.iii (3).

20 Ibid., A.ii (2).

21 Ibid., B.iii (iv).

22 Alcock tells his readers: 'Obedyence is thymage of a very heuenly man / [and] inobedyence thymage of a deuylleshe man.' Ibid., C.ii.

23 Although it is a very different text in many ways, *The abbaye of the holy ghost* offers its lay readership a similar textual participation in monastic life. It comments: 'Many men there be [that] wolde be in relygyon, but they may not be for diverse causes. Therfore they [that] may not be in bodily relygyon, may be in ghostly relygyon iff they woll, [that] is fo[n]ded in a place [that] is called Conscyence.' *The abbaye of the holy ghost* (Westminster: 1496?), STC 13608.7, A.iii / A.iii (v).

24 Ibid., E.ii (1).

25 Margaret Aston comments in relation to popular religion in the Middle Ages: 'There was a tension, latent or explicit, between the church defined as ecclesiastical hierarchy and the church defined as community of faithful believers.' It is possible that print intensified this tension by putting into the public realm texts that enabled the laity more easily to perceive themselves as members of a Christian community distinct from the church. Alcock's work, however, could be seen as an attempt to use the new technology in order to reduce the tension between laity and clergy by reaching out across Aston's potential divide. See Margaret Aston, *Faith and Fire: Popular and Unpopular Religion 1350–1600* (London: 1993), p. 1.

26 *The Contemplacon of Synners* (Westminster: 1499), STC 5643, A.iiii (v) The frontispiece of this work is a woodcut of a book, presumably *The Contemplacon of Synners*, being given to a bishop by another clergyman. This suggests that even if the author of this text was not himself a member of the clergy the work itself was meant to be read within a clerical context.

27 John Colet, 'Sermon 1511', in *English Historical Documents: V 1485–1588*, ed. C.H. Williams (London: 1967), pp. 652–660, p. 655.

28 Christopher Harper-Bill, 'Dean Colet's Convocation Sermon and the Pre-Reformation Church in England', in *The Impact of the English Reformation 1500–1640*, ed. Peter Marshall (London: 1997), pp. 17–37, pp. 17–18.

29 Colet, 1967, p. 658.

30 J.F. Davis comments: 'The persecution of Lollards on a hitherto unprecedented scale proves to be the background to the English Reformation in the early sixteenth century. These mass adjurations ... occurred in a number of places: under Bishop Fitzjames of London in 1510 and 1518; under Bishop Blythe of Coventry and Lichfield in 1511–12; under Archbishop Warham in 1511; under Bishop Smith of Lincoln in 1506–7; under

Literature and politics

Bishop Tunstall in 1527–28; and under Bishop Longland of Lincoln in 1521.' As has
been suggested, it is a matter of considerable contention among historians whether this
record displays an increased incidence of Lollardy or a new willingness on the part of
the authorities to look for *and* find it. See J.F. Davis, 'Lollardy and the Reformation in
England', in *The Impact of the English Reformation 1500–1640*, ed. Peter Marshall
(London: 1997), pp. 37–54, p. 41. For a very different view of the importance of Lollardy
in relation to the state of the pre-Reformation Church see Christopher Haigh, *English
Reformations: Religion, Politics, and Society under the Tudors* (Oxford: 1993), pp. 51–55.

31 The nature of sixteenth-century Lollardy has undergone considerable historical revision
since the 1980s. Having been regarded formerly as a vibrant popular religious
movement that had an important influence on the English Reformation, it has recently
been written off by revisionist historians as having only a negative effect on the English
Church after its defeat during the early years of the fifteenth century. Patrick Collinson
has, however, recently sought to restore some balance to the debate by suggesting
important similarities between the practices of early Tudor Lollards and Protestants.
See Patrick Collinson, 'Night Schools, Conventicles and Churches: Continuities and
Discontinuities in Early Protestant Ecclesiology', in *The Beginnings of English Protestantism*, eds Peter Marshall and Alec Ryrie (Cambridge: 2002), pp. 209–235.

32 G.R. Elton's dismissive view of *The Tree of Commonwealth* as a barren work has until
recently set the tone of discussions of Dudley's work. See G.R. Elton, *Reform and
Reformation: England 1509–1558* (London: 1977), pp. 1–2.

33 On Dudley see D.M. Brodie, 'Edmund Dudley, Minister of Henry VII', *TRHS*, 15 (1932),
pp. 133–161, and S.J. Gunn, 'Edmund Dudley and the Church', *JEH*, 51 (2000), pp.
509–526.

34 D.M. Brodie has argued: '*The Tree of Commonwealth* must be judged rather as a manual
for the education of a Prince than as a comprehensive political treatise.' However such a
separation is anachronistic in terms of Tudor political thought. D.M. Brodie, 'Introduction', in Edmund Dudley, *The Tree of Commonwealth*, ed. D.M. Brodie (Cambridge:
1948), pp. 1–17, p. 16.

35 Dudley's image of the commonwealth as a tree is a version of the common comparison
of the body of politic with the natural body of a man. One should note, however, that, as
Paul Achambault argues, during the early modern period this analogy was invariably
used with care and precision. See Paul Archambault, 'The Analogy of the "Body" in
Renaissance Political Literature', *Bibliothèque D'Humanisme et Renaissance*, 29 (1967),
pp. 21–53.

36 Dudley, 1948, p. 31.

37 Dudley is quick to gloss this association of the commonality with tranquillity, writing:
'There are two maner of fruites of tranquylite: the one is tranquilite in ease and
pleasure, But of this fruite I do no meane for ye comynaltie to medle therwith but vtterly
to refuse it as thei wold veneme or poison ... thother tranquilitie is ment for you, and
[that] is, to haue tranquilite to applie diligently with trew labours and honest diligens
and busynes.' (Ibid., p. 55).

38 Unlike his fifteenth-century predecessors John Fortescue and George Ashby, in whose
work social and political disorder is largely a product of monarchical weakness, in *The
Tree of Commonwealth* Dudley places social conflict at the centre of each order's identity.

39 Dudley, 1948, pp. 87–88.

40 Ibid., p. 88. John Ball is alleged to have delivered a sermon to the peasants in which he argued: 'We are descended from one father and mother, Adam and Eve. What reasons can they give to show that they are greater lords than we, save by making us toil and labour, so that they can spend?' (Jean Froissart, *The Chronicles*, Vol. 1, trans. John Bouchier (London: 1812), pp. 640–641).

41 See Neal Wood, *Foundations of Political Economy: Some Early Tudor Views on State and Society* (Berkeley: 1994), p. 82.

42 For Dudley's views on the church and how they compared with his behaviour when a royal minister see Gunn, 2000.

43 Dudley, 1948, p. 62.

44 Ibid., p. 64.

45 Arrogance's methods are inherited wholesale by his heirs, Popery and Heresy.

46 Robert Copland, *The Myrrour of the Chyrche* (1521), STC 965, F.iii (IV).

47 Robert Copland, *The Passyon of Our Lord* (1521), STC 14558, P. iii (I).

48 It is important to stress this point since popular religious writing like that of Copland has in the past been used to argue that English religious life before the Reformation was in some ways too materialistic or performative to be truly Christian. I have never really understood this argument. It seems to rely entirely on the assumption that a particular form of Protestantism can be regarded as normative in terms of proper Christian practice.

49 Robert Copland, 'The Seuen Sorowes that women haue when theyr husbandes be deade', c.1526, printed c.1565, STC 2734, in *Robert Copland: Poems*, ed. Mary Carpenter Erler (Toronto: 1993), pp. 83–124, p. 85. For the dating of this poem see Mary Carpenter Erler's discussion in her notes to the poem in this edition, pp. 109–110.

50 Ibid., p. 85.

51 Ibid., p. 85.

52 Ibid., p. 85.

53 Ibid., pp. 85–86.

54 Ibid., p. 88.

55 *A Hundred Merry Tales*, 1526, STC 23663, ed. Carew Hazlitt (London: 1887).

56 Garrett Sullivan and Linda Woodbridge point out that Tudor jests were written by and for the educated. Indeed, although they often claim to be based on the popular stories, in practice their content is largely derived from humanist and medieval exempla. See Garrett Sullivan and Linda Woodbridge, 'Popular Culture in Print', in *English Literature 1500–1600*, ed. Arthur F. Kinney (Cambridge, 2000), pp. 265–286. For the use of exempla in Tudor jest books see Stanley J. Kahrl, 'The Medieval Origins of the Sixteenth-Century English Jest-Books', *Studies in the Renaissance*, 13 (1966), pp. 166–183.

57 *A Hundred Merry Tales* (1526), B.iii (2v).

58 For this campaign and Skelton's involvement in it see Greg Walker, 'John Skelton, Thomas More, and the "Lost" History of the Early Reformation in England', *Parergon*, 9 (1991), pp. 75–85.

59 Andrew Hadfield, *Literature, Politics and National Identity: Reformation to Renaissance* (Cambridge: 1994), p. 46.

60 Seth Lerer comments that, 'Though he had been occasionally printed in his lifetime, Skelton seems to have had little interest in the new technology'. Lerer goes on to argue: 'Skelton ... represents himself as a poet of the scripted page rather then the printed book, a poet of the oratorical performance rather than disseminated documents of booksellers' (Seth Lerer, *Chaucer and his Readers: Imagining the Author in Late-Medieval England* (Princeton: 1993), p. 178).

61 John Skelton, 'Speke Parott', in *The Complete English Poems*, ed. John Scattergood (Harmondsworth: 1983), pp. 230–246, p. 231.

62 Ibid., p. 239.

63 The Parott's inappropriateness as an ambassador is also a product of his mimicry and parroting of other's words. Richard Halpern comments: 'The more speech is fed into Parott, the more uncanny and disconcerting he becomes ... Unlike those of *Phyllyp Sparowe*, the textual fragments shuttled through *Speke Parott* are not even subject to the constraints of a consistent poetic voice or persona; Parott shifts abruptly between languages and dialects, like a tape recorder gone mad ...' It would, however, be less anachronistic to see Parott as a mad printing machine spewing out fragments and scraps of text. See Richard Halpern, *The Poetics of Primitive Accumulation: English Renaissance Culture and the Genealogy of Capital* (Ithaca: 1991), p. 129.

64 Skelton, 1983, p. 246.

65 Greg Walker comments: 'in creating a poem which stresses the instability of authority, whether political or intellectual, Skelton comes close to describing a culture enmeshed in an insoluble crisis of authority'. Greg Walker, '"Ordered Confusion"? The Crisis of Authority in Skelton's *Speke Parott*', *Spenser Studies*, 10 (1992), pp. 213–228, p. 226.

66 John Skelton, 'A Replycacion Agaynst Certayne Yong Scolers Adjured of Late', in *The Complete English Poems*, ed. John Scattergood (Harmondsworth: 1983), pp. 373–386.

67 Ibid., p. 372.

68 On heresy see R.I. Moore, 'Heresy as Disease', pp. 1–11, and Gerard Verbeke, 'Philosophy and Heresy: Some Conflicts between Reason and Faith', in *The Concept of Heresy in the Middle Ages*, eds W. Lourdaux and D. Verhelst (Leuven: 1976), pp. 171–197. On the relationship between orthodoxy and heresy see R.N. Swanson, 'Literacy, Heresy, History and Orthodoxy: Perceptions and Permutations for the Later Middle Ages', in *Heresy and Literacy, 1000–1530*, eds Peter Biller and Anne Hudson (Cambridge: 1994), pp. 279–293.

69 Skelton, 1983, pp. 373–374.

70 At no stage in the poem does Skelton question whether or not Bilney's and Arthur's alleged views were actually heretical. This was perhaps a good thing since the extent to which Bilney in particular did hold heretical beliefs is a matter of dispute. See Richard Rex, 'The Early Impact of Reformation Theology at Cambridge University, 1521–1547', *Reformation and Renaissance Review*, 2 (1999), pp. 38–71 and Greg Walker, 'Saint or Schemer? The 1527 Heresy Trial of Thomas Bilney Reconsidered', *JEH*, 40 (1989), pp. 219–238.

71 Skelton, 1983, p. 376.

72 Sir Thomas More makes an identical accusation against Simon Fish, the author of *The Supplication of the Beggars* in *The supplycatyon of soulys*, *c*.1529, eds Frank Manley, Germian Marc' Harbour, Richard Marius and Clarence H. Miller, in *The Complete Works of St Thomas More*, Vol. 7 (New Haven: 1990), p. 136.

73 Skelton, 1983, p. 384.

74 For example John A. Alford has argued that in *Piers Plowman* William Langland uses grammar as a metaphor for truth because of its fixity and certainly. Alford comments, 'In the shifting word of fourteenth-century social and religious unrest, [grammar] was "a stake in a muyre ... for a trewe marke"' (John A. Alford, 'The Grammatical Metaphor: A Survey of Its Use in the Middle Ages', *Sp*, 57 (1982), pp. 728–760, p. 759).

75 The grammatical metaphor was ultimately an extrapolation of St Augustine's views on language. Augustine argued that all human language was marked by failure since it could not escape the effects of the Fall. The grammatical metaphor allowed a negotiation of this bleak view since it suggested that an aspect of language, its abstract eternal laws, escaped the effect of humanity's sinfulness. On Augustine's view of language, see Margaret W. Ferguson, 'Saint Augustine's Region of Unlikeness: The Crossing of Exile and Language', *Georgia Review*, 29 (1975), pp. 844–864.

76 See Thomas Hoccleve, 'Address to Sir John Oldcastle', in *Hoccleve's Works: The Minor Poems*, vol. 1, eds Frederick J. Furnivall and I. Gollancz, EETS e.s. 61 (London: 1970), pp. 8–24, p. 19.

77 Indeed is arguable that one of the effects of print was to highlight the materiality of words. Walter J. Ong points out, 'Print suggests that words are things far more than writing ever did' (Walter J. Ong, *Orality and Literacy: The Technologizing of the Word* (London: 1982), p. 118).

78 Vincent Gillespie argues that this sense of the generalised danger of the Bilney's and Arthur's heresy is an important element in Skelton's poem. He writes: 'an important part of Skelton's case against them [Bilney and Arthur], and one which is only implicit in the official process, is the disordering effect of their teaching on the body politic and on the body of Christ, which is the Church' (Gillespie, Vincent, 'Justification by Faith: Skelton's *Replycacion*', in *The Long Fifteenth Century: Essays for Douglas Gray*, eds Helen Cooper and Sally Mapstone (Oxford: 1997), pp. 273–311, p. 279).

79 The Preface to William Barlow's work, *A Dyaloge Descrybyng the Orygynall Ground of these Lutheran Facycons*, opens with a passage that represents Luther's heresy within the same discourse as that deployed by Skelton. Barlow writes: 'here is shewed their [the heretics'] monstrous maners and mutabilitie, theyr cankered contencions, and horrible ipocrisy, their develyshe devyses, and bytter blasphemye, and infinite lyke reliques of that raylynge relygion'. Heresy here fills up the text with words that describe and enact its linguistic disorder. This passage also, however, illustrates the extent to which representing one's doctrinal opponents in this way had a comic side. The reader of Barlow's work is expected to be shocked by its depiction of heresy but also take pleasure in the work's wit. See William Barlow, *A Dyaloge Descrybyng the Orygynall Ground of these Lutheran Facycons*, c.1531, STC 1461 (Amsterdam: 1974), p. 25.

80 On Tyndale's theology and in particular the influence of Lutheranism on his thought see Carl R. Trueman, *Luther's Legacy: Salvation and English Reformers 1525–1536* (Oxford: 1994).

81 For a judicious discussion of Tyndale's place in the history of the English Reformation see Patrick Collinson, 'William Tyndale and the Course of the English Reformation', *Reformation*, 1 (1996), pp. 72–97.

82 For the influence of Lutheran political thought on *Obedience of a Christian Man* see Quentin Skinner, *The Foundations of Modern Political Thought: Vol. 2 The Age of Reformation* (Cambridge: 1978), pp. 65–73.

83 William Tyndale, 'The Obedience of a Christian Man', 1528, STC 24446, in *Doctrinal Treatises and Introductions to Different Portions of the Holy Scriptures*, ed. Henry Walter (Cambridge: 1848), pp. 127–344, p. 331.

84 This tension is what complicates David Daniell's otherwise insightful comment that '*Obedience* is made of Scripture'. Certainly as Daniell goes on to point out there are whole paragraphs of Tyndale's text that are made up of Biblical sentences; however, papistry is not a scriptural term. See David Daniell, 'Introduction', in William Tyndale, *The Obedience of a Christian Man*, ed. David Daniell (London: 2000), p. xi.

85 Tyndale argues in this preface to his Old Testament, 'W.T. to the Reader': 'A thousand books had they lever to put forth against their abominable doings and doctrine, than that the scripture should come to light. For as long as they may keep that down, they will so darken the right way with the mist of their sophistry'. (William Tyndale, *Old Testament*, 530, STC 2350, ed. David Daniell (New Haven, 1992), pp. 3–4.

86 Tyndale, 1848, p. 343.

87 Ibid., p. 240.

88 Richard Y. Duerden, 'Justice and Justification: King and God in Tyndale's *The Obedience of a Christian Man*', in *William Tyndale and the Law*, eds John A.R. Dick and Anne Richardson, Sixteenth Century Essays and Studies, Vol. 25 (1994), pp. 69–80, p. 75.

89 Rudolph P. Almsy suggests that Tyndale's performance as a writer in *The Practice of Prelates* effectively elevates him '... as the authority – indeed, as the prophet of God – whose reading of the Old Testament must be accepted'. See Rudolph P. Almsy, 'Contesting Voices in Tyndale's *The Practice of Prelates*', in *William Tyndale and the Law*', eds John A.R. Dick and Anne Richardson, Sixteenth Century Essays and Studies, Vol. 25 (1994), pp. 1–10.

90 Given Tyndale's commitment to Augustinian Christianity, it would have been inconsistent for him to think that he could produce a version of Scripture totally free from his human sinfulness.

91 Tyndale, 1992, p. 150.

92 Ibid., p. 8.

93 Ibid., p. 7.

94 'A litel treatise ageynste the mutterynge of some papistes in corners', 1534, STC 19177, in *Records of the Reformation: The Divorce*, 2 vols, ed. Nicholas Pocock (London: 1870), vol. 2, pp. 539–552.

95 Ibid., p. 549.

96 On *King Johan* see Greg Walker, *Plays of Persuasion: Drama and Politics at the Court of Henry VIII* (Cambridge: 1991). On the important changes that Bale made to the text of *King Johan* see Peter Happé's introduction to John Bale, 'King Johan', c.1538, in *The Complete Plays of John Bale*, Vol. 1, ed. Peter Happé (Woodbridge: 1985).

97 The final five lines of Bale's list reflect the extent to which what is important about it is its demonstration of papistry's inherent diversity since the actual orders listed by Bale are a mixture of the real, the obscure and the nonsensical. Bale writes: 'Fulygynes, Flamynes, with Bretherne of the Black Alleye, / Donates and Dimysynes, with Canons of S. Mark, / Vestals and Monyals, a worlde to heare them barke, / Abbottes and doctors, with bysshoppes and cardynales, / Arche decons and pristes, as to their fortune falles' (Bale, 1985, p. 41).

98 Tyndale, 1992, p. 148.

99 Arthur F. Kinney has recently suggested: 'Rather than continue to separate Skelton's achievements from Tyndale's, we would do far better seeing them as oppositional voices coming from the same cultural moment, facing the pressures of the same cultural forces, and reaching out to the same audiences.' (Arthur F. Kinney, 'Skelton and Tyndale: Men of the Cloth and of the Word', in *Word, Church and State: Tyndale Quincentenary Essays*, eds John T. Day, Eric Lund and Anne M. O'Donnell (Washington: 1998), pp. 275–286, p. 286).

100 On the reductive effects of confessionalization see Reinhard, 1989, p. 391.

101 For an introduction to Sir Thomas More, see John Guy, *Thomas More* (London: 2000). For an introduction to More's thought see Brendan Bradshaw, 'The Controversial Sir Thomas More', *JEH*, 36 (1985), pp. 535–569.

102 R.R. McCutcheon points out that, 'the *Dialogue Concerning Heresies* is not an artless transcript but a thoughtful synthesis of the conventions – which include digressiveness – of classical literary dialogue'. See R.R. McCutcheon, 'Heresy and Dialogue: The Humanist Approaches of Erasmus and More', *Viator*, 29 (1993), pp. 357–384, p. 377.

103 Brian Cummings comments: 'The *Dialogue* opens with a preface of bewilderingly self-conscious fictionality, analyzing its own writtenness.' See Brian Cummings, 'Reformed Literature and Literature Reformed', in *The Cambridge History of Medieval English Literature*, ed. David Wallace (Cambridge: 1999), pp. 821–851, p. 837.

104 Sir Thomas More, *Dialogue concerning Heresies*, 1529, STC 18084, eds Thomas M.C. Lawler, Germian Marc' Harbour and Richard C. Marius, in *The Complete Works of St Thomas More*, Vol. 6 (New Haven: 1981), p. 21.

105 Ibid., p. 21.

106 Ibid., p. 23.

107 The editors of the Yale edition of the *Dialogue concerning Heresies* in their excellent Introduction comment: 'The structure of the *Dialogue* is the course of heresy itself, one digression or bypath leading to another, farther and farther from the common way.' The reader, however, can at any time escape the digressive maze of heresy simply by putting their faith in the teachings of the Church and leaving the doubt-filled world of More's work (Ibid., p. 443).

108 For a discussion of More's involvement in the case of Bilney see E. Gow, 'Thomas Bilney and his Relations with Sir Thomas More', *Norfolk Archaeology*, 32 (1958), pp. 292–340. For More's involvement in the controversy over whether or not Bilney did confess his faults before being executed see Brian Cummings, 'Swearing in Public: More and Shakespeare', *English Literary Renaissance*, 27 (1997), pp. 197–232.

109 More, 1981, p. 257.

110 Ibid., pp. 257–258.

111 The word frame could also equate Bilney's actions with the work of weavers who also used frames in the production of textiles.

112 More, 1981, p. 268.

113 See Sir Thomas More, *The Last Letters of Thomas More*, ed. and intro. Alvaro De Silva (Michigan: 2000), p. 86.

114 Chaucer's Old Man tells the three rioters who accost him on their way to find Death

and kill him: 'For I ne kan nat fynde / A man, though that I walked into Ynde, / Neither in citee ne in no village, / That wolde chaunge his youthe for myn age; / And therefore moot I han myn age stille, / As longe tyme as it is Goddes wille. / This walke I, lyk a restelees kaityf [wretch] / And on the ground, which is my moodres gate, / I knokke with my staf, bothe erly and late.' Chaucer's Old Man cannot find Death but his rioters do, by killing each other. Their deaths are a result of a piece of misreading akin to Bilney's as reported in More's work, since like him they mistake the allegorical for the literal. See Geoffrey Chaucer, 'The Pardoner's Tale', in *The Riverside Chaucer*, ed. Larry D. Benson (Oxford: 1987), pp. 196–202, p. 199.

115 Lee Patterson, 'Chaucer's Pardoner on the Couch: Psyche and Clio in Medieval Literary Studies', *Sp*, 76 (2001), pp. 638–680, p. 673.

116 More, 1981, p. 435.

117 Ibid., p. 435.

118 Recent research has made More's Bilney a more plausible figure, since it is now clear that many of the leading early Protestants came from those most deeply involved in the Church and committed to a Christian way of life. Richard Rex comments: 'The relative success of the Reformation among the friars is merely a particular instance of the general truth that support for the new religion came not from those most alienated from the old religion, but precisely from those who had hitherto been most engaged in it' (Richard Rex, 'Friars in the Reformation', in *The Beginnings of English Protestantism*, eds Peter Marshall and Alec Ryrie (Cambridge: 2002), pp. 38–59, p. 58).

119 This emphasis on reading is an aspect of More's engagement with the thought of St Augustine. On Augustine's hermeneutics, see Brian Stock, *Augustine the Reader: Meditation, Self-Knowledge, and the Ethics of Interpretation* (Cambridge, Mass.: 1996), p. 196.

120 For More's basically optimistic view of reading in this work, see Craig D'Alton, 'Charity or Fire? The Argument of Thomas More's 1529 *Dyaloge*', *SCJ*, 33 (2002), pp. 51–70, p. 55.

121 It should also be noted that this confidence seems to have deserted More in much of his latter polemical work, and in particular in his exchanges with Tyndale.

122 Sir Thomas More, *A Dialogue of Comfort Against Tribulation*, c.1534, eds Louis L. Martz and Frank Manley, in *The Complete Works of St Thomas More*, Vol. 12 (New Haven: 1976).

123 Ibid., p. 315.

124 Alistair Fox, in the only detailed literary critical study of More's work, points out, 'The allegory of the Turk is polysemous rather than simple'. See Alistair Fox, *Thomas More: History and Providence* (Oxford: 1982), p. 224.

125 Germen Gardynare, *A letter of a younge gentleman named mayster Germen Gardynare, wryten to a frend of his, wheron men may se the demeanour [and] heresy of John Fryth late burned* (1534) STC 11594.

126 John Frith was an early English Protestant. A colleague of Tyndale's, he was tried and executed in London in 1533. For the details of Frith's life see A.G. Dickens, *The English Reformation*, second edition (London: 1989), p. 101.

127 Gardynare, 1534, D.v. (2).

128 Ibid., E.v.

129 For the identification of the friend as Edward Fox, see C. Butterworth and Allan G. Chester, *George Joye 1495–1533: A Chapter in the History of the English Bible and the English Reformation* (Philadelphia: 1962), pp. 104–105.

130 Gardynare, 1534, A.iii (v) / A.v.

131 Frith's demeanour is also at the center of John Foxe's account of him in *Acts and Monuments*. Foxe presents him as a model of Christian humility and decorum. See John Foxe, *Actes and Monumentes* (London: 1570), STC 11223, p. 1176.

132 Gardynare, 1534, D.iii.

133 The failure of the friend to hunt heresy, and indeed even to spot it, is alluded to a number of times in Gardynare's text. Commenting on the company that Frith kept Gardynare writes that it included 'wyllyam Tyndale, George Joy'. He goes on to speculate that his frend will surely sigh at the name of Joy', 'seeing your self to haue ben so deluded with the hope whych ones ye conceyued of hym' (Ibid., A.iii).

Chapter 1

◆

Pilgrims, poets and politics: the Henrician Reformation

Could we, if we knew what we did, go against King Henry VIII, of whom I will say nothing but this: that His Grace's fame and praise cannot fall but when all good letters fall, which cannot be before men leave the earth and the earth men. (*A Remedy for Sedition*, Sir Richard Morrison, 1536)[1]

Sir Richard Morrison's *A Remedy for Sedition* was part of the Henrician government's propaganda response to the Pilgrimage of Grace. It is a sophisticated work with many classical and biblical references all designed to defend Henry VIII's Reformation, and in particular the Royal Supremacy, against the Pilgrim's criticism. Morrison's tract is also, however, exemplary in terms of mid-Tudor official written responses to popular rebellions or protests. Its basic ideology is identical to Sir John Cheke's *The hurt of sedicion* (1549) or John Christopherson's *An Exhortation to all Menne to ... Beware of Rebellion* (1554).[2] Despite the fact that these works were produced in response to very different events, they all repeat the same basic motifs; rebellion's inherent disorder, its subversion of order and lack of reason. For Morrison, as for his fellow government apologists, the voices of the commons should only enter the public sphere in a mediated form, ventriloquized by their betters. Otherwise they are simply a noise, a jumbled mass of shouts, words and cries – meaningless, violent and anarchic. In place of this babble Morrison proposes the singular legitimizing lucid voice of the King. In *A Remedy for Sedition*, obedience to the King provides the foundation for social harmony. In particular, the Royal Supremacy is portrayed as both legitimate and legitimizing; it is right in itself and confers legitimacy upon Henry's kingship. All the social tensions and antagonisms of Tudor society, of which the Pilgrimage of Grace was in Morrison's eyes simply a symptom, would vanish if everyone accepted Henry's ability and right to speak for, and as, the entire commonwealth; the potency of his supreme royal voice crossing, indeed dissolving, all boundaries, aristocrat / commoner, private / public, temporal / spiritual.[3] *A Remedy for*

Sedition is a piece of utopian propaganda. It represents as normative or proper an idealized state in which the monarch's power – Henry / Utopus – is total and totalizing; in which an ordered perfect commonwealth can be produced by the totalizing potency of the ruler's command.[4]

There are, however, a number of tensions running through *A Remedy for Sedition* that undermine its defence of the Royal Supremacy. Morrison represents his work as an address to the Pilgrims. Its tone is often that of a tired schoolmaster trying to explain something obvious to a dull child. *A Remedy for Sedition*, however, is only nominally aimed at the Pilgrims. By explicitly addressing them in his polemic Morrison invites his other non-rebellious readers to identify with him in condemning the Pilgrims and accepting the validity of his defence of the Royal Supremacy. He tells his readers: 'We must conquer our lusts and compel the appetites to obey all such statutes as reason and honesty shall think worthy to be enacted.'[5] In the context of Tudor society this is a banal argument, but polemically effective. The fact that no right minded Tudor reader could disagree with this statement is intended to create a more general acceptance of the validity of *A Remedy for Sedition*'s arguments. Morrison, however, goes on to argue: 'The King's Grace shall never have true subjects that do not believe as His Grace doth.'[6] This might look like a simple statement of the principle *Cuius regio, eius religio*; however, it is important to note that this principle, that the faith of the people should be that of their ruler, was developed in the context of the German Reformation and the contest between two emerging public religious confessions, Lutheranism and Catholicism. This was not the case in the England of 1536. The only fixed point in the post-Reformation religious landscape in England was Henry's absolute commitment to *his* Royal Supremacy and the congruent rejection of the papacy. Certainly Henry justified his reformation on the grounds that its aim was to return the English Church to the truth of Catholic Christianity, but what did this mean?[7] Morrison's tract reflects this situation by constantly bringing questions of religious truth back to the necessity of obedience to the Royal Supremacy.[8] But obedience to what? Morrison's work effectively collapses reason and honesty into Henry as supreme head – to be reasonable and honest one must not only accept the Royal Supremacy but also allow no difference to exist between one's beliefs and those of the king. This was an almost impossible state for anyone to be in, particularly in the context of Henry's failure, possibly deliberate or resulting from genuine personal uncertainty, ever fully to explicate or fix his beliefs and therefore those of *his* church.[9]

A Remedy for Sedition constantly asserts the legitimacy of the Royal Supremacy as the source of true religion without giving it detailed positive content. This could be a deliberate decision in terms of Morrison's polemical agenda since it allowed potential readers who held very different religious views nonetheless to accept the validity of his arguments. At the same time Morrison consistently rejects the possibility of treating the rebels' demands as meaningful or worthy of discussion. He writes: 'O lightness of commons, who can say so much against thee but he may seem to have said nothing?'[10] The Pilgrims' demands are so ridiculous, indeed they are themselves so 'light', that to attempt to answer them would be simply to produce nothing. It is perhaps for this reason that Morrison fills his work up with classical allusions; he cannot attack the rebels' demands directly without producing nothing (or even worse, making them appear as more than nothing) and he chooses not to defend the Royal Supremacy except by assertion. *A Remedy for Sedition* ultimately reveals the hollowness of the Henrician Reformation; that at its centre was simply a command to obey.

Richard Rex has recently commented:

> If there was any consistency to the various policies which Henry imposed on his church, it is to be found in the image of kingship which he adopted together with the royal supremacy. Once his kingship was recast by the supremacy propaganda into the image of the Old Testament monarchs, he sought to play the part.[11]

Rex's argument brings into sharp relief the extent to which Henry's Royal Supremacy was quite incompatible with the political and religious norms of Tudor England. How would an Old Testament king have coped with an institution like Parliament, with the common law, or perhaps more pertinently with Christ's teachings? These questions directly reflect the crisis of legitimacy at the heart of the Henrician Reformation. John Guy has discussed in detail the three-way fudge at the centre of the Royal Supremacy.[12] The legal basis of the Supremacy was the Act in Restraint of Appeals (1533). This legislation, however, simply asserted that the English kings had always been supreme heads of the church within their domains.[13] It did not address the status of the Supremacy in legal, political or religious terms.[14]

The Henrician Reformation created a crisis of legitimation within the Tudor polity that is reflected in the writings of the 1530s at a number of different levels. This chapter will first discuss Sir Thomas Elyot's work *The Boke named The Governour*. In this text Elyot advocates a programme of civic humanism – political reform on the basis of a number of key humanist principles. This chapter will then move on to discuss the Pilgrimage of Grace and the various government responses to it, in particular Wilfred Holme's poem *The fall and euill sucess of Rebellion from time to time*. It will conclude by examining the courtly poems of Sir Thomas Wyatt in the political context of the 1530s. All of these texts illustrate the extent to which the Royal Supremacy introduced new and radical possibilities into Tudor political praxis that were ultimately incompatible with existing political norms and ideals. Henrician kingship as it emerged from the changes of the early 1530s was tyrannous and at its centre sat a tyrant whose behaviour transgressed all accepted, and acceptable, boundaries of royal power and authority.[15]

SIR THOMAS ELYOT'S *THE GOVERNOUR*

Sir Thomas Elyot was born in c.1490. During the 1520s he worked for Cardinal Thomas Wolsey and by the end of this decade had reached a position of relative prominence. Although Elyot appears to have supported Henry's divorce and the Royal Supremacy, he did not play a leading part in the post-Reformation regime. Elyot produced a number of important works during the 1530s including *The Boke named The Governour* and the first Latin–English dictionary. The former was an extremely popular work of political theory which applied classical learning to the problem of early modern governance. It has recently been argued by a number of scholars, in particular Greg Walker, that Elyot's post-Reformation work can be read as a coded critique of the political regime of the 1530s. Walker suggests that throughout this period Elyot's work is marked by his religious and political conservatism.[16] This is undoubtedly the case.[17] The work that Elyot produced during the 1530s, however, also reflects the radicalism of the Henrician Reformation, its basic lack of legitimacy and the damage confessionalism did to English political praxis.

Elyot's major work, *The Boke named The Governour*, was first published in 1531. It has traditionally been discussed as an example of the genre exemplified by Castiglione's *Book of the Courtier*.[18] Eloyt's work, however, also needs to be seen as part of an English tradition of political writing which, John Guy has suggested, included the work of Sir John Fortescue, who wrote in the 1460s and 1470s, and that of Sir Francis Bacon.[19] *The Governour* is an attempt to apply humanist ideals to Tudor England.[20] In particular it privileges counsel within the polity as good in itself. This is because for Elyot dialogue and debate allow the collective political nation to create wisdom or, perhaps more accurately, reason. *The Governour* appears on the surface to be a rather staid conservative application of humanist ideas to Tudor England. In practice it is a self-reflective piece of political theory whose valorization of counsel and wisdom in the context of the Henrician Reformation makes it a subversive and radical work.

The Governour opens with a Proheme which includes a protestation by its author concerning its range and scope. Elyot writes:

> protestynge vnto your excellent maiestie [Henry VIII], that where I co[m]mende herin any one vertue or disprayse any one vyce I meane the general description of thone and thother, without any particular mening to the reproche of any one persone: to the whiche protestation I am nowe driven throughe the malignite of this present tyme, all disposed to malicious detraction.[21]

In this passage Elyot is attempting to control the way in which his book is read.

In particular, he is seeking to forestall any wish by his readers to apply the general concepts and ideas discussed in *The Governour* in a specific or topical way.[22] Elyot, however, gives his protestation a historical justification, arguing that it is the malignity of the present that forces him to steer his readers away from applying the ideas in his work directly to living people or current events. The implication of this is twofold. At one level Elyot is suggesting that it is only the state of the country in 1531 that means he has to attempt to control how his work is read in order to protect it, and its author, from malicious detraction. There is, however, a more specific and potentially radical reading of this passage which is that the malignity of the present time takes a particular hermeneutic form – that of malicious reproachful readers who in their reading make the move from the general to the particular in such a way as to destroy the integrity of a writer's work. Elyot ends his protestation by asking the King to protect *The Governour* and its author from attack.

> I moste humbly beseche your highnes to dayne to be patrone and defendour of this lyttlle warke / agayne the assaultes of maligne interpretours which fayle nat to rente and deface the renoume of writers, they them sefles beinge in nothinge to the publyque weale profitable.[23]

This passage sums up Elyot's authorial intention in *The Governour*. He clearly intends the work to advertise its author's usefulness to Henry as someone 'profitable to the public weal'. *The Governour* itself is part of this profit since in its detailed description of what it means to rule with virtue, how future rulers should be educated and how the polity should be organized, it participates in the defence and reform of the commonwealth.

Eloyt's protestation, however, also reflects a tension at the heart of *The Governour*. Elyot opens his work warning readers against applying its lessons directly to any 'one person', implying that it is Henry who should be regarded as beyond the pale in terms of *The Governour*'s meaning. Elyot's work, however, consistently incites its application to the Tudor polity and in particular to Henry's kingship. This takes place at a number of levels. *The Governour* consists of three books, each of which is divided into a number of chapters addressing various political issues. For example the First Chapter of the First Book is entitled, 'The signification of a Publicke Weale, and why it is called in latin Respublica'. Each of these chapters is typically made up of classical, historical and biblical examples with more general comments from Elyot as way of introduction and conclusion. This structure, however, creates a potential hiatus or delay between Elyot's argument and his examples. It is in this gap that the reader is expected to work in terms of *The Governour*'s reforming agenda. One of the central arguments of Elyot's work is that rulers, existing and potential, need to be wise and that the way to achieve this wisdom is through active participatory reading of *The Governour*.[24]

The political implications of this structure can be illustrated by Chapter 2 of Book 1 of *The Governour* entitled: 'That one souraigne gouernour ought to be in a publike weale. And what damage hath happened where a multitude hath equal authoritie without any souraygne.' The examples Elyot uses in this chapter, however, simply fail to illustrate this argument. Instead they subtly change the nature of the problem from the need for a single governor to how this person should be chosen.[25] For example Elyot uses Agamemnon to support his argument, asking his reader: 'The Grekes, which were assembled to reuenge the reproche of Menelaus ... dydde nat they by one assent electe Agamemnon to be theyr emperour or capitain: obeynge him as their souerayne during the siege of Troy?'[26] He goes on to discuss the way in which the Romans at times of war elected a Dictator as 'chyefe of all other'.[27] Finally Elyot turns to English history and conjures up a shocking image of the pre-monarchical Saxon England again framing his text as a question to its readers:

> Who wolde than haue desired to haue ben rather a man than a dog: whan men eyther with swerde or hu[n]ger peryshed, hauynge no profite or sustynance of their owne corne or catell, which by mutuall warre was contynually destroyed? Yet the dogges, either takynge that that men coulde nat quietly come by, or fedynge on the deed bodies, which on euery parte laye scatered plentously, dyd satisfe theyr hunger.[28]

This horrific image of a sovereign-less England in which it is better to be a dog than a man seems to leave no room for argument regarding the desirability of monarchical rule. However at the end of the chapter Elyot introduces a coda to the preceding discussion. He writes:

> But for as moche as I do wel perceiue that to wryte of the offyce or duetye of a souraygne gouernoure or prince, farre excedeth the compasse of my lernyng ... I wyll therfore kepe my penne within the space that is descrybed to me by the thre noble maysters, reason, lernynge, and experience.[29]

As a reader, how is one meant to bring the disparate parts of this chapter together? One is presented with examples intended to support the contention that rule by one person is natural and desirable but which also seem to suggest that this individual should, or perhaps more accurately in the past has been, elected to this position. One is then confronted with the horrific image of the state of Saxon England before the advent of 'noble king Edgar'. Finally Elyot explicitly excludes sovereign governors and princes from the scope of his study by placing in the foreground *The Governour*'s textual status – the extent to which its boundaries are policed by reason, learning and experience. *The Governour* is an attempt to create a new political language for the rulers of Tudor England. This language will encourage them to be virtuous and to govern on the basis of wisdom. The effect of Elyot's exile of sovereign princes from the space of his work is to place them beyond this new political discourse. Instead they become an external, God-given but also absent, point of order keeping at bay the forces of anarchy and violence.[30]

This point is emphasized at the beginning of Book 2, where in the first chapter Elyot creates an image of the total and remorseless publicness of the governor. He writes:

> They shal also consyder that by theyr preeminence they sit, as it were on a pyller on the top of a mountayne, where al the people do beholde them, nat only in their open affaires, but also in their secrete pastymes, priuie dalyaunce, or other improfytable or wanton conditions; which sone be discouered by the conuersation of their most familyare seruantis, which do alwaye imbrace that study wherin their mayster delyteth.[31]

In this passage Elyot's reader is presented with an image of the pre-eminent governor sitting above his subjects but constantly being the object of their gaze. There is no space in this representation for a governor to have a legitimate hidden or private life. This is partly because Elyot's words suggest equivalence between secret desires, privy dalliances and wantonness. It is also, however, because the nature of governorship means that secrecy is impossible – all will in the end be exposed by the gossip of the governor's familiars. This passage creates a potential relationship between pre-eminent governors and the 'maligne interpretours' who were the objects of Elyot's protestation, since a governor who has secret desires is also unprofitable to the commonwealth. Sovereign princes and malign readers are placed by Elyot beyond the space of his text, and yet they constantly return to disrupt *The Governour*'s surface. This is because they represent sources of power, and in particular violence, that escape the bounds of the political discourse that Elyot is seeking to produce in *The Governour*.

The relationship between these two enemies to Elyot's political agenda is stressed later in Book 2 when Elyot discusses the importance of 'placabilitie' to a governor and the tyranny produced by its absence. He writes:

> Who, beholdynge a man in estymation of nobylitie and wysdome by furie changed into an horrible figure, his face infarced with rancour, his mouth foule and imbosed, his eien wyde starynge and sparkelynge lyke fyre, nat speakyng, but as a wylde bulle, roring and brayinge out wordes despytefull and venomous: forgettyng his astate or condytion, forgettyng lernyng, ye forgettynge all reason ... Shal he nat wysshe to be in suche a man placabilitie?[32]

Elyot supports this image of a man undertaken by fury by referring to Ovid's work *The Craft of Love*. This suggests that Elyot's image of a furious governor can be viewed as that of a tyrant and even particularly as someone who resembles the tyrannical Cupid of Ovid's poem. This has important implications in terms of the politics of *The Governour*, since one of the determining characteristics of Cupid as tyrant in Ovidian texts is his corrupt wilful reading.[33] Elyot's tyrant is an animal, a wild bull, lost to reason and learning. His fury places him outside the pale of *The Governour*'s political community. At the same time the reference to Ovid's work suggests that Elyot's tyrant is similar, if not identical, to the malicious, malign and wilful reader against whom Elyot protested in *The Governour*'s Proheme.

Elyot's political agenda in *The Governour* can be summed up as an attempt to protect the commonwealth from malicious readers and tyrants. This is a reflection of *The Governour*'s humanism but also of its place within a tradition of English political writing.[34] Elyot's detailed discussions of how the children of nobles should be educated and the moral attitudes that a governor should possess are all directed at producing rulers / readers who place the good of the public wealth before their personal will. There are two key positive elements to the Elyot's political agenda in *The Governour*, which are the importance of friendship and counsel.[35] Elyot's emphasis on friendship, or *amicitia*, reflects at one level the influence of Cicero's works *De Amicitia* and *De Officiis* on his writings.[36] For Elyot *amicitia* functions as a nexus of virtue and certainty in a world of disorder, ambition and tyranny. He writes:

> In god, and all thynge that co[m]meth of god, nothing is of more greatter estimation, than loue, called latine *amor*, whereof *Amicitia* commeth, named in englyshe frendshyppe or amitie, which taken awaye frome the lyfe of man, no howse shall abide standinge, no fyelde shall be in Culture. And that is lyghtly perceyued, if a man do remembre what commeth, of dissention and discorde, finally he semeth to take the sonne from the worlde, that taketh frendshyppe from mannes lyfe.[37]

Elyot's argument here goes through a number of stages. Having equated *amicitia* with *amor* or love, he goes on to expand friendship's scope to the entire social field. Without *amicitia* society would collapse, discord would reign and men's lives would become sunless. Indeed one is reminded of Elyot's description of pre-monarchical Saxon England. *Amicitia* in *The Governour* is the opposite of discord and dissention. Its scarcity in Tudor England can be related to the issues raised by Elyot in his protestation. Clearly those who read with malignity and reproach have placed themselves beyond the scope of *amicitia*.

In *The Governour*, *amicitia* functions as a point of ideological closure. All the various virtues that Elyot discusses during the course of his work are brought to fruition in true friendship. As importantly, *amicitia* as a concept implies performance. One cannot be a true friend in the abstract. This relates *amicitia* directly to the form of *The Governour*. Elyot's work invites its readers to participate in the production of its meaning through its juxtaposition of examples with more theoretical discussions. The implication is that one can not read *The Governour* correctly without producing the kind of learned active reflection on the polity that Elyot is advocating. Reading *The Governour* properly means becoming part of its discursive community – it means recognizing within oneself one's potential as a virtuous governor. Indeed it ultimately means having a relationship with Elyot and his work that is based on *amicitia* and which stands in opposition to malign and tyrannous readers.[38]

Elyot's discussion of counsel is immediately proceeded by a chapter dealing with the dangers of detraction. This is an unusual section for Elyot's work, since on the whole *The Governour* focuses on the positive qualities that are necessary for a man to be equipped to play his proper role in the commonwealth.[39] One reason for this focus soon becomes apparent in this section, since Elyot's discussion of detraction can also be read as a guide on how to detract. Elyot argues:

> If a man, be determined to equitie, hauynge the eyen and eares of his mynde, set onely on the trouthe and the publike weale of his contreye, wyll haue no regarde to any requeste or desyre, but procedeth directely in the admynistration of iustyce, eyther he, whiche by Justyce is offended, or some his fautours, abbettours, or adhere[n]tes ... as soone as by any occasion, mention happeneth to be made of hym, who hath executed Justice exactly, forthwith they imagine some vyce or defaut, be it neuer so lyttel, wherby they maye mynysshe his credence, [and] craftily omittyny to speake any thynge of his rygour in Justice, wylle note and touche somme thynge of his maners, wherin shall eyther seme to be lyghtnes or lack of grauitie, or to moche sowernes or lack of Ciuilytie; or that he is nat beneuolent to hym in auctoritie, or that he is nat sufficient to receyue any dygnitie, or to dispatche matters of weigthye importa[n]ce, or that he is superfluous in wordes, or els to scarse.[40]

By the end of this passage it appears that the virtuous man is caught in a perilous linguistic state in which his words, indeed even how much he speaks, can be used to undermine his position within the polity. The implication of this is twofold. It suggests a polity in which virtue is not rewarded, or rather in which it is not in itself sufficient to protect one from the danger of detraction. It also, however, implies a criticism of those who listen to and act on the whisperings and hints of the detractors; those prepared to forget a man's rigorous administration of justice on the basis of gossip and rumour. Again *The Governour* creates an image of political breakdown and failure that is inherently linguistic and relates directly to the question of interpretation. Indeed it is hard to read this section of the work without thinking of Elyot's friend, Thomas More.

At the end of the chapter on detraction Elyot places its antidote in the judgement of the individual, arguing that:

> truste is not to be giuen to an other mannes iudgement, moche lesse to the malice of an accuser. But euery man shall reteyne to him selfe the power to enserche out the trouthe, and leauyng the enuye or dyspleasure to the detractour, shall ponder or waye the matter indifferentely, that euery thynge, in suche wise beinge curiously

inserched and proued, he maye at his pleasure eyther loue or hate hym, whom he hath soo substauncially tried.[41]

This process has, however, clearly failed in the past since Elyot goes on to comment:

> Of one thinge I am sure, that by Detraction as wel as many good wittes haue ben drowned, as also vertue, and paynefull study unrewarded, and many zelatours or fauourers of the publyke weale, haue ben dyscouraged.[42]

These passages seem to invite the kind of reading that Elyot objected to in his protestation. Elyot's readers are here incited to use their judgement, as individuals, in order to judge their fellow governors. At the same time this concluding remark suggests that governors have failed to do this in the past, and that the author of *The Governour* knows of specific examples. Clearly as a reader one's first response to these passages is to immediately attempt to fill the gap in Elyot's text with examples of one's own of men whose wits have been drowned by detraction or whose virtue has not been adequately rewarded.

The final section of *The Governour* is taken up with a discussion of the importance of counsel to the public weal. Elyot writes: 'This thinge that is called Consultation, is the generall denomination of the acte, wherin men do deuyse to-gether and reason, what is to be done. Counsayle is the sentence or aduise particulerly giuen by euery man for that purpose assembled.'[43] *The Governour* constructs counsel as public, reasoned and collective.[44] It is the centre, in geometric terms, of Elyot's model of the perfect polity and is the end of 'al doctrine and study'.[45] Elyot's discussion of the importance of counsel is, however, limited. It is hampered by the difficulty, if not impossibility, of explaining counsel's actual operation within the English polity without at once suggesting a limit to royal authority and power.

The Governour is a sophisticated and detailed work of political theory. It is not particularly radical. The ideals it aspires to, the proper education of future governors, *amicitia* and counsel, are not utopian. They were, however, completely out of place in the post-Reformation Henrician polity despite the fact that Henry often paid lip-service to them. Advocating reason and wisdom as the basis for political action was meaningless in post-Reformation Henrician England. At the same time Elyot's emphasis on the linguistic nature of tyranny, in particular his equation of malign readers with tyrants, reflects the tension between humanism and confessionalization. In a confessionalized world reading and writing was a potentially lethal endeavour.[46] It is this new confessional context that is reflected in a many of the letters and texts Elyot wrote during the 1530s and 1540s.

In March 1536 Elyot wrote to Thomas Cromwell concerning the recent proclamation against seditious books.[47] This letter is replete with themes and tropes that seem to have been drawn directly from the pages of *The Governour*.

Elyot constructs Cromwell as someone with whom he shares *amicitia*. He is, however, concerned that he has been a victim of detraction.[48] At the same time the basic purpose of Elyot's epistle could not be further from the world of *The Governour*. Elyot is writing to Cromwell asking for advice on how to deal with the 'few' seditious works he has in his library. He writes:

> As touching suche bookes as be now prohibited contayning the busshop of Romes authorite, some in deede I have; joyned with diverse other warkes in one grete volume or twoo at the moste, which I never found laysor to reade. Notwithstanding if it be the kinges pleasure and yours that I shall bringe or sende theim I will do it right gladly.[49]

Elyot goes on to ask Cromwell whether he should send him the complete volumes or should cut out the offending works. Elyot's letter reflects a world in which knowledge and texts are not only subject to control but can be subjected to retrospective prohibition.[50] Later in the same year Elyot wrote again to his friend Cromwell expressing the fear that he did not have the King's trust in matters of religion. He wrote:

> I am animate to importune your goode lordship [Cromwell] with most harty desyres to continue my goode lorde in augmenting the kinges goode estimacion of me, whereof I promise you bifore godd your lordship shall never have cause to repent. And where I preceyve that ye suspect that I savor not truely holy Scriptur, I wold godd that the king and you mowght see the moste secrete thowghtes of my hart.[51]

It is almost as though in this letter Elyot was asking to be treated as a heretic – to be examined in such a way that Henry could see, or perhaps more accurately read, his innermost thoughts and beliefs.

The prefaces that Elyot attached to his Latin–English dictionary can be read as a continuing attempt to demonstrate in the public his loyalty to the Henrician Reformation. The Preface to the 1538 edition of Elyot's dictionary celebrates Henry's notorious performance at the trial of John Lambert.[52] Elyot writes:

> above all thinges, I have mooste in admiration, the majestie of you, whiche be verye kynges raygnyng in Justice, whan I consider, that therin semeth to be a thynge supernaturall, or (if it may be spoken without derogation unto goddis honour) a divine influence or sparke of divinitie: which late appered to all them that behelde your grace [Henry VIII] syttyng in the Throne of your royal astate, as supreme heed of the churche of England nexte under CHRIST, about the descision and condemnation of the pernicious errours, of the moste detestable heretyke John Nicolson, callyd also Lambert ...[53]

It seems impossible that anyone reading this passage could doubt Elyot's support for the Royal Supremacy. In this passage Elyot repeats a common theme of Henrician propaganda, which was that the Royal Supremacy was an essential bulwark against the spread of heresy. Unfortunately this argument was effectively undermined by the problem of defining heresy in the period after 1530. For example, in the 1542 edition of his Latin–English dictionary Elyot added definitions of heresies and the names of heretics. He told his readers:

> I ... thought it necessary to enterlace [in this Dictionary] the detestable heretykes, with theyr sundry heresyes, concernynge the substance of our catholyke faythe justly condemned by the hole consent of all true christen men, to the intent that those heresyes beinge in this wyse divulgate, may be the sooner espied and abhorred in suche bokes, where they be craftily enterlaced with holsome doctrine.[54]

What were the heresies that Elyot thought his readers needed to be made aware of so that they could spot them when writers sought to sneak them into their works? Was it the Adamitæ who, according to Elyot, believed that all men and women should go naked? Or was Elyot concerned that Tudor England might become a breeding ground for the heresy of the Caiani, which was based upon the worship of Cain, or that the teachings of Basilides would find a sympathetic reception, that it was not Christ but Simon of Cyrene who was crucified on Good Friday?[55]

Elyot supported the Royal Supremacy as a tool for the production of religious order and as a protector of orthodoxy. But what were orthodox and heterodox beliefs in 1542? Despite his commitment to religious orthodoxy, Elyot found that he could only define its opposite, heresy, tentatively and with extreme caution, in effect only daring to define as heretical beliefs that were so extreme that even Henry would never espouse them.[56]

The Henrician Reformation created a state of ambiguity as to what were orthodoxy, heterodoxy and heresy. Peter Marshall has recently discussed in detail the case of the friar John Forest who was executed in 1538 as a heretic. As Marshall suggests, this makes Forest's case very unusual since supporters of papal power were far more usually condemned as traitors, not heretics. Marshall goes on to comment:

> Forest's punishment points to a different, yet more dogmatic and doctrinaire route the Henrician church might have taken; yet it also illustrates the acute sensitivity of the authorities to how that church was perceived from outside, as does the rapid abandonment of this radical extension of the heresy law.[57]

The problem with condemning Forest as a heretic was the implication that all supporters of the Papacy across Europe were also considered heretics by the Henrician Church. This was clearly too radical and dangerous a policy for Henry to adopt. The timidity and incoherence witnessed in the case of Friar Forest reflect the extent to which the Henrician Reformation was a parochial affair, quite lacking the coherence and integrity of other emerging religious confessions. G.W. Bernard has recently suggested: 'When Henry VIII confronted the fact of religious diversity, he declared that he wanted unity based on a mean.'[58] But this pursuit of a mean was neither moderate nor successful, primarily because, as Bernard goes on to argue, Henry insisted upon his right to define the confessional 'mean' between Catholicism and Protestantism, base it upon his own partial and limited understanding of these emerging confessional identities, and change it whenever it suited him. Henry's mean was violent and unprecedented, and it completely failed to deliver religious order and unity. It claimed confessional integrity, asked to be judged alongside other emerging confessions and in the process revealed its limited, incoherent and banal nature. Alec Ryrie has recently pointed out the one thing that all observers of the English religious scene could agree in 1540 is that after almost a decade of the Royal Supremacy 'religious discord had become endemic'.[59] And this was the ironic product of a Henrician Reformation whose watchwords were moderation, unity and accord.

THE PILGRIMAGE OF GRACE

Reading through the letters, documents and confessions relating to the Pilgrimage of Grace in *Letters and Papers of the Reign of Henry VIII*, one can not help but be struck by the discontinuity between the recorded words of the Pilgrims and those of the government.[60] While the former constantly invoke a political culture entirely compatible with early Tudor political thought, and one in which the programme mapped out in Elyot's *The Governour* would have made sense, the latter seem to come from a different world. In the case of one of the leading personalities of the Pilgrimage, Robert Aske, one can read in these documents the effect of moving from the world of the Pilgrims to that of the court. Aske's progression from active committed leader of a mass political movement to passive defeated supplicant of the King's mercy can be seen as a microcosm of the effects of Henrician tyranny on the Tudor body politic.[61]

The events that came to be known as the Pilgrimage of Grace started with a popular protest in Lincolnshire in October 1536. Even before this had been dealt with, however, the government was confronted with a far larger and more dangerous mass political movement which spread throughout Yorkshire and the far north during the winter of 1536/37. Faced with such a dangerous popular uprising, and with no military force at hand to oppose it, Henry had little choice but to negotiate with its leaders. This led to an agreement between the Pilgrims and the government, which in turn resulted in a truce being declared and most of those who had been involved in the Pilgrimage returning to their homes. However when a second revolt broke out, Henry used this as an excuse to repudiate the earlier agreements and in particular the pardons that had been issued to the leaders of the Pilgrimage. He could then take the bloody revenge that had been his aim from the moment that the revolt broke out.[62]

There has been considerable historical debate concerning the causes of the Pilgrimage of Grace and its status – was it a religious movement, a mass popular revolt, a court conspiracy gone wrong or a social protest against unscrupulous landlords? M.L. Bush has suggested that: 'Two basic concerns sustained the Lincolnshire Uprising and the Pilgrimage of Grace: the subversion of Christ's religion and the decay of the commonwealth.'[63] The existing partial notes from the conference held by the Pilgrims at Pontefract in December 1536 provide important evidence of the Pilgrim's views on the Royal Supremacy and Henrician government in general.[64] The items discussed at Pontefract display a concern with the status of oath-taking under Henry's government, reflecting a situation in which language itself is seen as being corrupted by government policy.[65] These articles also raise the obvious and indeed unanswerable objection to the Royal Supremacy: that Henry's status as a temporal man meant that his authority could not legitimately be extended to spiritual matters.[66] What runs throughout the Pilgrims' articles is a concern for good governance. For example, a number of the items drawn up by the Pilgrims address the need for Parliament to be a truly representative body whose members were free of royal control.[67] This concern with parliament was reflected in the actual practice of the Pilgrimage of Grace as a political movement. Ethan Shagan comments: 'The very essence of the Pontefract council was that it was performed as a *parliament*, representing the combined will of the estates of the realm before the king.'[68] The Pilgrimage of Grace criticized Henry's government not only in word but also in practice. It created a functioning polity sustained by an active and participatory public sphere whose legitimacy was based upon the failure of royal government to be either sufficiently public or consensual. This is not to suggest that the Pilgrims were in any sense revolutionaries. What they wanted from Henry was for him to rule within accepted bounds. Indeed this is illustrated in the case of the English Church where the Pilgrims were prepared to see an extension of royal power, provided it was legitimate and fitted into the norms of English government.

A Petition of advice to the Pilgrims at Pontefract, attributed to Sir Thomas Tempest, reflects the Pilgrimage's concern with the order of the commonwealth.[69] It shows that at least some of the Pilgrims were sufficiently politically knowledgeable to mount a fundamental critique of Henry's government.[70] The *Petition* rejects the idea, advanced forcefully in the government's first response to the Pilgrimage, that it was inappropriate for subjects to comment on the membership of the King's council.[71] It comments:

> Where yt ys alegyd that we shulde not tayke upon us to assyne his Gr[ace's Council] yt ys nessary that vertuus men that luffythe the communwelthe schulde be of his [council] ... suche vertus men as woylde regarde the communwelthe abuffe their princys lo[ve?] ...[72]

What is being articulated here is precisely the split between the needs of the commonwealth and those of the prince that Henry's government seemed intent on denying. It is also important to note the extent to which the blame for the emergence of the Pilgrimage of Grace is here being placed on Henry. The point about the royal council is not that the Pilgrims think it should be appointed by anyone but the king, *provided* he does not pack it with sycophants who love their prince more then the commonwealth.[73] To sustain this argument the author of the *Petition* turns to English history and refers to Edward II and Richard II as monarchs who suffered because their councils were filled with favourites whose advice they followed. The choice of these two monarchs is significant since it suggests a model of corrupt kingship based on flattery that can be directly related to Elyot's Ovidian image of tyranny in *The Governour*. A key element in the tyranny of Edward and Richard was the extent to which they ruled on the basis of their personal wills, and that their favourites enjoyed relationships with them that were at best inappropriate and at worst sodomitical.[74]

The *Petition* spends a considerable amount of time on the need for a free Parliament. It makes the radical claim that the recent Reformation Parliament was not a real parliament, commenting: 'a parliament they have devised that men may not speke off the Kynges vycys whysch ... men may say trewly had moste nede to be spokyn on, and reformyd of [all] thyng, [for if] the hede ayke how can the body be hole.'[75] Elyot's *The Governour* equates the possibility of a pre-eminent governor having a private life with secret dalliances and wantonness. The implication of this passage is that Henry has just the kind of private vices that need to be exposed and purged from the polity. The reference to the metaphor of the body politic in this passage reflects the conventionality of the political thought of the author of the *Petition*. It also, however, demonstrates how potentially radical conventional political imagery could be. Bringing the image of the polity into close proximity to a critique of the King's vices suggests that these are themselves bodily and therefore tyrannous. The political discourse of the Pilgrimage of Grace, as exemplified in this *Petition*, draws on ideas current within Tudor political thought in order to construct a sustained and coherent critique of Henry's rule. At the same time many of the issues raised in this document echo those discussed in Elyot's *The Governour*.

A rather different discourse is articulated in *The Ballad of the Pilgrimage of Grace*, possibily composed by the monks of Sawley Abbey in Lancashire. This text, which was one of a number of ballads supporting the Pilgrimage that circulated at this time, adopts an apocalyptic religious tone quite different to that of the Petition. It opens by explicitly linking the Pilgrimage of Grace with Christ's sacrifice on the Cross: 'Crist crvcifyd! / For thy woundes wide / Vs commens guyde!'[76] If this ballad was written by monks, it is interesting to note their preparedness to collapse any distinction between themselves and the commons. Indeed the whole ballad consistently constructs participation in the Pilgrimage as a religious act that embodies a potentially radical political Christian message. The *Ballad* argues that the state of the world is such that it is no wonder that the commons have been forced to rebel.

> Suche foly is fallen
> And wise out blawen
> That grace is gone
> And all goodness.
> The no marvell
> Thoght it thus befell,
> Commons to mell
> To make redresse.[77]

This verse reverses the logic of magisterial Tudor responses to mass popular movements. Instead of the disorder of the commons being a sign of their inherent lack of order, it is rather a proper and legitimate response to the prevalence of folly in the world and its supplanting of wisdom.[78] In such an upside-down world only the 'melling' of the commons can restore order, goodness and grace.

The *Ballad* goes on to criticize the behaviour of Henry with reference to his failure to live up to the precepts of Christian kingship as defined in the Bible.[79] It ends with a rousing statement of defiance.

> Crim, crame, and riche
> With three ell and the liche
> As sum men teache.
> God theym amend!
> And that Aske may,
> Without delay,
> Here make a stay
> And well to end![80]

There are a number of important aspects to this verse. The *Ballad* in these lines sets up a tension between Aske as a named individual and the Pilgrims' enemies, crim (Cromwell?), crame (Cranmer?) and riche (Rich), who are referred to in an oblique and riddling way. Indeed it maybe that these words refer as much to vices as to individuals, in particular avarice, the criminal cramming of riches. Whereas there is no ambiguity over the significance of the name Aske as the leader of the Pilgrimage, interpreting who crim refers to is an inherently provisional and partial act. The opening lines of this verse invite its readers to participate in determining the enemies of the Pilgrimage, those in government in need of amendment. This may have been intended to protect the authors of the *Ballad* from being accused of directly criticizing the King. The use of the term 'liche', meaning like or others, however, does appear to extend the scope of those needing amendment to Henry, at least to the extent to which he follows the polices of crim and crame. The *Ballad* and the *Petition* seem to exist in quite different political, and indeed religious, worlds. Indeed one could see the differences between these texts as reflecting the ultimately incoherent nature of the Pilgrimage of Grace. This would, however, be a mistake. What united the authors of these texts, and indeed all the Pilgrims, was an urgent sense of concern for the state, political *and* religious, of the commonwealth of England and a common acceptance that things had got so bad that radical political action was required to address the state of the realm.

In their study, *The Defeat of the Pilgrimage of Grace*, Michael Bush and David Bownes make the essential point that in 'early December 1536, [the Pilgrimage] stood on the verge of victory'.[81] The Pilgrims' success was, however, undermined by a number of factors, in particular the postpardon revolts that broke out in the North at the beginning of 1537. It is, however, clear that Henry was always committed to defeating the Pilgrims and exacting revenge. It sends a shiver down one's spine to read the letters the royal government sent to its representatives in the north during the winter of 1536 with instructions on how to deal with the Pilgrimage. On the 2nd of December Henry wrote to the Duke of Norfolk and his colleagues telling them how to negotiate with the Pilgrims. This letter consistently counsels deception and manipulation. Having rehearsed a number of possible scenarios in terms of offers to be made to the Pilgrims, Henry wrote that, if the Pilgrims insisted on a free, general pardon and a Parliament,

> you shall promise as above, to be suitors with them, if they will set their hands to the articles thereof, engaging not to molest us with particular or public matters. And having concluded this you shall take an abstinence for six or seven days as if to send hither to us, and at the end of that time, declare you have by great suit obtained their petitions, and present them the general pardon which we now send by Sir John Russell.[82]

Not content with instructing his commanders in the field to lie, Henry also seems to have felt the need to imaginatively stage the process of deception in his own words – creating a fantasy image of Norfolk's and Russell's performance, lurking in their camp and then producing the pardon like magicians pulling a rabbit from a hat. What makes this letter even more exemplary of Henrician kingship in the 1530s is its tone. Constantly in this letter, and in others written in this period, Henry complains about the defeatism of the letters he has received from his commanders in the field. He comments: 'We wonder you all write in such desperate sort as though the world would be turned upside down if we did not agree to the petitions of the rebels, especially for a free general pardon and a parliament.'[83] This theme is repeated at the end of the letter when the king complains again, 'it is much to our marvel to receive so many desperate letters from you'.[84] He goes on to comment, 'we could be as well content to bestow some time in the reading of an honest remedy as many extreme and desperate mischiefs'.[85] Henry not only sends his servants in the field detailed instructions on how they should treat with the Pilgrims dishonestly, he also tells them he does not want to read any more bad news. What is striking about this is that by complaining in this way Henry's behaviour matches an important image of tyranny in Tudor culture – the moment when Herod beat the messengers who told him that Christ and his family had escaped into Egypt.[86] Obviously Henry is not deliberately playing the role of Herod – or at least one assumes not – but one wonders what the king's servants made of Henry's behaviour. What did Norfolk make of the King's demand for good news? Was he meant to lie? Would that be better than telling the King the truth? What kind of rulers punished the messenger and ignored the message?

The fraught nature of Henry's kingship and in particular his religious policies during this period can be further illustrated by examining two texts, Wilfrid Holme's *The fall and euill success of Rebellion* and Stephen Gardiner's *The Oration of True Obedience*, written to support the Henrician Reformation. Wilfrid Holme wrote his poem in 1537 in the immediate aftermath of the Pilgrims' defeat. It was, however, not published until much later when it appears to have been printed as part of the Elizabethan response to the Northern Rebellion in 1570. It is unclear why Holme's poem was not published when it was written.[87] It is an extended allegorical political-religious text. Although Holme's starting point is the Pilgrimage of Grace and the poem is structured around a response to the Pilgrims' articles, it also covers a wide range of other topical issues. A.G. Dickens comments that, having addressed the events of the Pilgrimage of Grace, *The fall and euill success of Rebellion* 'broadens out into an elaborate essay upon the political and theological principles at stake during this supreme crisis of the English Reformation'.[88] Holme's poem opens with the narrator meeting an allegorical figure for England, Anglia, who commands him to tell a history of rebellions, classical, biblical and English. Having completed this task, Holme goes on to give a detailed poetic account of the events in Lincolnshire and the North in the winter of 1536. In the process he makes the conventional accusation, made by all magisterial writers against popular mass movements in the sixteenth century, that the Pilgrims sought to turn the world upside down. Holme claims that the Pilgrims:

> Ascribed a Cater to a king coequall in degree,
> With coshe Crommoke coshe, I would we had thee here
> Like sauage beastes loosed and put to their libertie,
> Enioyng in the splendent after obscuritie,

> Deuishing and inuenting Articles presumptuous
> Euery one discording from the other verily[89]

In this verse Holme gives the conventional magisterial argument made whenever there were popular revolts, that such movements simply reflected the populace's infantile desire for violence and disorder, a specifically Henrician twist. The Pilgrims' in *The fall and euill successe of Rebellion* produce a confused mass of articles which they then fall out over. It is noticeable that Holme suggests that this orgy of article-making is initially a source of enjoyment among the Pilgrims whose liberty and disorder is performed through the production of numerous divergent articles. *The fall and euill successe of Rebellion* constructs the Pilgrimage of Grace implicitly, and presumably unwittingly, as an alter-image of the Henrician Reformation, which was also marked by the production of numerous articles which in their turn became the source of debate and discord.[90]

The emphasis on the linguistic disorder of the Pilgrims is continued when Holme turns to his detailed critique of their articles. For example the Pilgrims' seventh article demanded the removal and punishment of heretical bishops. Holme replies to this article by recounting a beast fable allegedly told by Demosthenes during a siege of Athens in response to an offer from the besiegers to give up if the Athenians surrendered ten wise men.[91] Holme goes on to apply this fable directly to the Pilgrimage of Grace, while giving it an explicitly linguistic twist. He argues that if the Pilgrims had achieved their aims and had those bishops who they call heretical removed, they would have followed Demosthenes' fable.

> Deuouring the elect all Chrystes lawes mitigant,
> Depriuing the truth, to rumpe euery sillable
> By craftie Silogysmes and reasons variable
> With counterfet gloses, and sense tropologicall
> Craftily sophisticate with reasons applicable,
> Making them to appeare to seeme anagogicall.[92]

Holme's attack in this verse on the reason and learning espoused by the Pilgrims is entirely conventional in terms of Reformation polemic. In particular, in these lines, and throughout the poem, Holme deploys tropes and motifs from Henrician Reformation polemics, for example *A litel treatise* (1532), in combination with a reworking for radically different ends of John Skelton's representation of the effects of heresy on language. As in the work of other pro-Henrician and anti-papist writers, the most obvious example being John Bale, Holme criticizes the language of papistry and performs its corruption of language in his own text by piling up obscure abstract terms whose meaning is clearly of less importance than their ability to fill up textual space, to confuse the reader and make interpretation difficult if not impossible. In this verse *The fall and euill successe of Rebellion* performs its version of papist corruption. It represents one of the key dangers of the Pilgrimage as linguistic, arguing that if the Pilgrims had won then their wolves, scholastics and logicians, would have devoured Christ's laws with their variable reasons and crafty syllogisms.

As Holme works through the Pilgrims' articles, however, a number of passages indicate possible reasons for the poem's non-publication in 1537. Indeed, as soon as *The fall and euill successe of Rebellion* moves from criticising the Pilgrims to giving the Henrician religious settlement positive support, it enters dangerous territory. For example, Holme rejects the Pilgrims' defence of the doctrine of Purgatory but he does so in words that sound suspiciously Lutheran, writing: 'And by him [Christ] we are righteous, perfectly justified, / And to make right no right, it is no veritie, / Thus nought is their purgatori which they haue specified.'[93]

The English Church in 1537 had not, however, embraced the doctrine of justification by faith alone. Rex has pointed out that the Ten Articles that were issued in the summer of 1536 explicitly rejected Lutheran teaching on justification.[94] These articles expressed a degree of scepticism over some aspects of Purgatory, but only in terms of popular custom and papal practice. They do not explicitly provide a justification for Holme's rejection of purgatory as a concept.

The problems that Holme potentially faces in answering the Pilgrims' item on Purgatory are, however, minor compared with the issues he faces when addressing the place of the Church within the commonwealth of England. He opens this section of the poem by arguing that the existence of three estates – clergy, temporality and commons – has been the cause of 'much heresy'.[95] The solution he proposes is the complete eradication of any difference between the various groups that make up the commonwealth.

> Therefore I think in myne imagination
> It were well done we all were called spirituall,
> By names thus following by this protestation
>
> The spiritualtie of the eternall ministration
> The spiritaultie of the temporal justification,
> The spiritualtie of the mundane occupation
> Nowe these men are one, but not their occupation.[96]

Holme's proposal may seem bizarre but it is actually a relatively sophisticated attempt to address the crisis of legitimation at the heart of the Henrician Reformation. As has been suggested, a basic tension ran through Henry's religious policies in the 1530s over whose authority, the King's, Parliament's or the clergy's, gave them legitimacy? In this section of *The fall and euill successe of Rebellion*, Holme answers this question by denying any separate or special sphere for the clergy or indeed for the Church itself. In doing so he is simply spelling out something which, being extremely radical, was only implicit in the Henrician Reformation, namely that the King, despite his temporal status, had complete power over the Church – not only in secular matters but also religious. Holme reduces all members of the English common-wealth to the same status in order to make sense of the situation created by the Royal Supremacy – if all the King's subjects are basically the same, then the problems raised by competing jurisdictions and sources of authority, parti-cularly between the temporal and spiritual, simply disappear.

Having answered all the Pilgrims' articles in turn, *The fall and euill successe of Rebellion* then returns to the actual events of the Pilgrimage of Grace, giving a potted history of the movement's defeat. Holme comments:

> Yet this ought to be marked in time of vacation
> Or [before] the pardon was gyuen by the kings magnificence,
> V thousand Cotes of fence [mail] by the countryes preparation
> Was wrought and made for their corporall defence
> And Boyes went a procession[n] as they wold make pretence
> And Mynstrels soong songs with many allusions
> More lyke beastes than men to make so great offence,
> To vitipend their prince with such naughtie illusion.[97]

Holme's intention here is to place the blame for the breakdown of the agree-ments of December 1536 squarely on the Pilgrims' shoulders, and not the desire of the King for revenge. Unfortunately this verse looks less persuasive in hindsight, since we now know that those Holme accuses of preparing to defend themselves would have been wise to take such measures. Indeed this verse is marked by tension between its emphasis on the seriousness of the North's preparation for further war and the carnival atmosphere which Holme claims prevailed in the postpardon period. The reference in this verse to the allusions of the minstrels' songs serves as an introduction to the final section of *The fall and euill successe of Rebellion*, which includes a detailed discussion of why the prophecy known as the Mouldwarp could not be applied to Henry.[98]

Holme's *The fall and euill successe of Rebellion* is an exemplary Henrician text. It deploys the full range of anti-papal, and anti-clerical, propaganda in support of the Royal Supremacy. It also includes a detailed refutation of the articles of the Pilgrimage of Grace. However as has already been pointed out, it was not published until the reign of Elizabeth when much of it, particularly its detailed account of the events of the Pilgrimage of Grace, would have been completely redundant, if not meaningless. Holme's poem illustrates the extent to which the Henrician Reformation created a political and religious situation in which even a text written purposely in support of Henry's religious policies contains moments that slip beyond its author's pro-Henrician agenda.

Stephen Gardiner's *The Oration of True Obedience* was written during the 1530s in support of Henry VIII's religious policies. The main argument of *The Oration* appears to be that subjects have a duty of obedience to their princes.[99]

In this text Gardiner produces a far more sophisticated response to the Henrician Reformation's crisis of legitimacy than Holme did when he simply expanded, and effectively rendered meaningless, the category of spiritual by including within it every member of the commonwealth.[100] At the same time it is possible to read *The Oration* less as a whole-hearted endorsement of the Royal Supremacy and more as a coded and partial critique of Henry's religious policies.

The Oration opens by stressing the need to return to the purity of unadorned scripture. Gardiner writes:

> God is the truthe (as scripture recordeth) wher in he geveth his chiefe lighte unto us so much that who so euer seketh it in any other place and goth about to sette it out of mennes puddles and quallmyres and not out of the moste pure and clere fountayne it self they drawe and bringe up now and than I wote not what foule and myrye geare uneffectual and to no purpose for the quenching of mennes thirstie desires which perteigneth all together properly unto the truth it selfe.[101]

Placing this valorization of scripture at the opening of *The Oration* reflects the extent to which in this text Gardiner is concerned with questions of truth and interpretation. During the course of the work, however, it never quite becomes clear who is authorized to interpret scripture. For example, Gardiner asks his reader: 'How often doo we reade / that the causes of heresie / haue ben debated before Emperors and Princes / and discussed by their tryall?'[102] This question appears to be an implicit justification of the role that Henry assumed during the trial of John Lambert; however, the key thing about Gardiner's words is the way in which they imagine the role of the Emperor or Prince as enabling but passive. In the past causes of heresy, not the examination of heretics, have been debated *before*, not *by*, temporal rulers. Later when discussing the interpretation of scripture Gardiner writes:

> Let vs than folowe the ordre / that God hath prescribed / and not goo about with our interpretacton / to confounde and preuerte the members of his body the church / which he hathe set / in ordre and disposed in particulares accordingly / that one in the congregacion shoulde teache / and an other haue preeminence which is appointed to princes / ...[103]

Gardiner ends this passage by stating that true obedience means following the truth of God's words, which can only be established and guaranteed if the separation of roles between Prince and teacher is respected.[104]

The potentially subversive nature of this separation in terms of the Royal Supremacy only really becomes apparent in the context of Gardiner's consistent articulation of the difference between earthly and spiritual law. He writes: 'Goddes lawe is constant / but mannes laws is euer subiecte unto vanitie / and so unto varietie.'[105] Indeed for Gardiner God's law is not only changeless but also limitless.

> What maner of limites are those / that ye tel me of seinge the scripture hathe non suche? But generally speaking of obedience / which the subiecte is bounden to doo vnto the prince / the wife vnto the husbande / or the seruant to the maister it hathe not added so muche as / one sillable of excepicion / but only hathe preserued the obedience due to God / safe and hole / that we should not harken vnto any mannes worde in all the worlde against God.[106]

This is a very typical passage from *The Oration*. It follows a passage which discusses whether there are any limits to how obedient subjects should be to their prince. Gardiner's initial answer to this question appears to be that scripture imposes no limits on subjects' obedience to their prince. By the end of this passage, however, it is obedience to God that is limitless, and therefore by implication there is a limit to princely power. Indeed the final comment that no man's word should be heard before God's suggests an equality of men before God; the limitless obedience that Christians owe to God levels out human or earthly distinctions.

The Oration ends with a parable. This is, however, an ending that Gardiner states he felt compelled to add in order to answer those who doubt his ability to teach true obedience. In particular, Gardiner claims that some people, seeing him breaking his oath of obedience to the Pope, have started to question the efficacy of all oaths, asking, 'Wher is keping of othes become / say they? Wher is fidelitie? What maye a man beleve now a dayes? Whom maye a man trust?'[107] Gardiner's answer to those who accuse him of being an oath-breaker, indeed a subverter of the power of oaths themselves, is to tell the story of a man who, having been married, thinks his wife has died, remarries and is then confronted by his first wife returned as it were from the grave. Gardiner tells his readers how this man tried his best to stay married to the second wife but in the end, having lost his case before the law, 'he gaue place to the truthe / and taketh his furst wife to him agayn by the iudgement of the churche.'[108] Gardiner argues that no-one could accuse this husband of breaking his oath to his first wife. Indeed he advances the slightly bizarre argument that the fact that the husband took a second wife, and did not fall to whores, itself shows his respect for oaths. Gardiner goes on to gloss this story further by suggesting that the second wife had a hand in the first's disappearance, and that she was herself no maiden but an evil woman. Finally he comments, 'if a man wolde consider this gaire / shal he not see / as it were in a glasse / the very ymage of that husbande in me.'[109] This story contains a number of Biblical tropes; however, the Protestant editors of the first English edition of *The Oration* could not resist making the obvious point that there is something a little odd about a celibate churchman comparing himself to a twice married man.

There are a number of other important implications to Gardiner's use of the parable of the twice married man to conclude *The Oration*. This is a work of political theory written in support of the Royal Supremacy – concluding it with a parable raises questions over interpretation and the role of the reader. Why does Gardiner choose to end his text with what he calls a 'tale'? Moreover, it is a story whose meaning is deferred in such a way as to invite the reader to try and work out for themselves what it means. When Gardiner glosses his tale and relates the fate of the twice married man to himself this is such a surprising textual move that it seems designed to make the reader question either Gardiner's reliability as a narrator or their own ability to fully understand what they have read. Indeed this tale does appear to have a far more obvious topical meaning than as an allegory of a celibate bishop's relationship to Christ's teaching. It is surely possible that a Henrician reader would see the twice married man as an image of Henry, particularly given the role of the second 'wife' in driving away the true and honest first wife through tricks and allurements. *The Oration* could therefore be seen as concluding with an allegorical prophecy that Henry would sometime in the future return to his true first wife.

Obviously it would be bizarre to argue that *The Oration* is an oppositional work. It was clearly intended by Gardiner to display his dependability on questions of religion in the context of the Henrician Reformation. In particular, it is relatively unambiguously critical of the Papacy, albeit lacking the violence of some of Gardiner's other Henrician tracts. What *The Oration* reflects is the effect of the Henrician Reformation on public political and religious discourse in England. Gardiner's tract is written as if there is a censor, or more accurately an inquisitor, perched on the author's shoulder. It is a work of political theory and religious polemic that demands to be read a number of times before its subtleties and ambiguities become apparent. It is a performance, and a brilliant one at that, of submission and compliance which subtly places question marks against the very positions and arguments that it was ostensibly written to support.

SIR THOMAS WYATT AND THE POETRY OF TYRANNY

Sir Thomas Wyatt was born at the beginning of the sixteenth century and by the end of the 1520s had held a number of offices at court. It was, however, during the 1530s that he rose to real prominence within Henry's court. This led to him being knighted in 1535, but also to his imprisonment in the Tower of London a number of times, in particular after the downfall of Anne Boleyn in 1536. Wyatt died in 1542 after a typically Henrician career, which included a spell as ambassador in Spain as well as another sojourn in the Tower. Wyatt's status as a writer rests largely on his court poetry, and in particular his adaptation of the sonnet form from its native Italian. Wyatt did not publish any of his poems during his lifetime. The reasons for this are unclear. It has been suggested that his failure to publish his work was a product of aristocratic prejudice against print, however, there is no firm evidence that Wyatt regarded himself as an aristocrat or that he held any principled reasons for not publishing his work. It is also important to note that Wyatt's status as a court poet does not mean that he was writing within existing social or cultural contexts. The Henrician court of the 1530s was a new institution.[110] It is an awareness of this newness that partly explains the edginess of Wyatt's poetry. It is, however, the Henrician Reformation that most profoundly shaped the poetry that Wyatt wrote during the 1530s.[111]

Two themes dominate the Wyatt's poetry, power and ambiguity. His work constantly reflects upon the problem of interpretation in a world in which the subject is required to produce meaning, but cannot. The narrators of Wyatt's lyrics exist in a pressurized, impossible state. They know that they are dependent on words to articulate their desires and sense of self while at the same time being acutely aware how unstable and duplicitous the meaning of even a single word can be. This frustrating and alienated state has often been read by literary critics as typifying that of the Tudor courtier. In this tradition Wyatt's poetry is constructed as perhaps the first example in English literature of courtly poetry. Gary Waller comments:

> [Wyatt's] is the first substantial body of work in the period in England through which the power of the Court speaks as the controller and creator not only of the dominant discourse but of alternatives to it, which however dimly apprehended and unable to find a place within it except by negation, none the less radically disrupt it.[112]

Waller describes Wyatt's poetry as simultaneously caught within the symbolic order of the court and striving to escape from its control. This tension can be seen in the conflict between the angst-ridden tone of the narrative voice of Wyatt's poetry, the violent, chaotic space that his narrators find themselves in, with its constantly expanding and constricting boundaries, and the formal rigidity of the poems themselves.[113] Clearly this can be seen as describing the claustrophobic and oppressive atmosphere within which courtiers existed in Henry's court; however, it can also be seen as reflecting the cultural pressures created by the Henrician Reformation. Wyatt's poetry enacts, in the conflict between the perplexing and endangered state of its narrators and the poem's formal fixity, the situation created by the Royal Supremacy with its demand for complete and total obedience to a constantly changing and arguably inherently ambiguous set of religious teachings and doctrines.

Brian Cummings has recently described the linguistic effects of the changes introduced by Henry VIII during the 1530s. He comments that under Henry writing literature was a dangerous business. Cummings goes on to argue: 'The Henrician regime created a literature of suspicion, on its guard against the imputation of treason and heresy.'[114] As has already been suggested, this situation was partly the product of the shifting definitions of orthodoxy, heresy and treason throughout Henry's reign. Its effects on Wyatt's poetry can be seen at a number of levels. In particular, in his poems Wyatt consistently subverts discourses that could represent sources of authority beyond the arbitrary, all-pervasive but undefined power that saturates his poetry.[115] The lyric, 'It maybe good', opens in a typically oblique way.

> It maybe good, like it who list.
> But I do doubt. Who can me blame?
> For oft assured yet have I missed
> And now again I fear the same.
> The windy words, and eyes' quaint game
> Of sudden change maketh me aghast.
> For dread to fall I stand not fast.[116]

In *Tottel's Miscellany* this poem is entitled, 'The lover, taught, mistrusteth allurements'; however, this is simply an example of way in which Wyatt's Marian editors sought to place his texts within a courtly love paradigm. In practice the poem does not make it at all clear to what 'it' refers. Indeed while the title added in 1557 suggests that the poem has an explicit message which can be related to a conventional courtly love narrative, the Henrician version of this text does not offer readers such clues or props to their reading. Instead one is confronted by a verse which depicts its narrator in a state of doubt over the 'goodness' of something whose nature is unclear, but which is in some important way caught up in a world of 'windy words' and 'eyes' quaint game / Of sudden change'. The perilous state of Wyatt's narrator is expanded upon in the poem's second verse.

> Alas, I tread an endless maze
> That seek to accord two contraries;
> And hope still, and nothing haze,
> Imprisoned in liberties;
> As one unheard and still that cries;
> Always thirsty ye naught I taste.
> For dread to fall I stand not fast.[117]

This verse makes clear that the prison in which Wyatt's narrator is caught is of a particularly linguistic nature.[118] The reference to 'an endless maze' echoes the representation of corrupt, redundantly productive language found in the religious polemics of writers like Bale and Skelton, for whom it is papists / heretics who are caught in a web of their own meaningless babble and empty syllogisms. This is not to suggest that Wyatt's narrator is a heretic or papist, but rather that he is portrayed as existing in a world in which the meaning of words has become so radically unstable that one's very sense of self is endangered by their protean quality.

Wyatt sums up the state of his narrator in the line, 'Imprisoned in liberties'. This can be read as one of Wyatt's typically oblique statements designed to reflect the frustrating status of a Tudor courtier empowered and simultaneously dis-empowered by his relationship to the monarch. At the same time this line can also be seen as reflecting a particularly Henrician state of being. The Royal Supremacy was constantly lauded by its apologists for freeing the English from the shackles of papal tyranny. In particular, the provision of the Bible in English was seen as the legitimizing achievement of the Henrician Reformation.[119] Now at last the English were able to read scripture in their own tongue free from the obscurity of Latin and the shackles of papal glosses. This liberty was, however, only a partial one, implicitly undermined by the regime's repeated insistence on obedience as a virtue in and of itself. Wyatt's poem reflects a culture in which the government coupled a claim to have liberated the reading and interpretation of scripture with constant attempts to constrain and direct this liberty. The Henrician Reformation embodied the fantasy of a fully transparent commonwealth, all of whose members freely gave complete unquestioning but informed obedience to the Royal Supremacy. At the same time the failure of this state to come into being created a latent paranoia within the regime, waiting for an excuse to break forth into a full-scale hunt for those who exploited the tension between the inner and outer man in order to hide their heresy / papistry.[120] It is in this world that the narrator of Wyatt's poem exists. He wants certainty, desires fixity, but cannot achieve it, paradoxically because of this very desire.

Wyatt's poem concludes with a radical statement of the narrator's loss of bearing in a world in which meaning has become impossible.

> Assured I doubt I be not sure.
> And should I trust to such surety
> That oft hath put the proof in ure
> And never yet hath found it trusty?
> Nay, sir, in faith it were great foly.
> And yet my life thus I do waste:
> For dread to fall I stand not fast.[121]

The only thing that Wyatt's narrator seems confident of is that he doubts. At the same time he knows that he needs to stand fast but fear of falling prevents him from doing so. Doubt prevents him from escaping the endless maze he is caught in and fear of falling stops him finding a safe place to stand. Wyatt's narrator is caught in a state that Sir Thomas Elyot would have recognized. As has been suggested, throughout the 1530s Elyot consistently tried to prove to Cromwell and Henry his complete loyalty to the Royal Supremacy, even to the extent of fantasizing that he be treated as a heretic so that he could be put to the test and show 'the moste secrete thowghtes of his hart'. Wyatt's narrator would surely also leap at the chance of being examined, of standing fast, as a way of escaping the endless buffeting of 'windy words' – were it not for the terror that he would fail.

The desire for examination as a way of escaping the disabling effects of linguistic slippage and textual ambiguity is a constant refrain throughout Wyatt's poetry. For example 'They Flee from Me', one of his most famous poems, concludes with an incitement to examination and judgement. Its embittered narrator tells a story of love and betrayal. Throughout the poem, however, there is a tension between the narrator's version of events and the language he uses to describe what took place. This poem has received a considerable amount of critical analysis. Stephen Greenblatt has argued that 'They Flee from Me' perfectly encapsulates the state of a courtier at the court of Henry VIII in its portrayal of 'the conflicting cultural codes that fashion male identity in Tudor court lyrics'.[122] Certainly this poem does articulate the tension at the heart of Tudor courtiership between desire for power and one's passivity in the face of it. Elizabeth Heale makes the important point that Wyatt, and other court poets of the period, used misogynist assumptions about female treachery and betrayal in order to assert – or at least attempt to – a coherent male identity.[123] That this poem clearly fails in this endeavour is partly a result of the way in which Wyatt constructs his narrator but is also a product of its articulation of a specifically Henrician concern over the production of meaning.

Wyatt's poem opens by the narrator placing its events within a specific architectural space.

> They flee from me that sometime did me seek
> With naked foot stalking in my chamber.
> I have seen them gentle, tame, and meek /
> That now are wild and do not remember
> That sometime they put themself in danger
> To take bread at my hand; and now they range
> Busily seeking with a continual change.[124]

Wyatt's narrator constructs himself as the still centre in the middle of an erotic drama. He represents women as at once tame and wild, as passive and active. In the past they have sought him out and placed themselves in his power, although recently they have abandoned him. The narrator represents himself as occupying a place of enclosure where what was once wild is tamed. In his chamber the narrator appears to have control, but beyond its bounds the birds' / women's wildness returns. By the end of the verse, the narrator has been left watching while his erstwhile lovers range far and wide. The first verse of 'They Flee from Me' constructs a tension between the narrator's chamber which is a place of order and the world outside it which is wild, dangerous but also full of desirable women.

The second verse of Wyatt's poem, however, disrupts this structure. Suddenly it is at the centre of the narrator's chamber that wild female power erupts. The eroticism of this text is located around this moment of reversal which colours the rest of the poem through its problematization of the narrator's own status and desire.

> Thanked be fortune it hath been otherwise
> Twenty times better, but once in special,
> In thin array after pleasant guise,
> When her loose gown from her shoulders did fall
> And she me caught in her arms long and small,
> Therewithal sweetly did me kiss
> And softly said, 'Dear heart, how like you this?'[125]

At the centre of the narrator's chamber, Wyatt's poem and indeed the story that the poem tells is a moment of female empowerment and male passivity.[126] The erotic play of the poem takes place around the multiple meanings of the final word 'this' and in the way that the text defers this moment. The reader has to wait to find out what kind of encounter they are witnessing and then is frustrated in their voyeuristic desire since 'this' could refer to a number of possibilities ranging from the symbolic and poetic to the physical and bawdy. In particular, at the centre of 'They Flee from Me' is an image of vocalized sexual female empowerment and complete, indeed infantile, male dependency.

In the final verse of the poem the narrator asks his readers to decide on the meaning of the events that he has recounted.

> It was no dream: I lay broad waking.
> But all is turned through my gentleness
> Into a strange fashion of forsaking.
> And I have leave to go of her goodness
> And she also to use newfangleness.
> But since that I so kindly am served
> I would fain know what she hath deserved.[127]

'They Flee from Me' concludes with the narrator asking its readers to pass judgement on the woman who he clearly feels has betrayed him. Wyatt skilfully suggests, however, that the narrator of the poem is far from unbiased and that his version of events is prejudiced. The potential irony of the narrator's use of the words 'goodness' and 'kindly' to describe what he sees as an act of betrayal reflects his unreliability as a narrator and witness.

'They Flee from Me' presents its masculine narrator as caught between activity and passivity in a situation suffused with arbitrary power. At times it appears that he is in control; however, it is clear to the poem's readers that these moments are largely illusory. Indeed there is a level at which this poem, and indeed much of Wyatt's poetic writing, positions its reader alongside the arbitrary power that fills the world of the poem. To read 'They Flee from Me' is to become part of the jury judging the poem's narrator and his lover. Michael McCanles has argued persuasively that this poem 'analyses masterfully the theme of love as power'.[128] But the poem also offers its reader the temptation to read the power that escapes its protagonist as their own. We, through our interpretative labour, our desire to know the truth of the narrator's story, are incited by Wyatt to participate uncritically in the process of inquisition and judgement that the narrator desires as the only way of producing certainty in his world of the unstable words, 'newfangleness' and ambiguity. It is this incitement to examine that gives 'They Flee for Me' its particular tone and makes reading it so uneasy. Greenblatt comments that in Wyatt's poetry:

> The audience is not being manipulated but invited to experience the movement of the poet's mind through assurance, doubt, dread, and longing. This painstaking rendering of the inner life seems to surpass any social game, though the poems remain clearly embedded in such a game.[129]

However it is not the poet's inner life that is under the microscope in works like 'They Flee from Me'; it is that of Wyatt's narrator. We as readers are invited to place ourselves outside the world of the text with its ambiguities in order to pass judgement. To read 'They Flee from Me' is to be offered a particularly Henrician, and indeed confessional fantasy – that of examining, interrogating and judging the inner life of a person as a way of producing certainty and fixity in a world of textual slippage and linguistic violence.

The political implications of this fantasy in the context of the 1530s can be illustrated by looking briefly at Robert Aske's 'Narrative of the events of October and November 1536'.[130] In this text Aske presents himself as an unwilling participant in the Pilgrimage of Grace. Clearly there were very good reasons for this, given that this narrative was written after the movement's defeat and under the shadow of almost certain execution. Aske's only hope, which was an extremely slim one, was to argue that his role in the Pilgrimage had been largely reactive and passive. For example Aske claims that at one stage during the early part of the movement he was hiding in a poor man's house 'to thentent not to haue been known'. However, as the text goes on to recount:

> the comyns had gotyn then knowledge of him, and sent for him, and so on the night, passed the water to the comyns in H(ou)denshir. Then being aboutes the hous of Sir Thomas Methun, knight, and in danger to haue burnt the same, and for the intent to saue the same (hous) the said Aske repared vnto them, and saued the said hous and so pacified the comyns, that they repared that nyght home to ther houses.[131]

It is hard to understand why the commons would allow themselves to be pacified by a man who they had just found hiding from them. Moreover this passage suggests that the commons had the ability to summon the gentleman Aske, although the phrase 'and so on the night' works to obscure this reversal of early modern social norms and the reasons why Aske obeyed the commons' order.[132] Aske's 'Narrative' creates an image of the Pilgrimage in which no-one is in real control or has authority. His text consistently finesses moments of decision and action in such a way as to make them appear spontaneous. Aske's narrative concludes with a passage in the first person.

> And thus, most drad soueryng lord, I haue declared to your grace the planes of the promisses, so fer as I cane now (call) to my remembrance, alwais willing (that) if I haue omitted any mater to declare the troth from tym to tyme, besuching your (grace of your) most (mercifull) pardon in the promisse.[133]

The meaning of this passage is in places obscure; however, it is clear that Aske concluded his narration of the early stages of the Pilgrimage of Grace with a promise of endless confession. At the same time Aske's words suggest that the truth he has just produced is in some way incomplete or flawed. Indeed Aske himself acknowledges that he has only told the truth as far as he can now remember it. There is therefore a tension in this passage between the truth that Aske imagines Henry as desiring, complete and total, and that which Aske as a flawed human being can now produce. Aske's solution to this problem is to emphasize the extent to which his sense of self is caught up in the need to satisfy the King's desire – his ever-readiness to confess the truth until it is complete. The one area where this narrative constructs Aske as active, as an author, is in the context of this preparedness to endlessly declare the truth to Henry. It seems incredible that the Aske that is praised in *The Ballad of the Pilgrimage of Grace* for readiness to stand fast is the same man who in this narration consistently represents himself as a passive victim of events. Obviously the Aske of this narrative is a mediated textual representation of the real man who led the Pilgrims with such skill and bravery – an Aske designed, either by the man himself or his interrogators, to please Henry. This Aske has no place, no discourse, to refer to beyond the King's will. His existence depends on his ability to endlessly confess. In a Christian context this is entirely unremarkable, but Aske's narration is a political document. It is as though in this offer Aske is performing the logic of the Royal Supremacy, collapsing Henry's temporal and spiritual roles, constructing him as someone who has the right to demand endless confession from his subjects.

There is a significant distinction to be drawn between Aske as a historical person and the narrators of Wyatt's poetry, but it is equally important to note the extent to which Wyatt consistently reflects in his work upon the nature of the world in which Aske found himself after the defeat of the Pilgrimage: one in which it appeared that only the King's will mattered.[134] Wyatt's sonnet 'Each man me telleth' perfectly articulates the symbolic world of the Henrician court and the wider state of public discourse in England during the 1530s. This sonnet opens with a typically ironic statement by Wyatt's narrator of his fidelity to changeability. 'Each man me telleth I change most my device, / And on my faith me think it good reason / To change purpose like after the season.' Wyatt stresses the outrageous nature of this opening through the use of the terms 'faith' and 'device'. The latter can refer to desire and strategy as well as badge, while Wyatt's use of faith in this context suggests oath-taking. The opening lines of this sonnet therefore combine signifiers of fixity with an assertion of the wisdom of changing one's purpose to fit the season. The narrator of Wyatt's poem goes on to celebrate his diverseness before finishing with another claim to firmness and stability, writing: 'Treat ye me well and keep ye in the same state; / And while with me doth dwell this wearied ghost, / My word nor I shall not be variable / But always one, your own both firm and stable.'[135] The self imagined in this poem is caught in a state of such constant flux that it has become for him the only possible state that he can imagine. Indeed, for Wyatt's narrator in this sonnet, change is the basis of stability. His sense of self is built on the inevitability of an ever-rising diverseness.

The narrator of 'Each man me telleth' is, however, aware that there are worlds beyond that in which he is trapped. The sonnet opens with a reference to proverbial wisdom with its paraphrase of the saying, 'A wise man need not blush to change his purpose'. This importation of a popular saying into a courtly setting, however, seems to strip it of all its power or indeed meaning. Certainly Wyatt's narrator appears scornful of its advice.[136] This is ironic, since he clearly finds his present state disabling and frustrating. The nature of the wearied ghost that dwells with the narrator is unclear. It does not appear to be the person to whom the sonnet is addressed; rather it seems to be an aspect of the narrator himself, an echo of who he was before he entered a world of ever-rising diverseness. The wearied ghost is the uncanny other of the narrator, who he used to be before he was caught in his present state of complete obedience to a state of constant flux. Aske in his 'Narration' is also accompanied by an uncanny other, the ghost of the man who in the balmy days of the Pilgrimage of Grace had authority and purpose. Wyatt's poetry consistently represents the self as the cynosure of meaning, but one formed entirely in the shadow of an arbitrary and violent power. His reader is incited to make coherent the speech of narrators caught in a world of windy words and faithless oaths. In these terms Wyatt offers his reader a specifically Henrician fantasy of examination and inquisition in which they have the opportunity to match his narrator's outer and inner selfs, to sit above the poem in judgement, penetrating the text's obliqueness and the narrator's partial words as part of an inquisitorial reading. Christopher Z. Hobson has recently suggested: 'through "veiling" his truth Wyatt shows that a personal core of integrity exists, that truth matters and is of value in his own life, and yet his emphasis lies elsewhere

– on the need to keep that core shifting and elusive, to conceal its workings'.[137] Wyatt's poetry does constantly hint at the existence of a core of inner belief, of a real self behind its complex surface, a true inner man veiled by the performance of a duplicitous outer man. This is, however, a fantasy. Moreover it is one that is specifically Henrician in the way that it allows and indeed validates a form of inquisitorial reading in which the truth of Wyatt's text, the inner 'self' of the poem's narrator, can be produced through a process of penetrative iconoclastic reading – smashing the shell to find the kernel of truth.

The convoluted opaque nature of Wyatt's court poetry is reproduced in his satires and his paraphrase of the Penitential Psalms. The latter have often been read as Protestant texts; this is however a mistake. In fact they reflect precisely the tortured and ambiguous nature of the Henrician Reformation. In a world in which orthodoxy and heresy are constantly being defined and then re-defined, Wyatt produces religious poems whose meaning circles around questions of textuality and meaning.[138] Wyatt's satires could have provided him with an opportunity to create a world beyond the court; however, this is not the case. Even in a text such as 'My mother's maids', where Wyatt explicitly claims to be drawing on popular culture for the basis of his work, the poem itself ends up returning to the Henrician world in which wearied ghosts wander a textual maze. The animal fable at the poem's heart performs the same function as the moral tale in Chaucer's *Pardoner's Tale*. It appears to be moralizing, to have a message, but readers who give in to their desire to produce meaning, to fix the tale's meaning, simply end up caught within the toils of the poem. There is no moral to the story of the town and country mice, although the poem makes one feel that there ought to be. Instead Wyatt gives his reader a story that ends with an exercise of arbitrary violent power.

CONCLUSION

In *The Governour*, Sir Thomas Elyot was working within a tradition of English political writing. In this work he discusses how governors should be educated and what role they should have within the commonwealth. Despite the fact that Elyot explicitly excludes supreme or pre-eminent governors from his work their absence, and perhaps particularly that of Henry VIII, is constantly felt in the text. *The Governour* is haunted by the shadow of a tyrannous wilful reader. Its valorization of *amicitia*, of counsel and the importance of reason are all designed at one level to address the problem of tyranny within the common-wealth. None of these solutions are open to the narrators of Wyatt's poems. Above all Elyot's argument that pre-eminent governors should beware since all their actions will ultimately be publicly known is reversed in Wyatt's poems. In these texts it is the actions of the subject that are offered up to the reader for public inspection and judgement. The narrators of Wyatt's poems only have a private life in order for it to be made public by his readers, to give them the inquisitorial pleasure of forcing it into the open.

The symbolic world of Wyatt's poetry is quite unique. It is marked by the unusual and tyrannous nature of Henry's kingship in the 1530s and 1540s. After 1547 Tudor writers returned to the discourses that Wyatt had found empty or inadequate as sources of authority. Robert Crowley emphasized friendship as an egalitarian ideal. Barnabe Googe used the idea of *amicitia* to imagine a bond of Protestant brothers united against the twin dangers of royal tyranny and popular disorder. John Heywood celebrated the world of the street and the market as sites of popular wisdom. Whereas for Wyatt proverbial sayings could not provide a source of linguistic stability or order, they enabled Heywood to imagine a world beyond Reformation conflicts and violence. The Tudor writer whose example is most illustrative in comparison to that of Wyatt is Miles Hogarde. In his work one can see the positive possibilities of confessionalization. Hogarde's Catholicism gives his work a sense of purpose, coherence and authority that enables him to critique Tudor culture and even implicitly the religious policies of Mary Tudor. For Wyatt there is no escape from the oppressive logic of Henrician kingship, not even in confessional Protestantism.[39] He is caught in a world in which the desire to stand fast is constantly undermined by the need to change one's device at the whim of a man to whom killing six men in one day, three as heretics and three as traitors, was consistent with the pursuit of a religious mean.

NOTES

1 Richard Morrison, 'A Remedy for Sedition Wherein Are Contained Many Things concerning the True and Loyal Obeisance That Commons Owe unto Their Prince and Sovereign Lord the King', 1536, STC 18113.3, in *Humanist Scholarship and Public Order: Two Tracts against the Pilgrimage of Grace by Sir Richard Morrison*, ed. David Sandler Berkowitz (Washington: 1984), pp. 109–146, p. 141.

2 John Cheke, *The hurt of sedicion howe greveous it is to a Commune welth*, 1549, STC 5109, and John Christopherson, *An Exhortation to all Menne to ... Beware of Rebellion*, 1554, STC 5207.

3 The exemplary pictorial image of this fantasy is the frontispiece of the Great Bible of 1539, where Henry is depicted in graphic terms as the centre and font of all language. For a discussion of the tensions within this woodcut see David Scott Kastan, '"The Noyse of the New Bible": Reform and Reaction in Henrician England', in *Religion and Culture in Renaissance England*, ed. Claire McEachern and Debora Shuger (Cambridge: 1997), pp. 46–68, pp. 54–59.

4 *Utopia* is a more sophisticated work than *A Remedy for Sedition*, but Morrison's work does reproduce the political fantasy at the heart of More's work – that of an all-powerful monarch as producer of an ordered society without conflict or antagonism. The most important difference between these two works in this context is that, while it is clear that More's work is intended to be ironic and potentially subversive, Morrison's almost

certainly lacks this critical aspect. In particular, in *Utopia* More creates a tension between the story of the origin of Utopia as an act of royal will, embodied in King Utopus calling his new land Utopia, and *Utopia*'s celebration of a form of Ciceronian republican politics.

5 Morrison, 1984, p. 128.

6 Ibid., p. 129.

7 Although this claim was very important in terms of legitimizing the Henrician Reformation, the fact that it appears to have satisfied both Stephen Gardiner and Thomas Cranmer must lead one to question its status, except as a tool to finesse unity and create the appearance of agreement.

8 Richard Rex, 'The Crisis of Obedience: God's Word and Henry's Reformation', *HJ*, 39 (1996), pp. 863–894, p. 894.

9 G.W.Bernard argues: 'Henry skillfully used ambiguity, even contradiction, to advance his own religious convictions.' G.W. Bernard, 'The Making of Religious Policy, 1533–46', *HJ*, 41 (1998), pp. 321–349, p. 334.

10 Morrison, 1984, p. 119.

11 Richard Rex, *Henry VIII and the English Reformation* (London: 1993), p. 173.

12 See John Guy's discussion of these issues in his study *Tudor England* (Oxford: 1991), pp. 133–134.

13 J.J. Scarisbrick comments: 'From the start ... there was some confusion as to whether the king enjoyed his Supremacy as a direct, personal divine grant, or whether it was held by king of Parliament. There was statutory evidence for both ideas. There was ideological ambiguity in the core of Henricianism.' (J.J. Scarisbrick, *Henry VIII* (London: 1981), pp. 393–394).

14 It is clear that Henry desired to expand the scope of the Royal Supremacy to give it priestly status. See John Guy, 'The Henrician Age', in *The Varieties of British Political Thought 1500–1800*, ed. J.G.A. Pocock with the assistance of Gordon J. Schochet and Lois G. Schwoerer (Cambridge: 1993), pp. 13–46, p. 41.

15 It is important to distinguish between Henrician tyranny and absolutism. Henry was a tyrant by either modern or, more importantly, early modern political norms; however, he never had anything like absolute power or authority. See Steven G. Ellis, 'Henry VIII, Rebellion and the Rule of Law', *HJ*, 24 (1984), pp. 513–531.

16 Greg Walker, 'Dialogue, Resistance, and Accommodation: Conservative Literary Response to the Henrician Reformation', unpublished paper (2000), p. 4.

17 There are a number of moments in *The Governour* when Elyot appears to align it with those who opposed Henry's divorce. In Book 3 Chapter 6 one of the key examples of truth and fidelity is located in Spain. Later in the same book Elyot's discussion of the need to trust histories repeats arguments made by More in the *Dialogue concerning Heresies*.

18 For Elyot's humanism, see Alistair Fox, 'Sir Thomas Elyot and the Humanist Dilemma', in *Reassessing the Henrician Age: Humanism, Politics and Reform 1500–1550*, eds Alistair Fox and John Guy (Oxford: 1986), pp. 52–73.

19 Guy, 1993, p. 14.

20 For a discussion of the intellectual context of Elyot's work in terms of humanism and the ideal of Respublica – the ideal of a political community flourishing under a just and

beneficial political order – see Brendan Bradshaw, 'Transalpine Humanism', in *The Cambridge History of Political Thought 1450–1700*, ed. J.H. Burns with the assistance of Mark Goldie (Cambridge: 1991), pp. 95–131, esp. pp. 98–101.

21 Sir Thomas Elyot, *The Boke named The Governour* (London: 1531), STC 7635, A.iii.

22 This concern is the one that occupied John Heywood in his allegorical history *The Spider and Fly*.

23 Elyot, 1531, A.iii / A.iii (v).

24 F.W. Conrad points out: 'Elyot's decision to follow his defense of sovereign monarchy with an assertion of the necessity of inferior governors based upon [a] passage of Aristotle was deliberate: instead of simply promoting Henry's imperial style, the opening chapters of *The Governour* sought to explore its *bounds*.' (F.W. Conrad, 'The Problem of Counsel Reconsidered: The Case of Sir Thomas Elyot', in *Political Thought and the Tudor Commonwealth: Deep Structure, Discourse and Disguise*, eds Paul A. Fideler and T.F. Mayer (London: 1992), pp. 75–107, p. 85).

25 Peter C. Herman has recently pointed out that John Rastell's *Pastyme of People* (1529) 'consistently insists on the contractual nature of monarchy'. In this context *The Governour*'s discussion of the way in which kings, sovereign or sole rulers, have in the past been elected or selected could be seen as part of a continuum of political criticism of Henry's kingship stretching back at least to the late 1520s. See Peter C. Herman, 'Rastell's *Pastyme of People*: Monarchy and the Law in Early Modern Historiography', *JMEMS*, 30 (2000), pp. 275–308, p. 277.

26 Elyot, 1531, B (v).

27 Ibid., B.ii (v).

28 Ibid., B.iii / B.iii (v).

29 Ibid., B.iiii / B.iiii (v).

30 In theoretical terms Elyot constructs the sovereign prince as that which resists symbolization within the ideological field but which gives it consistency and order. See Slavoj Žižek, *For They Know Not What They Do: Enjoyment as a Political Factor* (London: 1991), p. 263.

31 Elyot, 1531, 1 M.v (3).

32 Ibid., O.v (1) / O.v (1v).

33 For a discussion of Cupid as tyrant in Ovidian discourse see James Simpson, 'Ethics and Interpretation: Reading Wills in Chaucer's *Legend of Good Women*', *Studies in the Age of Chaucer*, 20 (1998), pp. 73–100.

34 The key figure in this tradition is Richard II, whose tyranny was represented by contemporaries as a form of wilful reading. See James Simpson, *Reform and Cultural Revolution 1350–1547* (Oxford: 2002), esp. Chapter 4.

35 Stanford E. Lehmberg comments: 'Cicero's *De officiis* and *De amicitia* gave Elyot the basis of his "true description of amitie", and the tale of Titus and Gisippus with which he illustrated true friendship was ... translated out of the *Decameron*' (Stanford E. Lehmberg, *Sir Thomas Elyot: Tudor Humanist* (Austin: 1960), p. 84).

36 There has been considerable interest in the valorization of friendship or *amicitia* by Tudor humanists. See Alan Stewart, *Close Readers: Humanism and Sodomy in Early Modern England* (Princeton: 1997), esp. Chapter 4.

37 Elyot, 1531, R.iii. / R.iii. (v).

38 John Guy points out that the concept of *amicitia* in *The Governour* is socially exclusive and is effectively reserved for the nobility and landed gentry. In a sense only those who are potentially governors have a need for *amicitia* although it is less clear that they are the only ones who could aspire to it. See Guy, 1993, pp. 13–46, p. 18.

39 Although there are is no absolute bar in Elyot's work on women being governors, the whole thrust of the work is that it is directed at men. Certainly *amicitia* as a concept seems in Elyot's mind to have been inherently masculine.

40 Elyot, 1531, Ff. (2v) / Ff. (3).

41 Ibid., Gg.

42 Ibid., Gg. (v).

43 Ibid., Gg. (v) / Gg.ii.

44 Elyot's later work, *Pasquil the Playne*, can be read as a sustained argument for the necessarily public nature of true or good counsel in the context of its failure in relation to the Reformation Parliament. See Sir Thomas Elyot, *Pasquil the Playne* (London: 1533), STC 7672.

45 Elyot, 1531, Gg.iii (v).

46 For the extremely fraught relationship between humanism and confessionalization see Erika Rummel, *The Confessionalisation of Humanism in Reformation Germany* (Oxford: 2000).

47 The dating of this letter is disputed; however, K.J.Wilson's arguments for March 1536 are persuasive. See Sir Thomas Elyot, 'The Letters of Sir Thomas Elyot', ed. K.J. Wilson, *Studies in Philology*, 73 (1976) p. 28 (no. 5).

48 Ibid., pp. 27–28.

49 Ibid., p. 27.

50 The Proclamation that Elyot is writing to Cromwell about is almost certainly the one of 1st January 1536 Ordering Surrender of Bishop Fisher's Sermon, Books. See Paul L. Hughes and James F. Larkin, eds *Tudor Royal Proclamations. I: The Early Tudors 1485–1553* (New Haven: 1964), pp. 235–237.

51 Elyot, 1976, p. 30. Sir Thomas More expressed what appears to be a similar desire in a letter also written to Cromwell. He wrote: 'Never would I wish other thing in this world more lief, than that his Highness in these things all three [the Nun of Kent affair, the royal divorce and the primacy of the Pope], as perfectly knew my dealing, and as thoroughly saw my mind, as I do myself, or as God doth himself, whose sight pierceth deeper into my heart than mine own.' More here is, however, quite possibility being ironic, since the implication of this passage is that he wishes Henry had a godlike ability to know his desires and thoughts better than he knew them himself. The implication of More's letter is that behind Henry's persecution of him lay an infantile desire to possess such attributes – to be able to look into men's hearts and minds and see the truth. (Sir Thomas More, *The Last Letters of Thomas More*, ed. and intro. Alvaro De Silva (Grand Rapids, Michigan: 2000), p. 49).

52 This trial was deeply problematic for later Protestant writers like John Foxe, since during it Henry appeared to take on the role of judge and prosecutor. The account of the trial of John Lambert in the 1570 edition of Foxe's work represents Henry in a way that

is clearly intended to make any Tudor reader notice the similarities between him and that exemplary figure of tyranny in mid-Tudor political discourse, Herod. See John Foxe, *Actes and Monumentes* (London: 1570), STC 11223, p. 1282.

53   'Preface', *The Dictionary of Syr T. E. Knyght*, 1538, STC 7658, printed in Elyot, 1976, p. 61.

54   'Preface', *Bibliotheca Eliotae*, 1542, printed in Elyot, 1976, p. 67.

55   It is noticeable that Elyot even excludes Pelagius, presumably because any discussion of the relationship between good works and salvation was too dangerous in 1542. This omission is even more striking when one considers that, in the *Dialogue concerning Heresies*, More often includes Pelagius in his lists of ancient heretics.

56   It is worthwhile noting that at least two of the people condemned and executed as heretics during the reign of Edward VI, Joan Boucher and George van Parris, held beliefs that were included as heresies in Elyot's *Dictionary*.

57   Peter Marshall, 'Papist as Heretic: The Burning of John Forest, 1538', *HJ*, 41 (1998), pp. 351–374, pp. 373–374.

58   Bernard, 1998, p. 331.

59   Alec Ryrie, 'Counting Sheep, Counting Shepherds: The Problem of Allegiance in the English Reformation', in *The Beginnings of English Protestantism*, eds Peter Marshall and Alec Ryrie (Cambridge: 2002), pp. 84–110, p. 109.

60   On the Pilgrimage of Grace see Michael Bush, *The Pilgrimage of Grace: A Study of the Rebel Armies of October 1536* (Manchester: 1996) and Michael Bush and David Bownes, *The Defeat of the Pilgrimage of Grace: A Study of the Postpardon Revolts of December 1536 to March 1537 and their Effect* (Hull: 1999). For a recent discussion of the politics of the Pilgrimage see Ethan Shagan, *Popular Politics and the English Reformation* (Cambridge: 2003), Chapter 3.

61   Clearly this change in Aske's self-presentation maybe simply be a question of a change of circumstances; however, even if this were the case it is significant that political defeat in 1536/37 had to take place at the level of the subject. It was not enough to defeat Aske, his sense of self also had to be defeated.

62   MacCulloch and Fletcher point out that Henry's priority throughout his dealing with the Pilgrimage was 'to claim victims and display his victory' (Anthony Fletcher and Diarmaid MacCulloch, *Tudor Rebellions* (Harlow: 1997), p. 32).

63   M.L. Bush, '"Up for the Commonweal": The Significance of Tax Grievances in the English Rebellions of 1536', *EHR*, 106 (1991), pp. 299–318, p. 299.

64   These propositions, however, may not fully reflect the concerns of all the Pilgrims. The Pilgrimage of Grace was a mass popular movement and was inevitably made up of a number of different groups with their own priorities and grievances. However it is wrong therefore to assume a basic incoherence in the aims of the Pilgrimage since, taken as a whole, the Pilgrimage of Grace embodied a coherent and indeed conventional view of the proper ordering of the English polity and the status of the English Church.

65   *LP*, XI, 1182.

66   Ibid.

67   Ibid., Items 14–17.

68   Shagan, 2003, p. 97.

69 *LP*, XI, 1244.

70 It is important not to make the assumption that there was a divergence based on class within the Pilgrimage in terms of its political aims. S.J. Gunn has pointed out that one should not assume that those below the gentry could not initiate and control disorder 'as skillfully as they ran their farms and workshops and led their parish guilds'. S.J. Gunn, 'Peers, Commons and Gentry in the Lincolnshire Revolt of 1536', *PP*, 123 (1989), pp. 52–79, p. 79.

71 *LP*, XI, 957.

72 *LP*, XI, 1244.

73 The Pilgrimage of Grace exemplified a typical move within Tudor politics in which the emergence of a strong public sphere, one that demanded to be acted upon, was justified by the failure of the norm, a weak public sphere which the centre only needed to listen to. See the discussion of this aspect of Tudor politics in Tom Betteridge, *Tudor Histories of the English Reformations 1530–1583* (Aldershot: 1999), esp. pp. 30–32.

74 This is important since the figure of the sodomite as the signifier of corrupt male friendship was the opposite of the ideal relationship embodied in the story of Titus and Gisippus and therefore, in the context of the kind of civic humanism articulated in Elyot's work, had a particular resonance in terms of Tudor political theory. For the dangerous tension between the male friend and the sodomite see Alan Bray, 'Homosexuality and the Signs of Male Friendship in Elizabethan England', *History Workshop Journal*, 29 (1990), pp. 1–19.

75 *LP*, XI, 1244.

76 'Ballad of the Pilgrimage of Grace (1536)', ed. Mary Bateson, *EHR*, 5 (1890), pp. 344–345, p. 344.

77 Ibid., p. 344.

78 This reversal can also be found in Robert Crowley's discussion of the popular disturbances of 1549.

79 *The Ballad* addresses Henry directly, telling him, 'Bot on thing, Kynges, / Esayas saynges / Like rayn down brynges / Godes woful yre, / Harrying the subiect / Ther dewtis to forget / The pryncez let / Of such disyre.' ('Ballad', 1890, p. 345).

80 Ibid., p. 345.

81 Bush and Bownes, 1999, ii.

82 *LP*, XI, 1227.

83 Ibid.

84 Ibid.

85 Ibid.

86 For Herod's treatment of messengers see *York Mystery Plays*, eds Richard Beadle and Pamela King (Oxford: 1984), pp. 92–93.

87 Obviously it is possible that an edition has been lost or that Holme's work was simply overlooked.

88 A.G. Dickens, 'Wilfrid Holme of Huntingdon: Yorkshire's First Protestant Poet', *Yorkshire Archaeological Journal*, 39 (1956–58), pp. 119–135, p. 119.

89 Wilfrid Holme, *The fall and euill successe of Rebellion from time to time. Wherin is contained matter, moste meete for all estates to rewe* (London: 1570), STC 13602, C.iii (v).

90 The idea that the process of reformation is the cause of diversity and violent debate is at the heart of John Heywood's poem, *The Spider and Fly*.

91 Demosthenes tells his fellow Athenians: 'Wolues sometime (quod he) fre[n]dship to shepherds profred, / On condition that they would deliuer their hou[n]ds to the[m] / For your dogs are those said they, which hath our fre[n]dship barred: / The[n] afterwards the wolues deuoured the[m] to their shame' (Holme, 1570, G.iii).

92 Ibid., G.iii. Whatever one thinks about Holme's poetic skills, there is something impressive in rhyming 'tropologicall' with 'anagogicall'.

93 Ibid., G.ii.

94 Rex, 1993, pp. 146–147.

95 Holme, 1570, E.iii.

96 Ibid., E.iii.

97 Ibid., H.i (v).

98 The application of this prophecy to Henry during the Pilgrimage of Grace was clearly an issue for the royal government. Richard Morrison in his *Exhortation to all Englishmen to the Defence of their countreye* takes a different approach to Holme in dealing with the Mouldwarp. Instead of simply denying its relevance he produces his own biblical prophecy which he applies to Henry's role in freeing the country from the shackles of the Papacy.

99 Quentin Skinner, *The Foundations of Modern Political Thought: Vol. 2 The Age of Reformation* (Cambridge: 1978), p. 97.

100 See Francis Oakley, 'Christian Obedience and Authority, 1520–1550', in *The Cambridge History of Political Thought 1450–1700*, ed. J.H. Burns with the assistance of Mark Goldie (Cambridge: 1991), pp. 159–192, pp. 162–163.

101 Stephen Gardiner, 'The Oration of True Obedience', in *Obedience in Church and State: Three Political Tracts*, ed. and trans. Pierre Janelle (Cambridge: 1930), pp. 67–169, p. 73.

102 Ibid., p. 119.

103 Ibid., p. 161.

104 This emphasis on the difference between the roles of Prince and teacher allows Gardiner even to imagine a relatively positive role for the Papacy. He comments, 'let the Bishop of Rome be chief in teaching and preaching Christ a fore other / and so longe let him have the supremacies of that kinde of office' (Ibid., p. 149). Gardiner makes this point as part of a sustained critique of the Papacy's failure to fulfil its proper role, but the implication of it is that a reformed Papacy could, and perhaps ought, to have supremacy over the teaching of Christ's message.

105 Ibid., p. 131.

106 Ibid., p. 99.

107 Ibid., p. 161.

108 Ibid., p. 165.

109 Ibid., p. 169.

110 See David Starkey, 'Intimacy and Innovation: The Rise of the Privy Chamber, 1485–1547', in *The English Court from the Wars of the Roses to the Civil War*, eds David Starkey, D.A.L. Morgan, John Murphy, Pam Wright, Neil Cuddy and Kevin Sharpe (London: 1987), pp. 71–118.

111 The dating of Wyatt's poems, and indeed their attribution, is difficult. All references to Wyatt's poems in this chapter are taken from Sir Thomas Wyatt, *The Complete Poems*, ed. R.A. Rebholz (Harmondsworth: 1978). For a discussion of the problems of attribution see R.A. Rebholz's preface to this edition.

112 Gary Waller, *English Poetry of the Sixteenth Century* (Harlow: 1993), p. 110.

113 This is particular true of Wyatt's sonnets. In these texts there is often a three-way tension between the Petrarchan original, the rigidity of the form and the narrative voice. For the relationship between Wyatt and Petrarch see Michael R.G. Spiller, *The Development of the Sonnet: An Introduction* (London: 1992), esp. Chapter 6.

114 Brian Cummings, *The Literary Culture of the Reformation: Grammar and Grace* (Oxford: 2002), p. 233.

115 Mary Thomas Crane has argued that Wyatt's status as a courtier created a basic tension in relation to the humanist use of moral sayings as a source of authorial validation. She argues: 'Sayings remain for Wyatt a sign of steadfast moral authority that he cannot achieve, and of the insubstantiality of his poetic self: thus, they engrave themselves in his mind only as a scar, a painful trace of the clash between two incompatible systems [humanism and the court] and the ambivalent subjectivity that they engender' (Mary Thomas Crane, *Framing Authority: Sayings, Self and Society in Sixteenth-Century England* (Princeton: 1993), p. 161).

116 Wyatt, 1978, pp. 120–121. In the interests of clarity I have retained Rebholz's modernization of Wyatt's punctuation.

117 Ibid., p. 121.

118 This has led some critics to read Wyatt's poetry in almost entirely linguistic terms. For example Jonathan Crewe argues: 'Whether Wyatt's craft finally consists in a struggle for or against identification, for or against appropriation, it emphatically constitutes doubleness – or, rather, the nonidentity of any identity – as the peculiar condition and undoing if all attempts at identification.' Crewe's language seems to repeat the opaqueness of Wyatt's, and indeed to offer a similar fantasy – that underneath there is a 'real' or 'true' meaning. Certainly Crewe is right to suggest that Wyatt's poetry produces a kind of hermeneutically disabling doubleness, and in doing so it reflects the historically specific world of the Henrician Reformation. See Jonathan Crewe, *Trials of Authorship: Anterior Forms and Poetic Reconstruction from Wyatt to Shakespeare* (Berkeley: 1990), p. 44.

119 Rex comments, 'from the very start the supremacy was bound up with the rhetoric of the "word of God"' (Rex, 1993, p. 124).

120 This tension was given particular meaning in the treatment of Friar Forest in 1538. Peter Marshall has suggested: 'Implicit in the savagery with which the "outward man" was dealt in 1538 was a recognition that the "inward man" could prove a more subtle and elusive adversary.' (Marshall, 1998, p. 374). It is important to note, however, that at times the regime appears to have colluded with those who sought to dissemble their beliefs. For a discussion of this aspect of the Henrician regime's religious policies see Alec Ryrie, *The Gospel and Henry VIII: Evangelicals in the Early English Reformation* (Cambridge: forthcoming, 2004).

121 Wyatt, 1978, p. 121.

122 Stephen Greenblatt, *Renaissance Self-Fashioning; From More to Shakespeare* (Chicago: 1980), p. 152.

123 Elizabeth Heale, *Wyatt, Surrey and Early Tudor Poetry* (London: 1998), p. 48.

124 Wyatt, 1978, pp. 116–117.

125 Ibid., p. 117.

126 For the way in which the female voice is eroticized in this poem see Barbara L. Estrin, 'Wyatt's Unlikely Likenesses: Or, Has the Lady Read Petrarch?', in *Rethinking the Henrician Era: Essays on Early Tudor Texts and Contexts*, ed. Peter C. Herman (Urbana: 1994), pp. 219–240.

127 Wyatt, 1978, p. 117.

128 Michael McCanles, 'Love and Power in the Poetry of Sir Thomas Wyatt', *Modern Language Quarterly*, 29 (1968), pp. 145–160, p. 155.

129 Greenblatt, 1980, p. 156.

130 Robert Aske, 'Narrative of October and November 1536', ed. Mary Bateson, *EHR*, 5 (1890), pp. 331–343. Mary Bateson discusses the provenance of this document and concludes that, while it is not in Aske's hand, it is almost certainly a copy of a version that he either wrote or dictated.

131 Ibid., p. 334.

132 It is a little unclear if it was an order or a request. The implication is that Aske did not want to be found by the commons but also that they simply asked him to accompany them.

133 Aske, 1890, p. 343.

134 It is noticeable that the Pilgrims refer to history in order to validate their position. James Simpson has recently pointed out this move seems quite beyond the narrators of Wyatt's poetry. Simpson comments: 'what we observe in the last two decades of the reign of Henry VIII are Ovidian postures wholly locked out of any possibility of reentering the current of history. In this poetry the poetic persona remains both threatened and mesmerised by an absolute power, unable to escape the historical dislocations and emotional circularities that such a position entails' (James Simpson, 'Breaking the Vacuum: Ricardian and Henrician Ovidianism', *JMEMS*, 29 (1999), pp. 325–355, p. 341).

135 Wyatt, 1978, p. 86.

136 Adrian O. Ward comments: 'the proverbial in Wyatt's courtly lyrics fails as a means of defining the courtier's experience, resolving his dilemma or directing his action in the sphere of complex intrigue' (Adrian O. Ward, 'Proverbs and Political Anxiety in the Poetry of Sir Thomas Wyatt and the Earl of Surrey', *English Studies*, 81 (2000), pp. 456–471, p. 464).

137 See Christopher Z. Hobson, 'Country Mouse and Towny Mouse: Truth in Wyatt', *Texas Studies in Literature and Language*, 39 (1997), pp. 230–258, p. 252.

138 Cummings argues, 'it is characteristic of Wyatt's *Psalms* that they are as much self-concealing as self-revealing'. This could be seen as prudent on the part of Wyatt or as another example of his tendency to place the self at the centre of the interpretative

process. In this case one can ask whether Wyatt's *Psalms* are not an outrageous attempt to provide his readers with an opportunity to fulfil the Henrician fantasy of interrogating religious writing to find the religious truth of its author, to put him on trial and make him speak the secrets of his heart (Cummings, 2002, p. 224).

139 Wyatt's *Psalms* can also be read as reflecting the effects on early English Protestantism of Henrician tyranny. Their tentative references to Luther's evangelical teaching reflects the extent to Henry's tyranny crushed and distorted Protestantism as a coherent positive religious movement.

Chapter 2

Edwardian politics and poetics

My counsailo[u]rs with suche other necessarie p[e]rsons [that] attend vppon me that daie [St Stephens?] must also be consydered / There maie be no fewer then sixe counsailo[u]rs at the least / I must also have a divine a philosopher an astronom[e]r a poet a phisician / a potecarie / a Mr of request[es] / a sivilian / a disard / two gentlemen ushers besides Juglers / tomblers / fooles / friers and suche other ... (Letter from the lord of misrule [George Ferrers] regarding arrangements for the Christmas entertainments of 1552 3)[1]

Send for all the council not abroad. Because many of the best are absent, take the advice of six of the most experienced. If you cannot deal with the matter with your men of war, send for the German horsemen at Calais, almost 4,000, who may be spared for a little. Have Lord Ferrers and Sir William Herbert bring as many horsemen as they can from Wales and those they trust ... Send for your own trusty servants. (Lord Paget to the Duke of Somerset advising him on how to deal with the rebellions of the summer of 1549)[2]

Images of carnivalesque misrule, player kings and false counsellors, conspiracies and tumults, hover in the wings of Edward VI's kingship. They provide a subversive mocking background noise to the celebration of Edward as a new Josiah sent to purge the land of papistry and create an ordered godly commonwealth.[3] The gap between the rhetoric of sixteenth-century politics and the reality, which was always large, seems at times during the years 1547–53 virtually to widen beyond even the capacity of Tudor writers to bridge. This is particularly true of the events of the summer of 1549 when Robert Kett sat under the Tree of Reformation on Mousehold Heath outside Norwich, surrounded by his councillors, and dispensed justice. The tumults of 1549 led directly to the downfall of the duke of Somerset and revealed a fundamental disjuncture between legitimacy and power within Tudor political praxis.

This chapter opens by examining briefly the events of the summer of 1549 in the context of the Edwardian regime's emphasis on counsel and debate. It then goes on to discuss the numerous polemical works produced by the Edwardian regime to support its religious policy. In these texts the honest unlearned Protestant ploughman is constantly held up as spokesperson for religious truth against the sophisticated but corrupt learning of the papists. The second section of the chapter develops the idea that the reign of Edward VI represented a profound break with that of Henry VIII by examining the work of its leading poet, Robert Crowley, and William Baldwin's animal fable, *Beware the Cat*. Thomas Wyatt's court poetry is exemplary of Henrician culture; it is convoluted, difficult and tortured – the perfect distillation of what it meant to be a member of a polity centred on a violent and vicious monarch. Crowley's work reflects the very real sense in which the Edwardian period was perceived by its supporters as one of political reform and liberation. In particular, the poetic self as it emerges in Crowley's poetry is expansive and empowered in comparison with its cramped and oppressed Henrician counterpart; it embraces a confessional Protestant identity as a source of authority in a way unimaginable to one of Wyatt's tortured narrators. William Baldwin's *Beware the Cat* was written during the twilight of Edward's reign in the spring of 1553, but was not published until 1570. It can be read as a summation and critique of the period 1547–1553. In particular, the textual complexity of *Beware the Cat*, its cynical politics and poetics, reflect the shock to the magisterial Protestant endeavour caused by the events of 1549 and the realization that in 1553 the reign of which so much had been expected was coming to an end – not with a bang but a whimper.

Edward VI's reign was an anomaly – not only because of the royal minority but also because its political culture was, and proclaimed itself to be, fundamentally different to what had gone before. In the process it raised expectations and hopes that were ultimately dashed. It was a dynamic period whose writing reflects the serious issues and conflicts that marked the years 1547–53. At the same time there was something strangely theatrical about Edward's reign. John Foxe, a great supporter of the Edwardian Reformation, in 1570 introduces his account of the reign of Edward VI with a celebratory comparison of the boy king with Josiah. He also, however, comments that with the advent of the Edwardian regime 'a new face of things began now to appeare, as it were in a stage new players co[m]ming in, the olde being thrust out.'[4] The players of Edward's reign were an odd collection – the Dukes of Somerset and Northumberland, Sir William Paget and Sir John Cheke, Robert Crowley and Robert Kett, John Bon and Papista, William Baldwin and Grimalkin – and all had their part to play in the drama of the Edwardian Reformation.

EDWARDIAN COUNSELLORS, PLOUGHMEN AND CAMPERS

Tudor political culture was obsessed with the problem of counsel. This was particularly so during Edward VI's reign when the royal minority meant that the monarch was incapable of providing a proper focal point for counsel. Stephen Alford in his study, *Kingship and Politics in the Reign of Edward VI*, comments: 'Counsel was fundamentally unsuited to the political conditions of minority – or at least counsel in its proper form. For royal government to work properly there had to be no distinction between the location of sovereign power and its proper exercise. An adult could achieve this but a boy, however precocious, could not.'[5] As Alford goes on to point out, however, this insoluble problem did not prevent Edwardian politicians from creating a complex scaffold of councils and counsellors around Edward.[6] At the centre of this edifice, however, was always a hollow centre; Edwardian counsellors were playing at giving counsel to a boy who they knew was not, yet, capable of acting upon it.

This was particularly problematic since it is clear that the men who came to power in 1547 were committed to the idea of counsel in both practice and theory. Edwardian politicians and intellectuals theorized and lauded counsel. In the winter of 1548–1549 William Paget sent Somerset a 'schedule' as a Christmas present. This was a collection of short sentences designed to advise the Protector on how to be a good governor. Paget's text opens with the following precepts: 'Delyberate maturely in all thinges. Execute quickely the delyberations. Do justice without respecte.'[7] Earlier in his letter Paget had explained to Somerset that he should treat the schedule 'as in a glasse', which 'if your grace will dayly loke ... youe shall so well apparell your selfe as eche man shall delight to behold youe'.[8] Paget's present to Somerset was an attempt to instruct the Protector in how to be a good ruler – or, perhaps more accurately, how to appear to be one. This is not, however, to suggest that Paget's advice should be seen as insincere or Machiavellian. His schedule was a genuine attempt to help Somerset properly fit the role of Protector. Its form illustrates the extent to which Paget valued counsel in terms of Tudor political praxis and his confidence that the written word could have a reforming effect upon a person's behaviour. Paget's schedule both embodies good advice and in its proposed application suggests the need for Somerset to return constantly to its source, explicitly the text itself, implicitly its author, Paget.

Paget's schedule was an attempt to give the Protector private advice; however, the Edwardian regime witnessed an outpouring of texts, in print and manuscript, treatise and sermons, whose aim was to advise the polity in public. Many of these works were aimed at leading members of the regime and were intended to address specific governmental problems. In the past historians have described the authors of these texts as 'commonwealth men', in order to emphasis the common interest in reform to be found in the writings of such men as Robert Crowley, Hugh Latimer, John Hales, Thomas Smith and John Cheke. G.R. Elton, however, has argued that the label 'commonwealth men' is inaccurate and misleading. He suggests that there is little 'common ground or intersecting argument' in the work of men like Crowley, Latimer and Smith.[9] However, while it may be a mistake to see the emergence in Edward VI's reign of a organized movement dedicated to the reform of the commonwealth, the Edwardian period did witness a surge in interest in social reform and political theory.[10] As Diarmaid MacCulloch points out, there clearly existed during the years 1547–53 a 'widespread ... commonwealth ethos and programme'.[11] Indeed the Edwardian Reformation itself embodied an implicit, and often explicit, programme of social reform that was coherent and potentially radical.

Elton and MacCulloch may disagree about the importance of common-wealth ideas during Edward VI's reign; however, both historians single out Thomas Smith's work *A Discourse of the Commonweal of this Realm of England* as an exemplary piece of mid-Tudor social commentary. Smith was an academic and politician who, though a secretary of state under Edward and Elizabeth, appears never to have achieved the degree of prominence he felt he deserved.[12] His modern editor, Mary Dewar, suggests that:

> *A Discourse of the Commonweal of this Realm of England*, written in 1549 and first published in 1581, was the most brilliant and most enduring of an overwhelming flood of pamphlets, books, sermons, poems, and treatises prompted by the severe inflation and changing economic patterns of Tudor England.[13]

Smith's text argues for the inherent good of reasoned public debate. Smith writes in the Preface to his work that 'that kind of reasoning seem, to me best for bolting out of the truth which is used by way of dialogue or colloquy, where reasons be made to and fro as well for the matter intended as against it'.[14] Given this argument, it is not surprising that *A Discourse of the Commonweal* is written as a dialogue between a Doctor (who is a clergyman), a Knight, a Merchant and a Capper during which the ills of the realm are discussed and various proposals put forward to cure them. In particular, Smith, through the person of the Doctor, advocates the restoration of the coinage.

The dialogue form of this tract is central to its reforming agenda, since what it allows is the expression of opposing ideas which can then be shown to be reconciled through public debate. *A Discourse of the Commonweal* advocates the reform of the commonwealth and performs it through its textual form. Smith's work articulates a potentially radically notion of the proper scope of debate. During a discussion of the role of the learned man in the common-wealth the Doctor points out that one of the reasons for the recent decay of learning is the trouble and vexations it leads to. He goes on to ask his fellows, 'have you not seen how many learned men have been put to trouble of late within these twelve or sixteen years and all for declaring their opinions in things that have risen in controversy?'[15] The Doctor's argument is that it has been particularly difficult to be a learned man and take part in the public discussion of important matters since 1533–37 – in other words since the Henrician Reformation. Obviously *A Discourse of the Commonweal* is not opposed to religious reform and in places is clearly written from a Protestant perspective.[16] However it does implicitly criticize the Henrician Reformation on the basis of its detrimental stifling effect on public debate and the circulation of learned counsel within the polity.[17]

The valorization of debate apparent in *A Discourse of the Commonweal* can also be seen in another exemplary Edwardian text, *A tragedie or Dialogue of the Bishop of Rome*.[18] The writer of this work, Barnadine Ochino, was one of the influential foreign Protestant reformers whose presence in England during the period 1547–53 was so important to the course of the Edwardian Reformation.[19] His *Dialogue of the Bishop of Rome* is a fascinating work. Like Smith's treatise it is written in the form of a dialogue, although with a much greater scope. Ochino's work opens with a dialogue between Lucifer and Beelzebub during which they discuss how to corrupt Christ's teaching. This exchange, however, commences without any of the elaborate prefaces or addresses to the reader that one might expect in such a work. Instead the reader is plunged straight into a discussion between Satan and his leading lieutenant. This implies that Ochino was confident in his reader's abilities to read critically. He seems to have no worries that his readers would have problems recognizing the evil nature of Lucifer's and Beelzebub's words despite their apparent reason and logic – from a worldly perspective. *A Dialogue of the Bishop of Rome* proceeds through a number of discrete dialogues which build up into a complete history of the institution of papal supremacy. The final two dialogues, however, take a different track and instead are potted accounts of the Henrician and Edwardian Reformations.

The eighth exchange in *A Dialogue of the Bishop of Rome* is between Henry VIII, Archbishop Cranmer and Papista – who is an allegorical figure representing a defender of papal supremacy. Ochino carefully locates this dialogue in private, which creates a disturbing equivalence between Henry's behaviour and that of the Pope and the Emperor's secretary who, when setting up the papal supremacy, also had their discussions in secret. The dialogue between Henry, Cranmer and Papista is also an extremely limited one. It is in effect in two parts. In the first section Henry attempts to get Papista to agree to the debate, but is constantly rebuffed. Papista simply refuses to discuss the matter with Henry, finally commenting: 'Bycause it semeth good to youre maiestye, that it be so [i.e. to have the debate], I for my part haue nothynge els to say, but that the byshoppe of Rome is Christes Vicar in earthe with full power.'[20] However the second part of this dialogue is at least as much a failure

as a dialogue as the first section, since it consists entirely of a lengthy mono-
logue by Cranmer proving that the papal supremacy is a fraud and concluding
with a description of the true Church. This creates a situation in which during
neither of the two parts of the dialogue does Henry actually engage in any real
debate, first because Papista refuses to and then because Cranmer's speech
does not require it. The eighth dialogue of *A Dialogue of the Bishop of Rome* can
be seen as an Edwardian rewriting of the Henrician Reformation in which the
king's role was simply to instigate the reform process but not to have any real
part in its development or nature.[21]

The ninth dialogue of *A Dialogue of the Bishop of Rome* is entitled as being
between King Edward VI and the Lord Protector, although the actual parties in
the text are the King and his Council. What is noticeable about this dialogue is
its concentration on the process of reformation, not its matter. Edward tells
his Council:

> We haue determined ... to pursue the famouse enterprise of oure famouse father,
> and not onely to plucke up by the rootes, and utterlye ba[n]ishe out of our kingdome
> the name Antichrist and his Jurisdicion: but also clearely to purge [the] mindes of
> oure subiectes from all wycked idolatry, heresie, and superstycyon and such lyke
> deuelishnes as by hym was brought in.[22]

There is something slightly sinister about the agenda mapped out in this
speech and in particular the aim of purging the minds of the king's subjects.
How does one purge minds without at the same time purging people? The
Edward of *A Dialogue of the Bishop of Rome* is aware that the process of
confessionalization will be difficult and divisive. Indeed he conceives himself
as the realm's physician restoring it to health by purging it of its corruptions.
He informs his council:

> We know ryght well that a sicke body, which is ful of corrupt humours, can not be
> purged, and clensed with out some commocion, and stirryng of the body and
> membres: and euen so is it of our kingdomes. And we also knowe that the gospel is
> a moste swete and pleasant medecine to the chosen of god, although it turne the
> stomake of suche, as be reiected.[23]

The Edwardian Reformation, as imagined in *A Dialogue of the Bishop of Rome*,
is a deeply divisive process leading to commotions and the violent purging of
the kingdom. The social harmony that *A Discourse of Commonweal* suggests
should be the end of good government is here replaced by a clear separation
between the saved and the damned. This introduction of the logic of
confessionalization into Ochino's work ultimately undermines its emphasis
on debate. Reform might be best pursued through discussion and counsel but
its ultimate end is the creation of a godly commonwealth about which there
could be no legitimate reason or justification for debate.

1549 was a momentous year for the Protestant agenda imagined in *A*

Dialogue of the Bishop of Rome.[24] The preceding year had witnessed the publication of proclamations ordering the removal of images and the suppression of a number of traditional religious practices, such as the ceremony of candles at Candlemas, regarded as superstitious by Protestant reformers. 1548 also witnessed the first tentative but deliberate steps by Archbishop Cranmer towards the modification of the central rite of the Church, the mass. The meeting of Parliament in the autumn of 1548 was preceded by an outpouring of works attacking the mass, many of which expressed far more radical doctrinal positions than those publicly held by Cranmer and his colleagues at this time. In the spring of 1549 Parliament passed the Act of Uniformity, which among other things made the use of the first Edwardian prayer book compulsory from Whit Sunday, 9th June. Diarmaid MacCulloch comments: 'The English Church reached a watershed when Parliament ended in March 1549. Now it was on the verge of adopting a fully vernacular liturgy, its clergy could legally marry, and its metropolitan [Cranmer] had openly declared his allegiance to an unmistakeably Reformed eucharistic theology.'[25] These changes, however, were taking place against a background of mounting political tension. This was primarily due to the failure of the Duke of Somerset's policy in Scotland but also to his apparent refusal to rule within expected limits or norms.

It is impossible to read Sir William Paget's letters to Somerset in this period without noting his growing sense of alarm at the government's direction. In February 1549 Paget wrote to Somerset to inform him, humbly, of his poor opinion of his proceedings and asking Somerset not to 'make me ... a Cassandra, that is to saie, one that told the trouthe of daungers before and was not beleved ...'[26] Paget was concerned with the entire range of government policy and the state of the country. He concluded his letter, however, by telling Somerset that if he followed the advice it contained order will be restored to the realm. Paget wrote:

> ... therby your grace shalbe feared in the service of the kinge, the noblemen shall be regarded, and everie other man in his place abrode in the world reputed as he ought to be, wherby quyet shall ensue amonge oure selfes, and takinge all disputacions from vs other then by lawes ys apointed or permytted, we shall no more saie thow papist and thoue heretique, for your lawe the laste yere for the sacrament, and this yere for the ceremonies will helpe moche the matter yf they be well executed.[27]

Paget returned to the issues raised in this letter in a set of articles apparently drawn up to be discussed by the Council in April 1549. In summing up the state of the realm he wrote:

> The greater officers [are] not greatlie feared, the people presuminge much of their goodnes.
> The inferior officers not regarded but contempned.
> The gentlemen despised and so nowe contented to endure.

> The common people to liberall in speche, to bolde and licentious in their doinges and to wise and well learned in their owne conceytes.[28]

Paget concluded this list by commenting that at the present time 'all thinges [are] in maner goinge backewarde'. This phrase, with its evocation of a carnivalesque world in which the natural order is turned on its head, seems to look forward to events of the late spring and summer of 1549.[29] Indeed it is clear that despite his wishes, Paget was here playing the role of Cassandra: correctly foretelling the course of future events to someone too proud or arrogant to act on his / her advice.

There were sporadic outbreaks of rioting and general disturbance throughout southern England in April and May 1549, which coalesced into a number of major sites of violent protest in the West Country, south-east England and East Anglia.[30] The protests in the West Country appear to have been the culmination of a number of years of complaint and unrest which took off with the imposition of the first Edwardian prayer book on Whit Sunday 1549. By mid-June a large number of rebels were engaged in the siege of Exeter. Having initially misjudged the extent and danger of rebellion, Somerset's government spent July desperately trying to scrape together sufficient forces to enable Lord Russell to put down the rebellion and restore order. He achieved this by raising the siege of Exeter on 6 August and followed this up by defeating the rebels a week later at Sampford Courtenay. Russell's success, however, could not hide the fact that for two months the government's writ had not run throughout Devon and Cornwall. If anything the regime's response to the disturbances that took place slightly later in the year across south-east England and East Anglia was even more incompetent. The summer of 1549 saw 'camps', mass gatherings that combined the atmosphere of a protest meeting, an unruly football match and a carnival, being set up throughout East Anglia and south-east England.[31] In Norfolk there was trouble in Wymondham in early July which saw the emergence of Robert Kett as the leader of the commons. By the middle of July, Kett was encamped with his followers on Mousehold Heath overlooking the city of Norwich. Somerset's government initially went to extraordinary lengths in attempting to placate the protesters. This was perhaps because it was unclear if the campers were engaged in anything more than popular demonstrations. Certainly it appears that all the camps apart from that on Mousehold Heath dispersed without violence and with almost no punishment being meted out to the protesters. Anthony Fletcher and Diarmaid MacCulloch have argued that the main reason that events in Norwich took a more violent turn was due to the Marquis of Northampton's hopeless attempt to quell the protest which turned 'a vast popular demonstration ... into a full-scale rebellion'.[32] From this point it was only a question of time before the government assembled enough troops to defeat Kett and his followers. This duly happened on 26 August when a royal army commanded by the Earl of Warwick defeated Kett's forces at Dussindale.

Although Somerset's regime fumbled its response to events in Cornwall and Devon, it was Kett's Rebellion which caused it real trauma.[33] This was primarily because the main aims of those who took part in the Western Rebellion, essentially the return of the English Church to the doctrines and practices of the reign of Henry VIII, could be fitted neatly into the regime's political and religious assumptions. For men like Cranmer, the apparent desire of the West Country rebels to reject the Edwardian Reformation simply indicated the influence of papistry in their ranks and their own benighted ignorance.[34] Magisterial English Protestants knew from the historical writings of men like John Bale that the papists were past masters at stirring up the poor ignorant people in order to protect their corrupt practices and superstitions.[35] This is one reason why, when the West Country man, Philip Nichols, wrote a semi-official response to the rebels' demands, he constantly used the influence of papistry to explain the fact of rebellion. Nichols tells the rebels:

> Your fault, good countrymen, though it be very hainous, yet it is not utterly incurable if ye will in season reform yourselves. Your blindness is miserable but yet possible to be brought again to light, if yourselves shall not love the darkness of wicked popery more then the clear light of God's most holy word and gospel.[36]

It is noticeable, however, that in this passage, and indeed the entire tract, Nichols uses papistry not only to explain why the rebellion happened but also to provide his fellow West Country men with an excuse for their traitorous behaviour. *The Answer to the Commoners of Devonshire and Cornwall* is suffused with images of the people's blindness and gullibility in the face of the blandishments of the papists. Nichols makes the Western Rebellion fit precisely into the paradigm created by Bale in such works as his play *King Johan*, in which the papist clergy blind the commons in order to prevent them from coming to the aid of the play's eponymous hero.[37] This is not to suggest, however, that Nichols is applying Bale's text in a simplistic or crass way to an actual event. Rather the key point to make about his answer to the rebels is the way it deploys the notion of papistry as the cause of social unrest in order to create the possibility of a negotiated return to order in which blame for the disturbances is located outside the body of the realm – with the papists and papistry. This is precisely the argument one finds in *King Johan* and indeed in much English Reformation literature. It reflects the magisterial ideological fantasy that Tudor society would be non-antagonistic and harmonious, and in particular the populace would be happy with their lot, were it not for the corrupting presence of outsiders, alien forces, within the commonwealth. Nichols' text illustrates the utility of such labels as papistry or heresy to Tudor culture and the way they enabled it to explain away, to finesse, social unrest and conflict. In particular the effectiveness of the ideological fantasy that it was the papists, or for that matter the heretics, who were the cause of social conflict or disorder was based on the papistry's point of origin being beyond the realm's boundaries. Papistry was an inherently alien, albeit amorphous, thing or concept whose protean quality was part of its ideological attractiveness. Since papistry could never be fully defined or caught, it was always there to be found and blamed for the country's ills. *The Answer to the Commoners of Devonshire and Cornwall* illustrates perfectly the function of papistry as a fantasy, a myth, for Tudor writers; the fact that in this case rejection of Protestantism does appear to have been one of the main causes of social disorder simply made it easier for Nichols to use the term to explain away the actions of his fellow West Country men.[38]

Kett's rebellion, however, could not be successfully explained away by reference to evil papists.[39] This created tensions that were reflected in two different registers, the political, in terms of the fall of Somerset, and ideological, in relation to the legitimacy of the Edwardian Reformation. It is clear that Somerset's handling of the protests in East Anglia was one of the main reasons for his fall in October 1549. Certainly this was the position formally and publicly adopted by the Privy Council when they wrote to the ambassadors to explain Somerset's fall.[40] The councillors stressed in their letter that Somerset's role within the Edwardian regime should have been that of their 'mouthpiece'. The implication was that Somerset as Protector should have been the passive voice of the Council's collective wisdom. It is important to note that this construction of Somerset's role draws on conventional sixteenth-century ideas concerning the central and legitimatizing role of counsel within the English polity. Tudor political writing constantly addressed the issue of counsel, who should give it, how it should be given and, most crucially, what its status was.[41] This emphasis on counsel was based upon the assumption that the monarch should take into account, although not necessarily act upon, the views and concerns of the entire political nation. In a perfectly functioning transparent polity the transfer of counsel and command between monarch and people would be immediate and frictionless; a fully competent monarch would take counsel from the entire nation, albeit mediated through appropriate channels, and his actions would be his considered singular response to this advice.[42] Clearly the situation during the minority of Edward VI was far from perfect, but Somerset appears to have made the situation worse by not listening to the advice of the Council, and in particular that of men like Paget, while giving the impression in 1549 of being prepared to listen to the demands of Kett and his fellow protesters. Ethan Shagan has pointed out that the letters from Somerset's regime to the East Anglian protesters 'invited the commons to think of themselves, not as passive recipients of enlightened policy, but as political allies of the government and as partners in the creation of that policy'.[43] To give the commons, and indeed his colleagues on the Privy Council, this impression was itself lethal; however what made Somerset's position untenable in 1549 was the potentially radical implications of his response to the protesters' demands. By talking directly to Kett and his comrades, Somerset created the horrific possibility that the periphery could talk to the centre without intermediate circles or points of contact.[44] His government's response to the East Anglian protesters cut through the layers of the polity like a bolt of lighting short-circuiting its normal channels. This explains the Council's otherwise apparently hysterical claim that Somerset was responsible for the summer's tumults since he aspired to destroy the nobility and all honest persons.[45] This was of course nonsense, except that at one level it would have been the effect of the continuation of the situation which arose during the summer of 1549 when it appeared that the voices of Kett and his followers were taking precedence over those of the gentry, nobility and Privy Councillors. What else but their destruction would it mean for England's nobility and gentry if they had lost their roles as mediators and advocates for their localities? Somerset's actions in the summer of 1549 seemed to the men of business gathered in the Edwardian Privy Council to endanger the very consistency of the Tudor polity.

The ability of the events of the 1549, and specifically those in East Anglia, to raise such questions, and provoke the fears that underlay them, also, however, reflects how far this was a moment of real ideological crisis. This is reflected in the tension between the regime's initially conciliatory response to the East Anglian protesters and the violence, actual and symbolic, that was finally deployed to defeat them. Obviously Tudor society was not about to collapse in 1549; however, that members of the totally dominant ruling magisterial class could even entertain the possibility that one of their number aspired to erase them in their entirety reflects the depth of the crisis that erupted in this year. Ernesto Laclau and Lilian Zac point out: 'Power loses its legitimacy when it is unable to ensure the social order; in that case it shows itself as *mere* power.'[46] Mere power, class hated and violence are certainly what largely characterised the magisterial response to the events in Norwich. Sir John Cheke's *The Hurt of Sedition*, written in the heat of the crisis of the summer of 1549, is full of magisterial anxieties and fears. Cheke was a leading member of Somerset's government, a reforming humanist and supporter of the Edwardian Reformation. His *The Hurt of Sedition* constructs itself as an attempt to explain to the protesters and rebels of 1549 why their actions were wrong. In the process, however, it has completely to distort the demands of those involved in the East Anglian protests, or at least of their leaders.

Cheke finds it relatively easy to dismiss the south-western rebels. In particular he asks them if they will take upon themselves more 'learnynge then the chosen Byshoppes and Clerkes of this realme haue?'[47] When he turns to the East Anglian protesters Cheke's text almost immediately seems to enter the realm of fantasy. Cheke claims that Kett and his followers wanted all things to be equal and goes on to ask them a set of rhetorical questions designed to show the ludicrous nature of this aspiration.

> But what meane ye, by this equalitie in the comune welth? If one be wiser then an other, wyl ye bannyshe him, because ye entende an equalitye of al thinges? If one be stronger the[n] another, wyll ye sleye him because ye seke equalitie of all thynges? ... If one haue a better utteraunce then an other, wyll ye pul out hys tonge to saue youre equality? And if one be rycher then another, will ye spoile him to mayntaine an equalitye?[48]

The important thing to note about this passage is the extent to which it completely ignores the actual articles drawn up by the East Anglian campers. Largely on the basis of these demands MacCulloch has argued that the people gathered on Mousehold Heath were 'determined to create a world in which gentlemen would be kept at arm's length, recapturing an imaginary past where society had been divided into watertight social compartments, each with its own function: a sort of medieval social apartheid.'[49] Cheke, however, in *The Hurt of Sedition* constantly emphasizes the anarchic tendencies of those involved in the Norfolk tumults.[50] He compares them to dogs and argues:

> no doubt therof ye [the protesters] would have falle[n] to slaughter of men, rauishing of wives, deflowering of maides, chopping of childre[n], firing of houses, beting downe of stretes, ouerthrowing of al together. For what measure have me[n] in [the] encrease of madnes, whe[n] thei cannot at the beginning stay the[m]selues fro[m] falling in to it.[51]

How does one explain the difference between the image of the protesters in *The Hurt of Sedition* and their actual words and deeds?

Certainly it would be difficult to argue that Cheke's text was written in total ignorance of the real nature of the protests. After all the government of which he was a part regarded the protesters, or at least their leaders, as sufficiently reasonable to be engaged in purposeful and meaningful debate.[52] Of course the letters that the regime sent to these people might simply be an indication that Somerset's regime was adopting the traditional Tudor approach to dealing with dangerous disorders: appear to give in and then strike back once the immediate danger has passed. However, this does not explain why Cheke in *The Hurt of Sedition* felt the need to represent the protesters in such a way as to invite the sixteenth-century reader to equate them with the Anabaptists who took over Münster with such violent and shocking consequences.[53] It is possible that in doing this Cheke was responding to the presence within the East Anglian camps of genuine religious radicalism.[54] Another answer to this question can be provided by suggesting that it is a mistake to see *The Hurt of Sedition* as a text addressed to the protesters in East Anglia. The people who needed to be told that the campers of the summer of 1549 were best understood by comparing them to dogs or that their actions would inevitably lead to violence were Cheke's fellow magistrates; it is their fantasy which Cheke is seeking to confirm in *The Hurt of Sedition*. The other people to whom this message might have been addressed were ironically men like Kett, the substantial men who led village life in Tudor England. In these terms Cheke's violent polemical work had a relatively subtle agenda which was to unite the governing classes of Tudor England, magistrates and yeomen, against the poor. *The Hurt of Sedition*'s representation of the protesters as violent crypto-communists also had the effect of making it appear that Kett and his followers were responsible for their own deaths. This process was completed in Nicholas Sotherton's almost contemporaneous account of the end of the Mousehold camp which argues that the tragic events of 27 August were caused by Kett's trust in 'faynid prophecies which were phantastically devised'.[55]

The Hurt of Sedition's representation of the East Anglian protesters, and especially those camped on Mousehold Heath, as violent communists intent on making all things common served the ideological function of making them fit into a magisterial view of the populace. Cheke assures his readers that the relative order of the camps was a sham and that sooner or later Kett and his followers would have become completely disordered, breaking all social boundaries and indulging in an orgy of meaningless violence. Clearly this image of the Norwich campers is an ideological fantasy in which Kett and his followers give expression to a disavowed element of magisterial Tudor culture.[56] In particular, Cheke's fantasy rebels embody, as an inversion, the violence and class power that sustained the social hierarchy of Tudor England.[57] It was not Kett and his followers who were responsible for violence in the summer of 1549, nor was it they who, when the chips were down, used violence to protect their social position. Ideology constantly seeks to create the illusion of closure. One way it achieves this is through the production of symbols and concepts that can be deployed to suture social and cultural conflicts. The fantasy that the use of violence to sustain class position was an exception, only to be found in moments of carnivalesque excess like that of Kett's brief kingship on Mousehold, performs just such a suture. Without the fig-leaf of papistry Cheke had to create a fantastical image of the East Anglian protesters, not to answer their concerns, which are ultimately unimportant to him, but to sustain a magisterial ideological view-point that *needs* to see organized protest from those outside its ranks as inherently anarchic and to obscure the ultimately violent nature of its own dominant social position.[58]

Ironically *The Hurt of Sedition*'s portrayal of Kett's and his followers' demands makes them more radical than they actually were, at least on paper. In particular, far from being anti-clerical, articles 8 and 20 of their petition ask for priests who can preach and teach the word of God.[59] To the extent that the protestors took a religious view in 1549, it was mildly Protestant, demanding that the Church give them competent religious teachers. This pragmatism is completely ignored by Cheke and indeed by the first historian of the tumults in Norwich, Nicholas Sotherton. In Sotherton's *The commoyson in Norfolk*, Kett is portrayed as a false carnival king, sitting under a tree of Reformation surrounded by his councillors and dispensing justice.[60] Sotherton in particular stresses the extent to which the people on Mousehold Heath were engaged in class warfare against gentlemen. He writes:

> within a ii or iii wekes they [the protesters] had so pursuyd the gentlemen from all parts that in noe place durst one gentleman keepe his house but were faine to spoile themselues of theyr apparell an lye and keep in woods and lownde placis where noe resorte was ...[61]

Sotherton's text constantly depicts Norwich as a place in which the gentlemen had been driven underground; a carnivalesque society in which the natural social hierarchy has been turned on its head. It is now clear that there were good local political reasons for this, not the least being that in reality many of Norwich's leading citizens played at best an ambiguous role in the events of the summer of 1549. Like Cheke, Sotherton's narrative deploys a carnivalesque fantasy to finesse the failure of Norwich's magistrates. By constructing the events of the summer of 1549 through the prism of carnival Sotherton makes them appear inherently temporary, aberrant and implicitly ridiculous; far better to make Kett a carnival king than allow the appearance on the pages of history of a popular political protest that was ordered, pragmatic and to a large extent peaceful.[62]

Cheke's and Sotherton's responses to the 1549 tumults can be seen as attempts to represent the East Anglian and Norwich protesters in a way that firmly locates them within a magisterial understanding of their status. The Norwich magistrate, Raynball, adopted a similar strategy when in his accounts he described Kett and his followers as being 'inkennelled' upon Mousehold Heath.[63] The ideological work that this new word 'inkennel' is doing here is important to note. Clearly it creates an image of the people on Mousehold Heath as animals, perhaps specifically dogs, and certainly ones that need to be contained. However one has to ask who was doing the 'inkennelling'? Obviously not Raynball and his fellow Norwich magistrates. Indeed the idea of Kett and his comrades being 'inkennelled' reflects the ideological fears of men like Raynball since the word implies a space or state that is temporary. What would happen once the beast escaped his kennel? Even worse what would it mean if the beast was not really beastly at all?

Cheke's portrayal of the East Anglian protesters in *The Hurt of Sedicion*, as at best deluded and stupid and at worst as violent and animalistic, is particularly striking since it appears to totally contradict the representation of the populace and their culture in many of anti-mass pamphlets produced in 1548.

Edward Spurgeon suggests that in this year at least 27 works were published attacking the mass.[64] It is inconceivable that such a large number of works on one subject would have been published without at least the tacit support and approval of the Edwardian regime of which Cheke was a part.[65]

Typical of the anti-mass works published in 1548 is the work, *John Bon and mast Parson*.[66] This pamphlet takes the form of a dialogue between the unlearned but wise John Bon and a Parson. It opens with John asking the apparently naïve question: 'But tell me, mast[er] parson, one thinge and you can; / What saint is copsi cursty a man, or a woman?'[67] The Parson responds by telling John that 'it was a man'. This does not, however, satisfy John who goes on to question the Parson further on the nature of the mass. In common with much magisterial Protestant polemic of the mid-Tudor period, *John Bon and mast Parson* contrasts the foolish learning of the clergyman with the unlearned wisdom of a ploughman figure.[68] John's wisdom is natural and spontaneous. He tells the Parson that because he is a plain man he will speak as cometh to his mind.[69] Despite this apparent lack of sophistication, however, John soon has the Parson on the defensive. In particular, it is precisely John's lack of learning that the Parson finds it difficult to cope with. He tells the reader: 'I had leauer wyth a doctor of diuinitie to reason / Than wyth a stubble cur that eateth beanes and peason.'[70] By the end of the dialogue John has of course completely exposed the Parson's inability to explain and defend the mass. He ends by telling his clerical companion that:

> By my trueth mast[er] parson, I lyke full wel your talke
> But mass me no more messings, the right way wil I walke.
> For thoughe I haue no learning yet I know chese fro[m] chalke
> And yche can perceiue your iuggling as crafty as ye walke.[71]

It is important to note that, despite John's alleged simplicity, *John Bon and mast Parson* deploys sophisticated concepts to make its point. For example in the passage quoted above John constructs the Parson's speech as pleasurable in performative terms, as he perhaps sarcastically puts it he likes the Parson's 'talk', while simultaneously suggesting that the cleric's words are simply a mass or mess of meaningless words. The conflict between pleasurable but meaningless text and simple but truthful words is ultimately based in this period on the grammatical metaphor that, for example, John Skelton uses to make a very similar polemical point in *A Replycacion*. The implication of *John Bon and mast Parson* is that the reader must go beyond the seductive surface of the text and that words or writing that are all surface, all pleasure and textual play, are inherently dangerous. At the same time, and like most mid-Tudor confessional writing, *John Bon and Mast Parson* valorizes textual simplicity and plainness over complexity, as if truthful language is defined less by its inner truth then its refusal of the surface / depth dichotomy.

It is not, however, simply the polemical message of *John Bon and mast Parson* that makes it an exemplary early Edwardian text. As important is its dialogue form which invites the reader to participate in the text's production of meaning. Much of the anti-mass literature published in 1548 incites its readers to adopt the kind of active reading that one would expect from a regime whose self-understanding included a commitment to debate and discussion.[72] Indeed one of the salient things about the pamphlets published in 1548 attacking the mass is their complexity and the different generic forms they take. There are a number of texts in which a personified Mass recants in a quasi-judicial way. In William Punt's *A New Dialogue called the endightment agaynste mother Messe* a collection of allegorical figures, principally Knowledge and Verity, put Mother Mass on trial. The humour in this work is provided by the way in which the Mass is slowly brought to the point where she is forced to confess that 'the scripturs be true'.[73] In the process of reading this work one becomes a knowing participant in the Mass' trial; implicitly a member of the jury. In the tract *Pathos, or an inward passion of the pope for the losse of hys daughter the masse* the narrator of the poem, the Pope, describes the Mass' train on her journey into exile,

> And pilgrimage
> Shal be your page
> Auricular confession
> And popishe procession
> Aboute ye ride
> On euery side
> The colettes by kynde
> Before and behind
> Your fote men shalbe
> Ful comely to se
> The cannone playne
> Your chamberlayne.[74]

At one level this is a simple allegory that invites the reader to imagine these various church practices as the Mass' servants. The readerly pleasure of this work depends on the reader's participation in the work's central poetic conceit, that it is being narrated by a terrified, sweating and quaking pope. In *A short treatyse of certayne thinges abused in the Popish Church, long used: But now abolished*, repetition of the word holy is used to suggest the linguistic corruption and sterility of papistry.

> In [the] stede of goddes word we had holy bred [and] water
> Holy palmes holy ashes, holy candles holy fyer
> Holy bones holy stones, holy crewittes at the aulter
> Holy censars holy banners, holy crones holy atyer
> Holy war holy pax, holy smoke holy smyer

.Holy oyle holy creame, holy wyne for veneration
Holy coope holy canepy, holy reliques in [the] quier
Thus gods word could not flourish [the] light of our salvation[n].[75]

This passage argues that holiness has been diluted in the popishe church and performs its own argument through repetition of the word 'holy'. Central to this text's success is its reader's preparedness to participate in its polemical strategy. For example, this passage at one level incites its reader to get lost in its textual play, the mechanical repetition of one word, while at the same time the reader is clearly meant to notice how meaningless the word 'holy' has become by the verse's conclusion. As a reader, one is being asked to reproduce at a microscopic level one of magisterial Protestantism's key accusations against papistry: that it seduces people through linguistic play while emptying key Christian words of their meaning. 'Holy' in this passage becomes entirely meaningless and in the process fills the space that should have been occupied by God's word. In one of his writings attacking Stephen Gardiner, John Hooper accused his opponent of being 'full of allegories while speaking nothing of the text'.[76] The notion that to be full of allegories is a form of falseness is endlessly reproduced in the polemical works of 1548, where papistry is constantly depicted placing the allegorical before the truthful.[77]

In all these works papistry is attacked but is also the site of textual pleasure. This is a common element of Edwardian polemical writing. Its corollary was the emphasis on the absolute and fixed nature of truthful religious teaching. This was also a stable of mid-Tudor magisterial Protestantism. Richard Tracy's short treatise, *A brief [and] short declaracyon made, wherbye every chrysten man maye knowe, what is a sacrament* tells its reader: 'The cause wherefore sacramentes were Instytuted, is to declare and set fourthe the benyfyttes of god exhybyted a[n]d done to us. And to prynte and grafte them yn owre Myndes.'[78] In Tracy's work the ideal reader is passive, a blank page, waiting to be inscribed, printed, with the truth of God's teaching. There is no need for individual interpretation or even understanding; indeed these would only clog up the press. *A brief [and] short declaracyon* is, as its title suggests, a short pamphlet. Its representation of the proper attitude one should adopt towards the sacraments, in particular, and true Christian teaching in general, however, is exemplary of mid-Tudor magisterial Protestant writing. John Bale, for instance, constantly associates papistry with textual play while arguing that the religious truth is self-evident and literal. This is not to suggest that the Edwardian Reformation was not intended by its advocates, and experienced by many people, as a period of personal religious excitement and discovery.[79] It is, however, to argue that there was a basic fault-line running through the reform programme between two different kinds of reading: an iconoclastic one when confronted by papistry's false allegories and an almost passive one in the face of the literal truth of Protestantism. These two aspects of the

Edwardian Reformation can be clearly seen in the anti-mass writings of 1548, since at one level these works ask their readers to adopt an active participatory role in religious reform while at the same time they hold up religious truth as being beyond debate or interpretation.

In these tracts it is often the ploughman, in all his various guises, who drives the allegorical and excessively textual off the page. The final speech of *John Bon and mast Parson* depicts the unlearned but wise protagonist parting with the Parson and hitching up his horses.

> I thank you sir for that you seme verie kynde
> But praye not so for me for I am well inoughe.
> Whistill boy, driue furth God spede and the plough
> Ha browne done, forth the horson crab!
> Reecomomyne, garled, with haight, blake ha
> Have a gayn bald before, hayght ree who!
> Cheerily, boy, cum of that whomwarde we maye goo.[80]

The godly ploughman goes to work to ree (plough) the old encrusted field, ploughing up the old allegories, glosses and weeds, in preparation for the new seed. But when in 1549 'real' ploughmen put their hands to the plough of reformation the result was violence and bloodshed. Magisterial Protestants reacted with fear and oppression, turning John Bon from a partner and fellow worker in the construction of the new temple into a mad animal intend on turning the world upside down and massacring the gentry.

The events of 1549, and particularly those in East Anglia, revealed a basic legitimation crisis within the Edwardian Reformation. The anti-mass pamphlets of 1548 argued that purging the realm of papistry would require the labour of the entire realm. Indeed in these texts it is the ploughman, and the popular wisdom and support that he embodied, who was expected to provide a key source of legitimation for the reforms of Edward's reign. However when real ploughmen, who of course were not actual ploughmen but rather the leaders of village society, tradesmen and small farmers, took the reformers at their word, the result was violence and oppression. The 'inkennelling' of the plough-men, however, had real political costs for the Edwardian regime which are reflected in the work of the period's leading poet, Robert Crowley, and in William Baldwin's mediation upon the events of 1549, *Beware the Cat*.

ROBERT CROWLEY'S POETIC VOCATION

Robert Crowley is one of the most unjustly neglected English poets of the sixteenth century. He was born in 1517 and received a fellowship at Magdalen College, Oxford, in 1542. However he left in the same year and by the end of Henry VIII's reign was working in London alongside the Protestant printer,

John Day. During the early years of Edward VI's reign he worked as a publisher, editor and book-seller. Crowley's own writing is one long attempt to hold up a mirror to his readers in order to provoke repentance and reform. Crowley adopted a prophetic poetic voice, identical to that to which John Skelton aspired, in order to comment on the state of the polity and country. He wrote a considerable number of works during the Edwardian period, although his output seems to have largely ceased after he was ordained in 1551.

Crowley's poetics can be summed up by the advice that he included in the Preface to one of his editions of *Piers Plowman*. Crowley writes that Langland's complex and obscure text could only be properly understood by those who will 'not sticke to breake the shell of the nutte for the kernelles sake'.[81] Crowley's iconoclastic approach to reading, and in particular to the understanding of allegories, is identical to the Protestant hermeneutic that sustained the anti-mass tracts of 1548. In both cases the reader is asked to smash the shell of the nut to find its truth, with, however, the important difference that in the case of papistry the truth is radically different from the outward appearance, while in that of *Piers Plowman* it has simply been obscured by the poem's dark and dated diction. At the same time, in neither case is the reader left to their own interpretative resources. The anti-mass tracts of 1548 are laden with interpretative clues and glosses.[82] John King has discussed in detail the way in which the interpretative tools provided by Crowley as editor of *Piers Plowman* allowed him to capture Langland's poem and 'reshape it into Reformation propaganda'.[83] The injunction to break the shell to find the kernel is therefore in some ways a redundant one since Crowley has already wielded the nutcrackers for his prospective readers. Crowley's poetics simultaneously demand an iconoclastic reading while at the same time seeking to make any other reading impossible.

In *The Confutation of the mishapen Answer to the misnamed, wicked Ballade, called the Abuse of [the] blessed sacrame[n]t of the aultare* Crowley produces a composite text made up of three discrete texts, the initial ballad, 'Abuse of [the] blessed sacrame[n]t of the aulter', Miles Hogarde's 'Answer' to this work and Crowley's 'Confutation' of Hogarde.[84] On the page these three texts are clearly differentiated. Typically one is presented with a few lines of the ballad, then considerably more of Hogarde's answer. Both of these texts are in verse while Crowley's 'Confutation' is in prose and invariably far longer than either of the other two works. It is important to note that this editorial decision works asymmetrically on the three texts that make up the finished work, cutting up the 'Ballad' and the 'Answer' and making them the matter of Crowley's 'Confutation'. This does not mean, however, that the complexity and wit of Hogarde's work is completely obscured. In the following 'exchange' Hogarde parodies the language of the 'Ballad' to subvert its use of the word popish.

The ballad.
Lord grau[n]t that our head, king Edward [the] sixt
May bury that dead God which is pixte
And get in his stead, thy [Christ's] supper not mixte
With abuse popishe.

The answere.
Lord grau[n]t that king Edward which ouer us hath
The chief primacie under christe Jesu
Truely to defend the catholike fayth
Which from the apostle dyd hole enseu
And all heresy and popishnesse to subdue.[85]

Hogarde's response to the 'Ballad' is designed to subvert both the meaning of the word popish and the Royal Supremacy. By printing these lines, and indeed the entire 'Answer', Crowley's *Confutation of the mishapen Answer* ironically becomes a site of resistance to the Edwardian Reformation. Indeed it appears, although this is impossible to know since no other copy exists, that Crowley does print the entirety of Hogarde's 'Answer'.[86]

The Confutation of the mishapen Answer embodies in textual form the emphasis of the Edwardian reformers on debate. It also illustrates the profound change in tone and scope of public discourse between the reign's of Henry VIII and Edward VI. Obviously Crowley's text is not at all neutral. His responses to Hogarde's poem are highly partisan. Crowley not only attacks the way Hogarde draws on scripture to support his argument, but also constantly mocks his opponent's writing, and in particular his abilities as a poet, complaining at one point that his lines have 'neither head or tail' but are simply a 'heape of words'.[87] Crowley also likes to mock Hogarde's lack of learning and class status, calling him at one point 'Hogherde'.[88] Despite all this abuse, however, the salient point about *The Confutation of the mishapen Answer* is that Hogarde's voice is heard.[89] The Henrician Reformation constantly sought to close down debate and silence any voices of dissent. Indeed, as has been suggested, at one level it embodied the pathological fantasy of a monological public sphere in which only the King's voice was heard. Crowley's *The Confutation of the mishapen Answer*, for all its vicious polemics, reflects that extent to which the Edwardian culture responded immediately to the lifting of the sense of restriction, containment and fear engendered by Henry VIII's kingship.[90]

This new sense of freedom and in particular the possibilities for writers can also be clearly seen in Crowley's poetry. In 1550 Crowley published a collection of epigrams, *One and Thyrtye Epigrammes, wherin are bryefly touched so many abuses*, whose scope ranges across the entire realm.[91] This volume opens with a bold assertion of the poet's authority and right to adopt a critical voice.

The Boke to the Reader.
If bokes may be bolde

To blame and reprove
The faultes of all menne,
Boeth hyghe and lowe,
As the Prophetes dyd
Whom Gods spirite did move,
Than blame not myne Autor:
For right wel I know
Hys penne is not tempered
Vayne doctrine to sowe
But as Essaye hath bydden
So muste he nedes crye
And tell the Lords people
Of their iniquite.[92]

Crowley's first epigram reflects his potentially radical comparison between his own role, and that of an Old Testament prophet. Entitled 'Of Abbayes', it is a critique of the use made of the lands and treasures of the monasteries at their dissolution. Crowley, however, does not directly criticize those who benefited from the abbeys' demise. Rather he points out that their treasure could have been used to provide good preachers for the people.

O Lorde (I thought then)
What occasion was here,
To prouide for learninge
And to make pouertye chere?
The landes and the jewels
That hereby were hadde,
Would haue found godly preachers,
Which might well haue ladde
The people aright
That now go astraye.[93]

Crowley's poetic voice in these epigrams is that of public teacher. There is no sense in which his advice is intended for an elite or restricted readership. The topics he addresses are extremely wide-ranging, from 'Allayes', to 'Bawdes', 'Flatterers' and the Exchequer. The implication of *One and Thyrtye Epigrammes* is that Crowley, like John Skelton, considered it his right as a public poet to comment on the entire realm, places, persons and classes.[94]

Crowley, however, did not share Skelton's apparent reluctance to see his work printed. His poetic vision is radically topical, reflecting the new possibilities created by print in terms of scope and ambition.[95] Mary Thomas Crane comments: 'Crowley presents his epigrams as an explicitly didactic work, and implies, by its organisation, that he assumes the stance of teacher or catechist addressing a young student.'[96] The poetic voice of the epigrams may be that of a teacher, as Crane suggests; however, it is clear that the class-room is the entire kingdom. In these poems Crowley builds up a detailed picture of a taught realm in which social order is based upon morality, the mutual recognition by various classes of their obligations to each other and plain speaking. The latter in particular is important to Crowley. In the epigram, 'Of Vaine Wryters, Vaine Talkers, and Vaine Hearers', he writes:

> Then slumbered I a little
> And thoughte that I sawe
> Thre sortes of vayne menne
> Condempned by Gods lawe.
> The one was a wryter,
> Of thynges nought and vayne,
> And an other a talker
> And thys was theyr payne:
> The wryter hadde the crowne
> Of hys heade opened,
> Whose braynes with a stycke
> The talker styrred
> And he wyth boeth handes
> Drewe that talkers tonge,
> So that wythout hys mouthe
> It as an handefull longe
> The thirde was an herkener
> Of fables and lyes
> Whose eares were almost
> Drawen up to his eyes.[97]

Crowley's attack on the corrupters of language clearly fits in well with Edwardian culture's emphasis on debate. It is noticeable, however, that Crowley felt the need to stress that these strange and disturbing images came to the poem's narrator in a dream. There are clearly limits to the scope of Crowley's poetic endeavour. The poet can be a teacher of the realm – indeed in Crowley's work, *The Opening of the Wordes of the Prophet Joell*, the poet explicitly takes on the mantle of preacher – but he has to control his imagination.[98] Placing the inspiration for the metaphorical images in this epigram in a dream works to distance them from the reasoned public world in which Crowley's poetic persona claims authority. Crowley in his epigrams asserts authority as a poet while at the same time producing poetry which seeks to downplay its poetic nature. *One and Thyrtye Epigrammes* is a celebration of the power of poetry as a force of reform which seeks to downgrade and reject such basic ingredients of the poetic as textual play, metaphor and linguistic complexity.

Crowley's public poetry of the Edwardian period gives the impression that the matters it is addressing are too important to be communicated in any voice other then that of the plain-speaking teacher and preacher. A similar sense of urgency permeates Crowley's prose works of this period. These texts have often been dismissed as medieval owing to their hierarchical and estates-based view of the commonwealth. This is, however, a problematic criticism. The assumption that an ordered commonwealth should be based on a rigid compartmentalization of the estates was shared by, among others, Robert Kett, Bishop Latimer and William Paget. It is difficult to see what it means to characterize Crowley's view of the commonwealth as medieval if most of his mid-Tudor contemporaries shared it.[99] In practice Crowley invariably adopts a radical approach to social issues. In his early work, *An Informacion agaynst the oppressors of the pore commons*, Crowley argues that, 'the whole earth ... (by byrth ryght) belongeth to the chyldren of men. They are all inheritors therof indifferently by nature'.[100] Crowley goes on to argue that this means the 'sturdy', the rich and powerful, have a moral duty to care for the poor and dispossessed. Crowley advocates stewardship as an appropriate model for the relationship of the rich to their possessions and friendship as the basis for a godly society. He writes that:

> The Philosophers who knewe nothyng of the bonde of friendshippe which Christe our maister and redemer lefte among us: affirmed that amonge frendes al thynges are co[m]mon, meaneyng that frendshippe woulde not suffer one frende to holde frome an other, the thynge that he had nede of. And what shal we saye? Are we not frendes? Surly if we be not frendes: wee beare the name of Christe and bee called christians in vayne.[101]

In this passage Crowley takes the humanist notion of friendship and deploys it in a radical way.[102] He extends the theory that true friendship should cut across social barriers radically by genuinely applying it across society. In the process he rejects the elitist assumptions one invariably finds in humanist discussions of friendship.[103]

The radicalism of Crowley's approach to social issues is most apparent when one compares his response to the tumults of 1549, *The Way to Wealth, wherin is taught a remedy for sedicion*, to John Cheke's *The Hurt of Sedition*.[104] As has been suggested, Cheke's work consistently makes the protestors of 1549 fit into a magisterial ideological fantasy in which they are the cause of social conflict and violence, and not Tudor culture's profound inequalities of power and wealth. *The Hurt of Sedition* represents the Norwich campers as endangering the whole of society with their infantile desire to create a world in which no rules or boundaries stand in the way of their bestial urges to take, rob, rape, murder and destroy. Crowley completely rejects this representation of the 1549 protesters. In *The Way to Wealth* he argues that the people responsible for the creation of a world without proper boundaries are the rich. Crowley tells his reader that if he asked the poor who were responsible for sedition they would 'tel me that the great fermares, the grasiers, the riche buchares, the men of lawe, the merchauntes, the gentlemen, the knightes, the lordes, and I can not tel who; men that haue no name because they are doares in al thinges that ani gaine hangeth vpon."[105] Crowley goes on to characterize these men as people who wish to erase all barriers in their relentless pursuit of wealth, describing them as:

> Men that would haue all in their own handes: men that would leaue nothyng for others; men that would be alone on the earth; men that been neuer satisfied. Cormerauntes, gredye gulles; yea, men that would eate vp menne, women, & chyldren, are the causes of Sedition.[106]

Crowley's cormorants are the direct counterparts of Cheke's mad dogs, and also Skelton's avaricious Wolsey. All want to create a world in which their desires have complete and free reign, a world in which boundaries only exist in order to be thrown down and erased.[107] In his prose works Crowley argues for a moral solution to the damage that his greedy gulls were doing to Tudor society. He deploys concepts like stewardship and friendship to imagine a world in which the 'possessors' freely accept limits to the play of their power and wealth, to the scope of their desire.

It is, however, in his major poem, *Philargyrie of Greate Britayne*, that Crowley's political vision is at its most radical and incisive.[108] In this work Crowley reflects upon all the major issues of Edwardian culture, in particular the nature of Tudor society, the place of counsel in the polity and the role of the poet. John King comments: '*Philargyrie* fuses two crucial questions: who is the ideal royal counsellor and how does one recognise him?'[109] Crowley addresses these questions in the context of an allegorical history of the Henrician and Edwardian Reformations. The scale of Crowley's ambition in *Philargyrie* is indicated by the historical scope of the poem which opens with the institution of society in Great Britain by the giant Philargyrie, an allegorical figure for avarice, who invites the brutish Britons to,

> Com unto me
> Whoso wyll (quoth he)
> There shall no lawe him bynde
> I wyll him make
> Free for to take
> All thynges that he can fynde
> Force and stronge hand
> By sea and lande
> Shall be his lawe and ryght
> He shall be bolde
> To take and holde
> Al thyngis by force and myght.[110]

In Crowley's poem it is avarice that produces society, albeit one based on force and fraud. The social order created by Philargyrie is, however, not sufficiently exploitative for his gigantic tastes. It does not produce enough gold to satisfy his endless hunger. This situation is only solved when one of Philargyrie's subjects, Hypocrisie, advises him that to get more gold,

> We muste pretende
> Some holy ende
> That maye the people please
> And so we shall
> Be Lordis of all
> And fyl oure baggis wyth ease.[111]

Hypocrisie is an allegorical representation of the papists. At first Hypocrisie's plan works, but in the end he realizes that Philargyrie can never be satisfied and starts to keep back some of the treasure he has raised through his papist tricks. In other words papistry here gulls avarice. Hypocrisie's treachery is, however, revealed by Philaute, self-love, who feeds Philargyrie with all of the wealth that Hypocrisie has hoarded. Inevitably there is never enough and Philaute ends up having to debase the currency. The poem concludes when the people appeal to God for help. He sends Trueth to the King with the message that he needs to drive Hypocrisie, Philaute and Philargyrie out of his realm.

The radicalism of this text is reflected in its portrayal of the Henrician Reformation as a crooked deal between a tyrant, Philargyrie, and a corrupt counsellor, Philaute. As John King has pointed out, the latter can clearly be seen as an allegorical representation of Thomas Cromwell.[112] Philaute defeats Hypocrisie by exposing Purgatory as a lie. He tells Philargyrie that,

> I wyll declare
> How madde they are
> To gyue him of theyr good
> To be made iust
> Sens all men muste
> Be made iust bi Christi bloud.[113]

Philaute's plan to satisfy Avarice is apparently to preach a mainstay of magisterial Protestantism, justification by faith. Clearly Crowley's poem is not criticizing this doctrine; however, it is suggesting that even one of the central planks of Protestant teaching could be used for corrupt ends. The implication of the representation of the Henrician Reformation in *Philargyrie* is that any good that came of it was entirely accidental. The people of the great city Nodnol, London, do embrace Philaute's teaching with alacrity but this is entirely because they 'loue to chaynge'.[114]

Throughout Crowley's poem counsel takes place in private. Hypocrisie and Philaute are depicted as flatterers intent on simply telling Philargyrie what he wants to hear. The nature of Philargyrie's lordship is also problematic since it appears to be based purely on his power as a giant. When people approach him they fall flat on their faces as if he were a god. This level of obsequious-ness, however, makes Philargyrie look dangerously like Henry VIII. At the end of the poem Trueth has to tell the King what has been going on his realm. This is hardly a flattering representation of kingship. At the end of *Philargyrie* a king is depicted as being completely unaware of what has been going on in his reign. His response to being told the truth is initially to grab his Bible and sword, but he appears then to be overcome with guilt, or perhaps even fear, at the size of the task that faces him.

> Then fell he downe
> And cast his crowne
> And diademe asyde
> And lokyng on hye
> Up to the skye
> To God aloude he cryed.[115]

Kingship in *Philargyrie* veers between being tyrannical, if over-reliant on private counsel and therefore susceptible to being hoodwinked, and looking rather pathetic, a figure who casts off all the trappings of office in a fit of guilty humility.

It is not simply in political terms that *Philargyrie* is a radical text. Its radicalism extends to the model of poetry and the role of the poet that it embodies. In Chapter 1 it was suggested that Thomas Wyatt's convoluted opaque poetry reflected the claustrophobic and oppressive atmosphere of the Henrician court and in particular, that the sense of poetic self that is articu-lated in Wyatt's courtly lyrics is the product of historically specific tyranny, the result of Wyatt having written during the reign of a king like Henry VIII. The scope and ambition of *Philargyrie* is a product of the greater freedom that poets like Crowley enjoyed during the reign of Edward VI. There was no need for the kind of textual games, for the poetic obscurity and subterfuge, that marks the writing of Wyatt and his contemporaries. Crowley's populist poetic style in *Philargyrie*, in particular his adaptation of a ballad measure, reflects a scale of ambition in terms of readership lacking from the work of most court poets. Indeed the end of *Philargyrie* strongly suggests that poets like Crowley were fundamental to the reform of the commonwealth and the expulsion of Philargyrie, Hypocrisie and Philaute. This is partly because God sends the King men who were determined 'oppression to expell' but it is also because the poem itself is clearly intended to be part of this process.[116] The intention of *Philargyrie* was to argue for reform and the rejection of the rule of avarice, and the poem announces that God will be sending people with this agenda to help the King in his godly mission.

In the same year that *Philargyrie* was published, 1551, Robert Crowley was ordained, and his next publication was not until 1559. It is possible that the radicalism of his allegorical history of the Henrician Reformation made it dangerous for him to publish; however, this seems unlikely. It seems far more plausible that, having been ordained, Crowley no longer needed to take on the role of poetic teacher and prophet since he was now a preacher in his own right. Crowley's Edwardian writings reflect the extent to which the years 1547–53 were for many a period of real intellectual freedom. It was possible in this period to argue that the rich were to blame for the woes of the realm, that the dissolution of the monasteries had been mishandled and that the Henrician Reformation had been nothing more than a confidence trick to get money from the gullible people. But despite this, the events of 1549 cast a shadow over Crowley's work. Who were the people at whom his works were aimed? Why did he write in a populist style? Who were meant to be the pupils for his lessons? Crowley's work argues for and imagines a coalition for reform crossing all class and social boundaries, bound together in a confessional reforming crusade. Unfortunately for Crowley this agenda fell foul of one of the great ironies of the years 1547–53. The Edwardian regime, which sought legitimacy from the populace for its religious changes, which prided itself on its openness and rejection of censorship, alone among Tudor governments managed to massacre its own supporters. There is no doubt that those who took part in the Pilgrimage of Grace, Wyatt's Rebellion or the Northern Rising were opposed to the governments of the day; the opposite appears to have been the case in 1549. Kett, and his fellow East Anglian campers, seem to have conceived of themselves as the regime's ploughmen, ready to put their shoulders to the wheel of godly reform. They appear to have been quite prepared to play the role set out for them in the anti-mass pamphlets of 1548 and in the writings of Robert Crowley. The cultural and ideological effects of their suppression can be clearly seen in William Baldwin's *Beware the Cat*. The political costs for the regime were felt in 1553 when these same people played a crucial role in bringing Mary Tudor to the throne.[117]

WILLIAM BALDWIN'S *BEWARE THE CAT* AND EDWARDIAN POLITICS

In many ways William Baldwin is a similar figure to Robert Crowley. He was an assistant to the publisher Edward Whitechurch in the same period that Crowley was working very closely with the printer John Daye. During the reign of Edward VI, Baldwin published a number of works including the extremely popular *A Treatise of Moral Philosophy* and a translation of the scurrilous tract *Wonderful News of the Death of Paul the Third*.[118] However, at another level Baldwin appears almost as Crowley's nemesis. While Crowley sought to create a role for himself as a poet and writer within the public sphere, Baldwin seems to have constantly sought to find a place for himself within the Edwardian establishment. This difference between the two men is brought into stark relief by Baldwin's novel *Beware the Cat*, which suggests a complete and irreconcilable breakdown of communication between the elite culture and the wider realm.[119]

The differences between Crowley and Baldwin are emphasized by the events of the winter of 1552–53. Baldwin explicitly places the production of *Beware the Cat* at the court, or rather in its fringes. Baldwin locates the genesis of his work in a discussion between a frankly rather disreputable collection of men sharing a bedroom while working on the court's Christmas entertainments.[120] The Argument of *Beware the Cat* opens with Baldwin, or at least his narrative voice, recounting that: 'It chanced that at Christmas last I was at Court with Master Ferrers, then master of the King's Majesty's pastimes, about setting forth certain interludes, which for the King's recreation we had devised and were in learning.'[121] Sharing the room with Ferrers and Baldwin were the former's Astronomer, Master Wilmot, and his Divine, Master Streamer. The bulk of *Beware the Cat* is told by Streamer. Clearly it would inappropriate to treat Baldwin's account of the genesis of his novel with anything but scepticism, particularly given that one of the work's objects of scorn is people who are too trusting readers or hearers. There is, however, a reference in the accounts of the Master of the Revels to a payment being made to a William Baldwin, who appears to have been working as a prop-maker producing a crown of gold-paper and buckram for an Irish prince.[122] It is in some ways facile to point out that it is impossible to imagine Crowley being paid for making such a prop, a pretend crown designed for a theatrical performance. Crowley does, however, comment in his *Epitome of Chronicles* directly on the entertainments that Baldwin was involved in. His entry for the year 1552 states that Edward, after going on a progress in the summer, returned in the autumn to London, 'and fro[m] thens he went to Grenewich, wher was prepared matter of pastyme a fort counterfaited, riding at the tylte, and goodly pastimes at Christmas, tyll the kyng had gotten a cough that brought hym to his ende.'[123] Crowley's attitude to the courtly entertainments provided by Baldwin and his colleagues is made even more explicit in his entry for the preceding year when he writes that after the duke of Somerset's trial and execution,

> The younge Kynge was entised to passe time in maskeyng and mumminge. And to that ende was piked oute a sorte of misrulers to deuyse straunge spectacles in the courte, in tyme of Christmas, to cause the yonge kynge to forgette, yea rather to hate, hys good uncle, who had purged the courte of all suche outrage ... This was the high waye, first to made an ende of the knynges uncle, and after of the kyng hymselfe.[124]

Baldwin's prefatory material to *Beware the Cat* places its conception squarely within the world of the misrulers, the devisers of strange spectacles, responsible, as far as Crowley was concerned, for the production of the lethal 1552–1553 Christmas entertainments. Indeed from this perspective Baldwin, as the counterfeiter of a prop Irish crown, performed a particularly dubious role.

Beware the Cat can therefore be seen as the opposite side of Edwardian culture from that expressed in Crowley's *Philargyrie*. While the latter expresses a confidence in the power of writing, and perhaps specifically print, to carry a radical reforming message throughout the country, Baldwin's text suggests that any such agenda is based on a complete misconception of the status of writing, the role of writers and the possibilities of print. *Beware the Cat* is an extended piece of prose fiction split into the three parts of Master Streamer's Oration. Streamer's role as the orator of the entire text should be a unifying factor; however, this is not the case. This is partly because it soon becomes apparent that Streamer is a terrible narrator as well as being an untrustworthy one. It is also, however, because narrative voice in *Beware the Cat* is extremely unstable. It tends to take the form of a series of regressions. For example at the opening of his first oration Streamer reports the words of a servant in a printing house concerning a speaking cat in Staffordshire; another servant then reports a tale about a strange incident in Ireland during which a cat spoke in Irish. Terence N. Bowers points out: 'Streamer's narrative ... is composed of many orally transmitted tales which tend to multiply uncontrollably.'[125] A key element in this multiplication of voices is Streamer's successful creation and consumption of a potion which enables him to understand the language of cats. As a result his third oration comprises largely of the reported speech of a cat, Mouse-slayer, who is defending herself before a judicial tribunal against the charge that she unlawfully rejected the advances of another cat, Catch-rat. Of all the voices heard in *Beware the Cat* Mouse-slayer's is the most transgressive. But at the same time it is also the most authoritative since it is in her account that the lies and deceits of mid-Tudor culture are laid bare.

Beware the Cat opens with a dedicatory epistle to Master John Young. This text contains a complex account of the production of the work which simultaneously stresses its distance from Streamer's original words and suggests that when Ferrers and Willot read it they will 'think they hear Master Streamer speak'.[126] This immediately sets up a tension between print and oral culture that runs throughout *Beware the Cat*. There is then another prefatory piece, 'The Argument', describing the location where and specific time when Streamer first told his tale. Finally the reader reaches Streamer's first oration. Even here things are not simple.[127] Streamer opens his oration by telling his listeners, in a throw-away comment, that he was lodged at a friend's house that 'hangeth partly upon the town wall that is called Aldersgate'.[128] At this point Streamer's narrative takes a wrong turn and becomes an extended digression on how the gates of London got their names. Streamer discusses Aldersgate, Moorgate, Newgate and Ludgate. He comments that, 'Moorgate took the name of the field without it, which have been a very moor; or else because it is the most ancient gate of the City, was therof in respect of the other, as Newgate, called the Eldergate'.[129] This comment is accompanied by a gloss in the margin 'Why Moorgate'. However, this is all nonsense. The one thing the text does not tell the reader at this point is why Moorgate got its name. Streamer here is clearly simply speculating, although he does buttress his words with historical references. In the opening words of Streamer's narrative, Baldwin is specifically mimicking the kind of historical investigation in which writers like John Leland were engaged during the mid-Tudor period. At a more general level the opening of *Beware the Cat* mocks the Edwardian vogue for learned and speculative 'commonwealth' works.[130]

Baldwin's novel opens reading and, importantly, looking like a work of learning. There are the glosses that run down the page, although on careful reading these are often completely pointless or frankly confusing. The text contains numerous Latin tags, which usually add nothing to its meaning. In particular, Streamer represents himself as a man of learning, someone whose voice should carry weight within the commonwealth. This self-presentation is, however, immediately revealed to the careful reader as nonsense.[131] Baldwin's portrayal of Streamer, however, does not simply reflect the dangers of reading uncritically and allowing oneself to be seduced by the appearance of learning. By deploying the possibilities of print to create a character defined by his charlatanism and lack of consistency, *Beware the Cat* also implicitly critiques the way in which writers like Crowley used print to construct a consistent and authoritative voice within the public sphere. The implication of *Beware the Cat* is that print is a capricious servant. In the Epistle the reader is told that the printing of *Beware the Cat* was undertaken in order to bring to a wider public Streamer's learning and to give him the recognition that he deserves. The comparison drawn is between Plato and Socrates, with Baldwin as editor and publisher, playing the role of Plato to Streamer's Socrates. However what is actually communicated to the reader is Streamer's foolishness, his lack of learning and judgement.

Beware the Cat presents itself as a work of learning and turns out to be nothing of the sort. A similar transformation takes place around its status as a moral tale. What does it mean to beware the cat? What is the cat? These questions are complicated by the way the role of the cats changes during the course of the work. In the First Oration cats only appear, and talk, in the context of reported tales. There is the story of the Staffordshireman hailed by a cat as he rode home through Kankwood. Failing to respond when the cat calls his name he is requested by his feline accoster: 'Commend me unto Tittan Tatton and to Puss thy Catton, and tell her that Grimalkin is dead'.[132] This brief story is then followed by a much longer one, told by a different man, which is set in Ireland and recounts the death of Grimalkin who is killed by an Irish kern.[133] These feline stories lead to a discussion over whether animals have reason. The second of Streamer's orations concerns his making of a potion in order to hear what the cats meeting under his bedroom window are saying at night. Streamer's third oration is largely the testimony of Mouse-slayer. She tells numerous stories of cat derring-do, most of which involve her exposing human stupidity and culpability. For example at one stage she is given walnut shell shoes and locked in an attic. The noise of her feet, however, makes the superstitious country folk and their ignorant papist priests think the house is haunted and that she is the Devil. Indeed when the priests catch sight of her at the top of the ladder they are so scared that complete chaos ensures.

> But when the priest heard me come, and by a glimpsing had seen me, down he fell upon them that were behind him, and with his chalice hurt one, with his water pot another, and his holy candle fell into another priest's breech beneath (who, while the rest were hawsoning me, was conjuring the maid at the stair foot) and all to-besinged him ... the old priest, which was so tumbled among them that his face lay upon a boy's bare arse ... which for fear had beshit himself, had all to-rayed his face, he neither felt not smelt it, nor removed from him.[134]

Mouse-slayer's stories tell of a world of popular religion and folklore which she, and her human owners, constantly manipulate for their own ends. It is a world without any real moral or ethical code. Indeed in many ways it resembles that of Chaucer's *Miller's Tale*, except that in Baldwin's work this world is treated with far less respect. The charm and ultimate harmony of *The Miller's Tale* is lacking from the world of Mouse-slayer which is made up only of fools, gulls, bawds and fallen gentlemen.[135]

All three parts of Streamer's narrative are made up of numerous different voices and discourses. The only stability is provided by the fact that they are all being reported by one man; however the reader is constantly reminded by Baldwin that Streamer is a far from trustworthy narrator. *Beware the Cat* could have as its sub-title 'beware the narrator', particularly one who claims learning, wit and authority. Streamer's status as an unreliable narrator means that the reader is forced to pay close attention to *Beware the Cat*'s generic status. Baldwin's work is at one level an animal fable, which might lead the reader to expect it to have a few relatively straightforward possible meanings. As soon as one starts to read Baldwin's work in terms of generic expectations, however, problems arise. To start with there are a number of possible candidates for the cats. Perhaps the most obvious one is Catholics. R.W. Maslen points out that Baldwin's 'cats exhibit a number of characteristics which Protestant propagandists attributed to the Catholic clergy: they are sexually promiscuous, inordinately greedy ... and given to meddling with magic'.[136] However, identifying the cats as Catholics is problematic. This is partly because Baldwin's cats look more like *papists* than Catholics.[137] More importantly, as Maslen goes on to point out, the fit between cats and Catholics does not quite work. He comments:

'Baldwin's cats are owned by Catholics and resemble Catholics, but they also disrupt the clandestine plots of Catholics.'[38] So who are the cats? John King suggests: 'The all-seeing vision of the cat may serve as a figure for both the providence of God and the vigilance of the devil.'[39] Baldwin's cats certainly have the ability to cross all boundaries and penetrate the secret recesses of the human world. They seem naturally to inhabit the periphery and the hidden. Maslen comments that 'cat culture occupies the spaces left vacant by human society'.[40] At the same time these places were an integral if peripheral part of the social fabric of mid-Tudor culture. It is almost as if the cats occupy the sinews of society, its unacknowledged but vital supporting scaffold. Ultimately, however, it is impossible to fix the meaning of the cats. They do at times seem to be agents of divine vengeance, particularly in regard to adultery, but at other times they appear to be clearly demonic. Equally Baldwin's cats do look papist but they constantly make fun of the mass and mock attitudes that Protestants regarded as inherently papist.

The slipperiness of Baldwin's cats makes the injunction of his title, *Beware the Cat*, look capricious. How can the reader beware of something that cannot be defined or fixed? This uncertainly is, however, precisely the point of Baldwin's text. Andrew Hadfield comments that: '*Beware the Cat* works by never allowing the reader to settle for easy answers and rest assured that the world can be neatly split up into sheep and goats.'[41] Baldwin's text makes its readers question the assumptions that they bring to it. To this extent it is an exemplary Edwardian text since Crowley, and the writers of the anti-mass works of 1548, all wanted to teach their readers to adopt a questioning and interrogative hermeneutic. This was particularly the case when a work was a fable or an allegory, since to be taken in by such a work, to focus one's reading on its surface or shell, would be to lose oneself in the text. But this is the inevitable result of reading *Beware the Cat*. The more one seeks to fix the meaning of Baldwin's work, and in particular to nail down the cats, the more lost one gets. Trying to break the cats' shell to find the kernel of their meaning is a pointless and endless endeavour. This is because at one level Baldwin's cat is his text. His reader needs to be beware since in the process of reading he, and given the femininity of the cats the implicit masculinity of the reader is important, will lose himself in the text's feline web.

It would be wrong, however, to regard Baldwin's text as simply a literary exercise. Annabel Patterson points out that in early modern England there existed a 'tradition of political fabling as a form of resistance to unjust power relations, which ran continuously alongside (or beneath) the more conventional and conservative notion that the content of fables was merely ethical ...'[42] *Beware the Cat* sets itself up as an ethical tale – hence the admonition in the title – but, as has already been suggested, it fails to deliver. As a political fable, however, Baldwin's work reflects on the events of 1549 and the response of

Somerset's government to the East Anglian protesters. *Beware the Cat* works at an ideological level to buttress a magisterial understanding of Tudor society in a far more sophisticated way than works like Cheke's *The Hurt of Sedition*.[143] Ernesto Laclau argues that the 'ideological effect *strictu sensu*' is 'the belief that there is a particular social arrangement which can bring about the closure and transparency of the community'.[144] The ideological danger implicit in the events of 1549 was that the basis of this belief in the context of Tudor political praxis, that the periphery, commons and outsiders, could not talk to the centre in a way that it could hear or understand without mediators, would be revealed as a nonsense. Cheke's response, along with that of many of his fellow magistrates, was simply to assert that, despite appearances to the contrary, the East Anglian protesters were incapable of being reasonable or ordered. The fact that the events in the West Country fitted much more easily into this paradigm owing to their 'papist' nature made Cheke's job much easier. *Beware the Cat* takes the argument of works like *The Hurt of Sedition* much further. It constantly implies, in a number of different registers, that it is quite impossible for the centre to hear or understand the populace or the periphery. For example, it is clear that the cats represent something outside the grasp of the reader – is it papistry, popular culture, folk wisdom? Who knows? And this is precisely the point. The more one tries to pin down the cats, the more lost one becomes. Ultimately one is forced to throw up one's hands and give up. The one person who does appear able to penetrate the cats' world is Streamer and he needs to consume a disgusting potion in order to do so. And what is the result of his endeavours? Only to hear stories, witty though they may be, of a world without morals, learning or wisdom. *Beware the Cat* inkennels Kett and his comrades in fable. It tells its readers that the centre cannot talk to the periphery, and, if it could, the latter would have nothing useful to say. The portrayal of the popular in *Beware the Cat* therefore represents a massive retreat from the optimism of the anti-mass pamphlets of 1548. In these works figures like Piers Plowman and John Bon are deployed as spokesmen for the wisdom of the people and their proper scepticism about the claims of the papists. In *Beware the Cat* the people are depicted as amoral gulls easily taken in by papists, bawds and tricksters. Not that the latter are portrayed as any less gullible or foolish. Only the cats display any real wisdom in this world. This is, however, entirely tainted by their animal status. Indeed by locating the wit and cunning of the popular in cats Baldwin's text is repeating its central ideological message since the implication of this is that folk learning is animalistic and amoral.

Beware the Cat articulates a weary and resigned attitude to the possibility of communication not only between the centre and periphery, people and cats, but also in a more general sense in terms of the reforming potential of print and the process of confessionalization. The kind of confidence and indeed arrogance that one finds in Crowley's Edwardian work, which is predicated on the power of the printed text as an agent of reform, is entirely lacking in Baldwin's work. Indeed the implication is that print will itself lead to the corruption of learning and culture by cats and their tales. It is no coincidence that Streamer's First Oration opens in a print shop. Elisabeth L. Eisenstein, in her work *The Printing Press as an Agent of Change*, comments approvingly on the way printing created a new type of person, the scholar-printer whose 'products introduced new interactions between theory and practice, abstract brainwork and sensory experience, systematic logic and careful observation'.[145] In *Beware the Cat* the milieu of the print house is that of gossip, folk tales and nonsense. Streamer, who is meant to be working on the production of a Greek alphabet, is distracted by the printer's talk from this laudable endeavour and ends up drinking a foul potion in order to prove whether or not cats talk. Printing for Baldwin seems to be far more of a mixed blessing than Eisenstein appears to regard it as; far from producing scholar-printers, it produces printed scholars, men of learning led astray and corrupted by their exposure to the print-house and its denizens. It would, however, be a mistake to take Baldwin's text too seriously on this point. Who can seriously believe that Streamer's Greek alphabet would have brought more pleasure and done more good than the text which took its place, *Beware the Cat?* Baldwin's work shares with much mid-Tudor writing an unacknowledged indebtedness to Erasmus' work, and in particular, his *Praise of Folly*. Cats, like Folly are everywhere; all men have a share in them; none are free. Indeed it is Folly / Cats that provide backbone for culture and civilisation.[146] After all are not Baldwin and his fellow misrulers cats in the eyes of men like Crowley? There they lie in their attic bedroom, swapping ridiculous stories, having just completed such essential tasks for the well-being of the commonwealth as making prop Irish crowns for a mumming.

CONCLUSION

Beware the Cat was not actually published until 1570.[147] Strangely the gap between composition, Christmas 1553, and publication does not make Baldwin's text look dated or anachronistic. This is primarily because, although it was written in the last years of Edward's reign, the events it depicts are represented as if they are already dated. The narrative opens in Christmas 1553 but Streamer immediately takes the reader back to 1549–50 when the Aldersgate was adorned with the quarters of executed traitors. The bulk of Mouse-slayer's testimony takes place between 'the time when preachers had leave to speak against the Mass, but it was not forbidden till half a year after', 1548, and 'Whitsuntide last', 1551.[148] This temporal specificity, however, runs counter to the general tenor of Mouse-slayer's narrative with its depiction of a timeless world unaffected by the passing of time. Even the banning of the mass seems strangely timeless, as though it had happened many years before. But then in Mouse-slayer's world it is almost academic when the mass is banned: the superstitious people and their foolish priests will not change their behaviour or beliefs. They are impervious to reform or change. David Loades has argued that one reason for the failure of Northumberland's attempted coup in 1553 was the general sense of failure and disillusionment among the intellectual and religious leaders of the Edwardian regime.[49] It is this sense of ennui that *Beware the Cat* perfectly captures. The shock of the events of 1549 led to the transformation of John Bon into Mouse-slayer. In 1548 the figure of the plough-man reflected a magisterial Protestant confidence in the populace as a source of honest learning and godly labour. By 1553 Bon's plainness and simplicity had been replaced by catty cunning and deviousness. In the process the danger-ous possibility glimpsed during the summer of 1549, of the involvement of the populace in the reform of the commonwealth, was safely suppressed, or perhaps inkennelled. Mouse-slayer, and her comrades, would never be naive or foolish enough to be found camping on Mousehold heath.

NOTES

1 Printed in *Documents Relating to the Revels at the Court in the Time of King Edward VI and Queen Mary*, ed. Albert Feuillerat (Louvain: 1914), p. 89.

2 *Calendar of State Papers Domestic Series of the Reign of Edward VI 1547–1553*, ed. C.S. Knighton (London: 1992), pp. 121–122.

3 For Edwardian kingship see Stephen Alford, *Kingship and Politics in the Reign of Edward VI* (Cambridge: 2002).

4 John Foxe, *Acts and Monumentes* (London: 1570), STC 11223, p. 1486.

5 Alford, 2002, p. 63.

6 See chapter 5 of Alford, 2002.

7 *The Letters of William, Lord Paget of Beaudesert, 1547–1563*, ed. Barrett L. Beer and Sybil M. Jack, Camden Miscellany, Fourth Series, Vol. 13 (London: 1974), p. 20.

8 Ibid., p. 20.

9 G.R. Elton, *Reform and Reformation: England 1509–1558* (London: 1977), p. 321.

10 This was partly because the mid-Tudor period was one of real economic crisis, in particular rampant inflation, caused in the short term by the debasement of the coinage and in the longer term by population growth.

11 Diarmaid MacCulloch, *Tudor Church Militant: Edward VI and the Protestant Reformation* (London: 1999), p. 125.

12 On Smith see Mary Dewar, *Sir Thomas Smith: A Tudor Intellectual in Office* (London: 1964).

13 Sir Thomas Smith, *A Discourse of the Commonweal of this Realm*, ed. Mary Dewar

(Charlottesville: 1969), p. ix. On the general intellectual context of the Tudor literature of social complaint see Helen C. White, *Social Criticism in Popular Religious Literature of the Sixteenth Century* (New York: 1965).

14 Smith, 1969, p. 13.

15 Ibid., p. 32.

16 For example at one point the Doctor asks his colleagues, 'Was there any sacrament so holy or so freely instituted of God but we [the clergy] devised a way to get some lucre by the same?' (Ibid., p. 129).

17 This is particularly the case, given that it is possible that the learned men being referred to here are in practice one learned man, Thomas More.

18 Barnadine Ochino, *A tragedie or Dialogue of the Bishop of Rome*, trans. John Ponet (London: 1549), STC 18770.

19 Diarmaid MacCulloch has pointed out the importance of its internationalism to the Edwardian Reformation (MacCulloch, 1999, p. 79).

20 Ochino, 1549, Y.iii (iv).

21 I find it impossible not to read Henry's silence in the face of Cranmer's speech without imagining the latter's smile when reading this work. How Cranmer must have wished the Henrician Reformation had taken place in front of an approving but silent king.

22 Ibid., Cc.i.

23 Ibid., Cc.iii.

24 The actual relationship of *A Dialogue of the Bishop of Rome* to the events of 1549 is unclear since it is not known when it was written. Depending on which edition one reads, the first features Somerset while in the second he is replaced by the council, it can be seen either as prophetic of this year's commotions or as a retrospective explanation of them.

25 Diarmaid MacCulloch, *Thomas Cranmer: A Life* (New Haven: 1996), p. 409.

26 Paget, 1974, p. 22.

27 Ibid., p. 25.

28 Ibid., p. 31.

29 On carnival see Mikhail Bakhtin, *Rabelais and his World*, trans. Helene Iswolsky (Bloomington: 1984). For an excellent introduction to the carnivalesque see Peter Stallybrass, '"Drunk with the Cup of Liberty": Robin Hood, the Carnivalesque, and the Rhetoric of Violence in Early Modern England', in *The Violence of Representation: Literature and the History of Violence*, eds Nancy Armstrong and Leonard Tennenhouse (London: 1989), pp. 45–76.

30 For the events in East Anglia see Diarmaid MacCulloch, 'Kett's Rebellion in Context', *PP*, 84 (1979), pp. 36–59, Barrett L. Beer, *Rebellion and Riot: Popular Disorder in England During the Reign of Edward VI* (Kent, Ohio: 1982); and Diarmaid MacCulloch, *Suffolk and the Tudors: Politics and Religion in an English County, 1500–1600* (Oxford: 1986). For the Western Rebellion see Joyce Youings, 'The South Western Rebellion of 1549', *Southern History*, 1 (1979), pp. 99–122.

31 I am grateful to Diarmaid MacCulloch for allowing me to read the revised chapter on the rebellions of 1549 that will soon be published as part of the fifth edition of his study

with Anthony Fletcher, *Tudor Rebellions*. Drawing on important new research by Amanda Jones, MacCulloch now argues that the commotions of 1549 affected all of lowland England, with the exception of London, and that they show unmistakable signs of planning.

32 Anthony Fletcher and Diarmaid MacCulloch, *Tudor Rebellions* (Harlow: 1997), p. 69.

33 The term 'Kett's Rebellion' is misleading since Robert Kett was only the ring-leader of the Norwich camp and it is now clear that there were camps across the whole of East Anglia, south-east England and much of the midlands.

34 Indeed the Western Rebellion could be seen as a perfect illustration of the argument of *A Dialogue of the Bishop of Rome* that there would be some people in the country who would respond to the advent of Protestantism with turned stomachs.

35 On the history writing of John Bale see Tom Betteridge, *Tudor Histories of the English Reformations 1530–1583* (Aldershot: 1999).

36 It should be noted that Nichols was writing before the final defeat of the rebels and that he was also a fellow West Country man. See 'Udall's Answer to the Commoners of Devonshire and Cornwall', in *Troubles connected with the Prayer Book of 1549*, ed. Nicholas Pocock, Camden Society (1883–1884) pp. 141–193, p. 144. For Nichols' authorship see Youings, 1979, p. 115. For a discussion of Cranmer's response to the rebels demands see Diarmaid MacCulloch, *Thomas Cranmer* (New Haven: 1996), pp. 439–440.

37 For a discussion of Bale's *King Johan* see Betteridge, 1999.

38 Indeed as papistry as a concept became more established within early modern English political discourse, writers started to take an event's lack of papistry as the clearest proof that the papists were involved. The classic example of this is the late seventeenth-century view of the English Civil War and the execution of the King as examples of papist plotting.

39 This did not prevent the attempt being made. For example one of the letters written to the protesters in East Anglia by Somerset's government warned them that if they were not careful 'naughtie papist priests' would seek to use their behaviour to 'bringe in the olde abuses and bloodie lawes wherof this realme is ... well delivered'. See Ethan Shagan, 'Protector Somerset and the 1549 Rebellions: New Sources and New Perspectives', *EHR*, 114 (1999), pp. 34–63, p. 56.

40 'The Council to the ambassadors', in Knighton, 1992, pp. 148–149.

41 See John Guy, 'The Rhetoric of Counsel in Early Modern England', in *Tudor Political Culture*, ed. Dale Hoak (Cambridge: 1995), pp. 292–310.

42 The idea of Somerset as the Council's mouthpiece echoes the models of kingship produced in the fifteenth century, in the face of the collapse of royal authority under Henry VI, by such writers as Sir John Fortescue. See John Watts, *Henry VI and the Politics of Kingship* (Cambridge: 1996).

43 Shagan, 1999, p. 49.

44 For a discussion of the Tudor polity see G.R. Elton, 'Tudor Government: The Points of Contact', in *Studies in Tudor and Stuart Politics and Government*, Vol. 3 (Cambridge: 1983), pp. 3–57, and Guy, 1991, pp. 166–167.

45 'The Council to the ambassadors', in Knighton, 1992, pp. 148–149. It should be noted

that it is possible that the Council were right to be suspicious of the behaviour of Somerset's government during the summer of 1549. See, for example, J.D. Alsop, 'Latimer, the "Commonwealth of Kent" and the 1549 Rebellions', *HJ*, 28 (1983), pp. 379–383.

46 Ernesto Laclau and Lilian Zac, 'Minding the Gap: The Subject of Politics', in *The Making of Political Identities*, ed. Ernesto Laclau (London: 1994), pp. 11–39, p. 22.

47 John Cheke, *The Hurt of Sedition howe greveous it is to a Commune welth* (1549), STC 5109, A.iii (2).

48 Ibid., B.i–B.i (v).

49 MacCulloch, 1986, p. 303. There has been considerable historical debate over the demands of the East Anglian protesters. G.R. Elton suggested that the demands were mainly for agrarian reform, while Barrett L. Beer has argued that the protesters' list of grievances implicitly called for the establishment of more representative local government. See Beer, 1982, p. 111, and Elton, 1977, pp. 348–349.

50 This is particularly unfair to Kett and the leaders of the Mousehold camp, since it appears that they worked to calm the situation and that some of their followers may have held far more radical views than they did.

51 Cheke, 1549, C.iiii (4).

52 Whatever the ultimate aim of the letters that Somerset's regime sent to the protesters, they clearly express an assumption that the two sides, the court and camp, were speaking the same basic language.

53 The events in Münster in 1533–35, and indeed the earlier German Peasants' War, were constant reference points for scaremongering Tudor political writers.

54 MacCulloch in *Tudor Church Militant* points out that the authorities during their inquiries into the commotions were on the look-out for radical egalitarian religious beliefs. See MacCulloch, 1999, pp. 140–141.

55 Nicholas Sotherton, '"The Commoyson in Norfolk, 1549": A Narrative of Popular Rebellion in Sixteenth-Century England', ed. Barrett L. Beer, *Journal of Medieval and Renaissance Studies*, 6 (1979), pp. 73–99, p. 97. Sotherton's reference here to 'faynid prophecies' is probably intended to remind the reader of the notorious letters whose circulation proceeded the Peasants' Revolt of 1381.

56 See Slavoj Žižek, *The Plague of Fantasies* (London: 1997), p. 9.

57 However, as Andy Wood has recently argued, the idea of carnivalesque inversion was an important element in the commotions of 1549. Its presence reflects the extent to which some among the rank and file had a more radical and violent agenda than that of their elder and richer leaders. See Andy Wood, 'Kett's Rebellion and the Piers Plowman tradition', unpublished paper, 2001.

58 The extent to which the events of the summer of 1549 created a crisis within magisterial Protestant ranks can be illustrated by the example of Thomas Smith. *A Discourse of Commonweal* was not his only response to the summer's tumults; writing to William Cecil, he advised that the protector should be severe and that the 'despatch of many of the boisterous would be no loss' (Knighton, 1992, p. 127).

59 These demands suggest that the Norwich protesters would have agreed with Paget when he told Somerset that the people needed instruction, although they contradict the

Secretary's implication that the people would resist such teaching. On the contrary Kett and his followers seem simply to have wanted it to be provided by priests with sufficient skill and learning to properly perform the role.

60 See Sotherton, 1979, pp. 82–85.

61 Ibid., p. 83.

62 Given the way in which Sotherton's narrative deploys carnivalesque tropes that are at times clearly literary, it is sobering to note the extent to which it has been read as a factual record of events in Norwich in 1549 – to do so is to read with same basic social and political assumptions as a mid-Tudor magistrate.

63 Raynball's account books are published in Frederic William Russell's *Kett's Rebellion in Norfolk* (London: 1859), pp. 184–196. The reference to Kett and his followers being 'inkennelled' is on p. 188.

64 Dickie Spurgeon, *Three Tudor Dialogues* (New York: 1978), p. xxviii.

65 This is particularly the case given the nexus of Protestant printers and patrons involved in the production of these texts. See John N. King, 'John Day: Master Printer of the English Reformation', in *The Beginnings of English Protestantism*, eds Peter Marshall and Alec Ryrie (Cambridge: 2002), pp. 180–208.

66 Luke Shepherd, attrib., *John Bon and Mast Person* (1548), STC 3258.5.

67 Ibid., no pag.

68 The use of the ploughman tradition by mid-Tudor polemicists has been discussed in a number of articles. See R.L. Kelly, 'Hugh Latimer as Piers Plowman', *SEL*, 17 (1977), pp. 13–26, and John N. King, *English Reformation Literature: The Tudor Origins of the Protestant Tradition* (Princeton: 1982), pp. 319–339.

69 *John Bon and mast Parson*, 1548, no pag.

70 Ibid., no pag.

71 Ibid., no pag.

72 Obviously the extent to which the Edwardian regime really wanted to encourage people to engage in debate is problematic. This is primarily because the regime adopted contradictory policies in terms of public debate, it removed censorship, presided over a massive increase in the number of works published on all subjects but also issued proclamations that sought to control the amount of discussion over matters of religion.

73 William Punt, *A New Dialogue called the endightment agaynste mother Messe* (1548), STC 20499 printed in Spurgeon, 1978, C.i.

74 *Pathos, or an inward passion of the pope for the losse of hys daughter the masse* (London: 1548), STC 19463, B.ii (5).

75 Peter Moore, *A short treatyse of certayne thinges abused in the Popish Church, long used: But now abolished* (1548), STC 18053, A.ii (v).

76 John Hooper, 'An Answer unto my lord of wynchesters booke intytlyd a dection of the deuyls Sophistrye wherwith he robbith the unlernyd people of the trew byleef in the moost blessyd sacrament of the aulter', in *Early Writings of John Hooper*, ed. Samuel Carr (Cambridge: 1843), pp. 97–247.

77 This apparent rejection of allegory as a form marks an interesting development in English Protestant writing from the relative sophistication of William Tyndale's

acceptance of the power of allegories to teach God's message to the Edwardian characterization of the form as inherently papist.

78 Richard Tracey, *A brief [and] short declaracyon made, wherbye every chrysten man maye knowe, what is a sacrament* (1548), STC 24162, no pagination.

79 Diarmaid MacCulloch has suggested that the Edwardian Reformation 'was a movement of hope and moral fervour, capable of generating a mood of intense excitement, so intense that by 1549 thousands of people over hundreds of square miles in south-east England were prepared to gather in "the camping time"' (MacCulloch, 1999, p. 126).

80 *John Bon and mast Parson*, 1548, no pag. It is perhaps no coincidence that the names of John Bon's horses suggest that they were once monks.

81 Robert Crowley, 'The Printer to the Reader', *The Vision of Pierce Plowman, nowe the seconde tyme imprinted by Roberte Crowlye* (London: 1550), STC 19907, *.ii (v)

82 One exception to this is Ochino's *A Dialogue of the Bishop of Rome*; however, this may be an indication that the readers of this work were expected to be learned people. The length of Ochino's work suggests that it was intended for people with plenty of reading time, although it would be patronizing to assume that this would inevitably restrict the readership of *A Dialogue of the Bishop of Rome*.

83 John N. King, *English Reformation Literature* (Princeton: 1982), p. 337.

84 Robert Crowley, *The Confutation of the mishapen Answer to the misnamed, wicked Ballade, called the Abuse of [the] blessed sacrame[n]t of the aultare. Wherin, thou haste (gentle Reader) the ryghte understandynge of all the places of scripture that Myles Hoggard (wyth his learned counsaill) hath wrested to make transubstanciacion of the bread and wyne* (London: 1548), STC 6082.

85 Ibid., F.v (3v).

86 *The Confutation of the mishapen Answer* is far from being the only mid-Tudor composite text. A work which is as complicated is John Bale, *The Apology of John Bale agaynste a ranke Papyst, answering both hym and hys doctours, that neyther their vowes nor yet their priesthode are of the Gospell, but of Antichrist* (London: 1550), STC 1275.

87 Crowley, 1548, E.i (v).

88 Ibid., A.iii (1).

89 Diarmaid MacCulloch makes the important point: 'The Edwardian Age began as one of glasnost, with the abolition of the heresy laws and the lapse of censorship, and it remained a period where there was an extraordinary degree of theological discussion, both formal and informal' (MacCulloch, 1999, p. 133).

90 The inclusion of large extracts from the work being attacked was common in religious polemics, the most obvious example being Thomas More's various works attacking William Tyndale. The fact that this technique became uncommon after the Henrician Reformation indicates the extent to which this event was uniquely restrictive in terms of public debate.

91 Robert Crowley, *One and Thyrtye Epigrammes, wherin are bryefly touched so many abuses* (London: 1550), STC 6088.3, in *The Select Works of Robert Crowley*, ed. J.M. Cowper, EETS e.s. 15 (London: 1872), pp. 1–52.

92 Ibid., p. 5.

93 Ibid., p. 7.

94 On Skelton's self-construction as an authoritative public poet see Andrew Hadfield, *Literature, Politics and National Identity: Reformation to Renaissance* (Cambridge: 1994), p. 46.

95 For this reason the orthodox literary critical view of Crowley as a medieval is anachronistic. Did any medieval poets comment on the dissolution of the monasteries or on obstinate Papists?

96 Mary Thomas Crane, '*Intret Cato*: Authority and Epigram in Sixteenth-Century England', in *Renaissance Genres: Essays on Theory, History and Interpretation*, ed. Barbara Kiefer Lewalski (Cambridge, Mass.: 1986), pp. 158–188, p. 174.

97 Crowley, 1550, p. 48.

98 Robert Crowley, *The Opening of the Wordes of the Prophet Joell, in his second and third chapters* (London: 1567), STC 6089. Although this work was not published until 1567, it was written in 1546. It opens with a call to repentance and an announcement of the imminent end of the world: 'Repent, repent / I say repent / You misse [and] it amende / Christes prophecie / Doth shew plainely / This world shall shortly ende.' (A.ii).

99 John King and David Norbrook have pointed out that the writers of the mid-Tudor period had an important influence on those that followed them, making the labelling of men like Crowley as medieval potentially profoundly misleading. See King, 1982, and Norbrook, *Poetry and Politics in the English Renaissance* (London: 2002).

100 Robert Crowley, *An Informacion agaynst the oppressors of the pore commons* (London: 1548), STC 6086, A.iii (4).

101 Ibid., A.iiii (v).

102 The radicalism of Crowley's move is clear if one compares his version of friendship with that praised by either Sir Thomas Elyot or the Elizabethan Protestant poet Barnabe Googe.

103 There has been considerable work on humanist friendship in Tudor culture but unfortunately this has largely concentrated on elite understandings of the concept.

104 Robert Crowley, *The Way to Wealth, wherin is taught a remedy for sedicion* (London: 1550), STC 25588 in *The Select Works of Robert Crowley*, ed. J.M. Cowper, EETS e.s. 15 (London: 1872), pp. 129–150.

105 Ibid., p. 132.

106 Ibid., p. 132.

107 Crowley's image of the power of money to destroy boundaries and dissolve social bonds would not be out of place in early writings of Karl Marx.

108 Robert Crowley, *Philargyrie of Greate Britayne* (London: 1551), STC 6089.5.

109 King, 1982, p. 346.

110 Crowley, 1551, A. ii (iv) / A.ii (2).

111 Crowley, 1551, B.ii.

112 King, 1982, p. 350.

113 Crowley, 1551, C.iii (5).

114 Ibid., D.iii (2).

115 Ibid., D.iii (5) / D.iii (5v).

116 Ibid., D.iii (5v).

117 Diarmaid MacCulloch has commented that: 'The events of July 1553 can be seen to some extent as the people's revenge on the aristocracy for the events of the summer of 1549.' (Diarmaid MacCulloch, 'A Rejoinder', *PP*, 93 (1981), pp. 165–73, p. 173).

118 For a concise biography of Baldwin see the Introduction to William Baldwin, *Beware the Cat*, eds William A. Ringler and Michael Flachmann (San Marino, California: 1988).

119 Describing Baldwin's work as a novel is potentially problematic; however, its length, explicit fictionality and narrative complexity means that it needs to be differentiated from other Tudor prose works.

120 Interestingly the actual men mentioned by Baldwin who can be traced do not appear particularly disreputable; however, the text certainly implies that their status is ambiguous.

121 Baldwin, 1988, p. 5.

122 Feuillerat, 1914, p. 142.

123 Robert Crowley, *An Epitome of Cronicles ... continued until the reigne of Elizabeth* (London: 1559), STC 15221, Eeee 2 (1v).

124 Ibid., Eeee 2 (1).

125 Terence N. Bowers, 'The Production and Communication of Knowledge in William Baldwin's *Beware the Cat*: Toward a Typographic Culture', *Criticism*, 33 (1991), 1–29, p. 10.

126 Baldwin, 1988, p. 3.

127 For the importance of these various introductory frames see Edward T. Bonahue, '"I Know the Place and the Persons": The Play of Textual Frames in Baldwin's *Beware the Cat*', *Studies in Philology*, 91 (1994), pp. 283–300.

128 Baldwin, 1988, p. 9. Streamer's words suggest strongly that he is in the house of the noted Protestant printer John Day.

129 Ibid., p. 9.

130 In particular, 1551 saw the first publication in English of Thomas More's *Utopia* whose translator and editor, Ralph Robinson, seems not to have realized that More wrote this work with his tongue firmly in his cheek. John Guy has pointed out that Robinson also reversed More's abolition of social degree in Utopia by adding magistrates, citizens, artificers and workmen. See John Guy, *Thomas More* (London: 2000), p. 93.

131 Nancy A. Gutierrez comments, 'Streamer's convoluted style of speech along with his failure to stay on topic nearly destroys comprehension'. Nancy A. Gutierrez, '*Beware the Cat*: Mimesis in a Skin of Oratory', *Style*, 23 (1989), pp. 49–69, p. 58.

132 Baldwin, 1988, p. 11.

133 Ibid., p. 14.

134 Ibid., pp. 48–49.

135 The extent to which *The Miller's Tale* ends in harmony is of course debatable. However as Lee Patterson has recently pointed out Chaucer goes out of his way in this text to present the world of the fourteenth-century English village as a self-regulating coherent entity. This is not the case with the world Baldwin depicts in Streamer's Third Oration. See Lee Patterson, '"No Man His Reason Herde": Peasant Consciousness,

Chaucer's Miller and the Structure of the Canterbury Tales', in *Chaucer: Contemporary Critical Essays*, eds Valerie Allen and Ares Axiotis (London: 1997), pp. 169–192.

136 R.W. Maslen, *Elizabethan Fictions: Espionage, Counter-Espionage, and the Duplicity of Fiction in Early Elizabethan Prose Narratives* (Oxford: 1997), p. 79.

137 Given that most magisterial Protestants in the mid-Tudor period regarded themselves as Catholics, it would be strange if Baldwin expected his readers to assume an unproblematic connection between cats and Catholics on the basis of the punning connection between the two words. At the same time *Beware the Cat* was produced at precisely the moment when the terms Protestant and Catholic were beginning to be used to label supporters and opponents of the Edwardian reform programme.

138 Maslen, 1997, p. 80.

139 King, 1982, p. 406.

140 Maslen, 1997, p. 79.

141 Andrew Hadfield, *Literature, Travel, and Colonial Writing in the English Renaissance 1545–1625* (Oxford: 1998), p. 146.

142 Annabel Patterson, *Fables of Power: Aesopian Writing and Political History* (Durham, NC: 1991), p. 47.

143 The bluntness of *The Hurt of Sedition* leads it into dangerous ideological waters. For example Cheke tells the Norfolk protesters: '... ye must think that living in a comune wealth together, one kind hath nede of an other and yet a great sort of you more nede of one gentleman, then one gentlema[n] of a great sort of you ...' Of course from a strictly economic point of view Cheke's point is back to front – it took the labour of a large number of Kett and his kind to support one member of the gentry. Indeed, given the order in the East Anglian camps, what is being asserted here yet again is not the need of the commons for gentlemen but the latter's need to be needed by them. John Cheke, *The Hurt of Sedition* (1549), STC 5109, F.iiii (3).

144 Ernesto Laclau, 'The Death and Resurrection of the Theory of Ideology', *MLN*, 112 (1997), pp. 297–321, p. 303. Laclau is using 'closure' here to mean the idea of a community free from social antagonism.

145 Elizabeth L. Eisenstein, *The Printing Press as an Agent of Change* (Cambridge: 1979), p. 251.

146 Folly claims, 'the whole of human life is nothing but a sport for folly'. Clearly Baldwin's cats could make an identical claim. Desiderius Erasmus, *Praise of Folly*, trans. Betty Radice, intro. A.H.T. Levi (London 1993), p. 42.

147 It is possible that its publication in this year was part of the Elizabethan establishment's polemical response to the Northern Rebellion. Certainly a number of other existing but unprinted potentially anti-Catholic texts were printed in response to the events of 1570. However, it is as likely that the printer of this first edition was simply trying to cash in on a vogue for anti-Catholic satire.

148 Baldwin, 1988, pp. 37, 50.

149 David Loades, *The Reign of Mary Tudor: Politics, Government and Religion in England 1553–58* (London: 1991), p. 97.

Chapter 3

Writing the Marian Reformation

> I have in my hands the chief thing that Christ gave me for your salvation ... I have the very special law of mankind. For there is need of this special law if you are to attain your salvation. This special law, however, is such that God did not even grant it to the angels who had sinned. But why do I delay in showing this? First of all, do penance! (Reginald Pole, *De Unitate Ecclesiastica*, 1536)[1]

Cardinal Pole regarded the Henrician Reformation as both a crime and a scandal. Not only did it make the English Church schismatic, but, as Pole pointed out, it placed an ungodly combination of temporal and spiritual authority in Henry's hands. The tone of *De Unitate Ecclesiastica*, however, makes it clear that, although Pole regarded the events of the 1530s as sacrilegious, he also thought their inspiration was ultimately frivolous: Henry's infantile desire to have things all his own way. Throughout *De Unitate Ecclesiastica* Pole assumes the role of a firm but fair teacher dealing with a truculent child who cannot grasp even the basic principles of Christian teaching.[2] When twenty years later, as Papal Legate, Pole returned to England with the task of rescuing the English Church from schism and heresy, he again took upon himself the role of school-master. In this case, however, the task was far greater and more daunting. Now the school-room was the entire realm and Pole had to instruct, not simply an errant boy, but a whole commonwealth of errant believers. Addressing the citizens of London in November 1557, he compared their desire to keep the wealth plundered from the Church during the preceding reigns to the actions of a small boy who, having stolen an apple, refuses to return it even though he knows that eating it will make him ill.[3] Pole did not, however, see either his role or that of his fellow clergymen as simply that of teachers. The Henrician Reformation was too serious a crime against the Christian Church to be remedied with simple instruction. It was for Pole and the rest of the Marian clergy as preachers and prophets, to demand that the English give up their infantile infatuation with heresy. It was their duty to call upon the people of England to repent, to put off their false idols and return to the sharp and difficult path of the true religion before it was too late. Pole conceived of the Marian Reformation as a collective act of penance in which the entire English nation was brought to recognize and repent the sins it had committed since the 1530s.[4]

Pole's insistence that penance was an essential element in the restoration of the English Church from its heretical schismatic state was shared by other leading members of Mary Tudor's regime. Stephen Gardiner, Bishop of Winchester, made sense of his often difficult experiences and controversial actions under Henry and Edward by using images of sleep, exile and dreams. His Advent sermon of 1554 is exemplary in this regard.[5] In this text Gardiner used the trope of sleep to suggest that the religious changes of the 1530s and 1540s took place without his conscious knowledge, as though he had been in a dream, a nightmare, for the last fifteen years and was only now waking from it.[6] He told his audience:

> It is time for us ... to wake – not the Queen, nor the King, nor my lord cardinal, who have never fallen asleep – but for us, us – I do not exclude myself from this number. I acknowledge my fault, and exhort all who have fallen into this sleep through me or with me, with me to awake![7]

Gardiner's use of sleep as a metaphor to explain his role in the religious changes of the 1530s and 1540s appears at first sight to undermine Pole's emphasis on penance. Can one, or perhaps more importantly, should one be held responsible for things that one commits in one's dreams? Indeed the central conceit of Gardiner's sermon, that he and the country had sleep-walked through the 1530s and 1540s, is at one level designed to write over, or dream away, the complexities and compromises of those years.[8] It would be a mistake, however, to see, as some historians have, a basic division between the unworldly radicalism of Pole and the pragmatism of men like Gardiner. Despite his construction of the Henrician and Edwardian Reformations as nightmares, dreamt in the uneasy sleep of heresy, Gardiner's sermon does not shy away from the need to ask for penance – Gardiner publicly and unambiguously acknowledges his fault. The Marian Reformation was, like those of the Queen's father and brother, an act of state and faith; it needed both spiritual and political leadership.

This chapter is in three parts. The first section briefly examines the historiography of the Marian Reformation before moving on to look in detail at number of key cultural and literary issues of the period 1553–58. In particular, three of the themes reflected in Gardiner's 1554 sermon will be discussed: the self, the social effects of Reformation, and Marian approaches to the interpretation of texts. What did Gardiner mean when he claimed in his Advent sermon that ceremonies were the candles to proper religious understanding? This chapter will then move on in its second and third sections to discuss in detail the work of John Heywood and Miles Hogarde. These writers can be seen as central to the Marian regime's attempts to create its own literary culture. Heywood's work embodies an anti-Reformation agenda that seeks to escape from the violent cultural effects of the religious changes of the 1530s, 1540s and 1550s. The work of his fellow Marian poet, Miles Hogarde, however, takes a very different approach to Reformation poetics. Hogarde's work, perhaps for the first time in English, expresses an explicitly confessional Catholic sensibility defined against Protestantism. Heywood wrote against the baneful effects of religious labels on English culture. In the process he reproduced one of the central planks of the Marian Reformation – the need for reconciliation and peace after the upheavals of the preceding twenty years. Hogarde's work, however, reflects the other side of the religious agenda of Mary's regime with its insistence on the importance of penance and its constant division of the world into the saved and damned. Ironically it is Hogarde, in his highly conscious and deliberate return to fifteenth-century poetic tropes and norms, who is the more modern of these two writers, his return to the past acknowledging the profound and traumatic effects of the Henrician and Edwardian Reformations. Heywood wrote for Gardiner's dreamers – Hogarde for Pole's prophets.

THE MARIAN REFORMATION AND ITS POETICS

Few periods of English history can have been portrayed so differently by modern historians as the reign of Mary Tudor. In one camp are scholars of the stature of G.R. Elton and A.G. Dickens for whom the period 1553–58 was at best a hiatus in the triumphant match of Protestantism and at worst a tragedy without any positive results.[9] On the other side historians such as Christopher Haigh and Eamon Duffy have recently argued that Mary's reign saw a real and potentially lasting return to pre-Edwardian Reformation religion in England.[10] One thing that has become clear from recent work is that the Marian regime's religious agenda was far from a simple return to the past. For example, historians and literary critics have argued that the conservatism of Mary's government led it to neglect print as a tool of government propaganda.[11] The evidence for this apparent failure is the relative paucity of Catholic polemical works printed between 1553–1558. Duffy, however, has pointed out that the regime of Mary Tudor as a matter of policy tried to move away from the kind of polemical writing that was produced during Edward VI's reign. He writes that the Marian regime did not see the 'blustering scurrilities' of their opponents as the best models 'for establishing truth and stabilising the religious life of the people'.[12] Duffy's argument illustrates a wider historiographical point which is the importance of studying the period 1553–1558 in its own right, and not simply in terms of its relation to the Protestantization of England. The Marian Reformation was a vital element in the confessional-ization of England. Like the reformations of the Queen's father and brother it aspired to fundamentally change the religious life of the English people, principally by restoring the mass and healing the schism with the papacy. As part of this reforming agenda the Marian Reformation produced its own cultural poetics – which continued to have an influence on Tudor literature long after 1558.

The Marian Church pursued a clericalist agenda of social and religious reform in the context of tensions over the relationship between clerical and temporal power. A key aspect of its clericalism was its commitment to the pastoral labour of ensuring religious orthodoxy and the pursuit of heresy.[13] It is the treatment of heretics / Protestants during Mary's reign that has been central to its historical reputation. Again it is possible, if a bit simplistic, to divide the historiographical tradition between those who have stressed the fundamental importance of the approximately 300 Protestants killed for their beliefs between 1553 and 1558 and those historians who have argued that their deaths were relatively insignificant or uncontroversial.[14] Not surprisingly it tends to be the same historians who are critical of Mary's religious policies who stress the importance of the Protestant martyrs, while those who argue that the Marian Reformation was potentially successful have a tendency to play down its persecutory aspects.[15] However both these approaches are prob-lematic. The Marian Reformation looked back to policies of the queen's father and forward to the process of Catholic confessionalization embraced at the Council of Trent. It is this dual focus that gives the reign its fractured appear-ance and partly accounts for the tragedy of the Marian persecution. Dickens has pointed out that it is almost certainly inaccurate to suggest, as has been, that many of those burnt to death for their beliefs under Mary would have suffered a similar fate at the hands of the Church of England had Edward VI survived.[16] Certainly the Elizabethan Church displayed a marked desire not to create religious martyrs before the 1580s. It would, however, be far more accurate to point out that most of those who suffered under Mary would also have done so under Henry VIII, who constantly exhibited a willingness to persecute anyone who rejected or even questioned his own extremely orthodox view of the mass.[17] The world had, however, moved on since 1547. Pursuing a Henrician policy as regards heresy in 1553–1558 inevitably meant that many more people were likely to be caught up in the inquisitorial process. Andrew Pettegree has argued that in a European context the Marian persecution appears 'intense and somewhat anachronistic'.[18] Indeed the policy of pursuing Protestants to death sat problematically with the Marian regime's emphasis on the restoration of order and the acceptance by a number of its leading figures, perhaps particularly Bishop Bonner, of the need actively to pursue

Catholic confessionalization.[19] On one hand Mary's apologists celebrated her as the restorer of peace and characterized her realm as a time of reconciliation, while on the other writers like Miles Hogarde or Leonard Pollard depicted Marian England as a battlefield on which the forces of truth and light were engaged in a fight to the death with ignorance, sin and heresy.

In his Advent sermon of 1554 Stephen Gardiner emphasized the need for his hearers, and himself, to wake from the dream of heresy. In the process he gave voice to the emphasis in the Marian period on escaping the heretical state, at the level of individual, community and realm. Gardiner, and other Marian writers, argued that being in a state of heresy meant one was simultaneously in danger of slipping into a state of sophistic individualism *and* of losing oneself in heresy's entanglements. Ultimately it meant being damned to an eternity in hell. Heretics oscillated between an insistence on the self to the detriment of all else – Church, state, family and society – and a collapse of self into the oblivion of heresy.[20] This understanding of the heretical state could be applied across categories, from the individual to the church and state. For example, Gardiner argued that England during the Edwardian period was a dream realm. In his Advent sermon Gardiner told his audience:

> Now ... it is time we awake out of our sleep, who have slept or rather dreamed these twenty years past. For as men intending to sleep do separate themselves from company and desire to be alone, even so we have separated ourselves from the See of Rome, and have been alone, no realm in Christendom like us; as in sleep men dream of killing, maiming, burning, and such beastliness as I dare not name, so among us one brother has destroyed another, half our money has been wiped away at one time, those who would defend their conscience have been slain or troubled; as in sleep all senses are stopped, so the ceremonies of the Church, which were instituted to move our senses, were taken away; as the candle is put out when a man would sleep.[21]

It is noticeable that Gardiner refers here specifically to the monetary cost of the Henrician and Edwardian Reformations. He also stresses the importance of the papal supremacy and ceremonies to the establishment of true religion in England. Above all Gardiner's words apply the trope of sleep across a number of registers – individual, state and church – conjuring up an image of a sleeping, but not resting, England. Instead the realm is fixed or caught in a violent dream, with each individual member of the commonwealth lost without the light of the Church's ceremonies or the company of the See of Rome. Without Church or Papacy, the schismatic English, and Gardiner clearly included himself in this group, could not awake and escape their violent dreams.

The Marian regime legitimatized itself as an awakening from the nightmare of heresy; a return to pre-Protestant order and quiet. This did not mean, however, as has already been suggested, that its religious policies were simply reactive to the Henrician and Edwardian Reformations. It was not possible to return to the past, and supporters of the Marian Reformation knew this. This is why they constantly produced texts which symbolically enacted the defeat of heresy and the restoration of true religion. Gardiner's sermon, with sleep as a metaphor for heresy, was just one of the many ways in which supporters of Mary Tudor sought to legitimate the Marian Reformation. Another key trope deployed by Mary's supporters to support her religious policies was an emphasis on heresy's corrupt reading and interpretative practices. This took a number of forms but the effect was the development of what could be called a Marian poetic which rejected both the Edwardian Reformation's emphasis on reading iconoclastically and the convoluted inquisitorial hermeneutic of the Henrician court. Instead Marian culture emphasized the need to withdraw the self from the reading process and privileged the social realm as an arena for textual interpretation. This meant that smashing the text to find its kernel or pawing over it to penetrate its secrets were rejected as proper or useful models of textual interpretation during Mary's reign. Instead Marian writers empha-sized the importance of respecting the integrity of the text itself. This new emphasis forms the basis of the advice given to the reader in the preface to one of the Marian editions of Stephen Hawes' *Pastime of Pleasure*.[22] The central argument of this Address to the Reader is that *The Pastime of Pleasure*, simply because of the kind of text it is, can teach its readers without inciting a dangerous level of curiosity in them.[23] It argues:

> by the secrete inspiracion of almighty God (all men in general) so insaciately thirsteth for the knowledge of wisdome and learnyng, that some for the very earnest desire therof (though nature grudgeth) cease not to spend their dayes and houres, with such co[n]tinuall and importune trauayle in sekynge the same, that hauyng no regarde to the ouer pressyng of Nature ... do sodainely bryng forth their owne confusion. Some contrariwise ... beyng discomforted wyth painefull [and] tedious study, rather chose to be drowned in the stinkyng floude of ignoraunce.[24]

This passage appears to present the reader with two equally unappetising approaches to learning: either one can give up and sink into ignorance or lose one's way by over-pressing nature.[25] The Address, however, goes on to suggest a third option, which is 'to sayle (wyth a by wynde) into the pleasaunt Islande of wisdome and science' with *The Pastime of Pleasure*.[26] The writer of the Address argues that, by reading Hawes' poem, 'thou mayest easelye fynde (as it were in pastyme) wythout offence of nature that thyng ... which many great clarkes wythout great paynes and trauayle ... coulde neuer obteyne nor get'.[27] In 1554 Hawes was understood by his Marian editors as an exemplary poet for the present and future, a modern, perhaps even a postmodern, writer whose text illustrated the way forward from the mistakes of the immediate past. In particular, *The Pastime of Pleasure* is represented as offering its reader the possibility of learning that escapes the dangers of ignorance or excessive curiosity.

Hawes' Marian editors clearly felt *The Pastime of Pleasure* could protect against the twin dangers of overemphasizing the role of the author or the individual reader in the production of meaning. Indeed the idea that one could misread by 'over-pressing nature' seems to be almost directed at the hermeneutics implicit in the writing of such poets as Crowley and Wyatt since both these writers, albeit in very different ways, produced texts that incited iconoclastic or inquisitorial models of reading, requiring readers to press texts to produce their meaning.[28] In the Address to *The Pastime of Pleasure*, Hawes' Marian editors were, however, simply applying to a poetic work ideas concerning interpretation and the role of the self developed in the anti-Protestant writings of leading members of the Marian regime. Pole in his sermon to the London citizens in 1557 told his audience:

> in sekynge God, if you hope to fynde him, you sholde utterlye leave your owne wyll, which restethe speciallye in ii poyntes: the one in the desyre of more knowledge than God hath lymyted unto us: wheryn our fyrste moother fyrste dyd disobeye: And the other poynt is touchinge the carnall pleasure of the bodye.[29]

Leonard Pollard argued that heresy's ultimate cause was the desire of individuals to produce their own knowledge of God. He wrote:

> the originall cause of heresy is the truste that man hath in his owne wytte, that is bycause he thynketh that he knoweth gods worde better, or hath a deeper syght in gods mysteries then other men haue, therfore choseth he to hym self a pryuate, and a newe understandynge of gods worde.[30]

Pollard's emphasis on heresy's private nature reproduces one of the central arguments of More's *Dialogue concerning Heresies* and harks back to Germen Gardynare's representation of John Frith in his *A letter of a younge gentleman*. It also illustrates the commitment of Marian writers to the idea that truthful interpretation was inherently public and communal. Not surprisingly, this led them to emphasize the role of ceremonies in the Church, not only in terms of their intrinsic worth but also because they were an essential aid to a proper understanding of Christ's teaching. Pole argued that 'the observatyon of ceremonyes, for obedyence sake, wyll gyue more light than all readynge of Scrypture can doe'.[31] It is important to notice that Pole's words here embody a hermeneutic that matches that advocated in the Address to the Reader printed as a preface to Hawes' *The Pastime of Pleasure*. In both cases what is emphasized is the requirement that one suspend the desire to know and that instead one is obedient, and therefore open, to the communal production of meaning.

The Marian emphasis on the suspension of the will or self in the production of meaning was articulated through a number of tropes. One important one was the distinction between true and false paths. John Christopherson in his work, *An Exhortation to all Menne to … Beware of Rebellion*, argued that heretics, having ignored the Church, the location of true religion, are engaged in a hopeless journey, during which 'they fynde many bywayes, [and] one sayeth this is the waye and another sayeth, that is the waye, and the thirde fyndeth the thirde waye, and euerye one taketh his owne waye'.[32] For Christopherson heresy was aimless but also productive. It created a meaning-less maze of false ways that all led away from God. Marian writers consistently emphasized the destructive and privatizing nature of heresy in relation to the teaching of the Church and, in particular, as regards its fabric, symbolic and literal. John Gwynnethe, a veteran anti-Protestant writer, in his dialogue between a Catholic and a heretic had the former ask the latter:

> How have thei [the heretics] handled the semeless garment of Christe? Not castynge lottes for the whole (as his persecutors did) to save the unitee therof: But a thousande folde wors, snatchyng at the parts therof, to tere, rent, [and] destroy it all together.[33]

It was, however, Miles Hogarde who gave this idea its most powerful expres-sion at the end of his poem, *The assault of the sacrame[n]t of the Altar*, in the image of Cranmer tearing at the teaching of the Church's doctors with his teeth, ripping it out of their books to chew into pellets and spit at Lady Faith.[34] Hogarde's argument here can be related to the Marian critique of the Protestant rejection of unwritten verities since, as far as people like Hogarde were concerned, this had the effect of destroying the fabric of the Church.[35]

Thomas Martin in his work, *A Treatise declaryng and plainly prouyng, that the pretended marriage of Priestes, and professed persones, is no marriage, but altogether unlawfull*, argued that the way Protestants approached scripture was inher-ently reductive.[36] He asserted that 'Gods word was written long time in mens hartes before it was written in bookes'.[37] Martin went on to argue that, 'the scripture it selfe cannot geue sentence, for asmuch as it can not speake nor heare'.[38] One of the things that Martin is criticizing here was the tendency among Protestants to argue that in some way scripture was open, plain and self-interpreting. For Martin the idea that scripture could interpret itself, or indeed that it could be limited to the printed or written word of the Bible, was one of the worst fallacies of Protestantism. He argues:

> If we doe reiect and sette aside customes and unwritten verities as vnprofitable or of no force and authoritie, we shal condemne imprudently many things that be necessary in the Gospel, for our salvation. Yea, we shall bringe the verye prechyng of our faith, but to a bare, [and] only name.[39]

Martin's argument reproduces very similar ideas articulated by other supporters of the Marian Reformation, including Gardiner and Pole.[40] As such it can be regarded as exemplary in terms of the regime's understanding of the relation-ship between Christ, the church and true Christian teaching. It is difficult to think of a clearer illustration of the difference between mid-Tudor Catholicism and Protestantism. While magisterial Protestants like Crowley or Bale argued that individual reading of the Bible was efficacious in itself, the Marian Reformation regarded this activity as at best of limited value, producing a restricted and reduced understanding of Christ's message, and at worst as inherently dangerous and almost inevitably leading to heresy.

In place of the Protestant emphasis on individual Bible reading, Marian writers stressed the role of the church as the keeper and propagator of Christ's message. Martin argues: 'many necessarye matters there be unwritten whiche were taught only by mouth, by christ to his apostles by thapostles to the church, by the churche to all christian people from age to age'.[41] Martin's defence of unwritten verities has important hermeneutic implications, since it suggests real limitations on the interpretative scope of individual readers and specific texts, even the Bible. Supporters of Mary Tudor's religious policies used gender-specific imagery to argue that the feminine Church, and by association Mary herself, were the proper guardians of a religious truth that was beyond man's reason. James Brooks argued that the Catholic Church was the mother of the Scripture, 'Whose pappes are the two Testamentes: Whose milke is the true sence of the word of God: Out of those her pappes onelye to be sucked, of al christian suckinges.'[42]

Brooks went on to develop this analogy, arguing:

> Even as all women have geue[n] unto theim by nature, sence to discerne the good temperature of their owne pappes, from the distemperature of the same, so hath the Church geuen her by God, authoritie to discerne the true Scriptures from the forged ...[43]

John Proctor used similar imagery when recommending to his fellow countrymen that they renounce the malicious harlot, heresy, and:

> Come home to this swete nourse [the loving mother church], that you maye sucke from her brestes the holsome foode of your soules healthe and comforte: and leave the stinkinge carren wherwith this whore feedeth you.[44]

Proctor's and Brooks' maternal imagery has important implications in terms of the poetics of the Marian Reformation.[45] The implication of their work was that the Church, naturally but at one level passively, would feed her children the milk of scripture without them having to do anything other than love her. The only really active person in this loving exchange of Christian teaching was Christ himself, whose teaching was what made the Church's milk nourishing.[46] The believer's role as imagined by these writers is that of a child instinctively sucking true teaching from their loving mother. Scriptural reading in this imagery is compared to the natural behaviour of an infant. In this exchange there is no room for interpretation or even the use of reason. Indeed to attempt to make sense of this exchange would be either foolish or to 'over-press nature' in a pointless desire to explain something clearly beyond or outside the scope of man's reason.

In the field of poetry one of the most interesting responses to the hermeneutics being advocated by writers like Proctor and Books is the collection of poems published in 1557 entitled *Songs and Sonettes written by the ryght honourable Lorde Henry Howard late Earle of Surrey, and other*, better known as *Tottel's Miscellany*.[47] Literary critics have long regarded the publication of this collection of Henrician court poetry as a key moment for Tudor poetry. Wendy Wall argues that with this publication Tottel 'changed the literary landscape and established the English lyric'.[48] The collection's Marian provenance has, however, received very little comment. This is unfortunate since in many ways *Tottel's Miscellany* is an exemplary Marian text. Its valorization of native English writing is a common polemical trope of Mary Tudor's reign and relates directly to the idea that the Queen's succession presaged the reassertion of England's sovereignty against the foreign corruption of Protestantism.[49] The publication of *Tottel's Miscellany* also illustrates the influence of the Henrician period on the culture of Mary's reign, however, with a number of significant differences. Above all Tottel in his editorship subtly but fundamentally changes the nature of the lyrics he publishes by giving them titles and 'tidying' their verse forms. The effect of these changes is to emphasize their status as public poetic texts, concerned less with the individual poet and more with such general themes as love or worldly success.[50] For example, Wyatt's sonnet, 'The pillar perished', often now read as a comment on the fall of Thomas Cromwell, is entitled in *Tottel's Miscellany*, 'The louer lamentes the death of his loue'. This has the effect of relating the poem to the generic theme of love and distancing the poem's relationship to its author as the idiosyncratic and individual source of its meaning. In the process Tottel subverts Wyatt's Henrician hermeneutic, replacing complexity and the individual, poet and reader, at the centre of the poem's meaning with the text itself, and in particular its formal consistency.[51] Giving all the poems titles and placing them in his Address to the Reader within a specific courtly setting also reduces the role of the author. Tottel's editorship at one level creates the outline of a narrative for the lyrics that make up the collection and in the process emphasizes social and generic context over the role of the individual author in terms of a poem's meaning. His rigorous application of iambic pentameter as an authorising poetic norm in this miscellany, 'correcting' poems that failed to keep to its rules, also has the effect of privileging the generic over the idiosyncracies of individual poets and their texts. In *Tottel's Miscellany*, linguistic and poetic order is privileged in a way that one can compare to the Marian Church's emphasis on ceremonies as the basis for the proper understanding of scripture. In both cases the effect was to downplay the active role of the individual, reader or believer, and emphasize the generic and social.[52]

The Marian Reformation developed an understanding of how texts should be read that was deeply sceptical of man's reason. It did this in response to the religious and cultural changes of the Henrician and Edwardian Reformations. This does not, however, make the culture of Mary's reign inherently backward or conservative. Instead one should see it as mounting a sophisticated challenge to the interpretative norms established during the preceding twenty years. Marian culture stressed the integrity of the text and withdrawal of the self, that of the reader and writer, from the process of interpretation. This had particular implications in terms of poetry since the existing dominant poetical modes valorized forms of penetrative and iconoclastic reading which emphasized the role of the individual, author and reader. The two leading writers of this period, John Heywood and Miles Hogarde, responded to this poetic agenda in very different ways. Heywood in his writings of the 1550s produced texts that in various ways resisted the kind of interpretative strategies demanded by the work of such writers as Wyatt and Crowley. Hogarde's response to the poetics of the Marian Reformation was, however, in some ways more radical, since what one sees in his work is a conscious attempt to rethink past poetic forms and tropes in the context of an emerging confessional English Catholic sensibility.

JOHN HEYWOOD'S ANTI-REFORMATION WRITING

John Heywood was a well-known playwright during the reign of Henry VIII producing a number of plays during the 1520s and 1530s.[53] In this period he also married into the family of John Rastell. His wife was the niece of Sir Thomas More. Given these family connections it is not surprising that Heywood's writing consistently adopts anti-Protestant positions. It is also, however, explicitly anti-confessional, consistently arguing for moderation and the pursuit of a mean as a way of escaping the conflicts produced by the Reformation. Heywood's writing career took a new direction in 1550 when he produced a collection of one hundred epigrams. This was the same year in which Crowley published his *One and Thyrtye Epigrammes, wherin are bryefly touched so many abuses.* Heywood went on to produce another five hundred epigrams which he published at intervals throughout the rest of his life. During the reign of Mary Tudor, besides *Two hundred Epigrammes* (1553) and *The Spider and Fly* (1556), Heywood also published a number of poems on topical events.

John Heywood's mid-Tudor writing has been largely neglected by literary critics. C.S. Lewis seems to have been appalled by most of it, in particular the epigrams. Lewis' distaste for mid-Tudor or, as he called it, 'drab' poetry is well known. Heywood's sin, as far was Lewis was concerned, was that not only was he a drab poet but he persisted in his drabness from choice and not from lack of talent.[54] Lewis dismissed Heywood because he did not fit into his account of literary change and development during the sixteenth century. This would have little relevance today, were it not for the fact that most contemporary literary critics still seem to be working, albeit tacitly, within critical parameters created by Lewis. Mary Thomas Crane has recently criticized literary criticism for focusing on a very small canon of Tudor poetry based largely on the way it articulates 'a self-expressive speaking voice'. She comments:

> The Derridean deconstruction of presence, the Freudian theory of the 'partitioned subject', the Marxist critique of bourgeois individualism, and the New Historicist focus on the cultural determinants of selfhood have not shaken our conviction that the most interesting and valuable poems of the sixteenth century are engaged in expressing a 'fully present' self.[55]

The writing of the reign of Mary Tudor has suffered a disproportionate neglect from this ahistorical and under-theorised concentration on the poetry of the self.[56] This is because, as has been suggested, Marian culture explicitly rejected the emphasis of Henrician and Edwardian Reformation literature upon the self, writer and reader, as the centre and producer of meaning.

Heywood's two major Marian works, *Two hundred Epigrammes* and *The Spider and Fly*, are anti-confessional works. Their target is not so much Protestantism itself as the forms of reading and writing that reformation as a process seemed to demand. Having published his first epigrams in 1550, the same year that Crowley produced his, Heywood published his second, and far larger, collection *Two hundred Epigrammes* in 1553, quite possibly as a direct response to Crowley's work.[57] Indeed Heywood's epigrams are a critique of the kind of prophetic public role claimed by poets like Crowley. This is not, however, because of a lack of scope or ambition in terms of topics discussed. *Two hundred Epigrammes* is as much a product of print culture as *One and Thyrtye Epigrammes*. In Crowley's case print is a vehicle for propagating his reforming message. Heywood, however, uses it to celebrate popular wisdom. His epigrams can be seen as an eruption of the wisdom of the street and market-place, of the wit of Mouse-slayer and her fellow cats, into the public sphere. Not only do they open with a popular saying, tag or comment, they also fail to contain, or inkennel, the popular wisdom expressed in these opening phrases. Heywood resists the temptation to use popular culture simply to allow him to display a sophisticated mocking 'reforming' magisterial voice. *Two hundred Epigrammes* subverts the norms of Tudor epigram writing from two directions. Humanist epigrams, such as those produced by Thomas More, tended to be based on Greek or Latin tags, while Protestant writers like Crowley retained the humanist emphasis on epigrams as didactic, but made them more explicitly topical. Heywood's poems simply deny the possibility of learning anything serious through the reading of epigrams.[58]

Two Hundred Epigrammes presents its reader with a potentially bewildering textual world in which one searches in vain for a point of order or authority. It is as though one has been dumped into the world of Baldwin's cats without Streamer as a guide. However the ideological message of Heywood's work is quite different to that of *Beware the Cat*. Heywood's text is a celebration of the popular and its valorization against the claims of Protestants, humanists and, by implication, confessionalized Catholicism. In *Two Hundred Epigrammes* the popular is constructed neither as needing reform nor simply as the material for comment; instead it is presented as a world of plenitude, of a wisdom that is in tune with the ups and downs of the world, one opposed to grandiose and totalizing world views. In particular, Heywood's epigrams express a Marian scepticism that reason or book-learning had anything to teach popular culture, or that the world of the street and market-place did not have its own valid wit and wisdom. When Protestant, and for that matter humanist, reformers looked up from their books they saw a world in dire need of order and reform; Heywood instead saw one of balance, harmony and laughter. Epigram 128 is entitled Measure.

> Measure is a merry mean.
> Which, filled with noppy drink,
> When merry drinkers drink off clean
> Then merrily they wink.[59]

Measure in Tudor culture implied order and moderation. Heywood's epigram subverts this meaning, implying that measure is relative: if filled with drink it will produce drunkenness. However, this is not the end of measure's epigrammatic journey. Heywood produces nine additional verses on measure, all entitled 'Otherwise'. The obvious joke here is that an epigram on measure is measureless. Initially these poems stay with the theme of drink.

> Otherwise (2)
> Measure is a merry mean,
> But inch, foot, yard, or ell,
> Those measure are not worth a bean;
> They measure no drink well.[60]

However, as the epigrams pile up their aim changes. In Otherwise 7 Heywood appears to be commenting on the ambiguous position of married clergy under Mary Tudor.[61]

> Measure is a merry mean:
> And measure is thy mate
> To be a deacon, or a dean:
> Thou wouldst not change the state.[62]

In Otherwise 9 Heywood seems to be reflecting on his own writing.

> Measure is a merry mean:
> In volumes full or flat;
> There is no chapter, nor no scene
> That thou appliest like that.[63]

With both these verses it is, however, hard to work out quite what is being said. In Otherwise 7 does 'state' mean clerical position or marriage? Or is the poem simply criticising those clergy who constantly seek to take a middle way in order to further their careers? Otherwise 9 is as opaque. Who does 'thou' refer to? Presumably the reader, but if this is the case the implication of the poem is that Heywood's readers are all incapable of reading with measure. It may be that 'thou' in this context should be related to those readers, implicitly Protestants, whose reading was not measured, who sought to 'over-press nature'. But this is far from clear. What these epigrams reflect is the limitations of Heywood's poetic agenda in the context of the Marian Reformation. Religious polemics and the advancement of a reform agenda required confessional texts that did take sides, that claimed to be authoritative and saw the world in black and white. Heywood's poetic vision was in some ways too generous and humane, it did not fit in a Reformation world of violent of religious controversy, persecution and confessionalization.[64]

Similar issues are raised by Heywood's other major work of the period 1553–58, *The Spider and Fly*, which is an allegorical poetic history of the Edwardian Reformation. It recounts the events that follow the ensnarement of a fly, 'the best and most luckiest of flies', in a spider's web. *The Spider and Fly* tells how the spiders and flies seek to resolve their differences through debate, law and finally battle. At the end of the poem, however, a completely new note is struck when the maid of the house appears, sweeping away cobwebs and killing the chief spider. The maid is explicitly equated with Mary and it is only at this point that it is made clear that the chief spider is a figure for a leading Protestant, probably Northumberland but possibly Cranmer.

The Spider and Fly starts by insisting upon its limits, even failures, as a text: its inability within its own symbolic order to solve the problems and conflicts it reflects. This is entirely compatible with Heywood's commitment to the Marian scepticism concerning man's reason. *The Spider and Fly* opens with an extended preface centred upon a parable concerning three women, Madge, Meg and Marion, and their inability to see the faults in their own appearance while being prepared to mock those of their fellows. Heywood then extends this parable to include the readers of his poem, writing:

> As glass lookers looked, if book readers look,
> He upon him, and he on him, to scan
> Since most and best, nay most and worst they can,
> Scanning who is spider, who the fly,
> Neither of either to himself t'apply;

> Scanning no whit, by scanning here to see,
> In case spiders, in case flies, all scanned may be,
> Glass looking and book reading, in such wise
> May well be scanned one like vain exercise.
> Who that this parable doth thus define,
> This parable thus is his and not mine.[65]

Heywood here is warning his readers against adopting precisely the kind of interpretative strategy advocated by Edwardian writers like Robert Crowley. Indeed to seek to read *The Spider and Fly* on an interrogative or iconoclastic basis, of breaking the nut for the kernel or over-pressing nature, would be to scan oneself into the poem as either a spider or a fly. It is only by resisting the temptation to pin specific historical meaning onto the struggle between the spiders and flies, a temptation, moreover, that Heywood's text consistently incites, that one can fully understand the poem.

Having established how he wants his poem to be read, Heywood embarks on the main body of his text. Chapter 1 of the poem opens with the narrator witnessing a fly being caught in a spider's net. Each of the poem's chapters is accompanied with a woodcut illustrating in detail the events that the chapter will discuss. Typically these woodcuts depict the narrator sitting at his desk watching the action taking place in the window that occupies the vast majority of the image. The poem opens with an invocation of *The Canterbury Tales* as the narrator walks through the spring countryside and then moves inside with the narrator observing a lustful fly being caught in a spider's web. Having been trapped, the Fly goes on to lament his fate: 'Alas, alas, alas and wellaway! / To cry aloud, alas! What cause have I! / Alas (I say) that ever I saw this day!'[66] Clearly at this early stage in the work it would be inappropriate to seek to identify the caught Fly with any specific historical figures, since the Fly's sudden fall is arbitrary and natural. As Heywood's poem progresses, however, it seems to get more historically specific and it certainly becomes far more complex. The Fly disputes the Spider's right to build his cobwebs in the centre of the window and the two creatures engage in a lengthy debate involving such issues as – did the Fly of his own will get caught in the Spider's web, who has the freehold of window holes (an interesting concept in itself given that the debate at this point suggests it is possible to have a freehold over nothing or air) and whether their dispute should be tried by common law or custom. These discussions are replete with the language of Tudor social commentary and indeed of Edwardian commonwealth writers, perhaps particularly Crowley in *The Way to Wealth*. They are also completely circular and sterile in terms of resolving the debate between the Fly and Spider. At one point in this debate the Fly critiques the relationship between spiders and flies as a form of social stratification.

And yet (I say) in bending our knees to fall:
Flies looking like lams: spiders lyke lions looke.
As though poore flies, were made for rich spiders all.
Of which: though foolish flies: for suffrance may brooke:
Wise flies can not brooke it: for thei finde in booke:
This demand written. When Adam dolue and Eue span,
Who was in those golden daies, a gentleman.[67]

Heywood here is playing with his reader's expectations and any desire they may have to use their knowledge of history to understand his poem. What are we meant to make of the Fly quoting John Ball's notorious saying – 'When Adam delved and Eve span, Who was then a gentleman?' Is the Fly a lower-class radical? Or is he simply using these words to score a polemical point? None of these questions are answered by the text. The fact that Heywood's Fly has read Ball's words in a book, and now readers of *The Spider and Fly* are doing the same, may be a critique of history itself as a source of practical learning. The Fly's knowledge of history, like that of the reader, does not help to solve social conflict, to decide who owns the holes in windows or escape fate; it is redundant in terms of producing either justice or meaning.

As the text progresses, it starts to reflect more closely specific events from the Edwardian period. Eventually the Spider and Fly agree to appoint two arbitrators, an Ant and a Butterfly, who are asked to hear and judge the case. However, when this arbitration does not seem to be going in their favour, the Spiders suddenly build a great castle in the cobweb. The Flies, on hearing of the Spiders' action, threaten to hang the Ant from 'the tree of reformation (as they call it)'. At this point Heywood's poem seems to have taken on an explicitly topical tone, with the events it is now depicting clearly being at one level those of Kett's Rebellion. At the same time, however, this topicality is far from simplistic. Indeed one of the things one needs to note about this historical turn is the extent to which it is brought at the expense of the disappearance of the narrator and the window from the poem's illustrations. This may of course be simply a question of space on the page, however, what this development does in pictorial terms is focus the reader's attention on the events inside the window, with the framing and distancing function performed by the details of the poet and the window being lost. This in turn creates a situation in which the kind of scanning rejected in the Preface becomes even more tempting; without the spatial order created by the presence of the narrator and the window in the earlier woodcuts, the reader is drawn more immediately and, if they allow it, less problematically into the pictures and the events they depict.

Finally the Flies decide to assault the cobweb and a terrific battle ensues. If one compares the woodcut depicting the Flies' attack on the Spiders' castle with the relative order of earlier illustrations it is clear that something has gone seriously wrong in the world of Spiders and Flies for the kind of disorder it depicts to break out. What Heywood's poem illustrates up to this point is a slow but steady decline from dispute, to argument and contention that ends in violence and armed conflict. In the process it recounts the emergence of two separate stories or narratives, of Spiders and Flies, which ultimately become the reason for the final breakdown of order. It is precisely at the moment when these separate stories start to take a clear form, when the arbitrator's role is effectively rejected by the Spiders, that poem starts to refer quite specifically to the events of Edward's reign. Certainly by the time the Flies are gathered around a tree of reformation to protest at the oppression of the Spiders, and while the latter are locked up in a castle built on probably illegally acquired land (although actually it is built on 'hole' or air), the poem's relation to the Edwardian period seems clear.[68] *The Spider and Fly* depicts a world, that of the window, slowly falling into violence and disorder owing to what are ultimately sterile and pointless debates, contentions and tumults. It is clear that within the discourse accepted as normative and authoritative by both the Flies and Spiders there can be no resolution of their differences. It is as though their world lacks an ultimate arbitrator, or even a language, that can resolve the conflict. Without this figure or discourse Spiders and Flies are forced to adopt ever more extreme arguments and methods which simply cause more conflict. One of the things that Heywood is arguing in this poem is that confessional reading of history, understanding the past within an insect-specific story or narrative, is itself a cause of violence. While the Fly at the opening of the poem simply reproaches fate for causing his downfall, by the time his comrades are assaulting the Spiders' castle two quite separate versions of recent events, and of their legitimacy, have emerged and these versions have themselves become a source of conflict.

The war between the Flies and the Spiders is ended by an ambiguous agreement to share the holes in the windows. This result, however, is not achieved without there having been considerable loss of life on both sides. Nor has all the debate, argument and fighting helped the original Spider and Fly who are left in exactly the same situation as they were at the start of the poem. Even at this late stage the Fly continues to dispute the Spider's right to eat him, until, having exhausted all possible arguments, and having said his goodbyes, the Fly accepts his fate. At this point, however, an entirely new figure suddenly enters the poem – the maid of the house. The advent of this figure changes the whole nature of the poem. Not only is the Maid a completely new element in the terms of the world of the window, her presence also subtly but significantly changes the nature of the poem's allegory since she is clearly a figure for Mary Tudor and her actions effectively make the chief Spider Northumberland.[69] Indeed one could go further than this and argue that the figure of the Maid also speaks for Mother Church (and her master –

Christ) – an alternative, and inherently neutral, site of authority able to effectively arbitrate between the competing claims and narratives of the Spider and Fly, a point of order and mediation conspicuously absent from the poem up until this point.

The Maid's status as ruler of the world of the window is made explicit when she instructs the Spiders and the Flies on how to order their lives. She tells them that:

> As God orderly created creatures all,
> So were they created, orderly to intent,
> To use themselves, each creature in his call.
> Of which created sort the creator meant
> Spiders and flies twain, to order to relent.[70]

The Maid goes on to comment that her master and mistress (Christ and his Church) have suffered grief because of the strife between the Spiders and Flies and that they should live within their degrees. Having restored order the Maid departs, leaving the window clear and swept. The poem ends at precisely the point at which it commenced, with the narrator watching an ordered world without cumbersome cobwebs or excessive flocks of flies. In these terms the message of Heywood's poem is that the Henrician and Edwardian Reformations were aberrations, mistakes, without long term or permanent results; despite the violence and conflict, the debates and disputations, nothing has really changed.

Having brought the poem to this point of resolution and completion, Heywood then goes against all his advice regarding how it should be read and provides it with a historically specific gloss. He makes explicit the Maid's relationship to Mary and that of the chief spider to Northumberland. Heywood writes:

> This merciful maiden took in hand to sweep
> Her window, this realm, not to kill but to keep
> All in quiet, on her bringing us thereto
> As that maid all spiders and flies showeth to do.
> And as under that maid spider died but one,
> So under this maid, save one (in effect) none.
> And as that one under that one maid did die
> Repentant, so this other repentantly,
> Under this other maid, the death meekly took.[71]

The Spider and Fly constructs Mary's succession as producing a new situation in which the dangers of excessive scanning warned against in its Preface are no longer applicable. Indeed Heywood, in the conclusion to the poem, makes it clear that it was only after Mary's succession that the poem could be finished.

> I have, good reader, this parable here penned
> After old beginning newly brought to end.
> The thing, years more than twenty since it begun,
> To the things more than nineteen years, nothing done.
> The fruit was green; I durst not gather it then,
> For fear of rotting before riping began.[72]

These words indicate that Heywood started writing *The Spider and Fly* during the 1530s but could only bring it to a conclusion, ripen it, after the restoration of what he regarded as orthodox Catholicism; the space of the poem could only be restored to order after a similar restoration had taken place in the wider realm. Obviously Heywood's reluctance to finish his poem may reflect concerns over its potentially contentious construction of the history of the period 1535–55. At another level, however, it is clear that, in terms of the hermeneutics advocated in its Preface, *The Spider and Fly* requires its allegory to be cleared and made literal by a figure who enters it from outside the world of Flies and Spiders; a figure who does not subscribe to either the Flies' or Spiders' histories of recent events. In a typically Marian move, Heywood makes the resolution of the allegory of his poem, the solution of the interpretative problems it embodies, possible only after the advent of Mary. At the same time Heywood's rejection of the kind of iconoclastic reading strategy advanced by Crowley means that for Heywood there can be no smashing the nut, the narrative, to reach the truth. Indeed in *The Spider and Fly* it is the existence of the shell, the story in all its convoluted and frustrating detail, that is itself the poem's must eloquent criticism of the Henrician and Edwardian Reformations;[73] the extent to which the story of the Fly and Spider is marked by pointless, barren debate between two fundamentally antinomic histories which the reader ultimately cannot make meaningful on the basis of his or her own knowledge. This reflects one of the central polemical aims of the poem, which is to make the reader aware of the sterility of Reformation debate.[74] *The Spider and Fly* is a text that seeks to delay interpretation, to defer the production of meaning, until the emergence of the only figure – Maid / Mary / Catholic Church – who is authorised to bring all the poem's disparate parts together into a meaningful whole. In *The Spider and Fly* history, the conflict between the Spider and the Fly, fills up the space of the window with unprofitable disputes and violence. It is the Maid who sweeps the window clear of cobwebs, the violent debate produced by the confessionalization of the conflict between Spiders and Flies, and restores order to a world in which Spiders and Flies may still fight but do not conceptualize their conflict in moral, historical or religious terms.[75]

Heywood's critique and rejection of the polemics of Reformation did, however, come at a political cost. At the beginning of 1557 one of the more bizarre events of Mary Tudor's reign took place, when a small band of Protestant exiles led by Thomas Stafford seized the castle at Scarborough. They were quickly defeated and indeed David Loades has speculated that the whole event may have been stage-managed, albeit from a distance, by Paget.[76] Heywood wrote a poem celebrating the defeat of the rebels entitled *A breefe balet touching the traytorous takynge of Scarborow Castell*.[77] Although this text does refer to Stafford and his followers as members of a 'traytorous sect', it constructs their behaviour within a generalized moralizing context. The penultimate verse is exemplary in this context. Heywood writes:

> To crafts that euer thryue, wyse men euer cleaue;
> To crafts that seeldwhen thryue, wyse men seeldwhen flee.
> The crafts that neuer thryue, a foole can learne to leaue.
> This thriftles crafty crafte [ie treachery] then clere leaue we.
> One God, one Kynge, one Queene, serue franke and free.
> Their Scarborow castell, let it alone.
> Take we Scarborow warnyng euerichone.[78]

Heywood's argument here, that rebels never flourish, is entirely conventional in terms of Tudor views of rebellion. What is noticeable in the context of the Marian Reformation is that this verse suggests a possible continuum from crafts that thrive, to those that do not, and to criminality and treachery. *A breefe balet* avoids fitting the taking of Scarborough Castle within a specific confessional narrative; it refuses to label Stafford and his men as Spiders or Flies. Indeed if it were to do so in terms of *The Spider and Fly*, one could argue that it would itself become the cause of further dispute and violence. Heywood's rejection of the discourse of Reformation polemics means that *A breefe balet* is left having to explain and condemn the treacherous actions of Stafford and his followers as simply a local instance of foolishness and craftiness (criminality).

Heywood's Marian works illustrate the extent to which reformation itself as a process leading to divisive confessionalization could be rejected in the mid-Tudor period. At the same time, the work Heywood produced during the 1550s reflects the productive nature of Reformation discourse for Tudor culture in terms of explaining social antagonism. The celebration of the popular in Heywood's *Two hundred Epigrammes*, of its common-sense wisdom and its rejection of totalizing world views, is clearly as much a magisterial fantasy as that of the honest ploughman so dear to Protestant writers. In particular, Heywood presents his reader with an image of a popular world marked by plenitude and humour; one in which the natural order is maintained without violence or coercion. However the mid-Tudor period was one of real hardship for many people. The world of the street and market-place was one in which wit and wisdom had to be deployed to survive within a deeply exploitative and coercive culture. Heywood does not see this; for him the popular is a world of church ales, bustling markets and shared values, a realm free from antagonism or conflict (except that produced by meddling Protestants and troublemakers), one of harmony and order.

PENANCE AND POETRY IN THE WORK OF MILES HOGARDE

Order and harmony were also ideals that Miles Hogarde aspired to; however, for him they could only be produced by militant action, personal sacrifice and religious warfare. Hogarde saw the Marian Reformation as a struggle between the forces of darkness and light. His poetry and prose is violently confessional. Not for Hogarde Heywood's almost quietist position on matters of controversy. Hogarde is never happier than when labelling people – indeed this is what his major prose work almost obsessively does, hence its title *The Displaying of the Protestants.*[79] At the same time it is important not to create too great a distinction between the work of these two Marian writers. In particular, both Hogarde and Heywood in their texts respond to the same Marian ideas concerning proper models of interpretation, the role of the self and the status of the text.

Miles Hogarde was a very unusual Tudor writer since he did not come from a magisterial background. Very little is known about Hogarde's life, although he was clearly active in anti-Protestant circles during the 1540s. Robert Crowley's attack on one of his early works in *The Confutation of the mishapen Answer* provides evidence of this.[80] Throughout this work Crowley mocks Hogarde's learning and suggests that he must be acting as the mouthpiece for other more learned men.[81] Crowley's patronizing argument reminds one of the magisterial assumptions regarding learning and the right to speak in public that Hogarde had to overcome in order to get his writings into print. One of the few modern commentators on Hogarde's work, J.W. Martin, has suggested that: 'Hogarde exemplifies for the modern historian such trends as the gradual spread of literacy and printing, and the rising importance of the laity in religious affairs, not to mention the enlarging circle of aspiring authors'.[82] Unfortunately it is impossible to say what Hogarde represents for the modern literary critic, as his work appears to have been almost entirely unread by them. This is extremely unfortunate. Hogarde's work demonstrates that the Marian Reformation developed its own hermeneutics based on a penitential working through of the self and an emphasis on the social or communal as the proper sphere for interpretation. Martin comments: 'For Hogarde the Gospel preacher is an outstanding villain, along with the iconoclast, the Bible-quoting apprentice, and others whom John Foxe was to enshrine in his Protestant martyrology.'[83] What all these figures shared for Hogarde, and indeed for other Marian writers, was an arrogant and individualistic approach to Scripture: a desire to make the word of God their own. In all his Marian works it is this desire, and the model of the selfhood that underpinned it, that Hogarde critiqued through an analysis of its costs, social, cultural and religious, for the body of the realm.

As has been suggested, Heywood's poetry reflects the extent to which the advent of Mary Tudor was seen as a restoration of the natural order; in Gardiner's terms a waking from the disordered nightmarish sleep of heresy. There was, however, another important aspect to the Marian regime's self-understanding, exemplified in Pole's writings, which was an insistence on the need for the country as a whole to do penance for the sins committed over the preceding twenty years.[84] The writers who emphasized this aspect of the Marian Reformation were also those most committed to precisely the kind of active engagement with Protestant arguments and polemics that Heywood, and indeed many other supporters of Mary's religious policies, effectively rejected.[85]

In his *Fyve Homilies* Leonard Pollard advocated an active polemical engagement with Protestantism that would have appalled Heywood. In the preface to this work, Pollard writes:

> It is not unknowen to your Lordeshyp [the Bishop of Worcester] the number of bookes and sermons that were made to deface the churche, and the number and diligentes of them that wold haue destroyed the churche, the which diligence of them or rather continuall ragynge of it shulde not be matched or with like diligence of our parte overcome and outmatched / it shulde be much to the reproach of us all.[86]

He goes on to argue:

> this is the tyme of harvest and of labour and not of reapynge and rest. If we reape before our tyme our corne wyll be greene. If we rest eare our busynes be done, we shalbe co[m]pelled to worke when we shulde rest, [and] yet it shal not auayle us. We must therfore (as the prouerbe is) take the tyme whyle tyme is, for tyme wyl away.[87]

Pollard's argument here in some ways does work against Gardiner's use of the trope of waking from a dream to explain England's escape from heresy. It is clear that for Pollard escaping the effects of England's sleep and waking from the nightmare of heresy is going to be a long and hard struggle. In his Homily entitled 'Of priuate and chiefe autorite' Pollard deploys a number of martial tropes to explain and justify the privileged role of priests within a Christian commonwealth. He asks his reader:

> What is the chiefeste defence that the souldyers have ageynst theyr enemies? Is it not the kepynge of theyr array? Is not the battell lost, when the aray is broken? And doth not saynte Paule call uppen us to kepe our aray when he sayth, let euery man abyde in that vocation that he is called in, whether he be Iewe or Gentyll.[88]

Pollard goes on to relate this equation of a battle to the social order, through the idea that being in array and following one's vocation are equivalent to the role and status of priests within a commonwealth.

> Euen so good people it is necessary in the Churche of God to haue heades and rulers, to kepe vs in an order whyles we feyght ageinst the deuyll that when so euer the deuyll shall labour eyther by vicious behaviour to brynge us in a damnable

condicion of lyuynge, or by wrong understandyng of the scriptures into heresy and misbeliefe, man maye be kept in theyr aray, [and] not every man suffered to do [and] say what hym lysteth, the lacke of which gouernaunce, what it hath done in this realme, and what confusyon we have bin brought into, al the whole realme to their great griefe doth feele.[89]

This passage constructs the role of priests as fundamental not only to the status of the Church but also to the order of the commonwealth. Indeed it is noticeable that during the course of this passage the scope of priestly power is implicitly increased. Pollard opens by stating that it is necessary to have leaders in the Church, but the lack of such leaders has effects that lead the entire realm to grief. The commonwealth needs clergymen who are the acknowledged leaders in the struggle against the devil; the social order, man's array, can only be maintained by the leadership of godly priests.[90] In Heywood's poetry the social order is represented as natural and self-regulating. It is only disrupted by the greed and ambition of people or spiders. Pollard's common-wealth is like an army engaged in a continual struggle with the devil; its array can only be protected if all its members keep to their vocation and respect the clergy's leadership. The emphasis Pollard places on the role of clergy can be directly related to the importance the Marian regime attached to the need for penance. In his sermon to the citizens of London, Pole argued that 'the right and pryncypal way to come to the light of the knowledge of God ... is not gotten by reading ... [it] ys to take away the impedyment of that light, which be oure synnes, which be taken away by the sacrament of penance'.[91] For Pole non-penitential scriptural reading was at best useless and at worst dangerous. Like Pollard, and indeed Thomas More, a key component in Pole's critique of Protestantism was the heretical nature of its hermeneutics, which encouraged people to rely excessively on their individual personal engagement with Scripture. Pole emphasized the role of ceremonies and the importance of the clergy as a way of countering the effects of Protestant incitements to the populace to indulge their 'liberty', their desire as fallen sinful people to frame scripture to fit their personal needs and desires.[92]

Much of the work that Hogarde published during the reign of Mary Tudor reflects the confessional religious agenda of Pole and Pollard: the need to engage polemically with Protestantism, the emphasis on penance and the critique of Protestant hermeneutics. Hogarde's major prose work, *The Displaying of the Protestants*, is a fascinating text. It combines the style of a Reformation pamphlet with moments of apparently accurate reportage. *The Displaying* opens with a short poem in which Hogarde attacks the effects of Protestantism.

> Which so with witte and wyll haue wrought
> As wrong hath wrested right,
> From frutefull faith, to fruteles wordes,
> And quenched vertue quyght.

> Belefe is brought to talk of tongue,
> Religion rackt amis,
> Open praier, lyp labour cald,
> Fasting folyshe fondness.
>
> Prelacy in popishe pompe,
> Vertuous vowes are vaine,
> Ceremonies curious toys
> Priesthood popery plaine.[93]

These verses are a poetic summation of the Marian critique of Protestantism. Hogarde in a few short lines manages to encapsulate serious Catholic objections to Protestant beliefs and practices, while also suggesting in a similar vein to Pole that Protestantism, like all heresy, is essentially frivolous and infantile, a childish reduction of the complexities of Christianity. In the process Hogarde mimics and mocks the popular Protestant texts of the Edwardian period with their macaronic jingles. Hogarde's attack on Protestantism in this preface reaches its apogee in the following verse:

> And what is founde in all your deades,
> But fruites of lyberty
> Wynde, and wordes, wilfull workes,
> A mase of mysery.[94]

Protestantism, like all heresies, is for Hogarde nothing more then a maze of meaningless words leading to sin and misery. It seduces its victims by inciting them to indulge their sinful desires, their liberty, and then traps them in its webs of 'wilful works' and 'windy words'. Indeed it is for Hogarde an exact mirror image of papistry as defined by writers like Bale or Crowley.

Hogarde's critique of Protestantism does, however, create a problem for him as an author since a central aspect of it is a criticism of Protestant book-reading and learning. What does this imply about the value of reading *The Displaying*? Or indeed any other of Hogarde's works? Hogarde, however, concludes this poem by addressing precisely this issue.

> Though in this booke, sharpe sense and wordes,
> May seme to some appeare,
> Remember that, longe festered sores,
> Sharpe corses doo requere.
>
> And you that reade, now reade to learne,
> Come not with myndes prepared,
> To fynde out fautes, or fansy fede,
> Let all delites be bard.

The first of these verses is directed, not at any hypothetical Protestant readers, but at those people, like Heywood, who supported the Marian Reformation while rejecting the need for a violent struggle with Protestantism. In the following verse Hogarde implies that it is only now, in other words since Mary's succession, that people who read to learn can do so profitably. In particular, Hogarde's rejection of reading to find out faults or to feed one's imagination, two forms of reading that Hogarde associates with pleasure, suggest that his model of reading relates directly to *The Displaying*'s sharp sense. Reading this work is not going to be a pleasure, instead it will be an act of penance, forcing the reader to confront the truth of Protestantism. This is why having prefaced his work with a poem, Hogarde then turns to prose as a more appropriate, perhaps less pleasurable, form for the rest of the text.

The Displaying attacks Protestants as heretics on a number of levels. In particular, Hogarde attacks the idea that Protestant victims of the Marian persecution were martyrs. He compares the way that the deaths of those who died for the Catholic faith live on in the collective memory of the faithful until the end of time with the oblivion that faces the memory of Protestants executed under Mary. Hogarde writes: 'the deathes of oure cranke Heretykes, lye dead and are buryed in the graue of cankred obliuion, couered with perpetuall infamye, excepte they be enrolled in a fewe threehalfepennye bookes, which steale oute of Germanye'.[95] Hogarde never questions the need or purpose of the Marian persecution. As far as he was concerned Protestants were a disease, or at least a symptom of the country's infection with heresy, and as such had to be purged from the body of the realm. He writes, 'A sparckle as soon as is doth appeare, ought to be quenched: rotten flesh ought to be cut awaye'.[96] By comparing Protestants to diseased flesh and cancer Hogarde is constructing them as beyond redemption, something that simply needs to be caught, labelled and destroyed.

The Displaying adopts a radically different approach to recent Tudor history to that expressed by writers like Cavendish, or for that matter William Baldwin in *The Mirror for Magistrates*, who wrote largely within the dominant 'Fall of Princes' tradition of history writing. For Hogarde the events of the preceding twenty years could and should be explained simply by the presence of heresy and heretics within the body politic. It was not pride, ambition or greed that caused the Henrician and Edwardian Reformations, but heresy. Hogarde asks his reader what caused the falls of, among others, Northumberland, Cromwell and Cranmer – and provides the answer, heresy coupled with treason. For example he writes: 'What was the cause of Crumwelles falle, but heresie begonne with the spoyle of Abbeis, [and] treason against the kyng himselfe.'[97] Hogarde's historical method here is the mirror image of that of his Protestant opponents, John Bale and John Foxe. For him heresy was the universal tool of historical explanation; for them it was papistry. *The Displaying* consistently and remorselessly hammers home the message that, in Hogarde's words, 'The Protestants be bastards by the deuil begotten upo[n] heresy'.[98] Hogarde's work is a sophisticated polemical defence of the Marian persecution; however, it is also in many ways a profoundly negative text. This is perhaps inevitable. Its aim was to display the faults of the Protestants to the eyes of its readers. In these terms it is similar to such works as John Bale's *The first two partes of the Actes or unchaste examples of Englyshe Votaryes*.[99] This work is an obsessive history of the English monasticism in which Bale shocks his reader with, but also incites them to take voyeuristic pleasure in, a catalogue of pregnant nuns and sodomitical monks.[100] Hogarde has less lurid tales than those told by Bale but he still manages to produce a work in which the reader is constantly regaled with shocking details of Protestant outrages. In particular, in *The Displaying* Hogarde focuses on the alleged effects of Protestantism on women, arguing not only that it incites them to indulge in unfeminine behaviour, rejecting their husband's authority, travelling around the country and speaking in public, but that it also encourages their basic female sinfulness. For example, Hogarde is critical of the Protestantism of the wives of London citizens while at the same time suggesting that it is simply a tool to get new husbands – by encouraging their husbands to be Protestants, they are setting them up to be burnt, clearing the way for a new husband. *The Displaying*'s treatment of women, and indeed Protestants in general, makes it in some ways almost a Gothic text. The reader is invited to be shocked by the exposure of the Protestants' sins. We are meant to be appalled and scared by the outrageous behaviour of their women. But at the same time one is clearly meant to feel a frisson of excitement and even pleasure in the displaying of the horrors of Protestantism.[101] Despite his earlier claims, Hogarde's text does not bar all delights – rather it invites its readers to consume, condemn and enjoy the fantasy Protestants, effeminate men and wanton women, that it displays.

Towards the end of *The Displaying* Hogarde recounts a journey he took with two companions to hear a sermon by 'Father Brown, the Broker of Bedlem'.[102] What is particularly interesting about this episode is that Hogarde uses Brown to illustrate the dangers of the Protestants' over-emphasis on Scripture. It is not clear what kind of Protestant Brown is or indeed if, strictly speaking, he is one, but he is certainly popular with London's Protestants. Hogarde claims this is because he has a 'cloake of gods word' that hides his shepehardes apparell and makes his peevish prophecies esteemed by them. Hogarde's account of his encounter with Brown reminds one of the stories reported in Baldwin's *Beware the Cat*. Hogarde and his companions enter a strange word, of taverns, stables and parlours in which only 'gospel' is spoken. Hogarde witnesses numerous comings and goings until finally Brown's 'congregation' is assembled and he preaches to them from horseback. The main thrust of his sermon is the difference between three kinds of religion, the Lord Chancellor's, which Brown regarded 'as naught, Cranmer's, Latimer's and Ridley's, which was not good, and Goddes religion, in other words Brown's, which was best'.[103] Hogarde finishes this episode by lamenting that Brown 'is suffred in this sort to range the countreis without restrainte, not only for corrupting the people with ill opinions, and also for disseminating his vaine Propehecies to excite rumours'.[104] Hogarde's final comment is clearly meant to link Brown to lower-class radicalism and specifically to the circulation of false prophecies which were commonly associated by Tudor writers with the 1381 Peasants' Revolt and all subsequent lower-class rebellions.

Hogarde's account of his visit to old Father Brown introduces a new note into *The Displaying*, in terms of content and, more importantly, form. In this section of his work Hogarde is not attacking his normal enemies, magisterial Protestants like Crowley, but lower-class heterodox popular religion. Brown represents the potential for real religious anarchy that the Protestants with their emphasis on individual scriptural reading had unwittingly encouraged. *The Displaying* seems to imply, however, that the world of Father Brown exists beyond and prior to that of Protestantism. Brown's world is that of Mouse-slayer and he shares many characteristics with Baldwin's eponymous cat. In particular, Hogarde offers his reader in this section a comparable pleasure to that offered in *Beware the Cat*. The reader of *The Displaying* experiences Hogarde's account of the Brown episode as a journey into a strange lower-class world, literally beyond London's boundaries but also symbolically outside Tudor literary culture. The reader follows Hogarde as narrator through the domestic setting of Brown's 'church' and in the process experiences Hogarde's encounter with Brown in a partial and episodic way. At no stage is either reader or narrator given an uninterrupted view or hearing of Brown. Like Baldwin's cats Brown always seems to be moving from room to room, his actions appearing random to the narrator / reader but clearly having their own logic and purpose. The implication of this episode is that the struggle between Protestants and Catholics is only one aspect of the Marian Reformation. Once the Protestants have been defeated, it will be necessary to take on Brown and his companions, to penetrate and reform the world of popular lore and wisdom from which Brown and his ilk have sprung. Hogarde, however, unlike Baldwin in 1553, still seems to think that such a programme could be successful. Or at least in *The Displaying* he articulates a clear desire to see a radicalization of the reforming aspects of the Marian Reformation, homiletic and inquisitorial, to extend beyond Protestantism and into the sinews of popular belief and superstition.[105]

The desire to see the process of Reformation extended beyond the world of the religious belief and practice is also expressed in Hogarde's poem *A newe ABC*. This text combines a number of different elements in order to articulate an almost identical set of social concerns to those championed by Crowley. Hogarde in this text is claiming the same public authoritative poetic role as reformer of the commonwealth that his Protestant opponents had during the

preceding reign. *A newe ABC* opens with an announcement of its author's
failings as a poet and a lament on the state of the commonwealth.

> Wherfore sith the worlde at this daye,
> Is tourned up syde downe,
> This A B C here tourne I maye,
> In some part wronge to sowne
> But now my wyll whole to expresse,
> My wit can not attayne.[106]

Hogarde then goes on to produce a critique of mid-Tudor society constructed
around the alphabet so that the first verse opens with the letter A.

> A hath fyrst place, which place I muste
> As cause of wo to stande
> Auarice and eke fleshely lust
> Alone destroyed this land.[107]

This theme is pursued throughout the poem along with the dangers of liberty,
money and usury. Hogarde manages to retrain the poem's form right up to
the last line of the last verse where he clearly found it impossible to write four
lines all opening with words beginning with Z.

Having completed his ABC, Hogarde's text then takes a new tack. He
concludes the ABC by stating that the only proper response to the decay of the
commonwealth and the sinfulness of its members is prayer. Hogarde goes on
to provide a number of prayers for his readers all of which are written in Latin
and English. The first of these is entitled 'Our unblessinge'. Hogarde writes:

> *In Nomine* of whome do we our workes beginne
> *Patris*, nay God knoweth to much we do sinne,
> *Et filii*, his wisedome so small we esteem,
> *Et spiritus sancti*, his grace eke so little deme,
> *Amen*, we can not saye till we amende, and then
> Being turned, enioying grace, then may we saye
> Amen.[108]

There is a tension in this verse between the simplicity of the Latin and the
complexity of the English. For example Hogarde argues that until 'we amende'
the word *Amen* can not be spoken. Penance in this verse is the key to speech;
only the penitent will receive God's grace and this will enable them to say
Amen. Hogarde is arguing here that meaning is a ultimately a product of
grace and therefore dependent on penitence – without them one is left in a
world in which the meaning has been lost and the two halves of the poem can
never come together. Hogarde goes on to apply this structure to a number of
other prayers and psalms, relating these texts directly to his earlier social
agenda.

> The psalme of *venite* wherein god calleth
> Us from couetousnes as I applie it.
> *Venite* worldly people, and with one minde
> *Exultemus* in vertue as god had assignde
> *In domino* we should trust, and not in richesse
> *Iubilemus* for his giftes which we do possesse
> *Deo* lift we our heartes from all vanitie,
> *Salutari nostro* eke most louing let us be.[109]

These texts are extremely unusual. At one level they can clearly be seen as a continuation of the educative agenda implied by the work's title, *A newe ABC*, with its evocation of Tudor primers.[110] These composite texts, however, reflect a more specifically Marian agenda. As has been suggested, Cardinal Pole consistently stressed the necessity of ceremony in the context of scriptural interpretation.[111] One can read Hogarde's Latin / English works as poetic responses to this idea, with the Latin embodying the formal world of ceremony while the English serves to expand and explicate its meaning. Pole's attitude to ceremonies was based on the need for Christians to express their beliefs as members of a community and under the auspices of the Church; ceremony enacted the authority of the Church and the individual believer's acceptance of it. *A newe ABC* constructs Latin as the ceremonial kernel that makes the English majority of the poem meaningful.

This is not to suggest that *A newe ABC* can be read simply as an expanded polemical primer. It is at one level a profoundly ironic text – can one have a 'new' ABC? If one did invent one, would it make any sense? The title of Hogarde's work can be seen as relating to the Marian critique of Protestantism's alleged tendency to subvert meaning and knowledge. In particular, for Catholics like Hogarde the effect of the Protestant emphasis on individual Bible reading and interpretation was the production of countless individual interpretations of the Bible; everyone could frame their own ABCs – all equally valid and pointless. Indeed the irony of Hogarde's title goes even further then this since its central message is far from new. *A newe ABC* argues that society has been corrupted by avarice and greed. This corruption is not, however, here blamed on the Protestants. *A newe ABC* is really a very old one since its target is human sinfulness. Its critical scope extends beyond Protestants to encompass the entire realm. In the process it implicitly raises questions over the performance of the Marian clergy and their status. Would it be necessary for Hogarde to write demanding social and religious reform if clergymen were doing their job? On what basis did he, as a layman and an artisan, claim the right to speak on these matters in public and with authority?[112]

These issues are also reflected in Hogarde's work, *A Treatise entitled the Path waye to the towre of perfection*.[113] This is an extended allegory depicting the narrator's journey to the Tower of Perfection. He is guided on his way by a

Bird of Faith. In the first part of the journey Hogarde's narrator meets three allegorical figures, Flesh, World and the Devil, who seek to turn him back. Having overcome their temptations, the narrator then has to pass through the Field of Penance before finally reaching the Tower of Perfection. Hogarde uses the narrator's progress to make a number of polemical points, particularly as regards the scriptural basis of penance. *The Path waye* opens with Hogarde explicitly stating its lack of sophistication.

> I study not for any eloquence,
> For if I dyd my labour were in vaine,
> First because I lacke the intelligence,
> The whiche thereunto doeth truly apertaine:
> Secondely if I coulde, little woulde it gaine,
> The simple folke to who[m] I haue this boke wil[e]d
> Which in eloquente speache, is litle skilde.[114]

Hogrde having made a virtue of his work's simplicity in his address to the reader, the poem itself opens by placing its genesis within custom and tradition.

> It hath bene saied in time gone and past,
> That what so euer doth in custome grow,
> Very hard it is that away to caste,
> Be it good or yll this all men dothe knowe,
> Experience partly dothe the profe showe,
> And some custome there is which is indifferent,
> And that in my selfe, I see evident.[115]

The opening lines of this verse seem to be a reference to the heated mid-Tudor religious debate over the value and status of custom. *The Path waye*, however, is not simply, or indeed primarily, a polemical work. It is an allegorical account of the narrator's journey to salvation. This opening verse ends by giving the evocation of custom a specific and individual meaning. In fact the custom that is being referred to here is that of Hogarde's narrator to walk abroad and take delight in the singing of birds.

The narrator of *The Path waye* goes on to tell how in the past he has been inspired by the bird's song to write and that in particular one bird had 'caused me my penne, to the booke to set'.[116] Having listened to the bird's singing, Hogarde's narrator falls asleep and while dreaming is visited by the bird who becomes his guide to the Tower of Perfection. This opening conceit clearly places *The Path waye* within a tradition of dream vision poems, and in particular *Piers Plowman*. Hogarde's text opens with a number of tropes, the denial of eloquence and the dreaming narrator, that reflect the extent to which *The Path waye* self-consciously places itself within a pre-Reformation literary tradition.[117] Indeed it may well be that Hogarde is in this text attempting to reverse the Protestant appropriation of works like *Piers Plowman*. *The Path waye*'s evocation of fourteenth- and fifteenth-century poetic tropes reflects the extent to which it expresses a critique of Protestant hermeneutics similar to those articulated by Pole and Pollard in their work. The opening of *The Path waye* creates a series of recessions in the process of authorship. The work opens with a denial of eloquence. The narrator then places the inspiration for his past works in birdsong before falling asleep and 'dreaming' the rest of the poem. At another level the opening verse clearly locates the poem's composition within an act of custom. This has the effect of further under-mining the narrator's authorial role since it implies that it is based on the performance of a physical act. The narrator's fidelity to his 'indifferent' custom is a condition of the poem's composition but not its genesis – which is provided by his vision of the bird of faith. Custom in the opening of *The Path waye* operates in the way that Pole suggests ceremonies do in relation to scriptural interpretation; it is only the narrator's observation of his custom, for obedience's sake, that leads to him embarking upon and completing his journey to salvation.

The Path waye's relationship to *Piers Plowman* goes beyond its opening. Langland's poem is an extremely complex and dense text. Two of the central issues that it is concerned with are the status of language, which it reflects upon in terms of its allegorical form, and the self. Hogarde's poem reproduces these concerns. It is sometimes assumed that allegory is a simple or even conservative generic form. This is far from the case. David Lawton comments that:

> Allegory deals in power, knowledge, authority; equally it can challenge and negate them. It constructs ideology, and can deconstruct it. It has a tendency to do so, to turn in upon itself, at any time when doubt is paramount about the nature of authority – hence about the naturalness of the 'natural order', about the justice of power, or about the truth of language.[118]

Hogarde's poem constantly reflects on the relationship between the self, inter-pretation and religious authority. Constantly his narrator fails to read the signs properly. When he meets a beautiful woman his first comment is that 'I never saw woman so faire'. She goes on to tell him,

> I am thy darling and euer hath bene,
> It greueth me to se the thus farre to fall,
> In the fondest foly that euer was seene,
> All pleasures bodily thou hast lost cleane,
> But those shall enjoye it, which doth it seeke,
> Take this waye [and] you shall haue it next weeke.[119]

It is only the intervention of the Bird and her instruction to call for grace that prevents the narrator from giving in to the enticements of this woman, who represents temptations of the flesh. This is despite the fact that this verse clearly implicitly undermines Flesh's authority. She starts her speech by deploying the language of salvation, the fall, and ends it by making the banal promise that if the narrator follows her he will enjoy all the pleasures of the body 'next week'. The juxtaposition of the language of religion with that of the market place illustrates Flesh's corrupt nature. However the narrator fails to see this. He is engaged on a journey to save his immortal soul and yet appears at this point prepared to give it up for a promise of bodily pleasures in a week's time.

In this episode, and throughout the poem, Hogarde uses the possibilities of allegory to critique forms of sophistic or closed interpretation. In this he is following in Thomas More's footsteps. *The Path waye* argues that proper or truthful interpretation has to be based on more than just the relationship between an individual reader and a text. Indeed the allegorical form makes the point that this economy can never produce fully, or even partially correct, interpretations of texts. These issues are reflected upon in *The Path waye* around the sacrament of penance. At one level Hogarde's poem can be read as a poetic defence of this sacrament, and in particular auricular confession, against the attacks of Protestant writers. As the narrator makes his way to the Tower of Perfection, he is confronted with a grim-faced wall that, the Bird tells him, encloses the field of penance. There are four gates in this wall which the narrator must pass through in order to reach his goal, contrition, confession, charity and satisfaction. At the gate of confession the narrator is confronted by a 'wofull lady' who holds 'her heart openly in her hande'.[120] His own heart quakes at this sight and he is about to turn back when she tells him:

> Come nere man quod she and be not afraied,
> Thou seist how I shewe my hart in the lyghte,
> So must thou also thy sinnes beinge waied,
> Shewe forth thy hart ma[n], why hast thou staid,
> For of all vices I am a confounder,
> And in thy soule, of vertue a grounder.[121]

Confession then goes on to explain to the narrator her scriptural basis and why the Protestants are wrong to think her a new invention. Hogarde's image of Confession seems designed to offend Protestant sensibilities, being a woman who embodies literally a teaching, auricular confession, which they abhorred. Even Hogarde's narrator seems to find Confession a shocking figure. Indeed the rhyme at the end of this verse, 'confounder' and 'grounder', reminds one of the juxtaposition of registers that marked Hogarde's portrayal of Flesh. *The Path waye* depicts vices and virtues in very similar ways, creating a situation in which the narrator constantly has to judge the status of what he sees on the basis of outside advice, from either the Bird or Grace.

At the end of *The Path waye* the narrator reaches the Tower of Perfection and finds it surrounded by a collection of lost souls. There are those who have inconstant minds and are constantly blown from path to path. Another group of lost travellers spread carpets along their route to make it easier while others make no progress at all in their desire for worldly praise. A fourth group rush madly about keeping no path, while a fifth are a great rabble whose commitment to the one way of error means that they can never agree the one way to truth. The final group is made up of discreet men. The narrator seems puzzled to see these men caught in the same maze as the other groups.

> Of all sortes quod I, that I did yet see,
> These men were most like in this towre to dwel
> They were so quod she [Faith], for these men only be,
> Those which in morall vertues did hye excel,
> As their lyues in writing doth us plainly tell,
> But yet because of faith they neuer had the light
> Ascende to this towre trulye they neuer might.[122]

Hogarde's narrator is shocked when he realizes how few have trod the same path as he.

> Then in this thornye way wherein I did go,
> I sawe some people walke, but in number small
> Alacke quod I for paine, that I see no mo,
> Walke the right pathe to the lyfe eternall,
> A great sort I see walke the way infarnall,
> Remember quod she, what Christes sayings be
> Many their be calde, but fewe chosen saith he.[123]

These final images reflect the scope and ambition of Hogarde's poem. Although many of the groups lost in the byways surrounding the Tower of Perfection embody faults that other Marian writers had directly associated with Protestantism, Hogarde does not spell this out. Instead he leaves such comparisons to be drawn by his readers. *The Path waye* is not intended to be a simple polemical work and its scope extends beyond the religious disputes of the mid-Tudor period. It is a general allegorical account of the way to salvation which it depicts as being only open to a small elect band of Christians whose election depends finally on their faith.

The Path waye is a poetic allegorical embodiment of the Marian Reformation. Above all its concern with the status of the self and the need for penance reflect important aspects of the religious agenda pursued by men like Pole between 1553 and 1558. It is, however, around this issue that the tensions inherent in Hogarde's religious agenda become apparent. *The Path waye* opens with a denial of eloquence and authorship. During its course, however, it consistently and eloquently articulates Marian Reformation ideas. Above all its presentation of the narrator's failures as a reader and his need to constantly have outside help to read properly, and its emphasis on penance, all reflect key aspects of the reform process advanced by Pole and his colleagues. There is therefore a tension between Hogarde's denial of authorship and his emphasis on the communal production of meaning and the extent to which *The Path waye* is a crafted work written by an individual layman. Indeed the intention of *The Path waye*, the instruction of simple folk, itself appears potentially problematic in the context of Marian Reformation's emphasis on the role of the clergy. Hogarde's text reflects the extent to which the years 1553–58 saw the emergence of a radical confessional Catholicism. A key aspect of its radicalism was the way in which it placed in the foreground active penance by the individual believer as a way of working through the temptations of the world and self. At the same time, as is apparent in Hogarde's case, confessionalization could have the effect of subverting clerical authority, since it created the situation in which people like Hogarde see themselves as 'better' Catholics, or Protestants, than the clergymen who shared their religious identity.

The Path waye critiques the emphasis in Protestant hermeneutics on the role of the self by deploying allegory with its inherent problematization of the process of interpretation. In his lyric 'O Hear Me, Lord, and Grant Mercy' Hogarde adopts a very different approach.[124] In this text one hears the voice of mid-Tudor Catholic piety working through the problem of the self in much the same way that later Protestant writers did, the obvious example being John Donne. Hogarde opens his lyric with a plea that God grant the narrator mercy. This appeal is then reiterated throughout the work. Verse four reads:

> Suffer not me, thy creature,
> O Lord, to peryshe in thy syghte!
> Thowe canst make clene that is unpure!
> Clense me, O Lord, a wofull wyght
> O here me, Lord, and grant mercye.[125]

Later the narrator enters a plea for mercy based upon God's role in his creation.

> O Lord, what wood it profit the,
> That thou made me to thyne owne lyknes,
> Yf I should now condemned be
> To hell, for myne owne wychednes?
> O here me, Lord, and grant mercye![126]

This poem's intensely penitential tone can also be found in a number of other Marian works. For example, in 1558 a collection of prayers by Cuthbert Tunstall, Bishop of Durham, was printed. The first prayer in the collection is entitled 'A general confession of sinnes' and contains the following passage.

I have offended greuously, and aboue the number of sandes of the sea, in pryde and vayne glorye, in anger and hatred, in enuy, i[n] couetuousnes, in slothefulnes, in glutteni, in lecheri, in negligee[n]ce of diuine honor, ... in slaunderyngs, in lies, ... in vaine lookes, in bearyng, in tastynge, in thoughts, and in words in dedes, and in all thynges, that the frayltye of man at anye tyme might haue offended in, the which thing, I confesses to haue done through mi faute.[127]

Tunstall and Hogarde in these texts construct the individual interior self as something that the true believer needs to work through as part of the process of moving towards Christ. In the process they are articulating a form of piety and construction of the self that some literary critics and historians have argued is inherently Protestant, and specifically Puritan. Tom Webster has discussed the central importance of the creation of a self-abnegating selfhood as a pre-condition for a life centred wholly on Christ in Puritan spirituality; Hogarde's and Tunstall's texts reflect the extent to which this was an ideal shared by godly mid-Tudor Catholics.[128]

Hogarde's work illustrates the extent to which Marian Catholicism included an emerging confessional Catholic identity. Indeed one could argue that Hogarde is the first 'real' English Catholic poet, the first person to write poetry that embraces the label Catholic defined against that of Protestant. Whereas Heywood can be seen as the last pre-Reformation poet, his Marian colleague took up the challenge issued by writers like Crowley and produced explicitly Catholic works that were reforming, original and profoundly modern.

CONCLUSION

Discussions of the Marian Reformation have often concluded by commenting upon its success or failure. In particular, would the restoration of Catholicism that took place between 1553–58 have succeeded if Mary had lived longer or had a Catholic heir? However many of the participants in these debates have started from the wrong place by assuming that the Marian Reformation was a reactionary attempt to return to a pre-Reformation past. As this chapter has illustrated, this was not the case. At another level the example of Heywood and Hogarde illustrates the redundancy of these discussions. As has already been suggested, Hogarde's concerns with the self find their echo in the work of Donne, and indeed other Stuart poets, while Heywood's celebration and idealization of popular wisdom reminds one of many Elizabethan writers, and perhaps in particular William Shakespeare. This is not to argue that either Donne or Shakespeare had read these Marian writers. It is to suggest is that the social conflicts reflected in the work of Heywood and Hogarde remained in existence long after their deaths and remained the basis for, and matter of, Elizabethan and early Stuart culture.

As for the success of Mary's Reformation, it is surely possible to imagine an Elizabethan Catholic Church imbued with the spirit of Heywood but in constant conflict with those like Hogarde who embraced confessionalization and argued that the process of reformation needed to address not only Protestantism but also popular heretical beliefs and practices. Were there people in Elizabethan England to whom Hogarde's activist confessional agenda, his insistence upon the examination of the self, the role of the godly in reforming the commonwealth and frustration with the established clergy, would have appealed? Mary's Reformation would have succeeded and failed just as much as Elizabeth's did, or indeed, for that matter, Edward's or Henry's. None of them could have produced the ordered harmonious and Christian commonwealth to which they all aspired, since none were prepared to tackle the social conflicts and antagonisms that reformation as a process worked to obscure and elide. It is for this reason that the neglect of Hogarde's work by literary critics is so unfortunate. Reading his work, one becomes aware of a melancholic or even resigned tone. This is not because Hogarde knew that the Marian Reformation would ultimately fail. Rather it is a product of his awareness that, despite his religious commitment, his skill as a writer, his originality and piety, he would always be to his opponents and contemporaries Myles Hogherd – someone whose social status would always place him beyond the pale of learned, literate and literary society; there is no place for hogherds in the canon.[129]

NOTES

1 Reginald Pole, *Defence of the Unity of the Church*, trans. and intro. Joseph C. Dwyer (Westminster, Maryland: 1965), p. 298.

2 For example Pole tells Henry: 'Even though you hope your own interpretation [of Scripture] might be valid, it contradicts all scriptural sense and does not offer even a single word upon which you can base your claim' (Ibid., p. 15).

3 Reginald Pole, 'Cardinal Pole's speech to the citizens of London in behalf of religious houses', in John Strype, *Ecclesiastical Memorials*, 3:2 (Oxford: 1822), no. LXVIII, pp. 482–510, p. 483.

4 The term Marian Reformation is used here to refer to the religious changes introduced by the regime of Mary Tudor. Given that these were of the same scope, and enforced with the same mechanisms as those used at different times by her father, brother and sister, it seems appropriate to refer to them as the Marian Reformation.

5 A composite text of Gardiner's sermon is printed in James Muller, *Stephen Gardiner and the Tudor Reaction* (London: 1926), pp. 264–266.

6 This argument appears ridiculous, particularly when being made by someone as close to the centre of power as Gardiner was throughout most of the preceding twenty years. However, when writing to James V Scotland, Henry VIII himself argued that the best way to pursue religious change was secretly in order to disarm any opposition. See *LP*, XV, 136.

7 From a sermon by Stephen Gardiner, Bishop of Winchester and Lord Chancellor, given at St Paul's Cross, the first Sunday in Advent 1554, quoted in Muller, 1926, pp. 265–

266. Gardiner's sermon was reported in a number of contemporary sources, all of whom agree over its general tone and content. For a brief discussion of the differences between the various versions, see Muller, pp. 384–385, no. 31.

8 For example it appears that in 1547 Gardiner held far more ambiguous views towards papal supremacy than those he articulated in 1554. In one of his famous letters to Protector Somerset he argued: 'Many co[m]monwealths haue continued without the bishop of Romes iurisdictio[n]: but without the true religio[n], and with such opino[n]s as Germany mainteined, no estate hath continued in the circuit of the world to us know[n] since christ came' ('Stephen Gardiner to the Lord Protector', printed in John Foxe, *Actes and Monuments* (London: 1563), STC 11222, p. 733).

9 See G.R. Elton, *Reform and Reformation: England 1509–1558* (London: 1977), chapter 17, and A.G. Dickens, *The English Reformation: Second Edition* (London: 1989), chapter 12.

10 Eamon Duffy, *The Stripping of the Altars: Traditional Religion in England 1400–1580* (New Haven: 1992), chapter 16, and Christopher Haigh, *English Reformations: Religion, Politics, and Society under the Tudors* (Oxford: 1993), chapter 12.

11 See for example David Loades, *The Reign of Mary Tudor: Politics, Government and Religion in England 1553–58* (London: 1991), p. 285, and John N. King, *English Reformation Literature: The Tudor Origins of the Protestant Tradition* (Princeton: 1982), pp. 413–414.

12 Duffy, 1992, p. 529.

13 Christopher Haigh has recently argued: 'The Marian Church was the Church of the 1520s writ later: a vigorous pastoral episcopate; high levels of clerical recruitment; best-selling works of pastoral edification and piety; active investment in parish religion ...' Haigh goes on, however, to make the essential point that the Marian Church also shared with the Church of the 1520s such issues as problems over clerical authority and heresy (Haigh, 1993, p. 217).

14 For example, Haigh argues that the persecution was a mistake that largely continued due to the 'determination of ordinary Protestants to witness to the truth, and the determination of ordinary Catholics to destroy error' (Ibid., p. 231).

15 G.R. Elton argued that 'the persecution set the seal on Mary's failure to restore the Church of Rome in England' (Elton, 1977, p. 388). This claim has the effect of making persecution the defining characteristic of the religious policies of Mary Tudor.

16 Dickens, 1989, p. 296.

17 Henry's highly traditional attitude towards the mass was almost identical to that of his elder daughter. Indeed despite the historical tradition that sees Mary as a 'poor' Tudor, she was in many ways very similar to her father. G.R. Elton described her as arrogant, assertive, bigoted, stubborn, suspicious and rather stupid. His point was that these characteristics made her an untypical Tudor but it is hard to think of an early modern English ruler, with the possible exception of James II, who was more arrogant, assertive, bigoted, stubborn and suspicious than that archetypal Tudor – Henry VIII. See Elton, 1977, p. 377.

18 Andrew Pettegree, *Marian Protestantism: Six Studies* (Aldershot: 1996), p. 161.

19 Catholic confessionalization did not preclude the kind of persecution adopted by the Marian regime but it did tend to emphasize more strategic long-term, and ultimately successful, approaches to the 'problem' of Protestantism.

20 This tension is fundamental to More's understanding of heresy in his anti-Lutheran

works. In particular, More often argues that Luther's interpretation of Scripture is at once overtly individualistic and lacking in all consistency.

21 Gardiner, 1926, p. 264.

22 This Address to the Reader is not found in the earlier, pre-Marian, versions of Hawes' work.

23 Ironically, while this Address asserts even more rigorously than the original versions of *The Pastime of Pleasure* the status of Hawes' text as containing its own glosses and guides to reading, it does not include the wood-cuts that were an essential part of the poem. Indeed all the Marian editions of *The Pastime of Pleasure* fail to reproduce all the wood-cuts found in the original early Henrician edition. One can perhaps see in this failure the effects twenty-five years of iconoclasm had on Tudor culture and its appreciation of the printed image.

24 Stephen Hawes, *The Pastime of Pleasure* (London: 1554), STC 12950, *.iii.

25 This passage seems to be referring quite explicitly to the idea that forms the basis of More's account of Bilney's fall into heresy. More argued that it was excessive private study that led Bilney to frame his own heretical religion.

26 Hawes, 1554, *.iii.

27 Ibid., *.iii.

28 Marian critiques of Henrician models of interpretation and subjectivity reflect the perspicacity of David Aers' question when he recently asked: 'What if subjectivity is more bound into microhistory that is less linear than the master narrative determining the story told by Burckhardt, Robertson, Barker, Belsey, Dollimore, Greenblatt ... and ... suggested too by Foucault?' See David Aers, 'A Whisper on the Ear of Early Modernists; or, Reflections on Literary Critics Writing the 'History of the Subject'', in *Culture and History 1350–1600: Essays on English Communities, Identities and Writing*, ed. David Aers (Hemel Hempstead: 1992), pp. 177–202, p. 197.

29 Pole, 1822, p. 508.

30 Leonard Pollard, *Fyve Homilies* (London: 1556), STC 20091, I.ii (v).

31 Pole, 1822, p. 503.

32 John Christopherson, *An Exhortation to all Menne to ... Beware of Rebellion* (1554), STC 5207, K.iii.

33 John Gwynnethe, *A Declaration of the state, wherin all heretickes dooe leade their lives* (London: 1554), STC 12558, N.iii (v).

34 Miles Hogarde, *The assault of the sacrame[n]t of the Altar* (London: 1554), STC 13556, E.ii. For a more detailed discussion of this poem see Tom Betteridge, *Tudor Histories of the English Reformations 1530–1583* (Aldershot: 1999), pp. 155–160.

35 See Peter Marshall, 'The Debate over "Unwritten Verities" in Early Reformation England', in *Protestant History and Identity in Sixteenth-Century Europe: Vol. 1 The Medieval Inheritance*, ed. Bruce Gordon (Aldershot: 1996), pp. 60–78.

36 Thomas Martin, *A Treatise declaryng and plainly prouyng, that the pretended marriage of Priestes, and professed persones, is no marriage, but altogether unlawfull* (1554), STC 17517.

37 Ibid., B.iii (v).

38 Ibid., D.iii.

39 Martin, 1554, B.ii (v) / B. iii.

40 Gardiner in one of his letters to Protector Somerset also critiques the Protestant
    valorization of the printed word. He did this in the context of the debate over the images
    by pointing out that at one level letters were also images. Gardiner wrote: 'if by reviling
    stocks and stones, in which manner images be graven, the setting of the truth (to be
    read of all men) shall be contemned: how shall writing continue in honour as is
    comprised in clouts and pitch, wherof and whereupon our books be made …?' ('Stephen
    Gardiner to the Lord Protector', printed in John Foxe, *Acts and Monumentes* (London:
    1570), STC 11223, p. 1522). Pole in his *Defence of the Unity of the Church* asked Henry, 'Do
    you think that the truth should be sough from silent books always offering material for
    contention for man's ingenuity, rather than from the agreement of the Church that
    never lacks the Sprit of God?' (Pole, 1965, p. 327).

41 Martin, 1554, B. iiii.

42 James Brooks, *A sermon very notable, fruitefull and Godlie* (London: 1553), STC 3838, A.iii
    (v).

43 Ibid., B.ii (I).

44 John Proctor, 'The Prologue to His Deer brethren and naturall countree men of
    Englande', in Vincent of Lerins, *The waie home to Christ and truth leadinge from Antichrist
    and errour* (1556), STC 24754, Ab (2v).

45 It is also interesting to note that the gender-specific imagery used by writers during the
    reign of Mary Tudor has received far less attention by literary critics then that of the
    following reign.

46 Bishop Bonner in his *A profitable and necessary doctryne, with certayne homilies adioyned
    thereunto*, commented that: 'when the catholyke churche sayeth, that the body of Chryst
    is to be receyued there [in the mass] spiritually, it meaneth not that therefore the verye
    body of Christ is not there receaued really [and] in very deade. For this worde, spiritually,
    doth signifye only the manner of receauyng, and doth not importe the substance of the
    thyng so receyued' (Edmund Bonner, *A profitable and necessary doctryne, with certayne
    homilies adioyned thereunto* (London: 1555), STC 3282, R.ii).

47 *Tottel's Miscellany*, ed. Richard Tottel (1557), STC 13860.

48 Wendy Wall, 'Authorship and the Material Conditions of Writing', in *The Cambridge
    Companion to English Literature 1500–1600*, ed. Arthur F. Kinney (Cambridge: 2000),
    pp. 64–89, p. 73.

49 The Marian period witnessed a concerted nationalist campaign which illustrates how
    problematic it is to claim, as many literary critics and historians have, that there was a
    causal relationship between Protestantism and the development of a national conscious-
    ness in England. Perhaps the most interesting example of this campaign is the family
    tree printed in John Christopherson's *An Exhortation to all Menne* which shows that
    King Philip was no stranger, but a member of the English royal family.

50 Tottel also emphasizes the educational value of lyrics that make up his miscellany,
    claiming that through reading them the 'unlearned' would learn to be 'more skilful'.
    Like Hawes' *The Pastime of Pleasure*, reading *Tottel's Miscellany* will in itself be a learning
    experience (Tottel, 1557, 'The Printer to the Reader', no pagination).

51 For an excellent specific example of the way in which Tottel's editing affected the tone of
    Wyatt's poems, in particular making them less Henrician see Michael R.G. Spiller, *The*

Development of the Sonnet: An Introduction (London: 1992), pp. 99–101.

52 David Norbrook comments that the Marian censor preferred 'poetry to deal with eternal human truths, not transient political issues' (David Norbrook, *Poetry and Politics in the English Renaissance* (London: 2002), p. 51). This is, however, to give Marian poetics a rather negative emphasis. The publication of the first printed English edition of Virgil's *Aeneid* suggests a positive side to the rejection of the kind of partisan poetry whose passing Norbrook seems to regret. See Donna B. Hamilton, 'Re-engineering Virgil: *The Tempest* and the Printed English *Aeneid*', in *The Tempest and its Travels*, eds Peter Hulme and William H. Sherman (London: 2000), pp. 114–120.

53 For Heywood's earlier career see Greg Walker, *The Politics of Performance in Early Renaissance Drama* (Cambridge: 1998), esp. Chapter 3.

54 C.S. Lewis, *English Literature in the Sixteenth Century Excluding Drama* (Oxford: 1944), pp. 145–146.

55 Mary Thomas Crane, *Framing Authority: Sayings, Self and Society in Sixteenth-Century England* (Princeton: 1993), p. 136.

56 Although literary critics have done much sophisticated work on the self, the central question Crane raises – why texts that appear to be concerned with the self should determine the canon of important Tudor writing – has not been properly interrogated.

57 John Heywood, 'Two hundred Epigrammes', 1555, STC 13296, in *John Heywood's Works and Miscellaneous Short Poems*, ed. Burton A. Milligan (Urbana: 1956), pp. 141–198.

58 Mary Thomas Crane comments that 'John Heywood ... departed consciously from the generic precedents set by the Humanists, but he [also] reacted against Crowley as well. He provided not only another vernacular version of the epigram but also a version that sought to subvert the aphoristic wisdom and return the genre to a stance of amateur frivolity' (Mary Thomas Crane, '*Intret Cato*: Authority and Epigram in Sixteenth-Century England', in *Renaissance Genres: Essays on Theory, History and Interpretation*, ed. Barbara Kiefer Lewalski (Cambridge, Mass.: 1986), pp. 158–188, p. 176).

59 Heywood, 1956, p. 167.

60 Ibid., p. 167.

61 The position of those clergy who married under Edward VI presented a real difficulty for Mary Tudor and her government. It was relatively easy to reassert the need for clerical celibacy but if all married clergy had been expelled from the priesthood the English Church would have faced a serious staffing crisis. For the issue of clerical marriage in this period see Helen Parish, *Clerical Marriage and the English Reformation: Precedent, Policy and Practice* (Aldershot: 2000).

62 Heywood, 1956, p. 168.

63 Ibid., p. 168.

64 Bill Wizeman has suggested to me that Heywood's attitude to popular culture may also reflect its revival under Mary Tudor. For this aspect of the Marian Reformation see Ronald Hutton, 'The Local Impact of the Tudor Reformations', in *The Impact of the English Reformation 1500–1640*, ed. Peter Marshall (London: 1997), pp. 142–166.

65 John Heywood, *The Spider and Fly*, 1556, STC 13308, ed. John S. Farmer (London: 1908), pp. 6–7.

66 Ibid., p. 29.

67 Ibid., p. 199.

68 The illegality of the site of the Spiders' 'new castle' can be read as a reference to the dissolution of the monasteries. In this context that fact that the Spider has built on a 'hole' can be read as an ironic comment on those who had bought ex-monastic land thinking it was a good investment.

69 Although Robert Carl Johnson has recently suggested that the chief Spider could represent a number of historical figures, Wolsey, Cromwell, Cranmer and Northumberland: Robert Carl Johnson, *John Heywood* (New York: 1970), p. 67.

70 Heywood, 1908, p. 412.

71 Ibid., pp. 426–427.

72 Ibid., p. 423.

73 In these terms Heywood's work reflects the influence within Marian culture of More's construction of the effects of heresy on the commonwealth.

74 One should note that for many critics, modern and Heywood's own contemporaries, it is the success of the poem in resisting interpretation that is the problem. Certainly as far as C.S. Lewis was concerned *The Spider and Fly*'s complexity and the apparent opaqueness of its allegorical figures simply served to confirm Heywood's drabness. Robert Carl Johnson comments: 'The problem [with The Spider and Fly] is that neither the reader today nor Heywood's contemporaries could penetrate the allegory' (Johnson, 1970, p. 67). I would argue, however, that it is precisely this kind of reading that desires to penetrate the poem's allegory that Heywood is seeking to critique in *The Spider and Fly*.

75 Alec Ryrie has suggested to me a reading of the poem in which the Flies signify clergy and the Marian restoration of order relates to the relationship between the laity and clergy.

76 In early 1557 the government, or at least the Queen, appear to have been keen to give Philip support in his struggle with France. Loades suggests that the attack on Scarborough may have been designed to provide the doubters in the council with a clear act of French provocation in order to justify a declaration of war. See Loades, 1991, pp. 304–308.

77 John Heywood, 'A breefe balet touching the traytorous takynge of Scarborow Castell', c.1557, STC 13290.7, in *John Heywood's Works and Miscellaneous Short Poems*, ed. Burton A. Milligan (Urbana: 1956), pp. 272–274.

78 Ibid., p. 274.

79 Miles Hogarde, *The Displaying of the Protestants* (London: 1556), STC 13557.

80 In this work Crowley suggests that Hogarde was active in the persecution of Protestants during the last years for Henry VIII. He writes: 'Remembre your self (frynde Hogherde) howe manie you have sette towarde Smithfield in the tyme of persecution. Men / thynke that frome the tyme of John Frith to the death of (the constante wytnesse of gods trueth) Anne askwe, ther was no bloude shed in Smythfylde, but your parte will be in it at the last daye' (Robert Crowley, *The Confutation of the mishapen Answer to the misnamed, wicked Ballade, called the Abuse of [the] blessed sacrame[n]t of the aultare. Wherin, thou haste (gentle Reader) the ryghte understandynge of all the places of scripture that Myles Hoggard (wyth his learned counsaill) hath wrested to make transubstanciacion of the bread and wyne* (London: 1548), STC 6082, A.iii (v) / A.iii (i)).

81 Indeed the title of Crowley's text with its reference to Hogarde's 'learned counsel' reflects this argument.

82 J.W. Martin, *Religious Radicals in Tudor England* (London: 1989), p. 83.

83 Ibid., p. 93.

84 For the importance of penance to the Marian regime see William Wizeman, 'Recalled to Life: The Theology and Spirituality of Mary Tudor's Church', Oxford PhD, 2002.

85 For a discussion of this aspect of the Marian Reformation see Duffy, 1992, pp. 529–532.

86 Pollard, 1556, A.ii–A.ii (v).

87 Ibid., A.ii (v).

88 Ibid., F.ii (1).

89 Ibid., F. ii (1).

90 This emphasis on the role of the clergy is similar to the role that Crowley gives preachers in his work *Philargyrie of Greate Britayne* or indeed to that they are encouraged to play in Edmund Dudley's *The Tree of Commonwealth*.

91 Pole, 1822, p. 504.

92 For an excellent discussion of the resonances of the concept of liberty in Reformation debates see Alec Ryrie, 'Counting Sheep, Counting Shepherds: The Problem of Allegiance in the English Reformation', in *The Beginnings of English Protestantism*, eds Peter Marshall and Alec Ryrie (Cambridge: 2002), pp. 84–110, pp. 100–101.

93 Hogarde, 1556, no pag.

94 Ibid., no pag.

95 Ibid., p. 69 (v).

96 Ibid., p. 61.

97 Ibid., p. 102 (v).

98 Ibid., p. 96.

99 John Bale, *The first two partes of the Actes or unchaste examples of Englyshe Votaryes* (London: 1560), STC 1274.

100 For a discussion of this text see Betteridge, 1999.

101 In this Hogarde was clearly writing within the same tradition of men like Foxe and many later Protestant writers who filled their works with accounts of papist plots and atrocities.

102 Hogarde, 1556, p. 121.

103 Ibid., p. 124 (v).

104 Ibid., p. 125.

105 Indeed it is clear that towards the end of the Marian period the authorities were starting to investigate and condemn lower-class religious radicals. It has been assumed that this was simply the inevitable effect of the persecutory process; however, it may represent a change of policy on the part of the Marian regime. If this were the case, then they would simply be acting on the desire to 'reform' popular culture expressed by all confessional early modern regimes. At the same time the Brown episode may reflect

an aspect of Hogarde's activist agenda that many in the regime, and certainly people like Heywood, would have found shocking.

106 Miles Hogarde, *A newe ABC* (London: 1557), STC, 13559, A.i. (v).

107 Ibid., A.ii.

108 Ibid., B.i.

109 Ibid., B.ii (v).

110 Diarmaid MacCulloch has suggested to me that they also imply a readership capable of understanding the relationship between the Latin and English parts of the poem. What such a reader would make of the first part of this volume is unclear. It may be that *A newe ABC* reflects the extent to which a knowledge of Latin was more widespread then has been assumed, or that a work like Hogarde's could expect a relatively mixed readership.

111 Hogarde appears to have received patronage from Bishop Bonner who produced a religious primer during Mary's reign.

112 Hogarde's radicalism in this section of *A newe ABC* is compounded by the fact that these poems are liturgical.

113 Miles Hogarde, *A Treatise entitled the Path waye to the towre of perfection* (London: 1554), STC 13561.

114 Ibid., A.ii.

115 Ibid., A.iii.

116 Ibid., A.iii.

117 David Lawton has commented that the 'true mark of a fifteenth-century poet is to deny being a poet – to abrogate, that is, any specialised status ... that poetry might bring'. This is clearly what Hogarde does in *The Path waye*; however, he is doing so within the context of the kind of grandiose claims made for poetry by writers like Crowley. See David Lawton, 'Dullness and the Fifteenth Century', *ELH*, 54 (1987), pp. 761–799, p. 771.

118 David Lawton, 'The subject of *Piers Plowman*', *The Yearbook of Langland Studies*, 1 (1987), pp. 1–30, p. 25.

119 Hogarde, 1554, B.i.

120 Ibid., D.i.

121 Ibid., D.i.

122 Ibid., E.i (v). The narrator's guides change during the course of the poem from the visionary Bird, to Grace and here Faith. This suggests a development akin to that which takes place in Dante's *Divine Comedy* and Langland's *Piers Plowman*.

123 Ibid., E.ii.

124 Miles Hogarde, 'O Hear Me, Lord, and Grant Mercy', in *The Moral Play of Wit and Science and Early Poetical Miscellanies*, ed. John Orchard Halliwell (London: 1848), pp. 107–109.

125 Ibid., p. 108.

126 Ibid., p. 108.

127 Cuthbert Tunstall, *Certaine Godly and Devout Prayers, Made in latin by the Reverend father in God Tunstall, Bishop of Durham, and translated into English by Thomas Paynell* (London: 1558), STC 24318, A.iii (iv)–A.iii (2).

128 Tom Webster, *Godly Clergy in Early Stuart England: The Caroline Puritan Movement c.1620–1643* (Cambridge: 1997), p. 125.

129 Unlike some sympathetic modern commentators on Mary's reign, Hogarde appears to have no illusions over the extent to which Tudor society would always privilege the maintenance of the social order over other considerations, including the confessional.

Chapter 4

Elizabethan poetics and politics

The Perills are many, great and imminent.
Great in respect of the Persons and Matters.

    Persons

The Quenes Majesty herself as Pacient.
The Pope, the King of France, and Spayne as Authors and Workers; and their Associates.
The Quene of Scotts as Instrument, wherby the Matters shall be attempted ageynst the Quenes Majesty.

    Matters

For the recovery of the Tirany to the Pope, which of late Years hath bene discovered and so weakened, as, if the gret Monarchies wer not his Mayntenors, and intended his Recovery, the same had shortly fallen, or bene reformed ... (William Cecil, *A Short Memoryall of the State of the Realme*, 1569)[1]

In 1558 Nicholas Throckmorton wrote to the new Queen advising her that 'it shall not bee meete that either the old or new [councillors] should wholely understand what you meane, but to use them as instruments to serve yourself with ...'[2] In 1569, however, one of the Queen's instruments, William Cecil, turned this metaphor on its head, depicting her as a patient passively waiting to be cut up by her enemies' instrument – Mary Queen of Scots. Cecil portrays himself in this unfolding medical drama as a concerned onlooker, by implication rendered impotent by the Queen's passivity. *A Short Memoryall of the State of the Realme* is brutal in its depiction of the perilous state of the country. Not only is the Queen a helpless patient, but the realm itself is in a weak condition beset by troubles abroad and at home.

The next Imperfections ar here ay home, which be these: The state of religion many weis weakened by Coldness in the trew Service of God, by Increase of the Nombre and Courage of Baptists, and of Derydors of Relligion, and lastly by the Increase of Nombres of Irreligious and Epicures.

> Then followeth the Decaye of Obedience in Cyvill Pollycy; which being compared with the Fearfullness and Reverence of all inferior Estates to their Superiors in Tymes past, will astonish any wise and considerate Person to behold the Desperation of Reformation.[3]

Reading *A Short Memoryall*, one would think that its author was a bitter excluded critic of the regime, not its leading member – the person, second only to the Queen, responsible for the country's state. However, it is important not to take Cecil's words at their face value. Were there really increasing numbers of Epicureans in early Elizabethan England? What was the basis for Cecil's claim that obedience had decayed?

A Short Memoryall is not intended to be a transparent depiction of the realm. It is a discussion document written to guide the deliberations of Cecil and his fellow councillors. Its rhetoric is aimed at them and perhaps even more pointedly at the Queen herself. Why describe her as a patient unless one wanted to produce a very specific, presumably violent, reaction? Would Elizabeth have enjoyed being depicted as the sick ruler of Europe? Of being stretched out on the operating table while her enemies sharpened their instrument? Cecil's comments on religion are also significant. Clearly Epicurus had no followers in Elizabethan England. The intended audience of *A Short Memoryall* would, however, have understood and appreciated this classical allusion. The reference to Epicurus is a marker of the shared political language that united leading members of the early Elizabethan regime. It also, however, reflects the ideological tensions embodied in Cecil's work, since it suggests that the English Church is threatened by people who are committed to a life of pleasure and are unconcerned with the state of their souls. In the process Cecil's text writes over the possibility of principled confessional opposition to the Elizabethan religious settlement. *A Short Memoryall* is an exemplary early Elizabethan political work in its emphasis on counsel, the status of Elizabeth's queenship and the condition of the realm. It was almost certainly written for a very restricted audience; however, throughout the 1560s a number of texts were produced, most noticeably *The Mirror for Magistrates*, that shared its basic political assumptions: in particular, the need for the monarch to receive and act upon counsel – private *and* public.[4] This assumption was not, however, unchallenged. Indeed Elizabeth herself seems to have held a far more Henrician sense of what it meant to be England's monarch. The 1560s witnessed a debate over the nature of the Elizabethan regime – in simplistic terms, was it Henrician or Edwardian?

This chapter is in three parts, with the first section discussing the political culture of the early years of Elizabeth's reign as reflected in such texts as *The Mirror of Magistrates*. The second part of this chapter will examine in detail the writing of Barnabe Googe, whose works represent an attempt to produce a specifically Protestant and magisterial combination of Henrician court poetry with Edwardian politics. The final part of this chapter will discuss John Foxe's *Acts and Monuments* and George Gascoigne's work *A Hundreth Sundrie Flowres*. It will argue that these two very different works produce similar ideological solutions to the problem of defining Elizabeth's queenship. In the process they illustrate the extent to which the culture of the later Elizabethan period was a product of the political and poetic debates of the early years of the Queen's reign.

EARLY ELIZABETHAN POETICS AND POLITICS

Elizabeth's triumphant entry into London in 1558 was a carefully staged event. The account rushed into print by Richard Tottel, *The Passage of our most drad Soveraigne Lady Quene Elizabeth through the citie of London to westminister the daye before her coronacion*, emphasizes the entry's scale and ambition.[5] Tottel's pamphlet recounts how, as the Queen made her way through London's streets, she was met with a number of elaborate allegorical pageants intended to celebrate her succession as a restoration of order, unity and true religion. The central message of *The Passage*, and of the event that it sought to commemorate, was that the advent of Elizabeth would bring a period of concord and peace to the country[6] At the same time, as John Guy has pointed out, there was a basic tension between this celebration of Elizabeth's succession as a restoration of order and the Protestantism of the religious agenda that lay behind the City's pageants.[7] *The Passage* itself embodies this tension. Different tensions form the back ground to the ballad, *The wonders of England*.[8] This work is an allegorical history of the Marian period. It opens by claiming that in 1553 God's wrath fell on the land, since as soon as Edward died darkness descended: 'The Bats [and] Owles from holes out came / Wolves and Beares, and cruel Caun / Did Englande inuade.'[9] *The wonders of England* goes on to paint a nightmarish picture of Marian England.

> Whe[n] darknes thus ech where was sen
> And nightly Vermin ruled the rost,
> No Birds might syng in the late euen,
> By land, by sea, or by the coast,
> But straight were brought to firy post,
> Or else to Lolers tower tost
>   And kept in cage,
> Frome meate and frend somtimes so bard
> That lomy Walles they fed on hard
>   Hunger to swage.[10]

The rule of the Owls continued until God was so moved by the blood of the martyrs and the plight of their families that he decided to withdraw his wrath. The period 1553–58 is presented in this text as one in which not only the realm but meaning itself was plunged into a nightmarish state of darkness and violence.[11] Elizabeth's succession announces the lifting of God's punishment. It is important to note that in this poem Elizabeth only succeeds after God has forgiven England. In *The wonders of England* it is not her succession that stops the persecution but the blood of the martyrs that pays the price for the country's sins and makes possible her succession. As in *The Passage*, Elizabeth is represented in this text as at once embodying God's purpose in restoring England to light – in terms of this text Edwardian Protestantism – but also as requiring counsel. *The wonders of England* ends with an image of unity and concord but also expresses an anxiety that Elizabeth might not obey God's command but will instead allow 'vermin' to remain within the land.

The tension embodied in these texts reflects the political problem confronting the Elizabethan regime during the 1560s, which was what kind of regime it was – Henrician or Edwardian. As far as one can tell, Elizabeth regarded as normative her father's view of the role of the monarch and the nature of Tudor kingship. Stephen Alford comments that 'Elizabeth defined herself as an imperial monarch'.[12] John Guy has pointed out that 'like her father and sister [Elizabeth] particularly stressed her royal prerogative'.[13] There were, however, serious problems that made it impossible for Elizabeth to adopt her Henry's model of kingship.[14] This was partly because of her gender, although, if it had been possible for Elizabeth to be a more Henrician ruler, this might have addressed some of the problems caused by her sex.[15] There were, however, a number of insurmountable hurdles that prevented Elizabeth adopting a Henrician model of kingship. Alford has pointed out that the members of the 1560 Privy Council were committed to a model of kingship based upon a mixed polity derived from their experiences under Edward VI. In particular, men like Cecil and his fellow councillors shared a common political creed that 'rested on the principle that both the Privy Council and parliament had a duty to counsel, guide and direct Elizabeth, even in matters of 'state' like the Queen's marriage, the succession to the kingdom, and England's religion'.[16] Elizabeth appears not to have shared this creed, or at least to have had a very different understanding of what it meant for her to be counselled, but it would have been impossible to fully reject it, given the need to staff her government with men with at least a modicum of experience and similar religious views to hers.

The field of religion provided another key break on the adoption of a Henrician model of kingship by Elizabeth. This was not in terms of doctrine. Although there is a level of ambiguity over Elizabeth's personal beliefs, it is clear that she was a Protestant.[17] As importantly, her succession at home and, crucially, abroad was seen as a victory for Protestantism. Andrew Pettegree comments: 'Contemporary observers on both sides of the religious divide quickly assessed Elizabeth's accession as a golden opportunity for Protestantism, and a disaster for Catholicism.'[18] Pettegree, however, goes on to point out that Elizabeth, in the eyes of many of her supporters, ultimately failed to fully grasp this opportunity. This failure can be related to her personal religious beliefs; however, in political terms it was a result of the Elizabethan regime's rejection of reformation as a continuing process of religious examination, persecution and control. This set it apart from all other mid-Tudor regimes. Above all, it distinguished Elizabeth's regime from that of her father which appeared at times obsessed with policing the inner and outer beliefs of its subjects in an often paranoid search for traitors and heretics. Eamon Duffy's work on the parish of Morebath has demonstrated very clearly the local impact of the various Tudor Reformations, all of which placed considerable, and in the case of the Edwardian impossible, burdens on parishes. This was not the case after 1560. Duffy comments that:

> Elizabethan Anglicanism used Edward's Prayer Book, rejected images, detested the pope. Nevertheless, after a draconian beginning, in most places it was far less abrasive than the Edwardian 'Tudor Church Militant' on which it was modelled. Elizabeth was a sincere Protestant, but she had none of her brother's precocious reforming zeal, and in her reign some of the deep rhythms of pre-Reformation religion, outlawed under Edward, were allowed to reassert themselves.[19]

Elizabeth's regime, despite the best efforts of some of its principal members, rejected confessionalization as an act of state, in other words reformation. It was Protestant, and it expected the country to follow its lead, but it turned its back on the process of imposing confessional orthodoxy except in the loosest sense. The Elizabethan regime treated reformation as an event with a beginning and end – not a process. This had the effect of restricting the legitimatizing potential of reformation as a defining characteristic of the Elizabeth's government. It also distinguished her regime from those of her father, brother and sister. At the same time this quietist aspect of the Elizabethan regime could in itself serve as a source of legitimation.

In 1570 Elizabeth was faced with a serious, albeit limited, rebellion based in the north of the country. The causes of this revolt appear to have been largely connected with the court and the machinations of various nobles, in particular the Earl of Leicester and the Duke of Norfolk.[20] The latter was scheming to marry Mary Queen of Scots but when Elizabeth found out and inevitably expressed strong objections to the match, the duke and his northern associates found themselves almost accidentally in revolt. The rebellion, once started, did take on a religious flavour with deliberate attempts made to invoke the Pilgrimage of Grace. The Northern Rebellion was, however, a far less serious event than the mass popular movement that had rocked Henry VIII's government in 1536.[21] Certainly it is hard to view Norfolk and his accomplices as a serious threat to Elizabeth, although this did not prevent the Queen from demanding the summary execution of seven hundred rebels. Fortunately this order seems to have been carried out with the usual Elizabethan lack of rigour or concern for obeying the Queen's orders to the letter.[22]

One important element of the government's response to the Northern Rebellion was the production of a proclamation entitled *A Declaration of the Quenes Proceedings since her Reigne*.[23] This work is a short history of the 1560s intended to justify Elizabeth's rule. What is noticeable about it is the extent to which is eschews Reformation polemic. Despite the religious colouring of the Northern Rebellion neither papists or papistry are mentioned in *A Declaration*. This is particularly significant since the document does explain the events of 1570 in terms that seem to call out for the use of these labels. *A Declaration* asserts that the rebellion was caused by seditious persons seeking to 'make alteration of the Quietness, whereunto of [God's] Goodness our Realme is now again restored'.[24] The success of theses traitors' lewd practices depended on both external support and the existence of secret allies at home:

> Whereas it hath appeared unto us, that although in some part there wanted not externall Incytements and Provocations to animate and stirr our People to withdrawe their naturall Dutyes from us and our Lawes, and to enter into Rebellion; yet could not the same so have prevailed, if there had not ben also therwith joined secret Practices of other malicious Persons, partly our Subjects born and partly residing within our Realme.[25]

It seems incredible given that one is dealing with a political culture within which an attempt was made to blame an event like Kett's Rebellion on papists that *A Declaration* does not deploy papistry to explain the causes of the rebellion. Indeed at one level it does. *A Declaration* places the blame for the Northern Rebellion on external incitements and the existence of secret internal enemies whose favoured method of subversion is the spreading of false and malicious rumours. This combination of factors reproduces exactly the depiction of papistry's *modus operandi* as endlessly represented in Henrician and Edwardian propaganda. But *A Declaration* fails, or more accurately refuses, to label the instigators of the Northern Rebellion papists. It is difficult to fully explain the reasons for this reticence. It is possible that there was a concern within the government that the use of too overtly religious language would inflame the situation. A more significant explanation is, however, provided by the way in which *A Declaration* justifies the Elizabethan regime as one in which obedience is *given* by subjects and not *exacted* by the regime.[26]

Of course one always needs to be careful with texts written in the heat of rebellion or its immediate aftermath. However, *A Declaration*'s rejection of the exaction of obedience does reflect an important reality about the early Elizabeth regime. It was clearly an issue for Cecil, since in *A Short Memoryall* he argues that one of the weaknesses of Queen's realm was the 'overmuch Boldnes growne in the Multitude of hir Subjects by her Majesties soft and remis Government'.[27] The exaction of obedience was a key characteristic of Reformation government. The decision of the Elizabethan regime not to deploy the language of confessionalization in 1570 reflects its rejection of reformation as an ongoing process. The cost of this in 1570 was that the regime's ability to exact obedience, to legitimatize itself in confessional terms, was limited.[28] At the same time, as *A Declaration* shows, the rejection of confessionalization as the regime's defining purpose, could provide its own source of legitimation. However it did mean that it was impossible for Elizabeth to rule as her father had. No one could ever describe Henry VIII's rule as being tender or question the extent to which he was prepared to exact obedience.

A final brake on a Henrician Elizabethan regime was the development during the 1550s in Protestant circles of a radical critique of Henry VIII's rule as tyrannical because of its violent restriction of public debate and its dubious religious status. In his *Admonition to England and Scotland to call them to repentance* Anthony Gilby characterized the Henrician changes in religion as a 'deformation', not a reformation', and called Henry a tyrant and lecherous monster.[29] He went on to argue that the shocking events of the summer of 1540, when three Protestants were burnt and three Catholics hung, 'clearly paynt [Henry's] beastlynes, that he cared for no manner of religio[n]'.[30] Gilby concludes his critique of the Henrician Reformation by pointing out that it created a church within which all that was heard was the King's voice, his books, homilies and proceedings taking the place of God's word.[31] Like *An Admonition to England and Scotland*, John Ponet's *A short treatise of politike power* was a product of the Marian Protestant diaspora.[32] In this work Ponet describes tyranny in the context of when it is lawful for subjects to resist wicked rulers. He writes that in a time of tyranny:

> ther is no doing, no gesture, no behaueour, no place can preserue or defende innocency against suche a gouernours crueltie; but as an huntour maketh wilde beastes his praie, and useth toiles, nettes, snares, trappes, dogges, firrettes, mynyng and digging the grounde, g[u]nes, bowes, speares, and all other instruments ... wherby he maie come by his praye: so dothe a wicked gouernour make the people his game and praye, and useth all kindes of subtilties, deceates, craftes, policies, force, violence, crueltie ... to spoyle and destroye the people that be co[m]mitted to his charge.[33]

Ponet is writing here about Mary's persecution of Protestants. However it is impossible to read this description of tyranny without thinking of Thomas Wyatt's court poetry. Indeed the use of hunting as an image of tyranny echoes its use by Wyatt to characterize the experience of being a Henrician courtier. *A short treatise of politike power* explicitly states that subjects, Christian or pagan, do not owe obedience to such a ruler. It argues that the word nobility was first instituted to describe those who 'deliuered the oppressed people out of the handes of their gouernours, who abused their authoritie, a[n]d wickedly, cruelly tyrannously ruled ouer them'.[34] Whereas Gilby's attack on Henry's rule is specific, Ponet's target is far more general and theoretical. In effect Ponet is attacking the Reformation model of monarchy in which the subject's obedience is exacted by inquisition and examination, by hunting down and ferreting out any possible failure of the subject to 'give' the ruler their total and complete support. Both works argue that the collapse of religious and secular power was the basis for tyranny: *An Admonition to England and Scotland* makes this argument by reference to history, while *A short treatise of politike power* adopts a more theoretical approach to the problem. Ponet's description of tyranny as a form of hunting seems to characterize Reformation kingship as inherently tyrannical. In particular, the image of a monarch as a hunter, pursuing his subjects in order to exact obedience, is a perfect symbolic depiction of the persecutory regime inaugurated by the Henrician Reformation.

The succession of Elizabeth in 1558 made the radicalism of men like Gilby and Ponet suddenly deeply unfashionable among English Protestants. However the intellectual and historical context of their work could not be so easily ignored. Whatever Elizabeth's views on the proper status of the monarch, and her desire to model her rule on that of her father, men like Cecil, while rejecting the radicalism of writers like Ponet, clearly would not tolerate a return to Henrician methods of governance. Indeed one of the things that *A Declaration* does is implicitly to compare Henry VIII's methods and policies with those of his daughter in order to laud Elizabeth's for their moderation, order and lack of oppressive rigour – particularly in the field of religion. Stephen Alford suggests that one can read *A Declaration* as the Elizabethan regime's attempt to 'publicly define itself'.[35] This is certainly the case and one key aspect of this definition was that Elizabeth's rule was fundamentally different from, and better than, that of her father.

A Declaration, however, does not only reflect the extent to which the Henrician period provided a problematic political model for Elizabeth and the political nation during the 1560s. Having asserted the regime's moderation and its desire not to extract obedience from the Queen's subjects, *A Declaration* moves on to discuss the provision of justice within the realm.

> And notwithstanding this our naturall and private Dulcenes, yet we have not, for the Publick, and the Conservation of common Peace, and Lawe, mutually betwixt our Subjects of all Estats, neglected to our Power the due and derect Administration of Justice for the suppressing of Malefactors in all particular criminall Causes; having also therwith had carefull consideration to diminish and avoid the Multitude of such Offenders, wherwith this Age generally in all Contreys aboundeth; in such sort as by Records may appeare that the Judges criminall of our Realme have in no Tyme given fewer bloody Judgments.[36]

A Declaration is rejecting here any accusation of softness in the administration of justice while asserting the regime's success in reducing the number of laws being administered in the country. These two points seem to be almost contradictory. Why claim that one's judges were giving fewer 'bloody sentences' at the same time as asserting one's success in suppressing malefactors? The answer to these questions lies in the Edwardian experiences, and particularly those of the traumatic year 1549, of all the major players in the early Elizabethan polity. What was a central element in Paget's critique of Somerset's government? That it was hyperactive, doing too much all at once while at the same time failing to ensure the day to day business of government, and in particular the maintenance of order. Elizabeth's regime as defined in *A Declaration* is the complete opposite. It does less but what it does do is keep order. *A Declaration* represents the Elizabethan regime as not Henrician or Edwardian. It positions it between the twin poles of tyranny and anarchy, Reformation kingship and the populace, Henry VIII and Kett.

The Mirror for Magistrates reflects the political world of *A Declaration*. It is a complex text which went through a number of editions, the most significant of which are the aborted publication in 1554 and the first two Elizabethan editions of 1559 and 1563.[37] *The Mirror* is made up of a collection of verses, written by a number of contributors including Thomas Sackville, co-author of the play *Gorboduc*, and George Ferrers, the translator of the Magna Carta. Each of the work's verses deals with a historical character and the collapse in their fortunes. They are linked with short prose passages that serve to give the work a sense of coherence and narrative flow. All the early editions were edited by William Baldwin, author of *Beware the Cat*.

The Mirror has not had a good press from literary critics or been discussed in much detail despite the fact that it was one of the most popular works of English poetry published during the sixteenth century. In particular critics have tended to view *The Mirror* as a piece of dated poetry which expresses a conventional if not banal set of Tudor political commonplaces with little or no intrinsic value in itself. It has often been studied simply as a precursor to the work of writers like Shakespeare or Spenser. Andrew Hadfield, however, has recently criticized this approach to *The Mirror*, writing that for these critics, '*The Mirror* is the "drad" John the Baptist unfit to kiss the "golden" feet of those who came after it; it is the stunted boyhood of Shakespeare's histories.'[38] Given the people involved in its production, it would be strange if *The Mirror* was not concerned with serious political and poetic issues. Scott Lucas comments that, 'the known authors of the *Mirror* were some of the most important intellectuals of their day'.[39] He goes on to argue that 'the *Mirror* is a miscellany of often complex and subtle political commentary'.[40] Baldwin's decision to present *The Mirror* as a composite text with the prose passages announcing its collective and written status relates directly to the work's politics. *The Mirror* is intended as a guide for the nascent Elizabethan polity in its enactment of the production of shared political knowledge. It deploys such poetic genres as complaint and allegory because its aim is to engender inter-subjective communal reading. *The Mirror* locates the act of interpretation not at the level of the individual, reader or poet, but in terms of a far wider community: an imagined ideal Elizabethan public sphere.[41]

The Mirror opens with Baldwin stating clearly at whom the work is aimed and its intentions. The title page dedicates the work to the 'nobilitye and all other in office' and asks God to grant them 'wisedome and all thinges needful for the preseruacion of theyr Estates'.[42] *The Mirror* then goes on to represent itself as one of the things Elizabethan magistrates need in order to preserve the commonwealth in its current form. Baldwin tells his readers:

> here as in a loking glas, you shall see (if any vice be in you) howe the like hath bene punished in other heretofore, whereby admonished, I trust will be a good occasion to move you to the soner amendment. This is the chiefest ende, whye it [*The Mirror*] is set forth, which God graunt it may attayne.[43]

It is noticeable that Baldwin's introductory comments to *The Mirror* are addressed to magistrates and not rulers or monarchs.[44] It is the former that *The Mirror* seems to suggest are fundamental to the preservation of the social order. At the same time a number of British kings are discussed in the course of *The Mirror*. The implication of this is that it is Tudor magistrates, a loose term encompassing a large range of men from the nobility to the lesser gentry, who are responsible for social coherence. More radically in places *The Mirror* seems to construct the monarch as a potential source of political tension and conflict, alongside such dangers to the commonwealth as unruly commons or corrupt lawyers, all of which it claims to be able to teach its readers to negotiate successfully.

The first story or tragedy that *The Mirror* tells its readers is entitled: 'The fall of Robert Tressilian chiefe Iustice of Englande, and other his felowes, for misconstruyng the lawes, and expounding them to serve the Princes affections.'[45] The prose introduction that proceeds Tressilian's story places it in a clear post-Edwardian context. In this piece the collective authors of *The Mirror* are depicted discussing where they should start their history. George Ferrers concludes this discussion by commenting: 'therefore omytting the ruffle made by Jacke Strawe and his meyny, and the murder of many notable men which therby happened, for Jacke (as you knowe) was but a poore prince: I will begin with a notable example whiche within a whyle after ensured'.[46] *The Mirror* summons up the example of Jack Straw, and by implication the Peasants' Revolt of 1381, only in order to pass over it. Instead it tells the story of Robert Tressilian as warning to lawyers and judges not to treat the law like wax in order to make it serve the monarch's will. Tressilian tells *The Mirror*'s readers how he and his fellows climbed into Richard II's favour.

> The lawes we interpreted and statues of the lande,
> Not trulye by the texte, but nuly by a glose:

> And wurds that wer most plaine whan thei by vs wer skande
> We turned by construction lyke a welchmans hose,
> Wherby many one both lyfe and lande dyd lose:
> Yet this we made a mean to mount aloft on mules.
> To serue kings in al pointes men must sumwhile breke rules.[47]

Tressilian argues here that complete obedience to a monarch inevitably leads to the breaking of laws. The lesson of Tressilian's story is that corrupt reading, twisting or scanning a text to serve one's desire, is an inevitable price that subjects have to pay to monarchs who demand to be served in all points. The implication of *The Mirror*'s first tragedy is that particular forms of textual interpretation, and therefore texts, are associated with the misuse of royal power. Tyranny demands texts that are complex and if these are lacking it needs people, like Tressilian, prepared to warp the meaning of the plainest text. It is no coincidence that misinterpretation for politically corrupt ends is the topic of *The Mirror*'s first tragedy. The plainness of *The Mirror* reflects the work's politics. The commitment of Baldwin and his colleagues to plain language was a product of their espousal of the politics of counsel. Not for them a text that required glosses or was open to misleading scanning.

The Mirror's avocation of counsel as essential to the proper function of the polity is entirely conventional in terms of Tudor political writing. Baldwin's work, however, moves beyond convention in its emphasis on Parliament as the antidote to flattery and tyranny. Tressilian's downfall comes about only after the court has ceased to function as a site of counsel. Richard II's transcending of the limits of the law becomes so outrageous that all the wise and worthy people leave the court and the nobility of the land is forced to act.

> The Baronye of Englande not bearing this abuse,
> Conspyring with the commons assembled by assent,
> And seynge neyther reason, not treaty, coulde induce
> The King in any thing his Rygor to relent,
> Mawgree all his might they called a parliament
> Francke and free for all men without checke to debate
> As well for weale publyke, as for the princes state.[48]

This verse holds up as commendable a conspiracy between the nobility and commons which resulted in a meeting of a Parliament that, despite Richard's might, reformed the commonwealth after full and free debate. In particular, as the next verse makes clear, this Parliament decided to remove from the king his corrupt counsellors, including Tressilian. It is important to note the separation explicitly drawn in this verse between the public weal and the prince. The implication of *The Mirror*'s first tragedy is that it is permissible, indeed desirable, for magistrates to act on their own authority, or perhaps more accurately on the authority residing within the polity, as guardians of the public weal, and to forcibly reform a Prince's rigour by removing the corrupt counsellors responsible for its implementation.[49]

The Mirror's second tragedy is the story of the Mortimers. In the process of telling it, however, it has to 'cross' back over 1381 as if re-enacting the original decision to pass over Jack Straw and the Peasants' Revolt. The third tragedy returns to the issues raised in *The Mirror*'s account of Tressilian. It tells the story of Thomas, Duke of Gloucester, uncle to Richard II, and his unlawful murder. Gloucester's 'crime' was to take a lead in the events already described in the first tragedy and to force Richard II to give up his favourites. This tragedy extends the scope of its criticism of Richard beyond the details of his behaviour to the monarchy itself. One of the lessons of Gloucester's story is that it is extremely dangerous to try to control a prince's will or desire. To make this point Gloucester applies the fable of the cat's bell to Richard II and by implication to all monarchs.

> But as an olde booke sayth, who so wyll assaye,
> Aboute the Cates necke to hang on a bell,
> Had fyrst nede to cut the Cats clawes awaye
> Least yf the Cat be curst, or not tamed well
> She haply with her nayles may clawe him to fell:[50]

The 'old book' referred to in this passage is probably *Piers Plowman*, although Tudor Protestants did not distinguish clearly between Langland's actual poem and the ploughman literature that grew up around it.[51] Gloucester goes on to warn his readers not to busy their brains about 'the cat's bell'.[52] There is, however, a tension in the text at this point, since the use of an animal fable and the reference to Langland's allegorical work seem designed to incite just such speculation. Indeed to make sense of Gloucester's words one has at a bare minimum to read beyond the plain meaning of the text; clearly he has not suddenly changed topic from politics to pet care.

Gloucester's lesson to his readers is that it is exceedingly dangerous for subjects to presume to meddle with the power and desire of princes. At the same time his tale invites them to speculate on the events that it recounts by using an animal fable. Gloucester's use of the cat fable raises a number of dangerous questions. What did it mean to represent the monarch as a cat?[53] How could one bell one's prince? Indeed what would this 'bell' look like?[54] These questions illustrate the extent to which the third tragedy of *The Mirror* seems to contradict Baldwin's metaphoric construction of the work as a 'looking glass'. It is as though the advent of princely power, and in particular its control, leads to a sudden complication of *The Mirror*'s language. This is not, however, to argue that this is a moment of deconstructive collapse or an eruption of the subconscious. The use of a cat to represent royal power is entirely witting. *The Mirror*'s aim was to teach Tudor magistrates how to maintain the public weal. To do this they needed to learn the lessons of the past in terms of the performance of their roles, including the need to reflect upon the way royal power has been exercised *and* controlled. Gloucester's story teaches its readers that it is dangerous to seek to control royal power unless one does it properly.

The second early Elizabethan edition (1563) of *The Mirror* extends the work's scope to the reign of Richard III. In the process a number of significant new historical figures are included within the work. One of the most important is the poet Collingbourne who was executed during the reign of Richard III for 'making a foolish rime'.[55] David Norbrook comments that this story illustrates the dangers of 'politically committed poetry'.[56] Collingbourne's mistake was not, however, simply to have written the rhyme: 'The Cat, the Rat, and Lovel our dog / Rule all England under the Hog.' *The Mirror* makes it clear that the real problem was that he did this in a time of tyranny when the laws of treason and heresy had been confused and merged together. When Collingbourne protests against the severity of his sentence he does so by referring to the way heretics are treated. 'To Heretykes no greater payne is layed / Than to recant theyr errors or retract: / And wurse than these can be no wryters acte.' However this argument is roundly rejected by one of Richard's henchmen, William Catesby. 'Yes (quoth the Cat) thy rayling wordes be treason / And treason is far worse then heresye.'[57] Collingbourne rejects this argument and goes on to defend his rhyme on the basis that it could not be treason since it was the truth. This is in itself a potentially radical argument, particularly so when advanced in the context of a historical story that seems to refer, if only implicitly, to the reign of Henry VIII. Certainly Catesby's confusion of treason and heresy seems to refer back the reign of terror of the 1530s and the Edwardian critique of the effect of the Henrician Reformation on the polity. The lesson of Collingbourne's story that the truth cannot be treasonable is at one level entirely conventional, but also potentially radical since it raises questions over the definition of treason and the process by which it is defined.

The Mirror gives poetic expression to the ideals of a mixed polity shared by leading members of the Elizabethan regime including William Cecil. Given its authors, however, this is not at all surprising. Similar issues were addressed in the play *Gorboduc*, written by two men, Thomas Norton and Thomas Sackville, who formed part of the intellectual milieu that produced *The Mirror*.[58] Indeed Sackville contributed a number of verses to Baldwin's project while Norton's work the *Orations of Arranes* expresses a similar view of history to that articulated in *The Mirror*.[59] All these works reflect the political assumptions of the people who were instrumental in the creation of the Elizabethan regime of the 1560s and 1570s. Many of these men, like Cecil, had first started to be politically active during the reign of Edward VI. They shared the Edwardian critique of Henrician Reformation government, while at the same time the events of 1549 left them wary of any appeal to the populace. It is these twin influences that led to the emphasis on Parliament in such works as *The Mirror*. There was, however, a problem in rejecting a Henrician or an early Edwardian model of government. Henry's government had claimed legitimacy on the basis of its rigour, Edward's by appealing for popular support. In *A Declaration* the Elizabethan regime defined itself in an almost entirely negative way; it did not persecute, exact obedience from the Queen's subjects or pass many new, unnecessary laws. As is well known, the positive side of Elizabeth's rule was provided by the creation of the myth of the Virgin Queen. However, this was a development of the 1580s and 1590s. In the 1560s and 70s the work of Barnabe Googe, John Foxe and George Gascoigne reflect the extent to which the early Elizabethan period was marked by serious ideological problems and conflicts. One solution to these tensions was to perform a return to the cultural norms and forms of the Henrician and Edwardian periods. The Elizabethan regime of the 1580s and 1590s played at being Henrician but without the terror: it played at being Edwardian without the religious enthusiasm. Instead this performance allowed the regime to appear godly and rigorous, as much as anything to its own members, while retaining its commitment to the mixed polity of the 1560s. The alternative, briefly glimpsed in the poetry of the Barnabe Googe, was the development of an aristocratic Protestant public sphere defined against papistry, populace, but also the prince.

GODLY SHEPHERDS VERSUS CUPIDO

Barnabe Googe was born in 1540, the son of Robert Googe, a Lincolnshire man with important court connections. The most important of these was William Cecil, to whom Googe dedicated a number of his works. Googe spent much of his early life, after the death of his mother, at Canterbury in the household of Lady Hales, the wife of Sir James Hales. In 1560 he published a translation of Marecellus Palingenius' *Zodiacus vitae*. Googe produced a number of other translations during the course of his lifetime, as well as two volumes of his own poetry. His relationship with Cecil was very important to him and resulted in his receiving a number of favours and government posts. Googe continued to publish intermittently throughout the rest of his life and died in 1594.[60]

Googe dedicated his version of *Zodiacus vitae* to Cecil. The dedicatory letter clearly positions Googe's poetic vocation between the twin poles of Henrician court poetry and the reforming verse of writers like Crowley. Googe starts by claiming that the only way of remedying vice is through writing and that therefore writers have an essential part to play within the polity. This sounds very much like a justification for the kind of poetic agenda pursued by Crowley during the Edwardian period. Googe, however, is not interested in assuming

Crowley's role of the plain-speaking public poet. In his letter to Cecil he argues that textual complexity, and indeed dissimulation, can be as successful as plain speaking when it comes to attacking vice. Googe writes: 'what vice so odious can be remembered, or what crime so detestable may be reported, that they [the classical poets] with sugared sentences have not assaulted, with godly instructions battered, and thundering words exiled?'[61] Googe's argument here is impeccably Edwardian in terms of the public use of poetry to reform vice, but his methodology, the use of 'sugared sentences', is not. Indeed given the valorization during Edward's reign of public debate, even if it led to division and dispute, and the constant representation of papists as corrupters of language, people who subverted the truth of Christ's teaching by sweetening it with false unwritten verities, Googe's argument in this letter illustrates an important shift in Protestant poetics between 1548 and 1563. Googe goes on in this piece to explicitly ask for Cecil's protection – in specifically poetic terms:

> Humbly requesting that through your honour's learned protection and grave author-
> ity, the simple fruits of a young head may strongly be defended from the severe
> reprehensions of Momus and the malicious judgements of Zoilus.[62]

Googe asks Cecil to protect his work from malicious poets, Zoilus and Momus, the god of censure and ridicule. Googe's poetic project, the use of poetry to banish sin from the commonwealth, is threatened by other poets and not by such obvious misusers of language as papists. His use of these figures is at one level intended to advertise his learning and to demonstrate that he has mastered the humanist skill of classical allusion. At the same time it is noticeable that Googe, a committed Protestant, frames the enemies of his poetry in classical and non-confessional terms. Googe's reference to Zoilus performs the same ideological function as Cecil's reference to Epicurus does in his *A Short Memoryall*. In both cases a classical figure is deployed to signify a source of danger while at the same working to obscure the real nature of the conflict. Cecil's Epicureans stand in the place of Catholic opponents to the Elizabethan religious settlement. Zoilus and Momus simultaneously reflect and obscure a basic disjuncture within Googe's ideological agenda between its aim, the reform of the commonwealth, which needs to take place at a social level, and opposition to it, which Googe depicts as cultural and poetic.

Googe's *Eglogs, Epytaphes and Sonettes* (1563) addresses the same political and poetic issues as *The Mirror*. In particular, it articulates a Protestant male humanist identity against the evils of papist, popular and princely power. In Googe's work it is male friendship, *amicitia*, which provides the basis, the point of consistency, for a process of identification constantly endangered by slander, social disorder and the emasculating idolatrous tyrannical power of courtly love. *Eglogs, Epytaphes and Sonettes* presents itself as a poetic miscellany.

It is clearly modeled on *Tottel's Miscellany*, despite the fact that almost all of the poems it contains were written by Googe. The key similarity that it shares with Tottel's collection is that it offers its readers the fantasy of participating in a closed world. However, while *Tottel's Miscellany* did indeed make public texts which in the past had been largely confined to a restricted court coterie, *Eglogs, Epytaphes and Sonettes* has to write into itself the world that it then offers its readers; it has to create its own manuscript past upon which it can then claim to be based. This has poetic and political implications. *Tottel's Miscellany* contains a large number of works, in particular those written by Wyatt, which were produced under the shadow of Henrician tyranny. Their secrecy was at least partly a product of the political situation in which Wyatt and his fellow poets found themselves. One of the pleasures that *Tottel's Miscellany* offers its readers is the chance to read Henrician poetry as a previously hidden narrative of the Henry VIII's court. The conditions under which Wyatt wrote had an impact on the poetics of his work: under a tyranny one has to produce texts whose meaning is obscure; Henrician court poets wrote 'sugared sentences' because in their world plain unadorned words could have very bitter results. As has been suggested, the effect of the changes that Tottel made when he edited the poetry that made up his miscellany was, subtly but pervasively, to make it more public and less personal, emphasizing general themes and form over the individual poet and the historically specificity of his work. Googe in his volume builds on Tottel's poetic agenda but gives it a specifically Protestant direction.

There is another crucial distinction, however, between the poetics and politics of *Tottel's Miscellany* and of Googe's *Eglogs, Epytaphes and Sonettes*. The former presents itself to its readers as opening the lid on the private space of the Henrician court, while the latter offers those who read the chance of participating in a world that is defined not as courtly but rather as Protestant, humanist and masculine. In particular, while Tottel claims to be making public existing, implicitly private, manuscripts, Googe's volume creates the impression that although its transformation from manuscript to print happened without its author's permission, the texts it contains were never intended to circulate only within a restricted coterie. Tottel's collection is in some ways a historical document, revealing to its readers the truth of the no longer extant Henrician court. *Eglogs, Epytaphes and Sonettes* does have a historical side as it contains a number of poems that refer directly to the events of the reigns of Edward and Mary. However there is no sense, as there is in *Tottel's Miscellany*, of a clear separation between the reader's present and the work's. Googe expects his readers, like those of *The Mirror*, to understand and act upon *Eglogs, Epytaphes and Sonettes*. Googe's miscellany is a poetic representation of an ideal Tudor polity that combines a magisterial Protestantism, informed by the lessons of the past, with Elyot's civic humanism. *Eglogs, Epytaphes and Sonettes* creates an image of a textual world, a political sphere, made up of learned Protestant male friends, a band of brothers united in their fight to reform the realm against the dangers of papistry, tyranny and social anarchy. Where *Tottel's Miscellany* presents its readers with a closed private courtly world, the implication of *Eglogs, Epytaphes and Sonettes* is that those who read it, and understand it properly, can become part of its world, members of Googe's poetic public Protestant bond. Despite its title, *Eglogs, Epytaphes and Sonettes* is a politically radical volume. It deploys courtly genres and forms to imagine a political world whose coherence and virtue is based on the exclusion of prince, papistry and populace.

Eglogs, Epytaphes and Sonettes opens with a number of introductory texts, two poems, a letter and an address to the Reader. All these pieces are designed to locate Googe's collection very specifically within Elizabethan Protestant culture. The opening poem was written by Alexander Neville, who was the author of a Latin history of the events in Norwich in 1549.[63] Neville's poem tells Googe to ignore the criticisms of 'defaming minds' and instead to seek patrons whose judgement has been taught by time and practice. His attack on the former is particularly violent.

> Such crabfaced, cankered, carlish chuffs,
> within whose hateful breasts
> Such malice bides, such rancour broils,
> such endless envy rests,
> Esteem thou not. No prejudice
> to thee: nor yet opprest
> Thy famous writings are by them.
> Thou livest and ever shalt.
> Not all the sland'ring tongues alive
> may purchase blame or fault
> Unto thy name, O worthy Googe.[64]

Who was the actual target for this vitriolic rhetoric'? Neville does say that 'they' are like Momus' monstrous brood, giving them a classical and possibly learned status, but the phrase 'carlish chuffs' implies Googe's enemies come from a specific class since 'chuff' means churl, rustic or clown. There is a tension in Neville's poem between its classical references and its imagery of lower-class violence and ignorance.

This tension is reflected in the epitaphs that form an important part of Googe's volume. The first epitaph is to Lord Sheffield, one of the few victims on the government's side of the events in Norwich in 1549. Googe's poem not surprisingly reproduces the image of Kett and his followers found in such works as Cheke's *The Hurt of Sedition*. He writes:

> When brutish broil and rage of war
> in clownish hearts began,

When tigers stout in tanner's bond
unmuzzled all they ran,
The noble Sheffield, Lord by birth
and of courage good,
By clubbish hands of crabbèd clowns
there spent his noble blood.[65]

Googe here represents Kett and his followers as animalistic violent clowns. In the process he is clearly drawing on the same discourse as that used by Neville to describe the 'carlish chuffs' who, he suggested in the opening poem of the collection, threatened Googe's poetry with harsh and malicious criticism. This creates a parallel, albeit a slightly strained one, between the actual fate of Sheffield and the potential one of *Eglogs, Epytaphes and Sonettes* at the hands of crabbèd clowns and crab-snouted beasts.

Googe's next epitaph is to M. Shelley who died fighting the Scots at Musselburgh while setting an example of bravery to his fellow Englishmen. Both Sheffield and Shelley are presented by Googe as English heroes cut down well fighting against overwhelming odds. It is noticeable, however, that Googe does not use the same kind of language against the Scots as he does when describing Kett and his followers. Indeed there is a suggestion in the 'Epitaph to M. Shelley' that the war with the Scots was unnecessary. Googe writes that when the Scots denied their promise, of Mary Stuart's hand in marriage to Edward VI, and raised an army against the English, the latter decided to try their breach of faith not with truth but with 'trothless shields'.[66] The two other epitaphs included in *Eglogs, Epytaphes and Sonettes* mourn the passing of Thomas Phaer, the translator of the first English edition of Virgil's *Aeneid* printed under Mary, and Nicholas Grimald, whose poetry formed part of *Tottel's Miscellany*.[67] Googe celebrates these men for their wit and learning. Alongside Sheffield and Shelley they are part of Googe's Protestant, magisterial and humanist pantheon – the honoured dead whose example Googe is recommending to his readers.

None of the epitaphs published in *Eglogs, Epytaphes and Sonettes* commend the victims of the Marian persecution. The terrible events of the period 1553–1558 are, however, directly addressed in the opening part of the volume. Googe's eclogues are among the first examples of the genre in English. In these poems Googe juxtaposes three competing and conflicting themes – desire, tyranny and martyrdom. He uses the same language, however, when addressing each of these topics so that the reader is constantly unsure what is being discussed – politics, love or religion. The first eclogue takes the form of a dialogue between Daphnes and Amintas during which the latter fulfils on an earlier promise to tell his friend the 'state of love'. At one level Amintas' description of love draws on entirely conventional poetic tropes. The dialogic context of a Googe's eclogue, however, gives it a crucially different inflection in comparison to the work of such poets as Wyatt or Surrey. While the work of these poets, in James Simpson's words, 'repetitively fails to generate civic solidarities from within the experience of Cupid's tyranny', Googe deploys pastoral conventions precisely in order to imagine an alternative discourse in opposition to that of the God of Love.[68] Amintas starts his description of love by describing the process by which a person falls under Cupid's spell.

> A fervent humor (some do judge)
> within the head doth lie,
> Which issuing forth with poisoned beams
> doth run from eye to eye,
> And taking place abroad in heads
> a while doth firmly rest
> Till frenzy framed in fancy fond
> descends from head to breast,
> And poison strong from eyes outdrawn
> doth pierce the wretched heart,
> And all infects the blood about
> and boils in every part.[69]

For Amintas love, or rather Cupid's fiery love, is a potential madness which lies dominant within a person's mind until awakened by the exchange of lustful looks with another. It is this act of mutual gazing that gives love the potency to overpower a man's reason and leave him oppressed and in bondage. Amintas' love is clearly recognizable as Petrarchan, however, the pastoral context in which it is articulated also gives it an Ovidian emphasis. This is important since it suggests both the extent to which Googe's use of this language is political and the ways in which he imagines a solution to Cupid's tyranny. Amintas' description of love, moreover, also suggests class and religious tyranny. The lover is held in 'slavish servile yoke' suggesting that one of the effects of this love is to reduce its victim to that of one of Neville's 'carlish chuffs'. Finally the lover's behavior, caught in the flames of Cupid's fiery love, also reproduces imagery associated with the depiction of Protestant martyrs in John Foxe's *Acts and Monuments*.[70] Amintas' lover, like Foxe's martyrs, is caught in a flame that he cannot escape, indeed which he does not desire to escape if this would mean renouncing the object of his love.

Googe's third eclogue makes this comparison between the flames of love and those of the martyr's pyre far more explicit. The two speakers of this eclogue are Menalcas and Coridon, who has inherited the flock of Dametas, 'the martyr'.[71] Menalcas asks Coridon to tell him of the town's estate and this prompts a long account not only of the town's corruption but also of recent English history. Coridon tells Menalcas that the town (probably London) has become a place where Sir John Straw and Sir John Cur rule, a place in which class distinctions have been eroded by inappropriate social mobility.[72] Coridon is quick to point out that it is not their lack of birth that is the basis of his criticism of men like Sir John Cur. He tells Menalcas that:

> I would not them envy
> If any spot of gentleness
> in them I might espy.
> For if their natures gentle be,
> though birth be never so base,
> Of gentlemen (for meet it is)
> they ought have name and place.
> But when by birth they base are bred
> and churlish heart retain.
> Though place of gentlemen they have
> yet churls do remain.[73]

This 'churlish' state is exemplified by the chief man in the town, who is confusingly also called Coridon. This personage is associated both with the subversion of class boundaries and the Marian restoration of Catholicism. The poem at this point takes on an explicitly historical tone as Coridon tells Menalcas how his alter ego, because of the churlish cruelty that remained in his heart, reversed the effects of the Edwardian Reformation by forcing the silly sheep to leave their newly found sweet pastures and return to their old stinking dales and corrupted grasses.[74] Googe's language here reminds one of Gilby's critical depiction of Henry VIII as a boar destroying the flowers of godly teaching. Coridon goes on to produce an allegorical representation of the Marian persecution.

> And with the sheep, the shepherds good
> (O hateful hounds of hell)
> They did torment, and drive them out
> in places far to dwell.
> There dièd Daphnes for his sheep
> the chiefest of them all,
> And fair Alexis flamed in fire
> who never perish shall.[75]

In Coridon's speech, Googe places the Marian persecution in a pastoral classical context which is at the same time Protestant and magisterial. This locates Googe's representation of the Marian persecution between the two main competing Elizabethan historical constructions of Mary's reign: the Foxian emphasis on religion and in particular the status of *all* the martyrs as Protestant heroes and on the other side, the more traditional histories of writers like Thomas Cooper who, in his *Coopers Chronicle*, treated the executions of Mary's reign as simple, prosaic historical events – comparable to royal marriages or natural disasters.[76] Googe's third eclogue stresses the importance of the Marian persecution, and indeed its horror, while at the same time its classical pastoral form enables it to avoid the populist implications of *Acts and Monuments*. All of Googe's eight eclogues deal with various kinds of love. The first seven take as their subject various forms of disabling, failed or violent love. Googe's final eclogue places the preceding discussions of the dangers of love in quite a different, specifically religious, context when one of its participants, Cornix, tells his fellow shepherd, Coridon, that:

> Both place and time, my Coridon,
> exhorteth me to sing,
> Not of the wretched lovers' lives,
> but of the immortal king.[77]

Cornix goes on to give this choice, between wretched lovers and God as fit subjects of poetry, a specifically political emphasis.

> Of Him, therefore, me list to sing,
> and of no wanton toys,
> For Him to love, and Him to praise,
> surmounts all other joys.
> O shepherds, leave Cupido's camp,
> the end whereof is vile;
> Remove Dame Venus from your eyes
> and harken here a while.[78]

Cornix's argument here is that the shepherds should leave behind worldly objects of desire and concentrate instead on heavenly love. This change is given both spatial and visual meaning with the shepherds being encouraged to physically leave Cupido's camp and to withdraw their gaze from Venus. In this verse Cornix is telling his fellow shepherds that they should turn their backs on idolatry and its home, the court. Instead they should concentrate their poetic efforts on worshipping and praising God.

Googe's *Eglogs, Epytaphes and Sonettes* reproduces the forms and poetic discourses of Wyatt mediated through *Tottel's Miscellany* in the service of a specifically Elizabethan political and religious agenda. Googe takes the disempowering and disabling discourse of Petrarchan love as articulated in Wyatt's work and makes it the other of a godly Protestant masculine identity. At the same time *Eglogs, Epytaphes and Sonettes* extends further the poetic developments implicit in *Tottel's Miscellany*. As has been suggested, Tottel's collection privileged the social and generic over the individuality of either text or author. Googe gives this new emphasis a particularly Elizabethan political slant by locating a godly Protestant identity within the form of his eclogues, and indeed in *Eglogs, Epytaphes and Sonettes* as a whole. It is the dialogic nature of Googe's eclogues, and the way in which his shepherds experience the dangers of love within a communal framework, in particular that of male friendship, that ultimately allows them the possibility of escape that was denied the various narrators of Wyatt's poems. A similar change takes place in terms of the status of the reader. Wyatt's readers are constantly in danger of following his narrators into the textual toils that entrap them. *Tottel's Miscellany* offers its readers the fantasy of safely penetrating the dangerous world of the Henrician court by creating the outline of a narrative of courtly love through which readers can read the poems. *Eglogs, Epytaphes and Sonettes* encourages its readers to view themselves as participants in its godly agenda. Cornix's argument that the shepherds should turn away from Cupid's court and stop gazing upon Dame Venus is also directed at Googe's readers – indeed there is a level at which reading *Eglogs, Epytaphes and Sonettes* in itself performs this reforming act. To keep one's gaze locked on the goddess of love, to remain in Cupid's court, would be to succumb to the dangers of idolatry and voluntarily place oneself under a tyranny. Lurking behind these twin dangers are those of the 'bad' Coridon with his martyr's pyres and Neville's 'carlish chuffs' with their anarchic violence.

The key difference between *Eglogs, Epytaphes and Sonettes* and much later Elizabethan poetry is that it does not leave its reader on his own to negotiate the dangers of Petrarchan love and all that it represents. Instead Googe provides a clear alternative to the world of courtly love in the form of godly male friendship enacted through humanist tropes, in particular the exchange of texts. The middle section of *Eglogs, Epytaphes and Sonettes* contains a number of poems written by Googe to his friends and their replies. The effect is to create a parallel between the behaviour of the participants in the eclogues and that of Googe and his poetic friends. The implication is that the readers of Googe's work could also become part of this exchange of lyrics – provided they are prepared to share Googe's godly magisterial identity. One of the people addressed in the middle section of *Eglogs, Epytaphes and Sonettes* is the famous Protestant polemist and writer John Bale. Googe's poem is written as a piece of advice to this veteran of the Henrician and Edwardian Reformations. He writes:

> Good agèd Bale, that with thy hoary hairs
> Dost yet persist to turn the painful book,
> O Happy man, that hast obtained such years,
> And leav'st not yet on paper pale to look!
> Give over now to beat they wearied brain,
> And rest thy pen that long hath laboured sore.
> For aged men unfit, sure, is such pain,
> And thee beseems to labour now no more.
> But thou I think Don Plato's part will play,
> With book in hand to have thy dying day.[79]

Googe's representation of Bale as a Tudor Plato would surprise anyone acquainted with his writings whose violent polemical tone earned him the sobriquet of 'bilious Bale'. Placing Bale within a classical context has the effect of making him fit more readily into an early Elizabethan context. In the process it performs a symbolic rewriting of Edwardian Protestantism. The 'painful book' that Bale laboured on in the past, and is still prepared to study, refers to his work exposing papistry and perhaps in particular its history. Googe's poem constructs Bale's pre-Elizabethan work in specifically textual terms. In the process it implicitly strips it of any radical or social meaning. The comparison of Bale with Plato performs a similar symbolic move. It subtly suggests that Bale's kind of Protestant polemics are no longer vital or even relevant. *Eglogs, Epytaphes and Sonettes* is an explicitly Protestant text, but one that illustrates the effect on magisterial English Protestantism of the events of Edward's reign. In 'To Doctor Bale' Googe personifies the popular and violent past of English Protestantism in the person of the young John Bale. He argues that while Bale's labours should be recognized his moment has passed; that Elizabethan Protestants should turn their backs on the kind of popular polemical Protestantism that was once exemplified by men like 'bilious' Bale.

Eglogs, Epytaphes and Sonettes concludes with an extended allegorical dream vision entitled, 'Cupido Conquered'. In many ways this is a traditional piece, heavily influenced by Chaucer. The poem opens with its narrator in a state of melancholy. He decides to go for a walk in the lovely summer countryside in order to forget his pains of love. Having listened to the singing of the birds, he falls asleep and has a vision in which Mercury visits him. 'Whilst I lay thus in slumber deep, / I might perceive to stand / A person clothèd all in white.'[80] Mercury upbraids the narrator, who at this moment appears to be very clearly a figure for Googe himself, for taking too much to heart criticisms of his poetry. The god reminds Googe that even such poets as Chaucer have been accused of producing doltish rhymes. The purpose of Mercury's discussion of poetry only becomes apparent, however, at the end of 'Cupido Conquered'. The main part of the poem is taken up with the narrator's journey to a symbolic castle within which is the court of Diana. The narrator witnesses the arrival of a Messenger who has come to report that Diana's realm is under violent attack by Cupido and his fellows. The Messenger's description of what happens to those who fall under Cupido's power is particularly violent and again deploys images that seem designed to make the reader think of the suffering of Christian martyrs at the hands of pagan persecutors. 'Some [of Cupido's victims] anchor cast on crossèd beams / to rid themselves from strife / And hang themselves full thick on trees / to end a wretched life.'[81] Confronted with this threat, Diana dispatches an army led by Hippolytus which defeats Cupido after a violent battle. The poem ends inconclusively since the narrator wakes immediately after Cupido has begged for his life, before sentence is pronounced.

Although 'Cupido Conquered' is a conventional poem, it does contain a number of significant departures from the tradition in which it is written. Above all, in Googe's work Cupido is defeated. The poem concludes on a self-reflective note with the narrator telling the reader that after a night's sleep:

> When Phoebus rose, to pass the time
> and pass my grief away,
> I took pen and penned the dream
> that made my Muses stay.[82]

'Cupido Conquered' therefore ends at its beginning. It is as though Googe is concerned to emphasis the fictionality of his work, the extent to which it is a self-knowing piece of writing with a clear didactic aim. Indeed it is in these terms that the politics of Googe's poem become apparent. 'Cupido Conquered' could have as an alternative title 'Wyatt Conquered'. This is a poem about resistance to becoming caught in the toils of the kind of poetry that Wyatt and his contemporaries wrote. It is this which makes the defeat of Cupido so significant. Whereas Wyatt's narrators cannot imagine a language which would allow them successfully to defeat the god of love Googe makes his defeat the narrative motivation of his text. This also explains Mercury's discussion of poetry at the beginning of the poem. For Googe to stop writing because of the harsh words of his critics would be to leave Cupido undefeated. The inconclusive end of the vision also has important political implications since, by suspending judgement on Cupido, Googe implicitly places responsibility for it with the reader. However, unlike in Wyatt's poetry, here the reader has all the facts to reach a reasoned judgment. 'Cupido Conquered' is at one level a warning against wilful reading. Its allegorical form is designed to force the reader to slow down and make sure that they have worked through all the meanings of its images without being seduced by the text's surface brilliance. Indeed allegory as a form inherently problematizes the production of meaning. To reach a proper judgement on Cupido one needs to weigh up all the facts without being unduly or excessively influenced by Googe's own powerful imagery, the skill of his poetry or the pleasure of reading it; one needs instead to read as a member of an informed Protestant public sphere.

Eglogs, Epytaphes and Sonettes can be read as a poetic Protestant version of Sir Thomas Elyot's *The Governour*. Certainly they are very different texts but in both the ideal of informed debate by a select group of friends, a bond of brothers, is advanced as a political necessity. Perhaps more significantly, however, both texts are directed against malign readers and tyrannical rulers represented through Ovidian tropes, above all the equation of tyranny with corrupt wilful reading. In Elyot's text it is public debate and counsel that is advanced as the key antidote to tyranny, while in Googe's work it is allegory as a form which demands a particular kind of reading. Obviously there are important differences between the politics of *Eglogs, Epytaphes and Sonettes* and *The Governour*. Most significantly the former bears the scares of the mid-Tudor period. It is clear that for Googe *amicitia* can only really exist between learned Protestant men.[83] *The Governour* is concerned with the production of order and articulates a firm commitment to the existing social order. In particular, the representation of malign readers in Elyot's work consistently suggests they are fellow magistrates. *Eglogs, Epytaphes and Sonettes* shares *The Governour*'s concern with tyrannical reading by pre-eminent rulers, but is at least as concerned with the dangers of lower-class anarchy and papist persecution; the combination of prince, populace and papists as malign wilful persecutionary readers is what haunts Googe's poetic and political vision in this volume.

In 1569 Googe produced an extended allegorical poem entitled *The Shippe of Safeguarde*. As an appendix to this text he also published translations of two passages from Eusebius, 'The death of S. Polycarpus' and 'A Priest of Apollo straungely converted'.[84] *The Shippe of Safeguarde* is an allegorical voyage through various moral and spiritual dangers whose final destination is the port of godly living. It includes lengthy descriptions of Heresy and Idolatry, as well as an extract from Chaucer's *Romance of the Rose* which Googe uses to illustrate hypocrisy. All the poetry that Googe produced during the 1560s was committed to the creation of a godly Protestant England. Its enemies, as imagined by Googe, were an anarchic populace, papist idolatry and Cupido's tyranny. Googe's poetics are inseparable from his politics with their emphasis on the active role of the reader in the production of meaning and a concomitant rejection of the hermeneutics of Wyatt or Baldwin in *Beware the Cat*; Googe was not interested in giving his readers the pleasure of interrogation or exciting them with the fantasy of losing themselves in a web of feline tales. Googe's poetic and political agenda remained as a possibility within Elizabethan, and indeed Jacobean, culture. For example one can argue that the Bond of Association of 1584 enabled in the field of politics the emergence of the kind of Protestant bond of brothers that Googe imagined in *Eglogs, Epytaphes and Sonettes*. The Bond bound together the committed Protestant members of the Elizabethan polity in a voluntary association ostensibly solely concerned with the defense of the Queen. In practice, as Collinson has argued, the Bond was a 'quasi-republican statement' designed to create a Protestant political organization based, in Cecil's words, on 'fellowship and societie' – Googe's bond of godly Protestant shepherds committed to the defeat of papistry, popular anarchy and, by implication, princely tyranny.[85]

NARRATIVE AND FICTION IN *ACTS AND MONUMENTS* AND
A HUNDRETH SUNDRIE FLOWRES

The political and poetic issues that Googe addressed in the work he produced in the 1560s are also reflected in John Foxe's *Acts and Monuments*.[86] Foxe was a godly Protestant committed to the further Protestantization of the English Church. He played a minor role in the Edwardian Reformation and fled abroad when Mary came to the throne. The first two Latin versions of *Acts and Monuments* were produced while he was in exile. After his return to England Foxe went on to produce four quite distinct English versions of *Acts and Monuments*, those of 1563, 1570, 1576 and 1583.[87] *Acts and Monuments* is an extremely complex and very long work. In this chapter I shall only have time to touch briefly on some of the most important aspects of the 1570 edition of Foxe's work. This texts shows that Foxe shared the concerns of writers like Baldwin or Norton over the twin dangers of Henrician rigour and Edwardian anarchy. Foxe's response to these dangers is not, however, symmetrical. He explicitly rejects Henrician kingship as an appropriate model for Elizabeth's rule while his response to the dangers of popular enthusiasm takes place at the level of textual form.

It is easy to forget, given the work's anti-Catholic polemics, that one of the central messages of *Acts and Monuments* to its Protestant *and* Catholic readers is that all persecution is anti-Christian.[88] Indeed the idea of exacting obedience is itself alien to Foxe's work. V.N. Olsen comments that: 'Foxe's great work, the *Acts and Monuments*, especially the editions with woodcuts, could not but impress its readers with the fact that a persecuting church could not be the true church.'[89] In this case the message of *Acts and Monuments* and *A Declaration of the Quenes Proceedings since her Reigne* is the same, particularly for Catholic readers – the Elizabethan regime is legitimate because it does not persecute. Foxe's critique of Henry's kingship relates directly to his status as a persecutor. He describes the appearance and behaviour of Henry at the trial of John Lambert in terms that remind one specifically of Sir Thomas Elyot's description of a ruler who is without 'placabilitie'. Foxe writes:

> the kyng, his looke, cruell countenance, and hys bowes bent unto seuerity, did not little augment this terror [Lambert's] playnly declaryng a minde full of indigna-tion[n] farre unworthy such a Prince, especially in such a mater and against so humble and obedient a subiect.[90]

Foxe's critique of Henrician kingship is coupled with a more positive model of the proper ordering of the commonwealth. In the first of a number of prefaces to the 1570 edition of *Acts and Monuments*, Foxe writes:

> No man lyueth in that common wealth where nothing is amiss. But yet because God hath so placed vs Englishmen here in one commo[n] wealth, also in one

Church as in one shippe together: let vs not mangle and diuide the shippe, which being deuided perisheth: but euery man serue in hys order with diligence, wherin he is called. They that sit at the helme, kepe well the poynt of the nedle, to know how the shippe goeth, and whether it should. What soeuer wether betydeth, the nedle touched with the stone of Gods word will neuer fayle. Such as labour at the oares, start for no tempest, but do what they can to kepe from the rockes. Likewise they which be in inferior rowmes, take hede they moue no sedition, nor disturbance agaynst the rowers and mariners. No storme so daungerours to a shippe on the Sea, as is discord and disorder in a weale publicke.[91]

At one level Foxe's image of the commonwealth as a ship is entirely conventional. It is worthwhile, however, noting some of the subtleties of his version of this trope. This passage divides the commonwealth into three orders, mariners, rowers and inferior rowers. In addition it explicitly places the guidance of the commonwealth in the hands of those equipped to follow a compass 'touched by God's word'. The implication of this is that the commonwealth should be guided by the godly. It is hard to see in this image of the commonwealth the place for a monarch. Indeed this is particularly noticeable given that the trope itself seems to call out for a captain – but Foxe's ship of state is captain-less or has a crew of lesser captains.

This image of the England as a ship also has important poetic implications. Foxe in his writing consistently criticizes humanist utopianism. In his *A Sermon of Christ Crucified* he directly attacks More's *Utopia*. In this sermon Foxe discusses people who are quick to believe a bad report against their friend or neighbour and are 'so crabbed, that hardly or never will be reconciled after.' He goes on to comment:

Such stoicall stomackes [and] unsociable natures, which neither live here like Angels, nor yet reme[m]ber themselues to be but men amongst men, are to be sent '*ad rempublicam Platonis*' or to '*M. Mores Vtopia*' eyther there to liue with themselues, or els where as none may live to offend them.[92]

Foxe's critique of More's *Utopia* takes place in the context of a discussion of persecution. Foxe argues that there is a relationship between the desire for a totalizing order like the one imagined in *Utopia* and the acceptance of the need to persecute. Foxe's image of the commonwealth as a ship is noticeable for the way in which it accepts the reality that no one lives in a society without antagonism, in which nothing is amiss. The solution to this is not, however, as far as Foxe is concerned, to eradicate disorder but rather for the three orders that make up the commonwealth to work together.[93] He expects similar work from his readers. For Foxe, to read *Acts and Monuments* properly is to become a crew member in the godly ship of the English Protestant commonwealth.[94]

It would be a mistake, however, to see Foxe as anything other than a committed humanist. Indeed his humanism is perhaps most obvious in terms of his political thought as expressed in *Acts and Monuments*, when it often appears that he is drawing directly from Elyot's *The Governour*. For example, a key and difficult moment in Foxe's history was the reign of Edward VI and in particular the fall of the Duke of Somerset. Invariably *Acts and Monuments* explains events like those that rocked England in 1549 as the product of papist machinations and plots. Clearly this explanation would not work in terms of Somerset's downfall. Instead Foxe blames 'discord' within the Council, writing:

> So long as the Lords agreed in concord among themselves, Winchester and Bonner, with all that faction, was cut short, and began to condescend to good co[m]formitie. But afterward perceauing the states and nobles of the Realme to be amo[n]g themselues diuided, and [the] Lord Protector the Kings uncle displaced, and his brother the Admirall before beheaded, and the young King now left in that case, they bega[n] upon some hope to take hart unto them.[95]

However Foxe does not, or perhaps more accurately cannot, explain why discord breaks out.[96] He refers to the example of the Duke of Gloucester, who held the same position as Somerset during the minority of Henry VI, and was also driven from power. Unfortunately this historical example does not really help Foxe, since an essential element in Gloucester's positive reputation among English Protestant historians was that one of his main enemies during his protectorship was a cardinal. Foxe's explanation of the troubles of Edward's reign comes down to a tautology – the lack of concord within the Edwardian polity was caused by discord – and a moral assertion – the prosperity of Edward's reign and lack of persecution led to the people being corrupted by avarice.[97] Foxe's humanism leads him to see public debate as both the sign of a good commonwealth and a key element in its constitution. The failures of Edward's reign, and the difficulty of attributing them to papistry, led him to blame the operation of counsel, and in particular its subversion by discord, for the fall of Somerset and ultimately for the succession of Mary Tudor.

Another important element in Foxe's political thought, which again can be found in *The Governour*, is the emphasis in *Acts and Monuments* on Protestant friendship – confessional *amicitia*. Often Protestant martyrs are represented in such a way as to emphasis the close friendships they had with each other. For example in 1555 John Careless wrote to John Philpot to thank him for an earlier supportive letter.

> Ah my true louing frend, how soone did you lay aside all other busines to make a swete plaster for my wounded conscience, yea, and that out of a painefull pair of stockes ... But God hath brought you into a strait place, that you might set my soule at liberty. Out of your pinchyng and painfull seate, you haue plentifully poured upon me your precious narde, the sweet sauour wherof hath greatly refreshed my tried soule.[98]

In this passage Careless is using conventional Biblical tropes, drawn principally from the Song of Songs, to represent his friendship with Philpot as part of the larger relationship of Christ to the Church and the believer. Later in this same letter Careless produces an extended metaphor on Philpot's name.

> O my good master Philpot, which art a principal pot in deede, filled with most precious licuor, as it appeareth by the plenteous pouryng forth of the same: Oh pot most happy, of the high Potter ordained to honour, which doest containe such heauenly treasure in thy earthen vessell: Oh pot thrice happy, in whom Christ hath wrought a great miracle, altering thy nature, and turning water into wine, and that of the best, whereout the Master of the feast hath filled my cup so full, that I am become drunken in ioy of the spirit through the same.[99]

Careless' letter is his response to an earlier letter from Philpot, in which the latter wrote:

> Since God hath willed you at your Baptisine in Christ to be Careles, why do you make yourself careful? ... Behold the goodnes of God toward me. I am careles, being fast closed in a payre of stocks, which pinch me for very straitnes; and will you be carefull. I will not haue that unsemely addition to your name.[100]

What we see in these letters is the articulation of a friendship, *amicitia*, between two men based on the exchange of playful texts, albeit written in terrible conditions, embodying Biblical imagery that is clearly intimate and potentially erotic. In particular, the play that these men make with each other's name is noticeable. At one level this is can be seen as simply a typical piece of humanist display; however, one can also see it as an attempt to subvert the meaning that the Marian authorities had imposed or inscribed upon them. The meaning of the labels 'Careless' and 'Philpot' was a matter of dispute between these two men and their jailers. While the latter sought to make 'Careless' and 'Philpot' the names of notorious heretics, the letters that Careless and Philpot exchanged can be seen as part of an attempt to wrest back control of who they were from their jailers. And in this textual struggle the humanist discourse of male friendship proved an important weapon for Philpot and Careless.[101]

Foxe clearly presents the relationship between Careless and Philpot as exemplary. In the process he constructs their friendship as a source of strength which they drew on in order to resist their Marian opponents. In *Acts and Monuments*, as in *The Governour*, friendship is represented as offering its participants a place outside the existing power structures from which a sense of self could be constructed, uncontaminated by society's restrictions and bounds.[102] Collinson has suggested that there is the possibility 'that in the English Reformation life itself in the sense of character was more persuasive than doctrine', or than anything put into writing, except for the English Bible'.[103] This was certainly the case in relation to *Acts and Monuments*, particularly since Foxe took pains to ensure the homogeneity and coherence of the beliefs for which his martyrs died.[104] From a reader's perspective it is precisely the written lives of the martyrs that fill the pages of Foxe's work which provide the incentive to keep reading. In particular, it is in their letters that the impression is created that one is gaining a glimpse of the inner man that the Marian persecutors wanted to crush. It is this epistolary self that is preserved and celebrated in the work of Elizabethan writers like Foxe.[105] In this context *amicitia* functions to define and produce the ideal type of Protestant hero since it is in the intricacies of the written friendship of men like Careless and Philpot that one is allowed to read the inner life of the Marian martyrs and participate by proxy in their friendship.[106] *Amicitia* also, however, has an implicitly exclusionary function in *Acts and Monuments*. Although, like Elyot, Foxe does not state that only the literate can participate in true friendship, in practice it is only in the case of men like Philpot and Careless that the reader is offered a life to be read. This does not, however, mean that Foxe's work simply reproduces the norms of Tudor culture in terms of whose voice had a right to be heard. Careless, for example, was a weaver from Coventry.[107] The lives that *Acts and Monuments* held up to be read by its readers are shaped by Foxe's humanist and Protestant concerns. Learning and decorum, at the level of speech and the body, are essential components of a Protestant hero in *Acts and Monuments*. *Amicitia* allows the performance and display of both.

The poetics of *Acts and Monuments* are based upon a concern to display learning and decorum. This is particularly important in terms of the form of Foxe's work. The mid-Tudor period saw the development of narrative in the context of works like William Baldwin's *Beware the Cat* and *The Image of Idleness*.[108] These works, along with Miles Hogarde's *The Displaying of the Protestants*, inaugurated a new form into English writing marked by a relationship between domestic space and narrative motivation. *The Image of Idleness* is an epistolary satire which discusses the inherent fickleness of women. Its misogyny is reminiscent of the court poetry of writers like Wyatt as well as many of the stories that made up jest books like *A Hundred Merry Tales*. Misogyny and class tension are domesticated by the narrative form of *The Image of Idleness*.[109] In particular, this work allowed its readers the frisson of reading material that was potentially shocking and dangerous while at the same time its narrative form imposed a predictable order on the chaos and disorder that it seemed to celebrate. *The Image of Idleness*, like *Beware the Cat* and even the Father Brown episode of *The Displaying of the Protestants*, conjures up images of cat worlds, lower-class, heretical, papist, female, that have their own laws and rules and are dangerously close to, indeed often actually impinge upon, the ordered society of magisterial Tudor England. At the same time the narrative form of these texts works to assure their readers that these disturbing and exciting alien worlds can be safely domesticated, read and consumed.

One of the key problems that Foxe faced in *Acts and Monuments* was the need to create a symbolic space for his lower-class martyrs, in particular for their voices, which would not appear threatening to his readership. There was a danger, which remains in the wings of Foxe's work, that it would look like a literary Kett's Rebellion or Pilgrimage of Grace, a text without proper hierarchies or order in which carters would speak with the same authority as kings. Foxe avoids this through a number of strategies, but in particular the narrative form of his work allows him to impose an order on the disparate texts that make up *Acts and Monuments*.[110] Placing all the martyrs' stories within a grand overarching narrative of history reduces each individual story to an incident in this story.[111] Furthermore making some martyrs exemplary, such as Careless and Philpot, allows Foxe to manipulate the reader's experience of *Acts and Monuments* and the speed at which they read his text; as a reader one pauses, in a sense because one has to, over precisely those stories that Foxe regards as exemplary.[112] In shaping his material, making editorial and authorial decisions in terms of its appearance and how it would be read, Foxe inevitably gives it an order. In the process he reduces the authority of the competing voices and texts that make up *Acts and Monuments*; or, to be more accurate, his authorial voice claims the right to order these texts and voices so that they can take their place in a coherent, homogenous and unambiguously Protestant whole. The narrative frame of *Acts and Monuments* domesticates English Protestantism, and in particular popular religious radicalism, by emphasizing the legitimatizing nature of order in and for itself; in the same way that Googe's poem to John Bale simultaneously celebrates and contains Bale's reputation as a Protestant writer, *Acts and Monuments* celebrates Protestant heroes from the past while constructing them as part of an ordered historical narrative.[113]

To go from the godly pages of Foxe's *Acts and Monuments* to the profane leaves of George Gascoigne's *A Hundreth Sundrie Flowres* appears at first sight to be a bizarre leap. However, *A Hundreth Sundrie Flowres* in political and poetic terms can best be understood in relation to Foxe's work. George Gascoigne was a contemporary of Googe but his public and poetic career had a very different trajectory. Gascoigne was born *c.*1534. Unlike Googe, however, he lacked productive links to leading members of the early Elizabethan polity and seems to have a talent for getting himself into trouble. After a number of unsuccessful business and publishing ventures, including the publication of his poetic miscellany *A Hundreth Sundrie Flowres* (1573), Gascoigne did win employment with the Earl of Leicester, writing the entertainments that took place when Elizabeth visited Kenilworth in 1575. In the following year he finally secured government employment but died in 1577.[114] *A Hundreth Sundrie Flowres* was first published in 1573 but was almost immediately condemned as immoral. Two years later a 'reformed' edition was produced, in which Gascoigne presented himself to his readers as a prodigal son who has learnt the error of this ways. Despite this apparent repentance this volume was also censored.[115] Gascoigne's work has had a mixed reception by literary critics. The prose narrative, 'The Adventures of Master F.J.', which forms part of *A Hundreth Sundrie Flowres*, has long been recognized as an important example of early English fiction writing. As a poet Gascoigne has been viewed as one of the more interesting figures in the hiatus between Wyatt and Surrey and Sidney and Spenser.[116] Gascoigne's work can, however, be seen as the counterpart of Foxe's *Acts and Monuments* and as an answer to Googe's Protestant poetic agenda. *A Hundreth Sundrie Flowres* performs a similar act of domestication on court literary culture to that which Foxe enacts on English Protestantism. It is as a literary history of the Tudor literature, particularly court writing, that works to give it a particularly Elizabethan shape. *Acts and Monuments* orders and narrates the history of English Protestantism and in the process makes it palatable to magisterial Tudor England. *A Hundreth Sundrie Flowres* takes court culture as expressed in the poetry of writers like Wyatt and makes it fit the needs and desires of its audience. At the same time it turns its back on the godliness of Googe's work; for Gascoigne, Wyatt is not conquered so much as rendered harmless.

A Hundreth Sundrie Flowres opens with an address by the printer to the reader which gives a wonderfully complex account of the volume's travels from its author to its final publication. This piece ends with the bold claim that 'the worke [*A Hundreth Sundrie Flowres*] is so universal, as either in one place or other, any mans mind may therewith be satisfied'.[117] The universality of Gascoigne's work is, however, extremely limited. What it does offer its reader is a summation of Tudor court literature in an Elizabethan context. The first two works in *A Hundreth Sundrie Flowres* are translations, 'Supposes', a version of the Italian comedy *I Suppositi* by Ariosto, and 'Jocasta', from the Greek. Clearly at one level the inclusion of these works in the volume is designed to display Gascoigne's learning. 'Supposes', however, also has the important function of placing *A Hundreth Sundrie Flowres* within a specifically magisterial context. This play is a fantasy of social success and improvement. The play's prologue tells its readers:

> our Suppose is nothing else but a mistaking or imagination of one thing for an other: for you shall see the master supposed for the servant, the servant for the master: the freeman for a slave, and the bondslave for a freeman: the stranger for a well knowen friend, and the familiar for a stranger.[118]

The purpose of all this confusion is the pleasure that it brings to the reader in trying to suppose how all the play's 'supposes' will be resolved. The important thing about the 'supposes' of 'Supposes' is, however, that in the end they have no real effect on the social structure portrayed in the play. Indeed the conclusion of the play, when all the proper relationships between people are restored, suggests that the social order is beyond the scope of the play's supposes. In

'Supposes' social success is achieved through the ability to perform, to take on different identities, but in the context of the normative status of the existing social order.[119] The people who were being forced to take on new identities during the course of the sixteenth century in England, such as those who supported Kett in 1549, would probably not have found Gascoigne's 'supposes' very amusing. Indeed it is noticeable that, while the idea of playing with different identities is a constant one in Elizabethan comedy, the demand that the existing social order be respected and maintained was equally common in the demands of lower-class protesters during the Tudor period.

'Supposes' and 'Jocasta' are followed in *A Hundreth Sundrie Flowres* by 'A Discourse of the Adventures Passed by Master F.J.' After this narrative Gascoigne presents his readers with a substantial collection of lyrics entitled 'The Devises of Sundrie Gentlemen' before concluding the volume with the poem 'Dan Bartholmew of Bathe'. 'The Adventures' is in many ways a strange work even in this eclectic collection. It claims to recount the story of Master F.J. as told by his friend G.T. to another friend H.W., who, against all the injunctions of G.T., passed F.J.'s story on to a printer, A.B. H.W.'s justification for this double betrayal of G.T. and F.J. is that it amused him to 'sit and smile at the fond devises of such as have enchayned them selves in the golden fetters of fantasie, and having bewrayed them selves to the whole world, do yet conjecture that they walke unseene in a net'.[120] Of course the readers of 'The Adventures' are themselves soon caught in a web of fantasy. In particular it is extremely hard as one reads to keep sight of who is telling the story. G.T.'s account of F.J.'s escapes often seems so personal and intimate that it is easy to loose sight of the extent to which one is reading a report of a failed romance by an outside party. Ostensibly the prose details that G.T. provides are no more than massively expanded versions of the titles that Tottel added to Wyatt's lyrics and which work to place the Henrician poet's texts within a normative narrative of courtly love.[121] G.T. is simply providing the context for F.J.'s lyrics, but in the process he creates a complex text in its own right which also reflects directly upon Elizabethan political culture.

'The Adventures' tells the story of F.J.'s courtship of Elinor, the married daughter of the master of the house whose guest he is. This first act of betrayal is, however, only one of many in G.T.'s tale, which is shot through with lies and deceptions. The whole action takes place in the gardens, corridors and rooms of a manor house located somewhere in the north of England. As with *Beware the Cat*, 'The Adventures' implies that this domestic setting is perfect for the pursuit of illicit endeavours.[122] Gascoigne's text creates a metonymic relationship between the rooms, corridors and parks of this domestic setting and that of the Tudor court. It achieves this by locating a courtly romance within a gentry setting. It also, however, exploits the tension between G.T., the narrator, and F.J., the protagonist, in order to shape the reader's experience in a way that mimics Wyatt's construction of the reader's role in his work. Gascoigne's text offers its readers the pleasures of courtly love, complex ambiguous texts that require, and allow, one to interrogate their meaning.[123] However, unlike Wyatt's work, which was written under the shadow of a genuine tyranny, 'The Adventures' allows its readers to play at textual interrogation, to indulge their desire to penetrate the text's outer surface to find its inner truth, without this structure having a lethal counterpart in the real world of the Henrician Reformation.

Gascoigne is careful to create for his readers the frisson of dangerous reading. This is partly achieved through the constant suggestions that pepper 'The Adventures' that it is an account of real events and that this is why it can not name those involved. Of course what is really been enacted here is not the protection of F.J. and the rest of the protagonists of the tale, but rather a blatant incitement to the work's readers to relate the events of 'The Adventures' to a specific real situation of their choice. G.T. ends his narrative by commenting that:

> I have past it over with quod he and quod she after my homely manner of writing, using sundry names for one person, as the Dame, the Lady, Mistresse, etc ... I have thought it no greater faulte than pettie treason thus to entermyngle them, nothing doubting but you will easely, understand my meanings, and that is asmuch as I desire.[124]

G.T.'s final comment is ambiguous since it opens up the possibility that he desires the reader to go further than the text itself does in terms of naming its protagonists. Indeed the reference to 'pettie treason' suggests that this is what any honest reader ought to do.

Gascoigne's reference to treason at the conclusion of 'The Adventures' can be related directly to the story's northern location. The narrative opens with G.T. commenting on how F.J. 'chaunced once in the north partes of this Realme to fall in company of a very fayre gentlewoman whose name was Mistresse *Elinor*'.[125] The location of F.J.'s fall places it in the treasonable part of the country, while its form, courtly love, relates it to the other centre of treason in Elizabethan England, the court. This is not to suggest that 'The Adventures' is an allegorical history of the Northern Rebellion. What it is to argue is that Gascoigne is deliberately playing with the idea of treason in order to increase his reader's excitement. 'The Adventures'' bawdiness serves a similar purpose. At a crucial stage in the narrative F.J. goes on a nocturnal visit to Elinor conveying under his nightgown his naked sword. However when Elinor sees his weapon she asks him, 'what have I deserved, that you come against me with naked sword as against an open enemie?'[126] Later in this episode, however, F.J.'s naked sword is stolen by Lady Frances, another member of the household who is in love with him. Finally G.T. informs that reader:

dame *Elynor* (whether it wer according to olde custome or by wylie pollicie) found meane that night, that the sword was conveyed out of Mistres *Fraunces* chamber and brought to hirs: and after redeliverie of it unto F.J. she warned him to be more wary from that time forthwards.[127]

Later in the story the relationship between Elinor and F.J. turns sour, primarily due to the return of Elinor's secretary from London whose 'quils and pennes not worn so neer as they were wont to be, did now prick such faire large notes that his Mistres liked better to sing faburden under him, than to descant any longer uppon *F.J.* playne song.'[128] The symbolism of F.J.'s 'naked sword' and the secretary's 'pens' is so obvious that it is as though Gascoigne is playing with the reader's desire for this kind of bawdy punning. Indeed the initial bawdy reading of these passages is shown by the progression of the narrative to be at best limited and at worst wrong. Reading F.J.'s naked sword simply in bodily terms fails as soon as Lady Frances steals it – instead what Gascoigne makes plain is that the protagonists of his love story exist within the same discourse as his readers do while they are reading it. F.J.'s and Elinor's world is drenched with sexual imagery, but not sex, since this is appropriate for a textual love. Given this it is no wonder that the Secretary's pen works better for Elinor than does F.J.'s naked sword.

'The Adventures', despite the constant hints to the contrary, is never anything but a textual game. Unlike Wyatt's poetry, where the sense is constantly created that behind its surface complexity and the duplicity of its narrators there are real people and issues, all that is hidden behind G.T. is Gascoigne's knowing hand. Susan C. Staub comments that 'Gascoigne repeatedly sabotages the illusion of reality by presenting the working of the narrative [in 'The Adventures'] so near the surface. By allowing the seams of his narrative to show, Gascoigne invites us to watch him at his fiction making.'[129] This self-reflective fictionality is crucial to the politics of 'The Adventures'. Gascoigne's text, indeed the whole of *A Hundreth Sundrie Flowres*, is a rewriting of Henrician court literature as a game. There is a pretence of rigour, the creation of an atmosphere of treason and betrayal, of the dangers of textual slippage and ambiguity, but it is all an act or performance. The power that over-shadows Gascoigne's work is a pale imitation to that which terrifies and fascinates the narrators of Wyatt's poems.[130]

A Hundreth Sundrie Flowres offers its readers the opportunity to experience Henrician rigour as expressed in Wyatt's poetry as a game. In particular, the narrative form of 'The Adventures' allows Gascoigne to domesticate the terrifying world of the Henrician court. It is this which makes Gascoigne's text exemplary in terms of Elizabethan culture. Googe may have defeated Cupido but the danger in his work was that it effectively left no real place for the Queen. Gascoigne solves this problem by creating a text which retains Cupido's power, but only as a game. F.J.'s world is not really terrifying, but it looks sufficiently like that of Wyatt's narrators to give its readers the frisson of danger. *Acts and Monuments* allows its readers to enjoy the excitement of Protestant Reformation, indeed of the whole history of Protestantism as a triumph over persecution, while at same time domesticating its material for a magisterial Elizabethan readership.

CONCLUSION

Robert Crowley was very critical of the way in which the wealth of the monasteries had been dissipated by Henry VIII, with most of it ending up in the hands of the gentry. He argued that it should have been used to further the course of the Protestant Reformation. Foxe, however, in 1570 addressed Crowley's argument by defending on political grounds the transfer of the monasteries' lands to the gentry. He writes:

> If this throwing downe of Abbayes had happened in such free and reformed Cities or countryes, as are amongest the Germaines, where the state governed and directed by lawes, rather then rulers, remaineth alwayes alike and unmutable, who doubteth but such houses there standing still, the possessions might well be transposed to such uses abouesaid, without any feare or peril? But in such Realmes and kyngdomes as this, where lawes and Parlaments be not always one, but are subject to the disposition of the Prince: neither is it certaine always what Princes may come: the surest way therefore to send Monkery and Popery packyng out of the Realme, is to do with their houses and possessions as kyng Henry did, throughe the motion and Counsell of [Thomas] Cromwell.[131]

Foxe's argument is that the English polity is not sufficiently free or stable to guarantee the permanence of good or Protestant laws. This means that transfer of the lands of the monasteries to the gentry, which Foxe regards as the result of a deliberate policy by Cromwell, was essential to fix the religious changes of the 1530s. The implication of this passage is twofold. The most obvious is that English polity compares unfavorably with the government of German free cities. The more profound message of this passage is that for Foxe it was the transfer of wealth and in particular land to the gentry that was the best bulwark against any return of popery. This was because it meant that, while the sources of power at the centre – the prince, Parliament, even the law – were unstable and untrustworthy, out in the provinces there existed among the gentry an investment in the future of Protestantism that would ultimately guard against any capture of the organs of the state by popery. The domestication of the wealth of the monasteries, turning it into the homes and manor houses of the gentry, is for Foxe an essential point of stability within an English polity which otherwise would be dangerously open to unwelcome change and princely alteration. It is what creates the space, symbolically but also often literally, for the narrative scope and detail of *Acts and Monuments*.

The early Elizabethan writing discussed in this chapter displays a concern to navigate between the twin poles of Henrician tyranny and Edwardian popular anarchy. The solution proposed in texts like *Acts and Monuments* and *A Hundreth Sundrie Flowres* is to push these daungerous extremes to the edges of Elizabethan culture and at the same time domesticate them. Certainly Gascoigne's work reflects the possibility of a return of Henrician rigour while *Acts and Monuments* quite explicitly suggests in places that persecution could return to trouble English Protestants. Despite this, these works reflect an Elizabethan culture increasingly at ease with itself. The narrative form of *Acts and Monuments* and 'The Adventures' make the Henrician court and Protestant history something to be read, consumed and enjoyed by their readers as they sat in the safety of their manor houses and homes. In particular, the domestication of popular religion and court culture enacted in the work of Foxe and Gascoigne reflects the extent to which Elizabethan England wished to put behind it the traumas of the Reformation period.

NOTES

1 William Cecil, 'A Short Memoryall of the State of the Realme', in *A Collection of state papers relating to affairs from the reigns of King Henry VIII, King Edward VI, Queen Mary and Queen Elizabeth … left by William Cecil Lord Burghley*, ed. Samuel Haynes (London: 1740), pp. 579–588, p. 579.

2 'Sir Nicholas Throckmorton's Advice to Queen Elizabeth on her Ascension to the Throne', ed. J.E. Neale, *EHR*, 65 (1950), pp. 91–98, p. 98.

3 Cecil, 1740, p. 585–586.

4 For the importance of counsel within the Elizabethan polity, see Anne McLaren, 'Delineating the Elizabethan Body Politic: Knox, Aylmer and the Definition of Counsel 1558–88', *History of Political Thought*, 17 (1996), pp. 224–252.

5 *The Passage of our most drad Soveraigne Lady Quene Elizabeth through the citie of London to westminister the daye before her coronacion*, attributed to Richard Mulcaster, published by Richard Tottel (1558), STC 7390.

6 Sandra Logan comments on the way that *The Passage* insistently seeks to reveal the queen's monarchical capabilities and to shape them in accordance with its author's own perceptions. See Sandra Logan, 'Making History: The Rhetorical and Historical Occasion of Elizabeth Tudor's Coronation Entry', *JMEMS*, 31 (2001), pp. 251–282.

7 John Guy, *Tudor England* (Oxford: 1991), p. 251.

8 *The wonders of England* (London: 1559), STC 996.

9 Ibid., No Pag.

10 Ibid., No Pag.

11 Interestingly this reminds one of Stephen Gardiner's suggestion that during the period 1530–58 England had been asleep and dreamt the horror of heresy.

12 Stephen Alford, *The Early Elizabethan Polity: William Cecil and the British Succession*

Crisis, 1558–1569 (Cambridge: 1998), p. 38.

13 Guy, 1991, p. 251.

14 Elizabeth's personality was clearly a factor in the kind of regime she headed. It is, however, almost impossible to get a clear sense of her persona through the layers of performance that surrounded her and with which she cloaked herself. For a discussion of this aspect of Elizabethan kingship see Susan Doran and Tom Freeman, eds, *The Myth of Elizabeth* (Basingstoke: 2003).

15 For the importance of Elizabeth's gender in relation to the political culture of her reign see Anne McLaren, *Political culture in the reign of Elizabeth: Queen and Commonwealth, 1558–1585* (Cambridge: 1999).

16 Alford, 1998, p. 7.

17 Norman L. Jones comments: 'Elizabeth was a convinced Protestant. Though impatient with the theological quibbling, there is no doubt that she accepted the basic tenets of the reforming movement and did not believe in transubstantiation or the papal supremacy' (Norman L. Jones, 'Elizabeth's First Year: The Conception and Birth of the Elizabethan Political World', in *The Reign of Elizabeth*, ed. Christopher Haigh (Basingstoke: 1984), pp. 27–55, p. 28).

18 Andrew Pettegree, *Marian Protestantism: Six Studies* (Aldershot: 1996), p. 137.

19 Eamon Duffy, *The Voices of Morebath: Reformation and Rebellion in an English Village* (New Haven: 2001), p. 176.

20 Leicester, however, was not in any way involved in the actual revolt, despite the impression created by the recent film *Elizabeth*.

21 It is noticeable that among the works published attacking the Northern Rebellion were *Beware the Cat* (written 1553), *Gorboduc* (written 1561) and *The fall and euil successe of Rebellion* (1536). In the early 1570s it appears that the government or its supporters were prepared to publish anything that might be critical of the rebels' cause, however tangential or partial the reference. This suggests a regime that lacked confidence in its own ability to generate specific polemical responses to the Northern Rebellion. The rebels themselves also appear relatively unconvincing. M.E. James has, for example, suggested that one of their leaders, the Earl of Northumberland, blundered into rebellion. See M. E. James, 'The Concept of Order and the Northern Rising', *PP*, 60 (1973), pp. 49–83.

22 As with all Tudor rebellions and tumults, in 1570 far more blood was spilt by the government than by its opponents. For a discussion of the number of people who were executed in 1570, see Anthony Fletcher and Diarmaid MacCulloch, *Tudor Rebellions* (Harlow: 1997), p. 102–103.

23 See 'A Declaration of the Quenes Proceedings since her Reigne', in *A Collection of state papers left by William Cecil Lord Burghley*, ed. Samuel Haynes (London: 1740). pp. 589–593.

24 Ibid., p. 589.

25 Ibid., p. 589.

26 Ibid., p. 590.

27 Cecil, 1740, p. 580.

28 This is not to suggest that the legitimation of the Elizabethan regime was in itself a

problem, rather that the decision to eschew legitimation through reformation affected the nature and form of Elizabethan government.

29 Anthony Gilby, *An Admonition to England and Scotland to call them to repentance*, in *The Appellation of John Knox* (Geneva: 1558), STC 15063, p. 69 (v).

30 Ibid., p. 69 (v).

31 Ibid., p. 70.

32 John Ponet, *A Short Treatise of politike power, and of the true Obedience which subiectes owe to kynges and other civile Governors, with an Exhortation to all true naturall Englishmen* (Strassburg?: 1556), STC 20178.

33 Ibid., G.ii (v).

34 Ibid., G.v (2).

35 Alford, 1998, p. 208.

36 'A Declaration' 1740, p. 590.

37 Very little is known about the version of *The Mirror* that was suppressed in 1554, apparently upon the orders of Stephen Gardiner. For an excellent discussion of the edition of 1554 see Scott Lucas, 'The Suppressed Edition and the Creation of the "Orthodox" *Mirror for Magistrates*', *Renaissance Papers* (1994), pp. 31–54.

38 Andrew Hadfield, *Literature, Travel, and Colonial Writing in the English Renaissance 1545–1625* (Oxford: 1998), p. 81.

39 Scott Lucas, 1994, p. 52.

40 Ibid., p. 53.

41 For a discussion of this term and its applicability to Tudor England see Tom Betteridge, *Tudor Histories of the English Reformations 1530–1583* (Aldershot: 1999).

42 William Baldwin, et al., *The Mirror for Magistrates*, ed. Lily B.Campbell (Cambridge: 1938), p. 63.

43 Ibid., p. 64.

44 In this, as much else, *The Mirror* follows Sir Thomas Elyot's *The Governour* which is also directed at lesser governors while, like *The Mirror*, constantly bringing pre-eminent governors into its scope.

45 Ibid., p. 73.

46 Ibid., p. 71.

47 Ibid., p. 77.

48 Ibid., p. 78.

49 The meaning of the claim in this verse that the nobility conspired with the commons 'assembled by assent' is unclear. The implication appears to be that the commons had a corporate existence outside Parliament which gave assent for them to meet. The effect of the complexity of these lines, however, as *The Mirror*'s authors were no doubt aware, is to obscure the radical political implications of this verse's depiction of a Parliament being summoned against the wishes of the monarch.

50 Ibid., pp. 94–95.

51 For a discussion of the Protestant appropriation of *Piers Plowman* see David Norbrook,

Poetry and Politics in the English Renaissance (London: 2002), pp. 35–38.

52 Baldwin et al., 1938, p. 95.

53 This is a particularly interesting question in relation to Baldwin's *Beware the Cat*. Is there a relationship between 'cats' as representatives of papistry or popular culture and Gloucester's royal cat? One could argue that being caught between two potentially lethal cats, crown and populace, was the symbolic situation of the Tudor magisterial class.

54 Stephen Alford has provided a possible answer to this question with his fascinating work on Cecil's various schemes to force Elizabeth's hand over the succession question by using Parliament. Can one see parliamentary statutes as a way of belling the Queen / cat?

55 Baldwin et al., 1938, p. 347.

56 Norbrook, 2002, p. 50.

57 Baldwin et al., 1938, p. 356.

58 On the politics of *Gorboduc* see Susan Doran, 'Juno Versus Diana: The Treatment of Elizabeth I's Marriage in Plays and Entertainments, 1561–1581', *HJ*, 38 (1995), pp. 257–274 and Greg Walker, *The Politics of Performance in Early Renaissance Drama* (Cambridge: 1998).

59 Thomas Norton, *Orations of Arranes* (London: c.1560), STC 785. Norton argues that one reason for studying histories, and in particular historical orations is so that 'the use of eloque[n]ce in common weale should appeare, and the maner of applying of histories in consultation should be layd abroad for an example to the wise readers of histories, not only how to furnishe their own knowledge, but also howe profitably to deliuer the same to the information, warnyng and aduise of other' (A.iiii (v)). Norton is arguing here that the lessons of history pertain not simply to the individual but also need to be spread throughout the polity.

60 For the details of Googe's life see the editors' excellent introduction to Barnabe Googe, *The Shippe of Safegarde*, 1569, STC 12049, eds Simon McKeown and William E. Sheidley (Tempe, Arizona: 2001).

61 Googe's dedicatory letter is printed in Barnabe Googe, *Eglogs, Epytaphes and Sonettes*, 1563, STC 12048, ed. Judith M. Kennedy (Toronto: 1989), pp. 132–134, p. 133.

62 Ibid., pp. 133–134.

63 Alexander Neville was an important functionary within the Elizabethan Church, serving Archbishops Parker and Grindal. He wrote a Latin history of Kett's Rebellion as well as producing a number of other works including a translation of *Oedipus*.

64 Googe, 1989, p. 36.

65 Ibid., p. 79.

66 Ibid., p. 80. This aspect of Googe's poem may well reflect the fundamental change that took place in the relationship between England and Scotland after the withdrawal of French troops from Scotland in 1560. Its implicit criticism of Somerset's military campaigns against the Scots may also be a result of the relationship between Googe and Cecil who, as Stephen Alford has shown, was committed from very early in his political career to building a close working alliance with Scottish Protestants. See Stephen Alford, 'Knox, Cecil and the British Dimension of the Scottish Reformation', in *John Knox and the British Reformations*, ed. Roger Mason (Aldershot: 1998), pp. 201–219.

67 Grimald was a controversial figure because of his 'betrayal' of Nicholas Ridley.

68 See James Simpson, 'Breaking the Vacuum: Ricardian and Henrician Ovidianism', *JMEMS*, 29 (1999), pp. 325–355, p. 349.

69 Googe, 1989, pp. 46–47.

70 Foxe's work contains numerous stories and woodcuts depicting Protestant martyrs performing acts of faith from within the pyre's flames. For a discussion of the illustrations in *Acts and Monuments* see Tom Betteridge, 'Visibility, Truth and History in *Acts and Monuments*', *John Foxe and his World*, eds Christopher Highley and John King (Aldershot: 2002), pp. 145–159.

71 Googe, 1989, p. 52.

72 Ibid., p. 53.

73 Ibid., pp. 53–54.

74 Ibid., p. 54.

75 Ibid., p. 55.

76 Thomas Cooper, *Coopers Chronicle* (London: 1560), STC 15218. For a discussion of different early Elizabethan historical accounts of the Marian persecution see Betteridge, 1999, chapter 4. Perhaps the key difference between Foxe and Cooper is that, while the latter only names the major Marian martyrs, one of the main purposes of *Acts and Monuments* is to record the names of all those who is Foxe's eyes suffered for the truth of Christ's teaching.

77 Googe, 1989, p. 72.

78 Ibid., p. 73.

79 Ibid., pp. 84–85.

80 Ibid., p. 108.

81 Ibid., p. 116.

82 Ibid., p. 124.

83 In Googe's work there is also a new concern with the boundaries of *amicitia*. In the first eclogue as part of warning Daphnes of the dangers of passionate love, Amintas feels the need to add that, 'I shall not need (I think) to bid / thee, to detest the crime / Of wicked love that Jove did use / in Ganymede's time. / For rather would I (though it be much) / that thou should'st seek the fire / Of lawful love that I have told / than burn with such desire' (Googe, 1989, p. 49).

84 Googe, 2001.

85 Patrick Collinson, 'The Monarchical Republic of Queen Elizabeth I', in *Elizabethan Essays* (London: 1994), pp. 31–58, pp. 48–51. Collinson points out that the Bond had a divisive effect on the Elizabethan polity since, although it was in theory open to all, it was effectively a device for creating a committed Protestant party.

86 *Acts and Monuments* is a massive work which went through six editions, four in English, during Foxe's lifetime. For a discussion of the important differences between this version and the earlier English one produced in 1563 see Betteridge, 1999, chapter 4.

87 The complexity of the various different editions of *Acts and Monuments* is only now

becoming apparent due to the work being carried out by Tom Freeman, to whom I am greatly indebted.

88 Although there are moments when the iconography of *Acts and Monuments* does seem designed to create parallels between Elizabeth and Henry, overall Foxe's work is deeply critical of Henry's rule. For a more positive understanding of the relationship between Henry and Elizabeth as portrayed in *Acts and Monuments*, see Elizabeth H. Hageman, 'John Foxe's Henry VIII as *Justitia*', *SCJ*, 10 (1979), pp. 35–43.

89 V.N. Olsen, *John Foxe and the Elizabethan Church* (Berkeley: 1973), p. 210.

90 Foxe, *Actes*, 1570, p. 1281.

91 Ibid., iiii. (v).

92 John Foxe, 'A Sermon of Christ Crucified', 1570, STC 11242, in *The English Sermons of John Foxe*, ed. Warren Wooden (New York: 1978), p. 22.

93 In a comment printed in 1563 but edited out in all subsequent editions Foxe explicitly attacked the process of persecution. In particular he argued that reducing religion to a set of abstract articles inevitably led to the production of heretics. Foxe writes: 'neither is there any Article [of religion] which hath not his heresy annexed to him, as the shadow unto a body, insomuch that the matter is now come unto this point, that nothing can now be spoken of circumspectly, but that it shall tend to some snare of heresy, or at the least suspicion ... it were better that there were fewer Articles in the world and then the heresies would cease of their own accord.' For Foxe, defining heresy inevitably produces heretics: John Foxe, *Actes and Monuments* (London: 1563), STC 11222, p. 134.

94 It is now generally accepted that Foxe's focus was international. He was not concerned with the idea of England as an elect nation; far more important to him was the idea of Protestantism as an international pan-European movement of which the English Church was simply a branch.

95 Foxe, *Actes*, 1570, p. 1552.

96 Foxe, however, had no problem explaining the Western Rebellion of 1549. He avoided having to account for Kett's Rebellion by all but ignoring it.

97 Foxe writes that during the six years of Edward's reign the godly were spared all persecution. This, however, did not lead to a period of complete calm for English Protestants. Foxe writes: 'there was no da[n]uger to the godly, unlesse it were onely by wealth and prosperity, which many times bringeth more dammage in corrupting me[n], then any time of persecution or affliction' (Foxe, *Actes*, 1570, p. 1486).

98 Ibid., p. 2103.

99 Ibid., p. 2103.

100 Ibid., p. 2005.

101 Alan Stewart has argued that images of male friendship were sometimes deployed by mid-Tudor writers in order to obscure the politics of people's relationships and actions. See Alan Stewart, *Close Readers: Humanism and Sodomy in Early Modern England* (Princeton: 1997), p. 127.

102 Although as was pointed out below in the discussion of Sir Thomas Elyot's *The Governour*, *amicitia* was in practice something that could only exist between literate and magisterial men.

103 Patrick Collinson, '"Magazine of Religious Patterns": An Erasmian Topic Transposed in English Protestantism', in *Renaissance and Renewal in Christian History*, ed. Derek Baker (Oxford: 1977), pp. 223–249, p. 227.

104 It is clear that Foxe was prepared to suppress evidence of religious diversity among those who were executed for their religious beliefs under Mary Tudor. See Patrick Collinson, 'Truth and Legend: the Veracity of John Foxe's Book of Martyrs', in *'Clio's Mirror': Historiography in Britain and the Netherlands*, eds A.C. Duke and C.A. Tamse (1985), pp. 31–54.

105 Tom Freeman has done some outstanding work on the extant letters of the Marian martyrs which has revealed an interesting tension between a desire to ensure their orthodoxy and propriety post-1558 and an almost referential attitude towards them as artefacts. See Thomas S. Freeman, '"The Good Ministrye of Godlye and Vertuouse Women": The Elizabethan Martyrologist and the Female Supporters of the Marian Martyrs', *Journal of British Studies*, 39 (2000).

106 The possibility of this kind of participatory reading was one solution to the tension which Jane Facey has suggested, runs through *Acts and Monuments*. Facey writes: 'Foxe's analysis of the conflict between true and false churches had involved a direct opposition between the inward and outward forms of religion, between inner truths of scriptural doctrine and empty forms of human tradition and authority. That worked well enough when the true church was identified with small groups of true believers and the false church with the institutional structures and jurisdictional claims of the church of Rome. Now [i.e. during Elizabeth's reign], however, the English church was a national institution with claims and structures of its own, so how were these to be squared with the internal dynamic of true religion which had dominated Foxe's account of the true church thus far?' Readers of *Acts and Monuments* could negotiate this very real tension by identifying with those martyrs whom Foxe held out as exemplary. Self-fashioning based on Foxe's martyrs means having a godly inner life and locating oneself within the grand narrative of Protestantism. See Jane Facey, 'John Foxe and the Defence of the English Church', in *Protestantism and the National Church in Sixteenth Century England*, eds Peter Lake and Maria Dowling (London: 1987), pp. 162–192, p. 174.

107 Careless appears to have been released from jail to take part in the traditional Corpus Christi Weavers' plays in Coventry.

108 The modern editor of this work points out that its authors were very careful to disguise their identity, but it is possible that William Baldwin was involved in its writing. See *The Image of Idleness*, 1555, STC 25196, printed in 'The English Epistolary Novel: The Image of Idleness (1555). Text, Introduction and Notes', ed. Michael Flachmann, *Studies in Philology*, 87 (1990), pp. 1–75.

109 The full title of this work is, *A little treatise called The Image of Idleness containing certain matters moved between Walter Wedlock and Bawdin Bachelor, translated out of Trojan or Cornish into English by Oliver Oldwanton and dedicated to the Lady Lust*. Like *Beware the Cat*, this work pokes fun at humanist learning while offering its readers a salacious read.

110 The form of *Acts and Monuments* changes over the lifetime of the text. In particular, there is a significant change between the 1563 and 1570 editions, with the latter having a far clearer narrative form than the earlier text which is written in a chronicle style.

111 The use of narrative also had an important polemical aim. D.R. Woolf has argued that for Foxe, 'If unity is the watchword of the Reformed, division is that of Rome'. The

narrative thrust of *Acts and Monuments* was provided partly by the truth of Protestantism and this meant that within this narrative Rome and all that was associated with it could not fail to appear as a force of disorder; indeed as that which endangered the continuation of the text itself. See D.R. Woolf, 'The Rhetoric of Martyrdom: Generic Contradiction and Narrative Strategy in John Foxe's *Acts and Monuments*', in *The Rhetorics of Life Writing in Early Modern Europe: Forms of Biography from Canandra Fedde to Louis XIV*, ed. Thomas F. Mayer and D.R. Woolf (Michigan: 1995), pp. 243–282, p. 259.

112 Patrick Collinson comments: 'an analysis of Foxe's rhetorical and polemical art ... might depict a style in transition from the racy vulgarity of many of his sources and of his more polemical passages to the decorousness of a text designed for the edification of the pious world of what Louis B. Wright called Elizabethan "middle class culture"' (Collinson, 1985, p. 49).

113 This is not to suggest that Foxe was not committed to the further Protestantization of the country but that there is a tension in *Acts and Monuments* between the need for further reform and its form as a text. The nature of this tension changes across the various editions of *Acts and Monuments*, so that in the 1563 edition there is an assumption of further reform while by 1583 the sheer size of the work suggests consolidation and stability as fundamental characteristics of English Protestantism.

114 For the details of Gascoigne's life and career see George Gascoigne, *A Hundreth Sundrie Flowres*, 1573, STC 11635, ed. and intro. G.W. Pigman III (Oxford, 2000).

115 For a discussion of the second edition of Gascoigne's work see Felicity A. Hughes, 'Gascoigne's Poses', *SEL*, 37 (1997), pp. 1–19.

116 Gary Waller describes Gascoigne's poetry as 'undoubtedly the most interesting written in England between Wyatt and Sidney': Gary Waller, *English Poetry of the Sixteenth Century* (Harlow: 1993), p. 38.

117 Gascoigne, 2000, p. 4.

118 Ibid., p. 7.

119 On the title page of the play as printed in *A Hundreth Sundrie Flowres* it is claimed that 'Supposes' was performed at 'Grayes Inne' in 1566. If this attribution is accurate, and there seems no reason to doubt it, then it is difficult to imagine a more appropriate play for an audience of students and young lawyers. Gascoigne's play celebrates its hero's successful rite of passage to marriage and respectability despite his decision completely to neglect his studies and instead to rely on trickery and wit to win the hand of his love.

120 Gascoigne, 2000, p. 142.

121 Lorna Hutson argues that: 'Gascoigne's *Master F.J.* is organized less as a narrative conferring retrospective meaning upon events then as a contextualisation of F.J.'s discursive enterprise in gaining access to Elinor, the wife of the heir of the household' (Lorna Hutson, 'Fortunate Travelers: Reading for the Plot in Sixteenth Century England', *Representations*, 41 (1993), pp. 83–103, p. 93).

122 R.W. Maslen comments: 'The courtship of F.J. and Elinor resembles the bewildering interplay of torches and shadows in the rooms and corridors of an Elizabethan mansion, where the sudden flaring of a light serves only to dazzle the unwary passer-by' (R.W. Maslen, *Elizabethan Fictions: Espionage, Counter-Espionage, and the Duplicity of Fiction in Early Elizabethan Prose Narratives* (Oxford: 1997), p. 144.

123 Richard C. McCoy suggests that 'Gascoigne's purpose in *A Hundreth Sundrie Flowres* ... was to excite his reader to a state of "busie conjecture" and thus introduce them to the pleasures of courtly discourse'. See Richard C. McCoy, 'Gascoigne's " *Poëmeta castrata*": The Wages of Courtly Success', *Criticism*, 27 (1985), pp. 29–56, p. 41.

124 Gascoigne, 2000, pp. 215–216.

125 Ibid., p. 145.

126 Ibid., p. 168.

127 Ibid., p. 174.

128 Ibid., p. 199.

129 Susan C. Staub, '"According to My Sources": Fictionality in The Adventures of Master F.J.', *Studies in Philology*, 87 (1990), pp. 111–119, p. 119.

130 It is not only in terms of court power that Gasciogne's work reflects a change of atmosphere from the mid-Tudor period. R.W. Maslen has argued: 'Like Baldwin's *Beware the Cat*, Gascoigne's *Adventures* depicts an English society which is radically at odds with itself, riven with rival factions and competing languages; but in the *Adventures* the alternative political system devised by the genteel invaders of an aristocratic household is vastly more seductive than the furtive community exposed by Baldwin's feline informers.' This undoubted change can, however, be explained by the different historical moments in which Baldwin and Gascoigne were writing, and in particular the extent to which *Beware the Cat* reflects upon the serious events of 1549. The Cats, as Ketts, were a real danger to Tudor society, unlike Lady Elinor and her secretary (Maslen, 1997, p. 152).

131 Foxe, *Actes*, 1570, pp. 1350–1351.

Conclusion

Pan may be proud, the ever he begot
    such a Bellibone,
And Syrinx rejoyse, that ever was her lot
    to beare such a one.
Soone as my younglings cryen for the dam,
To her will I offer a milkwhite Lamb:
    Shee is my goddesse plaine,
    And I her shepherds swayne,
Albee forswonck and forswatt I am.
('April', Edmund Spenser, *The Shepheardes Calender*, 1579)[1]

The year 1580 is almost the exact mid-point of Elizabeth's reign. It therefore seems appropriate that in the years surrounding this date a number of texts were published that exemplify Elizabethan political and poetic culture. 1579 saw the publication of Edmund Spenser's *Shepheardes Calender* which built on the work of early English Protestant writers. In particular, Spenser combined in his volume Barnabe Googe's image of a band of godly shepherds with a celebration of Elizabeth's queenship. In *The Shepheardes Calender* Cupido becomes Cynthia, a fit object for the song of godly shepherds if not a full member of their bond. In 1583 William Cecil's *The Execution of Justice in England* and Sir Thomas Smith's *De Republica Anglorum* were published. These works can be read as exemplary representations of the Elizabethan regime as a *via media* between Henrician tyranny and Edwardian anarchy.[2]

The decade following the successful suppression of the Northern Rebellion in 1570 was a difficult one for the Elizabethan regime and its supporters. At home the campaign by godly Protestants to purge of the English Church of its residual papist elements continued but made only moderate headway in the face of Elizabeth's opposition. In 1577 Archbishop Grindal was suspended by Elizabeth for daring to suggest that as a clergyman he answered to a higher power than his prince.[3] The 1570s also saw the arrival in England of the first Catholic seminary priests and the continuing presence of Mary Queen of Scots – neither of which were conducive to the realm's peace.[4] There were also the contentious issues of Elizabeth's possible marriage and the question of succession. On the international scene the St Bartholomew Day Massacre in 1572, in which thousands of French Huguenots were murdered, shocked Protestant Europe. The Dutch Revolt and the position that England should adopt towards the rebels were constant sources of friction within the polity, pitting those who wished to intervene to help their fellow Protestants fight Spanish tyranny against colleagues, and the Queen, who wanted no part in a quarrel between a prince and his rebellious subjects. The fact that the membership of these two groups was constantly shifting did nothing to help the formulation of policy.[5] Despite these problems, the 1570s marked the beginning of an unparalleled period of political stability for England stretching from 1569–1642. The political settlement that emerged during the 1560s, articulated in such works as *The Mirror for Magistrates*, proved to be extremely stable, particularly in a European context.[6] The Elizabethan regime, however, experienced the 1570s and 1580s as decades of mounting worries and problems. In 1580 the Elizabethan culture was Janus-faced: at once growing in confidence and shot through with anxiety; Protestant but failing to impose confessional purity as an act of state. Elizabeth's queenship often looked Henrician but was not.[7] The gilded formality of the Elizabethan court looked nothing like Kett's camp on Mousehold Heath, but beyond the court's confines the alliance proposed by Cheke, in *The Hurt of Sedition*, between Kett's class and his own was becoming the basis for political stability and reform. Elizabeth's rule looked Henrician from the perspective of the court, and in this context issues like the queen's gender and the problem of counsel loomed large; in the localities it was looking more and more Edwardian.

William Cecil's *The Execution of Justice in England* is a short work. It does not claim to be anything more than a justification of the Elizabethan regime's treatment of Catholic priests and their sympathizers. It had a number of intended audiences. As with *A Declaration*, Cecil's text appears to be concerned to allay the fears of Elizabeth's Catholic subjects regarding the regime's attitude to those who did not share its religious views. Its message to such people is that the Jesuits and others the regime was torturing and executing were not dying as religious martyrs but as traitors. Another potential home audience was those among the Queen's subjects, Protestants as well as Catholics, who regarded the regime's response to the threat posed by seminary priests and their supporters as excessive. *The Execution of Justice in England* was also intended to have an impact on the continent. In particular, its claim that no-one was being persecuted for religion in England was aimed at those foreign powers who might be tempted to use Elizabeth's treatment of her Catholic subjects as a justification for invasion.

The main argument of Cecil's tract is that the Elizabethan regime had turned its back on Reformation politics and poetics. *The Execution of Justice in England* consistently avoids using the language of religious controversy. In particular, it argues that Elizabeth's regime can be distinguished from that of her predecessors by its refusal to persecute religious opponents. For example, Cecil lists all those Marian bishops and clergymen who, he claims, lived out their lives peacefully under Elizabeth despite their rejection of the religious settlement of 1558.[8] Cecil's tract insists that the Catholic priests being tortured and executed by the regime were suffering on the basis of their deeds and not their beliefs. Cecil writes:

> let these persons be termed as they list: scholars, schoolmasters, bookmen, seminaries, priests, Jesuits, friars, beadmen, Romanists, pardoners, or what else you will, neither their titles not their apparel hath made them traitors, but their traitorous secret motions and practices.[9]

This passage asserts a clear separation between religious identity and treason. Cecil argues that it is not beliefs that are treasonable but actions.[10] This argument was, however, completely rejected by Cecil's opponents.[11] It was also one that would have not made sense in the context of the Henrician, Edwardian and Marian Reformations. Cecil's polemical strategy in *The Execution of Justice in England* is to deny the applicability of a confessional discourse to Elizabethan culture. This argument is made at the level of content but also form. *The Execution of Justice in England* constructs Elizabeth's regime as non-confessional and this representation is supported by the tone of Cecil's tract, which eschews Reformation polemics. Cecil resists the temptation to deploy such labels as papists and popery. This is partly to avoid the danger of appearing divisive, but it also reflects his commitment to magisterial Protestantism and a civic humanism that Sir Thomas Elyot would have recognized. Edmund Spenser's *Shepheardes Calender* and Sir Thomas Smith's *De Republica Anglorum* are far more sophisticated works than *The Execution of Justice in England*, but they share the political ethos of Cecil's tract.

The Shepheardes Calender has been seen as an inaugural text creating a specifically Elizabethan poetic idiom. In particular, it has been argued that Spenser's use of pastoral tropes and settings in this work created a fashion that outlasted Elizabeth's reign.[12] Whatever the merits of these arguments, it is striking how far *The Shepheardes Calender* reproduces largely intact the poetics and politics of Barnabe Googe's *Eglogs, Epytaphes and Sonettes*. Spenser's work is addressed to the same band of Protestant shepherds that Googe imagined in his volume. *The Shepheardes Calender*, like *Eglogs, Epytaphes and Sonettes*, seeks to simultaneously depict in poetry a godly brotherhood and to teach its readers how to become members. Spenser's work also shares with Googe's a concern over the twin evils of popery and popular anarchy. The one real development that takes place between *Eglogs, Epytaphes and Sonettes* and *The Shepheardes Calender* is the incorporation of the monarch into the symbolic world of Spenser's work. In Googe's volume there appeared to be no place for a prince, apart from the tyrannous Cupido; however the April eclogue of *The Shepheardes Calender* is a celebration of Elizabeth's queenship.

The Shepheardes Calender is a supremely confident, indeed arrogant, work.

It takes existing poetic norms and claims to bring them all together in a new and original package. At the same time *The Shepheardes Calender* is marked in its details, its language and poetics, by an awareness of the potential for violence that existed in the sinews of post-Reformation Tudor society. In particular, the echoes of past traumas, 1540 (Henrician tyranny), 1549 (popular anarchy) and 1553 (popish rule), can be heard in the intricacies of Spenser's work. The form of Spenser's volume is provocatively all-encompassing. Each of the twelve eclogues that make up *The Shepheardes Calender* opens with a woodcut depicting the fictional moment of their composition. The poems themselves seem designed to show off Spenser's ability to write in numerous different styles and forms. The eclogues are each followed by a set of notes written by an unknown editor, E.K. From woodcut to gloss it appears at first glance as if Spenser is leaving nothing for his reader to do. This impression is, however, a deliberate illusion. For example the July eclogue, one of three that address religious issues, initially seems to be setting itself up as a simple polemical debate between a godly shepherd, Tomalin, and a proud pastor, Morrell. The woodcut depicts Morrell sitting on a hill in formal dress, talking down to Tomalin whose attire is far more homely.[13] The state of the two shepherds' flocks, however, reverses these differences since while Morrell's wander aimlessly Tomalin's are depicted at his back in an ordered group. The distinctions that structure this woodcut repeat graphic tropes common to English Protestantism. In particular, the frontispiece to John Foxe's *Acts and Monuments* deploys a similar, albeit much more complex, comparison between ordered godliness and the aimless wandering of papistry.[14] In comparison with Foxe's work, however, it does not work to attempt to apply the meaning of this woodcut to the poem it prefaces. Indeed to do so produces a reading that has to do more and more reductive damage to the actual dialogue between Morrell and Tomalin. Spenser in this eclogue incites his readers to expect a piece of religious polemic, only to dash this expectation. In the process he gives his readers a lesson in how to read in a religious context – with care and caution.[15]

The first sign that the distinction between Morrell and Tomalin is less than clear-cut comes when the latter turns down Morrell's invitation to join him on his hill. Tomalin tells his fellow shepherd:

> Ah God shield, man, that I should clime,
>   and learne to looke alofte,
> This reede is ryfe, that oftentime
>   great clymbers fall unsoft
> In humble dales in footing fast,
>   the trode is not so tickle.[16]

Tomalin sounds here like the voice of plain simple wisdom. But, as his speech continues, the limitations of Tomalin's view of the world are revealed. He goes on to comment that Morrell's hill lacks shade, a real problem since, as Tomalin points out, it is now the height of summer.

> And now the Sonne hath reared up
>   his fyriefooted teme,
> Making his way betweene the Cuppe,
>   and golden Diademe:
> The rampant Lyon hunts he fast,
>   with Dogge of noisome breath,
> Whose balefull barking bringes in hast
>   pyne, plagues, and dreery death.
> Agaynst his cruell scortching heate
>   where hast thou coverture?[17]

Tomalin's argument in this passage has a literal and figurative meaning since Morrell's hill-climbing also signifies his ambition. Occupying a position of prominence, in either the natural world or that of the Church, leaves one over-exposed to heat of the sun. There is, however, something quite disproportionate about Tomalin's description of the effects of the sun. E.K., in his gloss on the relationship between the Dogge and Lyon, comments: 'Thys is Poetically spoken, as if the Sunne did hunt a Lion with one Dogge. The meaning wherof is, that in July the sonne is in Leo. At which tyme the Dogge starre, which is called Syrius or Canicula reigneth, with immoderate heat causing Pestilence, drought, and many diseases.'[18] As is often the case, E.K. in this gloss explains the poetic text in a way that misses its central point. The key thing about Tomalin's use of these classical and astrological references is not their literal meaning but their contradiction of his earlier assumption of the voice of plain homely wisdom. The implication of this passage is that Tomalin knows about the dangers of prominence only in a poetic and classical context. It is this that explains his almost hysterical view that the sun brings 'distress, plagues and dreary death'.

Later in the poem Spenser stages another moment when the poem pushes towards a simple religious dichotomy only to end up frustrating this move. Morrell rejects Tomalin's criticisms of his hill-climbing telling him that:

> Syker, thous but a laesie loord,
>   and rekes much of thy swinck,
> That with fond termes, and weetlesse words
>   to blere myne eyes doest thinke.
> In evill houre thou hentest in hond
>   thus holy hylles to blame,
> For sacred unto saints they stond
>   and of them han theyr name.[19]

Tomalin will have none of this, telling Morrell that:

> Syker thou speakes lyke a lewde lorrell,
>   of Heaven to demen so:
> How be I am but rude and borrell,
>   yet nearer wayes I knowe.
> To Kerke the narre, from God more farre,
>   has bene an old sayd sawe.
> And he that strives to touch the stares,
>   oft stumbles at a strawe.[20]

Morrell's defense of his mountaineering appears suspiciously papist with its reference to saints and 'holy hills'. In particular, he seems to be confusing allegorical and literal hills. But is this case? Certainly Tomalin claims it is, but then his endorsement of the claim that the nearer one is to the Church the further one is from God repeats Morrell's hermeneutic blunder. Morrell might be a bit too close to papistry for his own good, but Tomalin's religious views lead him to make hasty judgements and imprecise pronouncements. Having criticized Morrell's attachment to hills, Tomalin goes on to give a potted pastoral history of Christianity. During the course of this Tomalin describes the first shepherd, who E.K. glosses as Abel. 'As meeke he was, as meeke mought be, / simple, as simple sheepe, / Humble, and like in eche degree / the flocke, which he did keep.'[21] Morrell's response to Tomalin's history is to comment: 'Here is a great deale of good matter, / lost for lacke of telling, / Now sicker I see, thou doest but clatter: / harme may come of melling.'[22] Morrell does not reject Tomalin's version of the history of the Church with its emphasis on the simplicity of the first shepherds. His criticism of it is aesthetic and social. Tomalin's 'melling' obscures the good matter of his history. The implication of Morrell's response is that Tomalin lacks the rhetorical skills to match his knowledge. If his history had been more ordered, more decorous, then its argument would have acceptable to Morrell. This eclogue famously ends with Tomalin's poetic misogynist account of Archbishop Grindal's fall from prominence.[23]

The July eclogue of *The Shepheardes Calender* is an argument for a moderate English Protestantism to unite members of the Elizabethan polity, from the magistrates to the churchwardens, against the forces of disorder. Although one of these is clearly popery, Spenser avoids in this poem indulging in typical Reformation polemics. His argument is no less confessional for all this but it is couched in terms that address the history of English Protestantism.[24] The struggle against popery needs to go on but it must not be conducted at a popular level. When Morrell raises the dangers of 'melling' in the context of religious reform, one can see this as a reflection of the Elizabethan rejection of the Edwardian model of Reformation, perhaps particularly the events of 1549. To mell means to mix and is associated with fighting and copulation. It has violent and irrational connotations, as well as lower-class ones. Mouse-slayer and John Cheke's Kett might mell, but not Googe's and Spenser's shepherds.[25] Indeed their existence is predicated on the need to avoid a melling like the one that broke out in 1549. *The Shepheardes Calender* is a poetic invitation to people from Kett's class to participate in Spenser's magisterial Protestant brotherhood. The price of admission to his bond of godly Shepherds is the internalization of the lessons of *The Shepheardes Calender* in terms of the work's emphasis on decorum and order.[26]

Spenser's volume, particularly its complex form with woodcuts and glosses, is an invitation to its readers to feel part of its symbolic code. E.K.'s often ham-fisted glosses play an important part in this process.[27] At one level it is important not to assume that they are all meant to be read as ironic or comic since they often do help to explicate Spenser's meaning. The reader has to learn care, however, when referring to E.K. Sometimes he is helpful while at other times he positively hinders the production of meaning. A similar tension exists in relation to the woodcuts. *The Shepheardes Calender* is a lesson on how to read with care, not rushing to make judgements or trusting too much on any one element of the work.[28] At the same time it is also designed to teach its readers how to be godly shepherds. In particular, the lesson in decorum that Tomalin needs to learn is one that the work is designed to teach throughout the Elizabethan public sphere.[29] The September eclogue, which concentrates on the dangers of popery, takes place between Diggon and Hobbinoll. The former has returned from a visit aboard where he hoped to find richer pastures but instead confronted the reality of popish corruption. He tells Hobbinoll:

> The shepherds there robben one another,
> And layen baytes to beguile her brother.
> Or theyr will buy his sheepe out of the cote,
> Or they will carven the shepherds throte.[30]

Diggon's account of his travels includes a comprehensive criticism of popery. Hobbinoll's response is sympathetic, but like Morrell he is critical of the way Diggon tells his story. At one point he interrupts Diggon to ask him 'speake not so dirke. / Such myster saying me seemeth to mirke'.[31] Thirty lines later, however, Hobbinoll is driven to interrupt Diggon again. 'Nowe Diggon, I see thou speakest to plaine: / Better it were, a little to feyne, / And cleanly cover, that cannot be cured.'[32] The obvious reason for Hobbinoll's caution is that in the preceding lines Diggon's criticisms have come very close to home.[33] In particular, Diggon attacks the effects on the Church of its plunder at the hands of secular lords.[34]

Having sailed too close to the winds with his plain talk, Diggon returns to the far safer topic of the Jesuit mission to England, telling Hobbinoll what is required to defeat them.

> But not good Dogges hem needeth to chace,
> But heedy shepheards to discerne their face.
> For all their craft is in their countenaunce,
> They bene so grave and full of mayntenaunce.[35]

Defeating Jesuits requires cautious attentive shepherds capable of looking beyond Jesuits' grave countenances to see their true wolfish faces. The argument of this poem is, however, that the importance of taking heed goes beyond any specific application to encompass the entire dialogue between Hobbinoll and Diggon. The latter learns during the course of this eclogue to be more heedful of his words, to walk the tightrope between being too dark and too plain. He has to appreciate that different levels of decorum are required at home and abroad. *The Shepheardes Calender* is a celebration of the virtues of heedfulness, in reading, writing and speech, as a bulwark against the forces of disorder – popery, hasty readers and speakers who mell their words. It is also an advertisement for its author's ability to play a crucial role in the creation of the 'heedy shepheards' needed to protect the country from popish wolves. In particular, the volume's impressive range of poetic styles and voices is designed to demonstrate the cultural and political utility of Spenser's linguistic skills.[36] The formal complexity of *The Shepheardes Calender* defers the use of generic expectations to short-circuit interpretation.[37] Only by reading with care can one appreciate the coherence of Spenser's work and earn the right to join the poet's bond of godly shepherds.

Sir Thomas Smith's *De Republica Anglorum* theorises the politics of *The Shepheardes Calender*.[38] This is despite the fact that it was written over ten years before Spenser's volume. At the centre of this work is an image of the English polity defined by the way in which counsel is conducted on the basis of order and decorum. Smith consistently emphasizes the decorous nature of English political debate against the dangers of popular anarchy and princely tyranny. *De Republica Anglorum* was written while Smith was serving as ambassador for Elizabeth in France in 1565 but not published until after Smith's death. It paints a picture of England as an entirely ordered commonwealth held together by the legitimacy of its laws. This leads Smith to assert: 'In no place shal you see malefactors go more constantly, more assuredly, and with lesse lamentation to their death than in England.'[39] This almost surreal claim relates directly to the central place of Parliament in Smith's conceptualization of the English polity. For him Parliament embodies the publicness of the English law. In particular, parliamentary debates, their conduct, order and reasonableness, make the laws of England in his eyes uniquely legitimate. This uniqueness has a nationalistic and historical side. *De Republica Anglorum* consistently contrasts the state of justice in England with what happens on the continent. In particular, for Smith the absence of torture in the English system reflects its legitimacy. He writes: 'The nature of out nation is free, stout, haulte, prodigall of life and blood: but contumelie, beatings, servitude and servile torment and punishment it will not abide.'[40] The other side to this celebration of English freedom is, however, reflected in Smith's emphasis on the necessary decorum of political debate within the polity. *De Republica Anglorum*, like *The Shepheardes Calender* and the work of Barnabe Googe, deploys the ideal of ordered speech in order to mark and simultaneously overwrite the shadow of 1549. The commonwealth of England in Smith's work is threatened by the danger of foreign tyranny and at home by those who would disrupt the decorum of its political sphere.

These dangers are given a historical twist when *De Republica Anglorum* discusses the maxim that 'the common wealth must be according to the nature of the people'.[41] Smith argues:

> If a contrary forme be given to a contrary maner of people, as when the shoe is too little or too great for the fote, it doth hurt and encumber the convenient use thereof, so that the free people of nature tyrannized or ruled by one against their wille, were he never so good, either faile of corage and wexe servile, or never rest until they either destroie and them that would subdue them, or be destroyed themselves.[42]

This passage appears to be relatively simple. Tyranny results from over-tight laws that do not fit a people's nature. But Smith's argument here depends on a tautology – what makes the shoe of tyranny pinch is its tyrannous nature. This passage appears on first reading to be an explanation for the existence of tyranny, but in fact it is a history lesson relating directly to the mid-Tudor period. What is being described here is the regime of Henry VIII and its effect on the country. This reading is reinforced when Smith goes on to describe what happens when the shoe of government is too loose fitting. He writes:

> And againe another sort there is which without being ruled by one prince but set at libertie cannot tell what they shoudle doe, but either through insolencie, pride, and idleness will fall to robbery and all mischiefe, and to scatter and dissolve themselves, or with foolish ambition and private strife consume one another and bring themselves to nothing.[43]

This passage depicts popular anarchy. In it Smith is drawing on the same basic ideological assumptions as Richard Morrison in *A Remedy for Sedition* and John Cheke in *The hurt of Sedition*. For Morrison, Cheke and Smith, writing at very different times and contexts, an excess of liberty will inevitably lead the people to defy all laws and erase all boundaries. Smith's argument in these passages is, however, asymmetrical. *De Republica Anglorum* depicts the dangers of tyranny in terms of a political class defined by its freedom, while the effects of liberty are felt at another social level entirely among the mass of the populace who without order will dissolve themselves into nothing. Smith's work depicts an English commonwealth in which politics is the bulwark against tyranny and popular anarchy. It describes a political class posed between these two evils and in the process follows in Cheke's footsteps by suggesting a common interest between aristocrats, gentry and those who Smith calls yeomanry.

The poetics of *De Republica Anglorum* reflect this agenda. At the conclusion of his work Smith compares it with 'feigned commonwealths like More's Utopia which never were or shall be except in the vaine imaginations of Philosophers'.[44] He argues that in comparison *De Republica Anglorum* should be read as a chart or map of England in the year 1565, writing:

> This being as a project or table of a common wealth truly laide before you, not fained by putting a case: let us compare it with common wealthes, which be at this day in esse, or doe remaine discribed in true histories, especially in such pointes wherin the one differeth from the other, to see who hath taken the righter, truer, and more commodious way to governe the people aswell in warre as in peace.[45]

The 'you' in this passage is Smith's reader. What is being incited in this passage is the use of *De Republica Anglorum* as a tool for informed political education. The emphasis in the work on discussion, however, gives this agenda a specific twist since the implication is that Smith's work would be best used as the basis for public debate over the relative merits of different commonwealths. *De Republica Anglorum*'s insistence on its non-polemical nature, its self-construction as a map, reflects the extent to which the work's form is designed to support its politics. Unlike Spenser's *Shepheardes Calender*, *De Republica Anglorum* is not a lesson in how to read but an example of how politics should sound.

The Shepheardes Calender and *De Republica Anglorum* have similar political agendas.[46] Spenser's work is intended to fashion a community of godly, heedful readers who reject the blandishments of popery and the dangerous pleasures of melling. Smith's work claims to be a simple, even non-textual, map of the polity. Its stated aim is to provoke its readers to political debate centred on the discussion of the merits of the English commonwealth. In both texts an ideal political community is imagined that is coterminous with the text's ideal readership and in neither could the Queen conceivably be a member. This does not make either *The Shepheardes Calender* or *De Republica Anglorum* an anti-monarchical work. Or perhaps more accurately it does not make them texts opposing Elizabeth. This would be a bizarre claim, given Smith's description of Elizabeth as noble and virtuous and Spenser's celebration of her in the April eclogue. At the same time Elizabeth's place in their symbolic worlds is tangential and in some ways strangely arbitrary. Do the political and poetic agendas of *The Shepheardes Calender* or *De Republica Anglorum* require a monarch at their centre? In fact would they not make more sense without a prince? What would the political world imagined in Spenser's and Smith's texts look like?

This political world does not, however, have to be imagined. It existed, and indeed was growing and developing throughout Elizabeth's reign. Paul Slack has suggested that one of the key effects of the dissolution of the monasteries and the general plunder of the Church throughout most of the Tudor period after 1530 was the growth of corporate and civic bodies. Slack argues that it was these bodies that inherited the commonwealth ethos of the Edwardian period after it 'withered away during the 1560s'. He writes: 'Though the history of English corporate bodies remains to be written, their survival and formal evolution were essential ingredients in the dissemination of civic and civil consciousness in the sixteenth century.' [47] It was this world of miniature public spheres which provides the context for the politics and poetics of works like *The Shepheardes Calender* and *De Republica Anglorum*. Peter Lake has recently suggested that one can see,

> the plethora of statutory regulations and wish lists produced by the parliaments of the later sixteenth century [as] an almost utopian vision, a state-based imaginary of order and control which, of course, was never fully enforced in the localities but was nevertheless securely based on abstract notions of parliamentary sovereignty, as the embodiment of the commonweal or the godly commonwealth.[48]

Lake's argument is that what linked Slack's corporate bodies and committees and Parliament was a shared, almost utopian, agenda for social reform driven by the image of a reformed godly commonwealth. This sounds Henrician in its utopianism, but with a crucial difference. In the world of Elizabethan politics as imagined in *The Shepheardes Calender* or *De Republica Anglorum*, it is Spenser's bond of godly shepherds or the members of Smith's class in political geography who are the repositories of the utopian vision – it is they who have inherited confessionalization with its ability to glue the spokes of the wheel of government together. Indeed given the collective nature of these imagined communities' confessionalization played a vital role in enabling and legitimatizing their pursuit of social reform and order. In the school boards and borough councils Cheke and Kett worked together in pursuit of a godly commonwealth and against disorder – popular, papist, heretical or, if necessary, princely.

NOTES

1 Edmund Spenser, 'The Shepheardes Calender', 1579, STC 23089, in *The Yale Edition of the Shorter Poems of Edmund Spenser*, eds William A. Oram, Einor Bjorvard, Ronald Bond, Thomas H. Cain, Alexander Dunlop, Richard Schell (New Haven: 1989), pp. 1–213, p. 74.

2 William Cecil, *The Execution of Justice in England*, 1583, STC 4902, ed. Robert M. Kingdon (Ithaca: 1965) and Sir Thomas Smith, *De Republica Anglorum: A Discourse on the Commonwealth of England*, 1583, STC 22857, ed. L. Alston (Cambridge: 1906).

3 On the Elizabethan Church see Patrick Collinson, *The Religion of Protestants: The Church in English Society 1559–1625* (Oxford: 1982).

4 The debate over what to do about Mary Queen of Scots continued throughout the 1570s. It is a background motif in the politics of this decade always ready to swell to a major strain at times of crisis.

5 John Guy argues that despite the real differences at the heart of the Elizabethan regime during the 1570s it is important not to over-emphasize these. Cecil and Francis Walsingham may have disagreed over intervention in the Netherlands but the latter was Cecil's chosen successor as secretary and they were united by far more than divided them. See John Guy, *Tudor England* (Oxford: 1991), pp. 275–282.

6 John Morrill has argued that the period 1569–1642 was exceptionally stable in the context of England's history. He comments: 'The period 1569 to 1642 was the longest period ever without major rebellion; the period 1605–1641 the longest without the conviction of a peer of a realm for treason; the number of trials for treason declined decade by decade from the late sixteenth century through to the 1630s. Where else [in Europe] in the early seventeenth century were few or no royal officials killed in discharging their duties? ... Were there not more dead bodies on stage at the end of a production of *Hamlet* than following any collective act of violence in the period up to 1642?' (John Morrill, *The Nature of the English Revolution* (London: 1993), p. 5).

7 Simon Adams points out that, compared to the governance of Henry VIII, Elizabeth's was mild and merciful. Indeed those at the centre of the Elizabethan regime knew that this was the case. They acted as if Elizabeth was another Henry, knowing that they and the Queen were all part of a performance of Henrician kingship. See Simon Adams, 'Eliza Enthroned? The Court and Politics', in *The Reign of Elizabeth I*, ed. Christopher Haigh (London: 1984), pp. 55–78, p. 76.

8 Cecil, 1965, pp. 10–11.

9 Ibid., p. 37.

10 Cecil's argument here is, however, incoherent since the way he typifies Catholic belief in terms of labels and apparel implies that it is inherently performative. This suggests that in practice anyone who is known by any of the labels Cecil lists here is taking part in a deceptive act.

11 William Allen argued that it was the regime's own inquisitorial processes that ultimately forced Catholics to call Elizabeth a heretic. He comments, 'This is to make traitors and not to punish treasons.' William Allen, *A briefe historie of the glorious martyrdom of XII priests* (1582), STC 369.5, c.iii. (v).

12 See Nancy Jo Hoffman, *Spenser's Pastorals* (Baltimore: 1977), and Patrick Cheney, 'Spenser's Pastorals: *The Shepheardes Calender* and *Colin Clouts Come Home Againe*', in *The Cambridge Companion to Spenser*, ed. Andrew Hadfield (Cambridge: 2001), pp. 79–105.

13 It is possible the Morrell is wearing clothes designed to look like Elizabethan clerical vestments.

14 The July woodcut also reproduces a traditional Protestant binary pictorial opposition, with godliness occupying the authoritative right hand-side of the woodcut in the person of Tomalin and papistry the weaker left-hand side.

15 David Norbrook argues that in *The Shepheardes Calender* Spenser 'draws attention to the

difficulties, and the political implications, of interpretation'. See David Norbrook, *Poetry and Politics in the English Renaissance* (London: 2002), p. 66.

16 Spenser, 1989, p. 122.

17 Ibid., p. 122.

18 Ibid., p. 130.

19 Ibid., pp. 122–123.

20 Ibid., p. 125.

21 Ibid., p. 126.

22 Ibid., p. 128.

23 Tomalin tells how Algrin, a figure for Grindal, was sitting on a hill when he was hit on the head by shellfish dropped by an eagle who mistook his bald head for chalk.

24 For the place of *The Shepheardes Calender* in the tradition of English Protestant poetry see John N. King, 'Spenser's *Shepheardes Calender* and Protestant Pastoral Satire', in *Renaissance Genres: Essays on Theory, History and Interpretation*, ed. Barbara Kiefer Lewalski (Cambridge, Mass.: 1986), pp. 369–398.

25 It is extremely unlikely that Spenser would have known the text of the 'Ballad of the Pilgrimage of Grace' but the authors of this text argue that the commons have been forced to mell by the foolishness of the world and that their melling is efficacious.

26 Andrew Hadfield has argued that Sir Philip Sidney was engaged in a similar project in his *Apologie*, arguing: 'Sidney may well have been a Protestant, as was Surrey, but the *Apologie*'s argument for a 'noble' poetic voice based on the poetry of Surrey was designed to kill off a vernacular Protestant literary tradition and replace it with a consciously aristocratic one.' The important difference between Sidney's and Spenser's agendas is that Spenser did not want to kill off the tradition personified in Tomalin so much as make it more decorous. See Andrew Hadfield, *Literature, Politics and National Identity: Reformation to Renaissance* (Cambridge: 1994), p. 143.

27 Evelyn B. Tribble has commented on E.K's importance to the way *The Shepheardes Calender* positions its reader to 'ally him/herself not with some transcendent poetic voice but with the community of readers' brought together by the relationship between gloss and poem. See Evelyn B. Tribble, *Margins and Marginality: The Printed Page in Early Modern England* (Charlottesville: 1993), p. 87.

28 This aspect of Spenser's work reflects the extent to which it eschews Reformation polemics. In these terms it repeats Sir Thomas More's agenda in the *Dialogue concerning Heresies*, albeit in a radically different religious context.

29 Louis Montrose has argued that Elizabethan pastoral performs important ideological work in its simultaneous acknowledgement and rejection of rural life. He suggests that: 'A social matrix for Elizabethan pastoral forms and practices may be located in the interstices between the categories of baseness and gentility, on that ambiguous social boundary that pastorals symbolically mark and transgress.' *The Shepheardes Calender* gives this boundary a particular linguistic emphasis. One knows that one is on the 'right' side of the line between gentility and baseness if one's speech is decorous and one's reading is cautious. See Louis Adrian Montrose, 'Of Gentlemen and Shepherds: The Politics of Elizabethan Pastoral Form', *ELH*, 50 (1983), pp. 415–459, p. 433.

30 Ibid., p. 153.

Literature and politics

31 Ibid., p. 155.

32 Ibid pp. 156–157.

33 The editors of the Yale edition of *The Shepheardes Calender* point out that, while the ostensible focus of Diggon's account is foreign popish lands, as it continues it becomes apparent that he is talking about Britain, and perhaps even more specifically the situation in the bishopric of Richard Daves in Wales. Ibid., p. 149.

34 Given that Cecil and Leicester were notorious offenders in terms of taking lands from the Church, Hobbinoll's, and Spenser's, caution over Diggon's discussion of this matter was certainly politic.

35 Ibid., 158.

36 Spenser's agenda here, his assumption of a privileged poetic voice speaking authoritatively within the public sphere, is identical to that of John Skelton in such works as *A Replycacion*.

37 In *Mother Hubberds Tale* Spenser plays with narrators and personas in order to make his reader take heed or care when reading this work. See Kent T. Van Den Berg, '"The Counterfeit in Personation": Spenser's Prosopopoia or Mother Hubberds Tale', in *The Author in His Work*, eds Louis L. Martz and Aubrey Williams (New Haven: 1978), pp. 85–102.

38 On Smith's work, see Patrick Collinson, '*De Republica Anglorum*: Or, History with the Politics Put Back', in *Elizabethan Essays* (London: 1994), pp. 1–30 and Anne McLaren, 'Reading Sir Thomas Smith's *De Republica Anglorum* as Protestant Apologetia', *HJ*, 42 (1999), pp. 911–939.

39 Smith, 1906, p. 105.

40 Ibid., p. 106.

41 Ibid., p. 28.

42 Ibid., p. 28.

43 Ibid., p. 28.

44 Ibid., p. 142.

45 Ibid., pp. 142–143.

46 These agendas could also be related to that pursued by men like Foxe in relation to Elizabethan religion. The editions of *Acts and Monuments* published after 1570, in 1576 and 1583, present themselves to their readers as guides to public discussion and debate. In particular, they incite their readers to compare the state of the English Church with that of the primitive Church. This comparison is, however, clearly represented in Foxe's work as taking place in public between those already sympathetic to the cause of Protestant reform.

47 Paul Slack, *From Reformation to Improvement: Public Welfare in Early Modern England* (Oxford: 1998), p. 27.

48 Peter Lake, 'Periodization, Politics and "The Social"', *Journal of British Studies*, 37 (1998), pp. 279–90, p. 287.

Bibliography

PRIMARY WORKS

The abbaye of the holy ghost (Westminster: 1496?), STC 13608.7.

Alcock, John, *Mons Perfeccionis: otherwyse in englysshe the hyl of perfeccon* (1497), STC 279.

Allen, William, *A briefe historie of the glorious martyrdom of XII priests* (1582), STC 369.5.

Aske, Robert, 'Narrative of October and November 1536', ed. Mary Bateson, *EHR*, 5 (1890), pp. 331–343.

Baldwin, William et al, *The Mirror for Magistrates*, ed. Lily B. Campbell (Cambridge: 1938).

Baldwin, William, *Beware the Cat*, 1570, STC 1244, ed. and intro. William A. Ringler and Michael Flachmann (San Marino, California: 1988).

Bale, John, 'King Johan', c.1538, in *The Complete Plays of John Bale*, Vol. 1, ed. Peter Happé (Woodbridge: 1985).

Bale, John, 'The Comedy of the Three Laws', c.1538, printed c.1548, STC 1287, in *The Complete Plays of John Bale*, Vol. 2, ed. Peter Happé (Woodbridge: 1986), pp. 64–123.

Bale, John, *The Apology of John Bale agaynste a ranke Papyst, answering both hym and hys doctours, that neyther their vowes nor yet their priesthode are of the Gospell, but of Antichrist* (London: 1550), STC 1275.

Bale, John, *The first two partes of the Actes or unchaste examples of Englyshe Votaryes, gathered out of theyr owne legendes and Chronicles* (London: 1560), STC. 1274.

Ball, John, 'Letters', in *The Peasant's Revolt of 1381*, ed. R.B. Dobson (London: 1983), pp. 380–383.

'Ballad of the Pilgrimage of Grace (1536)', ed. Mary Bateson, *EHR*, 5 (1890), pp. 344–345.

Barlow, William, *A Dyaloge Descrybyng the Orygynall Ground of these Lutheran Facycons*, c.1531, STC 1461 (Amsterdam: 1974).

Bonner, Edmund, *A profitable and necessary doctryne, with certayne homilies adioyned thereunto* (London: 1555), STC 3282.

Brooks, James, *A sermon very notable, fruitefull and Godlie* (London: 1553), STC 3838.

Calendar of State Papers Domestic Series of the Reign of Edward VI 1547–1553, ed. C.S. Knighton (London: 1992).

Cecil, William, 'A Short Memoryall of the State of the Realme', in *A Collection of State Papers Relating to Affairs from the Reigns of King Henry VIII, King Edward VI, Queen Mary and Queen Elizabeth ... Left by William Cecil Lord Burghley*, ed. Samuel Haynes (London: 1740), pp. 579–588.

Cecil, William, *The Execution of Justice in England*, 1583, STC 4902, ed. Robert M. Kingdon (Ithaca: 1965).

Chaucer, Geoffrey, 'The Pardoner's Tale', in *The Riverside Chaucer*, ed. Larry D. Benson (Oxford: 1987), pp. 196–202.

Cheke, John, *The hurt of sedicion howe greveous it is to a Commune welth* (1549), STC 5109.

Christopherson, John, *An Exhortation to all Menne to ... Beware of Rebellion* (1554), STC 5207.

Colet, John, 'Sermon 1511', in *English Historical Documents: V 1485–1588*, ed. C.H. Williams (London: 1967), pp. 652–660.

The Contemplacon of Synners (Westminster: 1499), STC 5643.

Copland, Robert, *The Myrrour of the Chyrche* (1521), STC 965.

Copland, Robert, *The Passyon of Our Lord* (1521), STC 14558.

Copland, Robert, 'The Seuen Sorowes that women haue when theyr husbandes be deade', *c.*1526, printed *c.*1565, STC 2734, in *Robert Copland: Poems*, ed. Mary Carpenter Erler (Toronto: 1993), pp. 83–124.

Cooper, Thomas, *Coopers Chronicle* (London: 1560), STC 15218.

Crowley, Robert, *An Informacion agaynst the oppressors of the pore commons* (London: 1548), STC 6086.

Crowley, Robert, *The Confutation of the mishapen Answer to the misnamed, wicked Ballade, called the Abuse of [the] blessed sacrame[n]t of the aultare. Wherin, thou haste (gentle Reader) the ryghte understandynge of all the places of scripture that Myles Hoggard (wyth his learned counsaill) hath wrested to make transubstanciacion of the bread and wyne* (London: 1548), STC 6082.

Crowley, Robert, 'The Printer to the Reader', *The Vision of Pierce Plowman, nowe the seconde tyme imprinted by Roberte Crowlye* (London: 1550), STC 19907.

Crowley, Robert, *One and Thyrtye Epigrammes, wherin are bryefly touched so many abuses,* London, 1550, STC 6088.3, in *The Select Works of Robert Crowley*, ed. J.M. Cowper, EETS e.s. 15 (London: 1872), pp. 1–52.

Crowley, Robert, *The Way to Wealth, wherin is taught a remedy for sedicion,* London, 1550, STC 25588 in *The Select Works of Robert Crowley*, ed. J.M. Cowper, EETS e.s. 15 (London: 1872), pp. 129–150.

Crowley, Robert, *Philargyrie of Greate Britayne* (London: 1551), STC 6089.5.

Crowley, Robert, *An Epitome of Cronicles ... continued until the reigne of Elizabeth* (London: 1559), STC 15221.

Crowley, Robert, *The Opening of the Wordes of the Prophet Joell, in his second and third chapters* (London: 1567), STC 6089.

'A Declaration of the Quenes Proceedings since her Reigne', in *A Collection of State Papers Relating to Affairs from the Reigns of King Henry VIII, King Edward VI, Queen Mary and Queen Elizabeth ... Left by William Cecil Lord Burghley*, ed. Samuel Haynes (London: 1740), pp. 589–593.

Documents Relating to the Revels at the Court in the Time of King Edward VI and Queen Mary, ed. Albert Feuillerat (Louvain: 1914).

Dudley, Edmund, *The Tree of Commonwealth*, ed. D.M. Brodie (Cambridge: 1948).

Elyot, Sir Thomas, *The Boke named The Governour* (London: 1531), STC 7635.

Elyot, Sir Thomas, *Of the Knowledge which Maketh a Wise Man* (1533), STC 7668.

Elyot, Sir Thomas, *Pasquil the Playne* (London: 1533), STC 7672.

Elyot, Sir Thomas, *The Dictionary of Syr T.E. Knyght* (London: 1538), STC 7658.

Elyot, Sir Thomas, *Bibliotheca Eliotae* (London: 1542), STC 7659.

Elyot, Sir Thomas, 'The Letters of Sir Thomas Elyot', ed. K.J. Wilson, *Studies in Philology*, 73 (1976), no. 5.

Erasmus, Desiderius, 'Erasmus' Letter to Carondelet: The Preface to His Edition of St Hilary', trans. John C. Olin, in *Six Essays on Erasmus*, ed. John C. Olin (New York: 1979), pp. 93–120.

Erasmus, Desiderius, *Praise of Folly*, trans. Betty Radice, intro. A.H.T. Levi (London: 1993).

Fish, Simon, *The Supplication of the Beggars*, 1529, STC 10883, ed. Edward Arber (London: 1878).

Foxe, John, *Actes and Monuments* (London: 1563), STC 11222.,

Foxe, John, *Actes and Monumentes* (London: 1570), STC 11223.

Foxe, John, 'A Sermon of Christ Crucified', 1570, STC 11242, in *The English Sermons of John Foxe*, ed. Warren Wooden (New York: 1978).

Foxe, John, *Acts and Monuments* (London: 1583), STC 11225.

Froissart, Jean, *The Chronicles*, Vol. 1, trans. John Bouchier (London: 1812).

Gardiner, Stephen, 'The Oration of True Obedience', c.1534, printed 1553, STC 11585, in *Obedience in Church and State: Three Political Tracts*, ed. and trans. Pierre Janelle (Cambridge: 1930), pp. 67–169.

Gardynare, Germen, *A letter of a younge gentleman named mayster Germen Gardynare, wryten to a frend of his, wheron men may se the demeanour [and] heresy of John Fryth late burned* (1534), STC 11594.

Gascoigne, George, *A Hundreth Sundrie Flowres*, 1573, STC 11635, ed. and intro. G.W. Pigman III (Oxford: 2000).

Gilby, Anthony, *An Admonition to England and Scotland to call them to repentance*, in *The Appellation of John Knox* (Geneva: 1558), STC 15063.

Googe, Barnabe, *Eglogs, Epytaphes and Sonettes*, 1563, STC 12048, ed. Judith M. Kennedy (Toronto: 1989).

Googe, Barnabe, *The Shippe of Safegarde*, 1569, STC 12049, ed. Simon McKeown and William E. Sheidley (Tempe, Arizona: 2001).

Gwynnethe, John, *A Declaration of the state, wherin all heretickes dooe leade their lives* (London: 1554), STC 12558.

Hawes, Stephen, *The Pastime of Pleasure* (London: 1554), STC 12950.

Heywood, John, 'Two hundred Epigrammes', 1555, STC 13296, in *John Heywood's Works and Miscellaneous Short Poems*, ed. Burton A. Milligan (Urbana: 1956), pp. 141–198.

Heywood, John, *The Spider and Fly*, 1556, STC 13308, ed. John S. Farmer (London: 1908).

Heywood, John, 'A breefe balet touching the traytorous takynge of Scarborow Castell', c.1557, STC 13290.7, in *John Heywood's Works and Miscellaneous Short Poems*, ed. Burton A. Milligan (Urbana: 1956), pp. 272–274.

Hoccleve, Thomas, 'Address to Sir John Oldcastle', in *Hoccleve's Works: The Minor Poems,*

Vol. 1, eds Frederick J. Furnivall and I. Gollancz, EETS e.s. 61 (London: 1970), pp. 8–24.

Hogarde, Miles, *The assault of the sacrame[n]t of the Altar* (London: 1554), STC 13556.

Hogarde, Miles, *A Treatise entitled the Path waye to the towre of perfection* (London: 1554), STC 13561.

Hogarde, Miles, *The Displaying of the Protestants* (London: 1556), STC 13557.

Hogarde, Miles, *A newe ABC* (London: 1557), STC 13559.

Hogarde, Miles, 'O Hear Me, Lord, and Grant Mercy', in *The Moral Play of Wit and Science and Early Poetical Miscellanies*, ed. John Orchard Halliwell (London: 1848), pp. 107–109.

Holme, Wilfrid, *The fall and euill successe of Rebellion from time to time. Wherin is contained matter, moste meete for all estates to rewe* (London: 1570), STC 13602.

Hooper, John, 'An Answer unto my lord of wynchesters booke intytlyd a dection of the deuyls Sophistrye wherwith he robbith the unlernyd people of the trew byleef in the moost blessyd sacrament of the aulter', 1547, STC 13741, in *Early Writings of John Hooper*, ed. Samuel Carr (Cambridge: 1843), pp. 97–247.

A Hundred Merry Tales, 1526, STC 23663, ed. Carew Hazlitt (London: 1887).

The Image of Idleness, 1555, STC 25196, printed in 'The English Epistolary Novel: The Image of Idleness (1555). Text, Introduction and Notes', ed. Michael Flachmann, *Studies in Philology*, 87 (1990), pp. 1–75.

Letters and Papers, Foreign and Domestic, of the Reign of Henry VIII, 1509–47, eds J.S. Brewer, James Gairdner and R. H. Brodie (1862–1932).

'A litel treatise ageynste the mutterynge of some papistes in corners', 1534, STC 19177, in *Records of the Reformation: The Divorce*, 2 vols, ed. Nicholas Pocock (London: 1870), Vol. 2, pp. 539–552.

Martin, Thomas, *A Treatise declaryng and plainly prouyng, that the pretended marriage of Priestes, and professed persones, is no marriage, but altogether unlawfull* (1554), STC 17517.

Moore, Peter, *A Short treatyse of certayne thinges abused in the Popishe Church, longe used: But now abolished* (1548), STC 18053.

More, Sir Thomas, *Utopia*, eds George M. Logan and Robert M. Adams (Cambridge: 1989).

More, Sir Thomas, *Dialogue concerning heresies*, 1529, STC 18084, eds Thomas M.C. Lawler, Germian Marc' Harbour and Richard C. Marius, in *The Complete Works of St Thomas More*, Vol. 6 (New Haven: 1981).

More, Sir Thomas, *The supplycatyon of soulys*, c.1529, eds Frank Manley, Germian Marc Harbour, Richard C. Marius and Clarence H. Miller, in *The Complete Works of St Thomas More*, Vol. 7 (New Haven: 1990).

More, Sir Thomas, *A Dialogue of Comfort Against Tribulation*, c.1534, eds Louis L. Martz and Frank Manley, in *The Complete Works of St Thomas More*, Vol. 12 (New Haven: 1976).

More, Sir Thomas, *The Last Letters of Thomas More*, ed. and intro. Alvaro De Silva (Michigan: 2000).

Morrison, Richard, 'A Remedy for Sedition Wherein Are Contained Many Things concerning the True and Loyal Obeisance That Commons Owe unto Their Prince and Sovereign Lord the King', 1536, STC 18113.3, in *Humanist Scholarship and Public Order: Two Tracts against the Pilgrimage of Grace by Sir Richard Morrison*, ed. David Sandler Berkowitz (Washington: 1984), pp. 109–146.

Morrison, Richard, *An Exhortation to all Englishmen to the Defence of their countreye* (1539), STC 18110.

Norton, Thomas, *Orations of Arranes agaynst Philip the treacherous kyng of Macedone ...* (London: *c.*1560), STC 785.

Norton, Thomas and Sackville, Thomas, *Gorboduc*, in *Two Tudor Tragedies*, ed. William Tydeman (London: 1992), pp. 52–125.

Ochino, Barnadine, *A tragedie or Dialogue of the Bishop of Rome*, trans. John Ponet (London: 1549), STC 18770.

The Letters of William, Lord Paget of Beaudesert, 1547–1563, eds Barrett L. Beer and Sybil M. Jack, Camden Miscellany, Fourth Series, Vol. 13 (London: 1974).

The Passage of our most drad Soveraigne Lady Quene Elizabeth through the citie of London to westminister the daye before her coronacion, attributed to Richard Mulcaster, published by Richard Tottel (London: 1558), STC 7390.

Pathos, or an inward passion of the pope for the losse of hys daughter the masse (London: 1548), STC 19463.

Pole, Reginald, *Defence of the Unity of the Church*, trans. and intro., Joseph C. Dwyer (Westminster, Maryland: 1965).

Pole, Reginald, 'Cardinal Pole's speech to the citizens of London in behalf of religious houses', in John Strype, *Ecclesiastical Memorials*, 3:2 (Oxford: 1822), no. LXVIII, pp. 482–510.

Pollard, Leonard, *Fyve Homilies* (London: 1556), STC 20091.

Ponet, John, *A Short Treatise of politike power, and of the true Obedience which subiectes owe to kynges and other civile Governors, with an Exhortation to all true naturall Englishmen* (Strassburg?: 1556), STC 20178.

Proctor, John, 'The Prologue to His Deer brethren and naturall countree men of Englande', in Vincent of Lerins, *The waie home to Christ and truth leadinge from Antichrist and errour* (1556), STC 24754.

Punt, William, *A New Dialogue called the endightment agaynste mother Messe*, 1548, STC 20499, printed in Dickie Spurgeon, *Three Tudor Dialogues* (New York: 1978).

Russell, Frederic William, *Kett's Rebellion in Norfolk* (London: 1859).

Shepherd, Luke, attrib., *John Bon and Mast Person* (1548), STC 3258.5.

Skelton, John, 'Speke Parott', in *The Complete English Poems*, ed. John Scattergood (Harmondsworth: 1983), pp. 230–246.

Skelton, John, 'A Replycacion Agaynst Certayne Yong Scolers Adjured of Late', in *The Complete English Poems*, ed. John Scattergood (Harmondsworth: 1983), pp. 373–386.

Smith, Sir Thomas, *A Discourse of the Commonweal of this Realm*, ed. Mary Dewar (Charlottesville: 1969).

Smith, Sir Thomas, *De Republica Anglorum: A Discourse on the Commonwealth of England*, 1583, STC 22857, ed. L. Alston (Cambridge: 1906).

Sotherton, Nicholas, '"The Commoyson in Norfolk, 1549": A Narrative of Popular Rebellion in Sixteenth-Century England', ed. Barrett L. Beer, *Journal of Medieval and Renaissance Studies*, 6 (1979), pp. 73–99.

Spenser, Edmund, 'The Shepheardes Calender', 1579, STC 23089, in *The Yale Edition of the*

Shorter Poems of Edmund Spenser, eds William A. Oram, Einor Bjorvard, Ronald Bond, Thomas H. Cain, Alexander Dunlop, Richard Schell (New Haven: 1989), pp. 1–213.

Spenser, Edmund, 'Complaints', 1590, in *The Yale Edition of the Shorter Poems of Edmund Spenser*, eds William A. Oram, Einor Bjorvard, Ronald Bond, Thomas H. Cain, Alexander Dunlop, Richard Schell (New Haven: 1989), pp. 216–457.

'Sir Nicholas Throckmorton's Advice to Queen Elizabeth on her Ascension to the Throne', ed. J.E. Neale, *EHR*, 65 (1950), pp. 91–98.

Tottel's Miscellany, ed. Richard Tottel (1557), STC 13860.

Tracey, Richard, *A brief [and] short declaracyon made, wherbye every chrysten man maye knowe, what is a sacrament* (1548), STC 24162.

Tunstall, Cuthbert, *Certaine Godly and Devout Prayers, Made in latin by the Reverend father in God Tunstall, Bishop of Durham, and translated into English by Thomas Paynell* (London: 1558), STC 24318.

Tyndale, William, 'The Obedience of a Christian Man', 1528, STC 24446, in *Doctrinal Treatises and Introductions to Different Portions of the Holy Scriptures*, ed. Henry Walter (Cambridge: 1848), pp. 127–344.

Tyndale, William, *The Obedience of a Christian Man*, 1528, STC 24446, ed. David Daniell (London: 2000).

Tyndale, William, 'The Practice of Prelates', 1530, STC 24465, in *Expositions and Notes*, ed. Henry Walter (Cambridge: 1849), pp. 237–344.

Tyndale, William, *Old Testament*, 1530, STC 2350, ed. David Daniell (New Haven: 1992).

'Udall's Answer to the Commoners of Devonshire and Cornwall', in *Troubles Connected with the Prayer Book of 1549*, ed. Nicholas Pocock, Camden Society (1883–1884), pp. 141–193.

The wonders of England (London: 1559), STC 996.

Wyatt, Sir Thomas, *The Complete Poems*, ed. R.A. Rebholz (Harmonsworth: 1978).

York Mystery Plays, eds Richard Beadle and Pamela King (Oxford: 1984).

SECONDARY WORKS

Adams, Simon, 'Eliza Enthroned? The Court and Politics', in *The Reign of Elizabeth I*, ed. Christopher Haigh (London: 1984), pp. 55–78.

Aers, David, 'Altars of Power: Reflections on Eamon Duffy's *The Stripping of the Altars: Traditional Religion in England 1400–1580*', *Literature and History*, n.s. 3:2 (1995), pp. 90–105.

Aers, David, 'A Whisper on the Ear of Early Modernists; or, Reflections on Literary Critics Writing the "History of the Subject"', in *Culture and History 1350–1600: Essays on English Communities, Identities and Writing*, ed. David Aers (Hemel Hempstead: 1992), pp. 177–202.

Alford, John A., 'The Grammatical Metaphor: A Survey of Its Use in the Middle Ages', *Sp*, 57 (1982), pp. 728–760.

Alford, Stephen, *The Early Elizabethan Polity: William Cecil and the British Succession Crisis, 1558–1569* (Cambridge: 1998).

Alford, Stephen, 'Knox, Cecil and the British Dimension of the Scottish Reformation', in *John Knox and the British Reformations*, ed. Roger Mason (Aldershot: 1998), pp. 201–219.

Alford, Stephen, *Kingship and Politics in the Reign of Edward VI* (Cambridge: 2002).

Almsy, Rudolph P., 'Contesting Voices in Tyndale's *The Practice of Prelates*', in *William Tyndale and the Law*, eds John A.R. Dick and Anne Richardson, Sixteenth Century Essays and Studies, Vol. 25 (1994), pp. 1–10.

Alsop, J.D., 'Latimer, the "Commonwealth of Kent" and the 1549 Rebellions', *HJ*, 28 (1983), pp. 379–383.

Archambault, Paul, 'The Analogy of the "Body" in Renaissance Political Literature', *Bibliothèque D'Humanisme et Renaissance*, 29 (1967), pp. 21–53.

Aston, Margaret, *Faith and Fire: Popular and Unpopular Religion 1350–1600* (London: 1993).

Bakhtin, Mikhail, *Rabelais and his World*, trans. Helene Iswolsky (Bloomington: 1984).

Beer, Barrett L., *Rebellion and Riot: Popular Disorder in England During the Reign of Edward VI* (Kent, Ohio: 1982).

Berg, Kent T. Van Den, '"The Counterfeit in Personation": Spenser's *Prosopopoia or Mother Hubberds Tale*', in *The Author in His Work*, eds Louis L. Martz and Aubrey Williams (New Haven: 1978), pp. 85–102.

Bernard, G.W., 'The Making of Religious Policy, 1533–46', *HJ*, 41 (1998), pp. 321–349.

Bernard, G.W., 'Vitality and Vulnerability in the Late Medieval Church: Pilgrimage on the Eve of the Break with Rome', in *The End of the Middle Ages? England in the Fifteenth and Sixteenth Centuries*, ed. John Watts (Stroud: 1998), pp. 199–233.

Betteridge, Tom, *Tudor Histories of the English Reformations 1530–1583* (Aldershot: 1999).

Betteridge, Tom, 'Visibility, Truth and History in *Acts and Monuments*', in *John Foxe and his World*, eds Christopher Highley and John King (Aldershot: 2002), pp. 145–159.

Bonahue, Edward T., '"I know the Place and the Persons": The Play of Textual Frames in Baldwin's *Beware the Cat*', *SP*, 91 (1994), pp. 283–300.

Bossy, John, *Christianity in the West 1400–1700* (Oxford: 1985).

Bowers, Terence N., 'The Production and Communication of Knowledge in William Baldwin's *Beware the Cat*: Toward a Typographic Culture', *Criticism*, 33 (1991), pp. 1–29.

Braddick, Michael, 'State Formation and Social Change in Early Modern England', *Social History*, 16 (1991), pp. 1–17.

Bradshaw, Brendan, 'The Controversial Sir Thomas More', *JEH*, 36 (1985), pp. 535–569.

Bradshaw, Brendan, 'Transalpine Humanism', in *The Cambridge History of Political Thought 1450–1700*, ed. J.H. Burns with the assistance of Mark Goldie (Cambridge: 1991), pp. 95–131.

Bray, Alan, 'Homosexuality and the Signs of Male Friendship in Elizabethan England', *History Workshop Journal*, 29 (1990), pp. 1–19.

Brodie, D.M., 'Edmund Dudley, Minister of Henry VII', *TRHS*, 15 (1932), pp. 133–161.

Brodie, D.M., 'Introduction' in Edmund Dudley, *The Tree of Commonwealth*, ed. D.M. Brodie (Cambridge: 1948), pp. 1–17.

Bibliography

Bush, M.L., '"Up for the Commonweal": The Significance of Tax Grievances in the English Rebellions of 1536', *EHR*, 106 (1991), pp. 299–318.

Bush, Michael, *The Pilgrimage of Grace: A Study of the Rebel Armies of October 1536* (Manchester: 1996).

Bush, Michael, and Bownes, David, *The Defeat of the Pilgrimage of Grace: A Study of the Postpardon Revolts of December 1536 to March 1537 and their Effect* (Hull: 1999).

Butterworth, C. and Chester, Allan G., *George Joye 1495–1533: A Chapter in the History of the English Bible and the English Reformation* (Philadelphia: 1962).

Cheney, Patrick, 'Spenser's Pastorals: *The Shepheardes Calendar* and *Colin Clouts Come Home Againe*', in *The Cambridge Companion to Spenser*, ed. Andrew Hadfield (Cambridge: 2001), pp. 79–105.

Collinson, Patrick, *The Elizabethan Puritan Movement* (Oxford: 1967).

Collinson, Patrick, '"Magazine of Religious Patterns": An Erasmian Topic Transposed in English Protestantism', in *Renaissance and Renewal in Christian History*, ed. Derek Baker (Oxford: 1977), pp. 223–249.

Collinson, Patrick, *The Religion of Protestants: The Church in English Society 1559–1625* (Oxford: 1982).

Collinson, Patrick, 'Truth and Legend: The Veracity of John Foxe's Book of Martyrs', in *'Clio's Mirror': Historiography in Britain and the Netherlands*, eds A.C. Duke and C.A. Tamse (Walburg: 1985), pp. 31–54.

Collinson, Patrick, 'De Republica Anglorum: Or, History with the Politics Put Back', in *Elizabethan Essays* (London: 1994), pp. 1–30.

Collinson, Patrick, 'The Monarchical Republic of Queen Elizabeth I', in *Elizabethan Essays* (London: 1994), pp. 31–58.

Collinson, Patrick, 'William Tyndale and the Course of the English Reformation', *Reformation*, 1 (1996), pp. 72–97.

Collinson, Patrick, 'Night Schools, Conventicles and Churches: Continuities and Discontinuities in Early Protestant Ecclesiology', in *The Beginnings of English Protestantism*, eds Peter Marshall and Alec Ryrie (Cambridge: 2002), pp. 209–235.

Conrad, F.W., 'The Problem of Counsel Reconsidered: the Case of Sir Thomas Elyot', in *Political Thought and the Tudor Commonwealth: Deep Structure, Discourse and Disguise*, eds Paul A. Fideler and T.F. Mayer (London: 1992), pp. 75–107.

Crane, Mary Thomas, '*Intret Cato*: Authority and Epigram in Sixteenth-Century England', in *Renaissance Genres: Essays on Theory, History and Interpretation*, ed. Barbara Kiefer Lewalski (Cambridge, Mass.: 1986), pp. 158–188.

Crane, Mary Thomas, *Framing Authority: Sayings, Self and Society in Sixteenth-Century England* (Princeton, NY: 1993).

Crewe, Jonathan, *Trials of Authorship: Anterior Forms and Poetic Reconstruction from Wyatt to Shakespeare* (Berkeley: 1990).

Cummings, Brian, 'Swearing in Public: More and Shakespeare', *English Literary Renaissance*, 27 (1997), pp. 197–232.

Cummings, Brian, 'Reformed Literature and Literature Reformed', in *The Cambridge History of Medieval English Literature*, ed. David Wallace (Cambridge: 1999), pp. 821–851.

Cummings, Brian, *The Literary Culture of the Reformation: Grammar and Grace* (Oxford: 2002).

D'Alton, Craig, 'Charity or Fire? The Argument of Thomas More's 1529 *Dyaloge*', *SCJ*, 33 (2002), pp. 51–70.

Davis, J.F., 'Lollardy and the Reformation in England', in *The Impact of the English Reformation 1500–1640*, ed. Peter Marshall (London: 1997), pp. 37–54.

Dewar, Mary, *Sir Thomas Smith: A Tudor Intellectual in Office* (London:1964).

Dickens, A.G., 'Wilfrid Holme of Huntingdon: Yorkshire's First Protestant Poet', *Yorkshire Archaeological Journal*, 39 (1956–58), pp. 119–135.

Dickens, A.G., 'The Early Expansion of Protestantism in England 1520–1558', *Archiv für Reformationsgeschichte*, 78 (1987), pp. 187–222.

Dickens, A.G., *The English Reformation: Second Edition* (London: 1989).

Doran, Susan, 'Juno Versus Diana: The Treatment of Elizabeth I's Marriage in Plays and Entertainments 1561–1581', *HJ*, 38 (1995), pp. 257–274.

Doran, Susan and Freeman, Tom, eds, *The Myth of Elizabeth* (Basingstoke: 2003).

Duerden, Richard Y., 'Justice and Justification: King and God in Tyndale's *The Obedience of a Christian Man*', in *William Tyndale and the Law*, eds John A.R. Dick and Anne Richardson, Sixteenth Century Essays and Studies, Vol. 25 (1994), pp. 69–80.

Duffy, Eamon, *The Stripping of the Altars: Traditional Religion in England 1400–1580* (New Haven: 1992).

Duffy, Eamon, *The Voices of Morebath: Reformation and Rebellion in an English Village* (New Haven: 2001).

Eisenstein, Elizabeth L., *The Printing Press as an Agent of Change: Communications and Cultural Transformations in Early-Modern Europe* (Cambridge: 1979).

Ellis, Steven G., 'Henry VIII, Rebellion and the Rule of Law', *HJ*, 24 (1984), pp. 513–531.

Elton, G.R., *Policy and Police: The Enforcement of the Reformation in the Age of Thomas Cromwell* (Cambridge: 1972).

Elton, G.R., *Reform and Reformation: England 1509–1558* (London: 1977).

Elton, G.R., 'Tudor Government: The Points of Contact', in *Studies in Tudor and Stuart Politics and Government*, Vol. 3 (Cambridge: 1983), pp. 3–57.

Estrin, Barbara L., 'Wyatt's Unlikely Likenesses: Or, Has the Lady Read Petrarch?', in *Rethinking the Henrician Era: Essays on Early Tudor Texts and Contexts*, ed. Peter C. Herman (Urbana: 1994), pp. 219–240.

Facey, Jane, 'John Foxe and the Defence of the English Church', in *Protestantism and the National Church in Sixteenth Century England*, eds Peter Lake and Maria Dowling (London: 1987), pp. 162–192.

Ferguson, Margaret W., 'Saint Augustine's Region of Unlikeness: The Crossing of Exile and Language', *Georgia Review*, 29 (1975), pp. 844–864.

Fletcher, Anthony and MacCulloch, Diarmaid, *Tudor Rebellions* (Harlow: 1997).

Foxe, Adam, *Oral and Literate Culture in England 1500–1700* (Oxford: 2000).

Fox, Alistair, *Thomas More: History and Providence* (Oxford: 1982).

Bibliography

Fox, Alistair, 'Sir Thomas Elyot and the Humanist Dilemma', in *Reassessing the Henrician Age: Humanism, Politics and Reform 1500–1550*, eds Alistair Fox and John Guy (Oxford: 1986), pp. 52–73.

Freeman, Thomas S., '"The Good Ministrye of Godlye and Vertuouse Women": The Elizabethan Martyrologist and the Female Supporters of the Marian Martyrs', *Journal of British Studies*, 39 (2000).

Gillespie, Vincent, 'Justification by Faith: Skelton's *Replycacion*', in *The Long Fifteenth Century: Essays for Douglas Gray*, eds Helen Cooper and Sally Mapstone (Oxford: 1997), pp. 273–311.

Gow, E., 'Thomas Bilney and his Relations with Sir Thomas More', *Norfolk Archaeology*, 32 (1958), pp. 292–340.

Greenblatt, Stephen, *Renaissance Self-Fashioning; From More to Shakespeare* (Chicago: 1980).

Gunn, S.J., 'Peers, Commons and Gentry in the Lincolnshire Revolt of 1536', *PP*, 123 (1989), pp. 52–79.

Gunn, S.J., 'Edmund Dudley and the Church', *JEH*, 51 (2000), pp. 509–526.

Gutierrez, Nancy A., '*Beware the Cat*: Mimesis in a Skin of Oratory', *Style*, 23 (1989), pp. 49–69.

Guy, John, *Tudor England* (Oxford: 1991).

Guy, John, 'The Henrician Age', in *The Varieties of British Political Thought 1500–1800*, ed. J.G.A. Pocock with the assistance of Gordon J. Schochet and Lois G. Schwoerer (Cambridge: 1993), pp. 13–46.

Guy, John, 'The Rhetoric of Counsel in Early Modern England', in *Tudor Political Culture*, ed. Dale Hoak (Cambridge: 1995), pp. 292–310.

Guy, John, 'Tudor Monarchy and its critiques', in *Tudor Monarchy*, ed. John Guy (London: 1997), pp. 78–109.

Guy, John, *Thomas More* (London: 2000).

Hadfield, Andrew, *Literature, Politics and National Identity: Reformation to Renaissance* (Cambridge: 1994).

Hadfield, Andrew, *Literature, Travel, and Colonial Writing in the English Renaissance 1545–1625* (Oxford: 1998).

Hageman, Elizabeth H., 'John Foxe's Henry VIII as *Justitia*', *SCJ*, 10 (1979), pp. 35–43.

Haigh, Christopher, *English Reformations: Religion, Politics, and Society under the Tudors* (Oxford: 1993).

Halpern, Richard, *The Poetics of Primitive Accumulation: English Renaissance Culture and the Genealogy of Capital* (Ithaca: 1991).

Hamilton, Donna B., 'Re-engineering Virgil: *The Tempest* and the Printed English *Aeneid*', in *The Tempest and its Travels*, eds Peter Hulme and William H. Sherman (London: 2000), pp. 114–120.

Harper-Bill, Christopher, 'Dean Colet's Convocation Sermon and the Pre-Reformation Church in England', in *The Impact of the English Reformation 1500–1640*, ed. Peter Marshall (London: 1997), pp. 17–37.

Heale, Elizabeth, *Wyatt, Surrey and Early Tudor Poetry* (London: 1998).

Herman, Peter C., 'Rastell's *Pastyme of People*: Monarchy and the Law in Early Modern Historiography', *JMEMS*, 30 (2000), pp. 275–308.

Hobson, Christopher Z., 'Country Mouse and Towny Mouse: Truth in Wyatt', *Texas Studies in Literature and Language*, 39 (1997), pp. 230–258.

Hoffman, Nancy Jo, *Spenser's Pastorals* (Baltimore: 1977).

Hughes, Felicity A., 'Gascoigne's Poses', *SEL*, 37 (1997), pp. 1–19.

Hughes, Paul L., and Larkin, James F., eds *Tudor Royal Proclamations. I: The Early Tudors 1485–1553* (New Haven: 1964).

Hutson, Lorna, 'Fortunate Travelers: Reading for the Plot in Sixteenth Century England', *Representations*, 41 (1993), pp. 83–103.

Hutton, Ronald, 'The Local Impact of the Tudor Reformations', in *The Impact of the English Reformation 1500–1640*, ed. Peter Marshall (London: 1997), pp. 142–166.

James, M.E., 'The Concept of Order and the Northern Rising', *PP*, 60 (1973), pp. 49–83.

Johnson, Robert Carl, *John Heywood* (New York: 1970).

Jones, Norman L., 'Elizabeth's First Year: The Conception and Birth of the Elizabethan Political World', in *The Reign of Elizabeth*, ed. Christopher Haigh (Basingstoke: 1984), pp. 27–55.

Kahrl, Stanley J., 'The Medieval Origins of the Sixteenth-century English Jest-books', *Studies in the Renaissance*, 13 (1966), pp. 166–183.

Kastan, David Scott, '"The Noyse of the New Bible": Reform and Reaction in Henrician England' in *Religion and Culture in Renaissance England*, eds Claire McEachern and Debora Shuger (Cambridge: 1997), pp. 46–68.

Kelly, R.L., "Hugh Latimer as Piers Plowman', *SEL*, 17 (1977), pp. 13–26.

King, John N., *English Reformation Literature: The Tudor Origins of the Protestant Tradition* (Princeton: 1982).

King, John N., 'Spenser's *Shepheardes Calendar* and Protestant Pastoral Satire', in *Renaissance Genres: Essays on Theory, History and Interpretation*, ed. Barbara Kiefer Lewalski (Cambridge, Mass.: 1986), pp. 369–398.

King, John N., 'John Day: Master Printer of the English Reformation', in *The Beginnings of English Protestantism*, eds Peter Marshall and Alec Ryrie (Cambridge: 2002), pp. 180–208.

Kinney, Arthur F., 'Skelton and Tyndale: Men of the Cloth and of the Word', in *Word, Church and State: Tyndale Quincentenary Essays*, eds John T. Day, Eric Lund and Anne M. O'Donnell (Washington: 1998), pp. 275–286.

Lake, Peter, 'Anti-Popery: The Structure of a Prejudice', in *Conflict in Early Stuart England: Studies in Religion and Politics 1603–1642*, eds Richard Cust and Ann Hughes (London: 1989), pp. 72–106.

Lake, Peter, 'Periodization, Politics and "The Social"', *Journal of British Studies*, 37 (1998), pp. 279–290.

Laclau, Ernesto and Zac, Lilian, 'Minding the Gap: The Subject of Politics', in *The Making of Political Identities*, ed. Ernesto Laclau (London: 1994), pp. 11–39.

Laclau, Ernesto, 'The Death and Resurrection of the Theory of Ideology', *MLN*, 112 (1997), pp. 297–321.

Lawton, David, 'Dullness and the Fifteenth Century', *ELH*, 54 (1987), pp. 761–799.

Lawton, David, 'The subject of *Piers Plowman*', *The Yearbook of Langland Studies*, 1 (1987), pp. 1–30.

Lehmberg, Stanford E., *Sir Thomas Elyot: Tudor Humanist* (Austin: 1960).

Lerer, Seth, *Chaucer and his Readers: Imagining the Author in Late-Medieval England* (Princeton: 1993).

Lewis, C.S., *English Literature in the Sixteenth Century Excluding Drama* (Oxford: 1944).

Loades, David, *The Reign of Mary Tudor: Politics, Government and Religion in England 1553–58* (London: 1991).

Logan, Sandra, 'Making History: The Rhetorical and Historical Occasion of Elizabeth Tudor's Coronation Entry', *JMEMS*, 31 (2001), pp. 251–282.

Lucas, Scott, 'The Suppressed Edition and the Creation of the "Orthodox" *Mirror for Magistrates*', *Renaissance Papers*, 1994, pp. 31–54.

McCanles, Michael, 'Love and Power in the Poetry of Sir Thomas Wyatt', *Modern Language Quarterly*, 29 (1968), pp. 145–160.

MacCulloch, Diarmaid, 'Kett's Rebellion in Context', *PP*, 84 (1979), pp. 36–59.

MacCulloch, Diarmaid, 'A Rejoinder', *PP*, 93 (1981), pp. 165–173.

MacCulloch, Diarmaid, *Suffolk and the Tudors: Politics and Religion in an English County, 1500–1600* (Oxford: 1986).

MacCulloch, Diarmaid, 'Henry VIII and the Reform of the Church', in *The Reign of Henry VIII: Politics, Policy and Piety*, ed. Diarmaid MacCulloch (London: 1995), pp. 159–180.

MacCulloch, Diarmaid, *Thomas Cranmer: A Life* (New Haven: 1996).

MacCulloch, Diarmaid, *Tudor Church Militant: Edward VI and the Protestant Reformation* (London: 1999).

Marshall, Peter, 'The Debate over "Unwritten Verities" in Early Reformation England', in *Protestant History and Identity in Sixteenth-Century Europe: Vol. 1 The Medieval Inheritance*, ed. Bruce Gordon (Aldershot: 1996), pp. 60–78.

Marshall, Peter, 'Papist as Heretic: The Burning of John Forest, 1538', *HJ*, 41 (1998), pp. 351–374.

Marshall, Peter and Ryrie, Alec, eds, *The Beginnings of English Protestantism* (Cambridge: 2002).

Maslen, R.W., *Elizabethan Fictions: Espionage, Counter-Espionage, and the Duplicity of Fiction in Early Elizabethan Prose Narratives* (Oxford: 1997).

Martin, J.W., *Religious Radicals in Tudor England* (London: 1989).

McCoy, Richard C., 'Gasciogne's "*Poëmeta castrata*": The Wages of Courtly Success', *Criticism*, 27 (1985), pp. 29–56.

McCutcheon, R.R., 'Heresy and Dialogue: The Humanist Approaches of Erasmus and More', *Viator*, 29 (1993), pp. 357–384.

McLaren, Anne, 'Delineating the Elizabethan Body Politic: Knox, Aylmer and the Definition of Counsel 1558–88', *History of Political Thought*, 17 (1996), pp. 224–252.

McLaren, Anne, *Political Culture in the Reign of Elizabeth: Queen and Commonwealth, 1558–1585* (Cambridge: 1999).

McLaren, Anne, 'Reading Sir Thomas Smith's *De Republica Anglorum* as Protestant Apologetia', *HJ*, 42 (1999), pp. 911–939.

Montrose, Louis Adrian, 'Of Gentlemen and Shepherds: The Politics of Elizabethan Pastoral Form', *ELH*, 50 (1983), pp. 415–459.

Moore, R.I., 'Heresy as Disease', in *The Concept of Heresy in the Middle Ages*, eds W. Lourdaux and D. Verhelst (Leuven: 1976), pp. 1–11.

Morrill, John, *The Nature of the English Revolution* (London: 1993).

Muller, James, *Stephen Gardiner and the Tudor Reaction* (London:1926).

Norbrook, David, *Poetry and Politics in the English Renaissance* (London: 2002).

Oakley, Francis, 'Christian Obedience and Authority, 1520–1550', in *The Cambridge History of Political Thought 1450–1700*, ed. J.H. Burns with the assistance of Mark Goldie (Cambridge: 1991), pp. 159–192.

Olsen, V.N., *John Foxe and the Elizabethan Church* (Berkeley: 1973).

Ong, Walter J., *Orality and Literacy: The Technologizing of the Word* (London: 1982).

Parish, Helen, *Clerical Marriage and the English Reformation: Precedent, Policy and Practice* (Aldershot: 2000).

Patterson, Annabel, *Fables of Power: Aesopian Writing and Political History* (Durham, NC: 1991).

Patterson, Lee, '"No Man His Reason Herde": Peasant Consciousness, Chaucer's Miller and the Structure of the Canterbury Tales', in *Chaucer: Contemporary Critical Essays*, eds Valerie Allen and Ares Axiotis (London: 1997), pp. 169–192.

Patterson, Lee, 'Chaucer's Pardoner on the Couch: Psyche and Clio in Medieval Literary Studies', *Sp*, 76 (2001), pp. 638–680.

Pettegree, Andrew, *Marian Protestantism: Six Studies* (Aldershot: 1996).

Reinhard, Wolfgang, 'Reformation, Counter-Reformation, and the Early Modern State: A Reassessment', *Catholic Historical Review*, 75 (1989), pp. 383–404.

Rex, Richard, *Henry VIII and the English Reformation* (London: 1993).

Rex, Richard, 'The Crisis of Obedience: God's Word and Henry's Reformation', *HJ*, 39 (1996), pp. 863–894.

Rex, Richard, 'The Early Impact of Reformation Theology at Cambridge University, 1521–1547', *Reformation and Renaissance Review*, 2 (1999), pp. 38–71.

Rex, Richard, 'Friars in the Reformation', in *The Beginnings of English Protestantism*, eds Peter Marshall and Alec Ryrie (Cambridge: 2002), pp. 38–59.

Rummel, Erika, *The Confessionalisation of Humanism in Reformation Germany* (Oxford: 2000).

Ryrie, Alec, 'Counting Sheep, Counting Shepherds: The Problem of Allegiance in the English Reformation', in *The Beginnings of English Protestantism*, eds Peter Marshall and Alec Ryrie (Cambridge: 2002), pp. 84–110.

Ryrie, Alec, *The Gospel and Henry VIII: Evangelicals in the Early English Reformation* (Cambridge: forthcoming, 2004).

Scarisbrick, J.J., *Henry VIII* (London: 1981).

Schilling, Heinz, *Religion, Political Culture and the Emergence of Early Modern Society* (Leiden: 1992).

Schilling, Heinz, 'Confessional Europe', in *Handbook of European History 1400–1600 Late Middle Ages: Renaissance and Reformation*, Vol. 2, eds Thomas A Brady, Heiko A. Oberman and James D. Tracy (Leiden: 1995), pp. 641–681.

Shagan, Ethan, 'Protector Somerset and the 1549 Rebellions: New Sources and New Perspectives', *EHR*, 114 (1999), pp. 34–63.

Shagan, Ethan, *Popular Politics and the English Reformation* (Cambridge: 2003).

Simpson, James, 'Ethics and Interpretation: Reading Wills in Chaucer's *Legend of Good Women*', *Studies in the Age of Chaucer*, 20 (1998), pp. 73–100.

Simpson, James, 'Breaking the Vacuum: Ricardian and Henrician Ovidianism', *JMEMS*, 29 (1999), pp. 325–355.

Simpson, James, *Reform and Cultural Revolution 1350–1547* (Oxford: 2002).

Skinner, Quentin, *The Foundations of Modern Political Thought: Vol. 1 The Renaissance* (Cambridge: 1978).

Skinner, Quentin, *The Foundations of Modern Political Thought: Vol. 2 The Age of Reformation* (Cambridge: 1978).

Skinner, Quentin, 'Sir Thomas More's *Utopia* and the Language of Renaissance Humanism', in *The Languages of Political Theory in Early Modern Europe*, ed. Anthony Pagden (Cambridge: 1987), pp. 123–157.

Slack, Paul, *From Reformation to Improvement: Public Welfare in Early Modern England* (Oxford: 1998).

Spiller, Michael R.G., *The Development of the Sonnet: An Introduction* (London: 1992).

Spurgeon, Dickie, *Three Tudor Dialogues* (New York: 1978).

Smith, Julia A., 'An Image of a Preaching Bishop in Late Medieval England: The 1498 Woodcut Portrait of Bishop John Alcock', *Viator*, 21 (1990), pp. 301–322.

Stallybrass, Peter, '"Drunk with the Cup of Liberty": Robin Hood, the Carnivalesque, and the Rhetoric of Violence in Early Modern England', in *The Violence of Representation: Literature and the History of Violence*, eds Nancy Armstrong and Leonard Tennenhouse (London: 1989), pp. 45–76.

Starkey, David, 'Intimacy and Innovation: The Rise of the Privy Chamber, 1485–1547', in *The English Court from the Wars of the Roses to the Civil War*, eds David Starkey, D.A.L. Morgan, John Murphy, Pam Wright, Neil Cuddy and Kevin Sharpe (London: 1987), pp. 71–118.

Staub, Susan C., '"According to My Sources": Fictionality in The Adventures of Master F.J.', *SP*, 87 (1990), pp. 111–119.

Stewart, Alan, *Close Readers: Humanism and Sodomy in Early Modern England* (Princeton: 1997).

Stock, Brian, *Augustine the Reader: Meditation, Self-Knowledge, and the Ethics of Interpretation* (Cambridge, Mass.: 1996).

Strauss, Gerald, *Enacting the Reformation in Germany: Essays on Institution and Reception* (Aldershot: 1993).

Sullivan, Garrett and Woodbridge, Linda, 'Popular Culture in Print', in *English Literature 1500–1600*, ed. Arthur F. Kinney (Cambridge: 2000), pp. 265–286.

Swanson, R.N., 'Literacy, Heresy, History and Orthodoxy: Perceptions and Permutations for the Later Middle Ages', in *Heresy and Literacy, 1000–1530*, eds Peter Biller and Anne Hudson (Cambridge: 1994), pp. 279–293.

Tribble, Evelyn B., *Margins and Marginality: The Printed Page in Early Modern England* (Charlottesville: 1993).

Trueman, Carl R., *Luther's Legacy: Salvation and English Reformers 1525–1536* (Oxford: 1994).

Verbeke, Gerard, 'Philosophy and Heresy: Some Conflicts between Reason and Faith', in *The Concept of Heresy in the Middle Ages*, eds W. Lourdaux and D. Verhelst (Leuven: 1976), pp. 171–197.

Walker, Greg, 'Saint or Schemer? The 1527 Heresy Trial of Thomas Bilney Reconsidered', *JEH*, 40 (1989), pp. 219–238.

Walker, Greg, 'John Skelton, Thomas More, and the "lost" history of the Early Reformation in England', *Parergon*, 9 (1991), pp. 75–85.

Walker, Greg, *Plays of Persuasion: Drama and Politics at the Court of Henry VIII* (Cambridge: 1991).

Walker, Greg, '"Ordered Confusion"? The Crisis of Authority in Skelton's *Speke Parrott*', *Spenser Studies*, 10 (1992), pp. 213–228.

Walker, Greg, *The Politics of Performance in Early Renaissance Drama* (Cambridge: 1998).

Walker, Greg, 'Dialogue, Resistance, and Accommodation: Conservative Literary Response to the Henrician Reformation', unpublished paper, 2000.

Wall, Wendy, 'Authorship and the Material Conditions of Writing', in *The Cambridge Companion to English Literature 1500–1600*, ed. Arthur F. Kinney (Cambridge: 2000), pp. 64–89.

Waller, Gary, *English Poetry of the Sixteenth Century* (Harlow: 1993).

Ward, Adrian O., 'Proverbs and Political Anxiety in the Poetry of Sir Thomas Wyatt and the Earl of Surrey', *English Studies*, 81 (2000), pp. 456–471.

Watts, John, *Henry VI and the Politics of Kingship* (Cambridge: 1996).

Webster, Tom, *Godly Clergy in Early Stuart England: The Caroline Puritan Movement c.1620–1643* (Cambridge: 1997).

White, Helen C., *Social Criticism in Popular Religious Literature of the Sixteenth Century* (New York: 1965).

Wizeman, William, 'Recalled to Life: The Theology and Spirituality of Mary Tudor's Church', Oxford PhD, 2002.

Wood, Andy, 'Kett's Rebellion and the Piers Plowman Tradition', unpublished paper, 2001.

Wood, Neil, *Foundations of Political Economy: Some Early Tudor Views on State and Society* (Berkeley: 1994).

Woolf, D.R., 'The Rhetoric of Martyrdom: Generic Contradiction and Narrative Strategy in John Foxe's *Acts and Monuments*', in *The Rhetorics of Life Writing in Early Modern Europe: Forms of Biography from Canandra Fedde to Louis XIV*, eds Thomas F. Mayer and D.R. Woolf (Michigan: 1995), pp. 243–282.

Bibliography

Youings, Joyce, 'The South Western Rebellion of 1549', *Southern History*, 1 (1979), pp. 99–122.

Žižek, Slavoj, *For They Know Not What They Do: Enjoyment as a Political Factor* (London: 1991).

Žižek, Slavoj, *The Plague of Fantasies* (London: 1997).

Index

Note: 'n.' after a page reference indicates a note number on that page.